GREAT CLOUD OF WITNESSES

OF

IN HEBREWS ELEVEN

Other Books by E. W. Bullinger:

The Book of Job

Commentary on Revelation

The Companion Bible

How to Enjoy the Bible

Number in Scripture

The Witness of the Stars

Word Studies on the Holy Spirit

GREAT CLOUD OF WITNESSES

IN HEBREWS ELEVEN

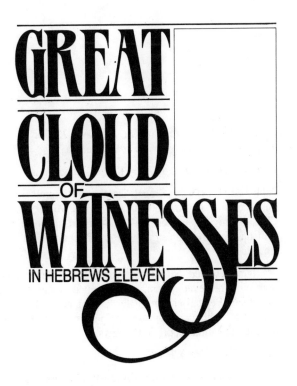

E. W. BULLINGER

Foreword by Warren W. Wiersbe

kregel
CLASSICS

Grand Rapids, MI 49501

Great Cloud of Witnesses in Hebrews Eleven by E. W. Bullinger, Foreword by Warren W. Wiersbe.

Foreword copyright © 1979 by Kregel Publications.

Published in 1979 by Kregel Classics, an imprint of Kregel Publications, P. O. Box 2607, Grand Rapids, MI 49501. Kregel Classics provides trusted and time-proven publications for Christian life and ministry. Your comments and suggestions are valued.

Cover Design: Don Ellens

Library of Congress Cataloging-in-Publication Data
Bullinger, E. W. (Ethelbert William), 1837-1913.
    [Great cloud of witnesses in Hebrews eleven. "Being a series of papers on Hebrews eleven."]
    Great Cloud of Witnesses in Hebrews Eleven/ E. W. Bullinger.
          p.   cm.
    Reprint of the 1911 ed. published by Eyre & Spottiswoode, London.
    1. Bible N.T. Hebrews 11—Criticism, interpretation, etc.—Addresses, essays, lectures. I. Title.
BS2775.B76   1979   227'.87'06—dc20   79-14425
                                                             CIP
ISBN 0-8254-2247-7 (paperback)

        7 8 9 10 11 Printing / Year 98 97 96 95 94

Printed in the United States of America

Contents

Foreword

Apart from the standard commentaries on Hebrews, you will not find many volumes devoted to the "heroes of faith" listed in Hebrews 11. Dr. G. Campbell Morgan's *The Triumphs of Faith* is an excellent series of sermons, but it is not an exegetical study of the chapter. The careful expositor of the Word needs exegetical tools that will help him mine the ore for himself, and then mint it into coins of truth for wide circulation.

One such tool is *Great Cloud of Witnesses in Hebrews Eleven* by Dr. Ethelbert William Bullinger. I know of no other book on Hebrews eleven in the English language that contains more solid spiritual teaching and practical truth than this one. Far from being an "ivory tower" commentary, this book touches life and makes living by faith an exciting and practical experience.

Dr. Bullinger held some doctrinal views that perhaps some of us might not agree with; but this disagreement must not rob us of the blessings of his written ministry. He was a careful student of the Word and a recognized scholar in the field of Biblical languages. In fact, the Archbishop of Canterbury granted him an honorary Doctor of Divinity degree in 1881 in recognition of his Biblical scholarship.

If this is your first meeting with Dr. Bullinger, you may be perplexed by his analytical outlines of Scripture passages. He was a great believer in the inspiration of The Scriptures and in the *order* in which God revealed truth. His massive work, *Figures of Speech Used in the Bible*, shows how carefully he examined the text and sought to unlock its meaning. To him, the analysis of the total passage and the exegesis of the individual words and phrases must go together. The complete working out of this principle is seen in his monumental volume, *The Companion Bible,* a valuable tool for the serious Bible student, even if he does not follow Bullinger's system of interpretation.

Bullinger was born in Canterbury, England, on December 15, 1837. His early training was in music, but his greatest joy was Bible study. He trained for the Anglican Church ministry at King's College, London, showing great skill in the study and use of Biblical languages. For a short time he served as curate at Bermondsley Abbey Church on Tooley Street in London, near the London Bridge. His personal views of Scripture led him into an independent ministry, including the publishing of a Bible study magazine, *Things to Come.* He died in London on June 6, 1913.

I predict that your use of this excellent book will not only make you a better student of the Word but also a better follower of the Lord.

Warren W. Wiersbe

Introduction

1. The Scope of Hebrews Eleven

WE trust that our readers are by this time duly impressed with the fact that we must not give an interpretation of any passage of Scripture, or even a chapter, apart from its context.

We have learnt also that the *Scope* of the passage must be gathered from its *Structure*. In other words, we must know what it is all about before we can find a clue to the meaning of the words : and we can find this out only by getting the *Structure* of the whole context.

As our subject here consists of a complete chapter, it will be necessary for us to see the exact place in which it stands in relation to the Epistle as a whole. We must therefore give the Structure of

The Epistle to the Hebrews as a whole :—

A | i.. ii., Doctrinal Introduction.

  B | iii. 1-iv. 13. The Mission of Christ.

    C | iv. 14-16. General Application ('Εχοντες οὖν. " Having therefore.") Boldness of access to God in heaven.

  B | v. i.-x. 18. The Priesthood of Christ.

    C | x. 19—xii. 29. Particular Application ("Εχοντες οὖν. " Having therefore.") Boldness of access to God in heaven.

A | xiii. Practical Conclusion.

1

The first thing we learn from this Structure is that the chapter we are to consider has not been "rightly divided" by man.

Its subject does not begin at the first verse of chapter xi., but at the nineteenth verse of the previous chapter (ch. x.), the member of which it forms part. That is to say, it begins at chap. x. 19, and ends with chap. xii. 29.

Heb. xi. therefore comes in the middle, and forms part of a larger portion of the Epistle. Consequently no exposition of it can be complete which treats it as beginning only at ch. xi. 1. We must go back to ch. x. 19 if we would see the part it bears in relation to the whole.

The commencement of this member, C, is marked off by the catch-words "Having therefore;" these are the same words which commence the corresponding member C (chapters iv. 14-16). The former of these two members (ch. iv. 14-16) contains the conclusion which follows from the establishment of the argument concerning *The Mission of Christ* (ch. iii. 1—iv. 13); while the latter (chs. x. 19—xii. 29) contains the conclusion which follows the argument concerning *The Priesthood of Christ* (ch. v. 1—x. 18).

It will be necessary now for us to note the Structure of the second of these conclusions, so that we may, by its being broken up, see what is the scope of the whole, and what is the special place of the chapter we are to consider.

Each of the large members given above (page 1), has its own proper and peculiar Structure, and is capable of being expanded, and of having its various sub-members exhibited to the eye. The sub-structure of C. (ch. x. 19-29) is as follows :—

The Structure of *C* (Heb. x. 19—xii. 29).

Particular Application of ch. v. 1—x. 18.

C | *D* | x. 19-23. Exhortation to draw near to God, and to "hold fast the confession of our faith without wavering," because Christ the High Priest is accessible in heaven and "faithful that promised."

    E | x. 24-25. Duties as brethren, to endure exhortation.

      F | x. 26-31. Warning in view of God being "the living God."

        G | *a* | x. 32-37. Exhortation to patience, in view of the promise.

          b | x. 38, 39. Living by faith.

        G | *b* | xi. 1-40. Examples of living by faith.

          a | xii. 1. Exhortation to patience in view of the examples of faith in the promise.

  D | xii. 2-3. Exhortations to look away from the above examples to Jesus, the Foremost and Last "example of faith," because He endured, and is accessible in Heaven.

    E | xii. 4-24. Duties as sons, to endure chastening.

      F | xii. 25-29. Warning, in view of God being "a consuming fire."

From the above Structure we see the true place of chapter xi.

We see also the true place of the member "*b*," and the relation in which it stands to the context.

The Scope of the whole passage is an exhortation to patient endurance in view of the promises. This exhortation is based on the faithfulness of the Promiser (ch. x. 23), and the examples of faith are shown in those who "lived by faith" (ch. xi.)

The pivot on which the whole turns is the quotation from Habbakuk ii. 4, "The just shall live by faith."

This is quoted three times in the New Testament, and each time the emphasis is on a different word :—

Rom. i. 17.   "The just shall live by FAITH."*
Gal. iii. 11.   "The JUST shall live by faith."
Heb. x. 38.   "The just LIVE by faith."

In the *first* of these (Romans i. 17) the subject is Faith or *Faith-principle* as being the principle of Justification, in God's Gospel, which is there being revealed.

In the *second* (Galatians iii. 11) the subject is *Justification*, which is by Faith-principle in contrast with law-principle.

In the *third* (Hebrews x. 38) the subject is *Living* by faith in God's promises, so as to be able to wait and watch with patient endurance.

This is the subject of Hab. ii. 1, 3, 4, which begins "I will stand upon my WATCH, and set me upon the tower, and will WATCH what he will say unto me. . . .

> For the vision is yet for an appointed time . . .
> But at the end it shall speak, and not lie :
> Though it tarry, WAIT for it ;
> Because it will surely come, it will not tarry. . . .
> The just shall LIVE through his faith."

This context is clear.   Faith in God's word can alone enable us to wait with patience for the fulfilment of His promise.

---

*Heb.   "The just shall live in (or by) his faith (or faithfulness").

This is the burden of the context of Heb. xi., and hence, in Heb. x. 37, the third verse of Hab. ii. is quoted as well as verse 4, while, in Romans and Galatians, this verse (*v.* 3) is not quoted; because patient *Waiting* is not the burden and object of the context in those two quotations of Hab. ii. 4.

The exhortation (Heb. x. 32-37) is to patient waiting through faith : " Cast not away therefore your confidence, which hath great recompense of reward. For ye have need of patience, that, after ye have done the will of God, ye might receive the promise." Then it goes on to quote Habbakuk : "for yet a little while," etc.

The whole burden of Heb. xi. is the patience of those who endured by faith, "not having received the promise" (*v.* 13) ; and of those who, " having obtained a good report through faith, received not the promise" (*v.* 39).

Now we are prepared to understand and appreciate

(1) The Definition of Faith in *vv.* 1-3, and

(2) The Exemplification of Faith in *vv.* 4-39.

THE DEFINITION OF FAITH

In Heb. xi. i. Faith is defined as being

" The FOUNDATION of *things hoped for,*
The CONVICTION of *things not seen.*"

There is no question as to the meaning of the word rendered " substance " in the A.V.; which, in the margin, gives " *ground, or confidence,*" as an alternative.

In the R.V. it is rendered " assurance," with "*giving substance to*" in the margin. The word is ὑπόστασις *(hypostasis) a setting* or *placing underneath.* Hence, its primitive meaning is *foundation*. The rendering "substance" comes from the Latin, *sub stans* (standing under). In the *Papyri* it is used of *title deeds*.

We all hope for many things, but the question is, What foundation or ground have we for our hope? What are our *title deeds?* All depends upon this.

As to our hope for eternity, it all rests on the faithfulness of God's promise. If there be no God; or, if His promise be not true, then we have no foundation whatever for our hope; all is baseless. Everything, therefore, depends upon the fact that God has spoken, and that what He has said is true.

Hence, the definition of faith in Romans x. 17.

"Faith cometh by hearing,
And hearing [cometh] by the word of God."

If we have heard nothing, there can be nothing to believe. There is neither place nor room for faith. We may think it, or imagine it, or hope for it; but we cannot possibly *believe* it, because we have not *heard* anything about it. Our hopes and thoughts and imaginations are all vain, being without any "foundation."

Hence, of Abraham's faith, the "father of the faithful," it is said.

"ABRAHAM BELIEVED GOD"

God had spoken; Abraham had heard; and he believed God.

What he had heard came "by the word of God: and his faith came by this hearing."

Abraham believed what God had said; God had "caused him to hope;" and hence, believing God, his faith in God's Word was the *foundation* or ground of that for which he hoped.

None can hope in vain who believe God.

This is why the common question, Do we believe? is so senseless. The real question is, not Do we believe? but WHAT do we believe? or rather, WHOM do we believe.

We believe many things that man says, and that man promises. But the question is, are they true?

It is not a question of the *sincerity* with which we believe, but of the *truth* of what we believe.

The more sincerely we believe what is not true, the worse it is for us. This holds good in every department of life. If what we hear be not true, then, to doubt it, means our safety.

When we give ear to man, we can never be certain that what he says is true. But when we give ear to God, we can set to our seal that "God is true" in what He says; and that "He is faithful" in what He promises. Faith is hearing God and believing what He says. This is the simple definition. But there are various expressions connected with this faith.

It is used with the Preposition ἐν (*en*) *in*. This means that our faith rests *in* the truth of what is said (Mark i. 15, etc.). It is the same when used with the Dative of the person.

It is used with ἐπί (*epi*) *upon*, which means that faith rests *upon* what we hear; and that what we hear is the *foundation upon* which our faith rests (Rom. ix. 33; x. 11, etc.).

It is used with εἰς (*eis*) *unto*, which means that faith goes *out to*, and is *directed to* Him of whom, or that of which we hear (John ii. 11; iii. 16, etc.)

There can thus be no mistake as to the meaning of the first part of the definition of Heb. xi. 1.

As to the second :—Faith is said to be

" THE CONVICTION OF THINGS NOT SEEN."

The A.V. renders this "evidence," while the R.V renders it "proving," with "*test*" in the margin.

The word is ἔλεγχος (*elengchos*) *a proof, that by which anything is proved* or *tested*; *logical proof, proof* that conveys a satisfying *conviction* to the mind. Hence, this is the best meaning to give the word here. It is the conviction produced by demonstration. In John viii. 46 the Lord says, " Which of you convicteth Me of sin ? " (not " convinceth," as in the A.V., but "convicteth," as in the R.V.) ; so in John xvi. 8, " When He [the Holy Spirit] is come, He shall convict the world in respect of sin," (not " reprove," as in A.V. margin, *convince*), but *convict*, or *bring in guilty*. None could do this of Christ ; but the Holy Spirit does this of the world. He brings it in guilty, and convicts it of sin. Why? For this very reason : "Because they believe not on Me."

This is the great sin. And this brings us back to our subject.

God hath spoken ; and the sin is defined as not believing what He hath said : for He was the Living Word, and through Him we believe in the Living God.

Hence the opening words of Isaiah i., which is the great indictment of Israel's sin :

> " **Hear, O heavens,**
> **And give ear, O earth :**
> **For Jehovah hath spoken.**"

This is the great fact for us who possess the Word of God.

GOD HATH SPOKEN

Do we believe what He hath said ? This is the one

abiding question. He has given to us, and made us exceeding great and precious promises. Do we believe Him? If we do, then, this faith is the "foundation" of all we hope for. It is the "conviction" of what we have heard but *do not see*. Thus Faith is the opposite of sight. Man says that "seeing is believing." This is one of his many fallacies. Faith is the demonstration to us of what we do not see. Hence, we live in, and by, this faith, "we walk by faith, and not by sight" (2 Cor. v. 7).

What we see is what we *know*.

What we believe is what we *hear*.

Hence the examples of faith given us in Hebrews xi. are those who, having heard God, believed what He said. Every instance of faith in this chapter comes under the category of "things hoped for," or of "things unseen."

Noah believed the truth of "things not seen as yet" (*v.* 7).

Others by faith saw the promises "afar off" (*v.* 13).

Moses "endured as seeing Him who is invisible" (*v.* 27).

This is faith. This was Abraham's faith. He "rejoiced to see Christ's day: and he saw it, and was glad" (John viii. 56). But he saw it, by faith, "afar off."

2. Reckoning by Faith (Verse 3)

HAVING given the true definition of faith, the Apostle proceeds to give examples of it; showing how men of God in past days lived by it: *i.e.,* how they conducted their lives according to it.

Those whom he calls "the elders,"* in Heb. xi. 1, he speaks of as the "great cloud of witnesses" in ch. xii. 1.

The scope of the whole passage (of which this chapter forms part) is, as we have seen, an exhortation to patience in view of the great tribulations these Hebrew believers were passing through, and of the faithfulness of God to His promises which He had made to them.

God's word was the foundation of all that they hoped for; His faithfulness was all that they had to rest upon.

He points his readers back to the great cloud of witnesses† who had borne such wondrous testimony to the power of a living faith in the living God: to those who had borne witness, not only in their faithful life, but in their martyr-death.

The word rendered "obtained a good report," in

The word is used in its Hebrew sense זְקֻנִים *ancients* (*zekunīm*). *See* Isa. xxiv. 23, which thus implies the *resurrection* of those who are referred to, *i.e.,* not older in age, but people who lived in olden times.

† The word is μάρτυς (*martus*), and is always used of *a judicial witness,* or *deponent; i.e.,* one who witnessed with his lips and not with his eyes. Hence the word comes to be limited, to-day, to the greatest of all such *witness,* a martyr's death.

The word for eye-witness is quite different. It is ἐπόπτης (*efoptēs*), *a looker on, spectator.*

Heb. xi. 2 and 39, and "witnesses," in Heb. xii. 1, are cognate.

In the former chapter it is the verb, and in the latter it is the noun. There is no word in the original about " good."

Verse 2 tells us that by (or through) this faith [of theirs] ; or by such a faith as this, they were *made witnesses* (by God), or *became* witnesses (for God), and could thus be called, in chap. xii. 1, " a great cloud of witnesses," by faith in the promises which they had received from God, and believing what they had " heard."

They were enabled to bear such wondrous witness ; and were strengthened to suffer, and conquer, and to wait patiently for the fulfilment of the promises which they saw, by this faith, " afar off."

It was this, and " by such faith as this," that their example was so necessary, and was such an encouragement for those to whom the Apostle was writing.

The scope of the whole section is (as we have seen), an exhortation and warning against apostasy ; and the words immediately preceding are, " We are not of those drawing back to destruction, but of faith, to the saving of the soul."

What it is to be thus, " of faith," is the subject of what follows in chapter xi. Faith has to do with that which is " not seen." The things we hope for are " not seen " : as it is written : " Hope that is seen is not hope : for what any one seeth, why doth he yet hope for ? But if we hope for what we do not see, then do we with patience wait for it " (Rom. viii. 24, 25). It is to this patient waiting under trial that these Hebrew believers were being exhorted.

Faith is thus the opposite of sight (2 Cor. v. 7). This is the essence of the whole of chapter xi. It begins, in verse 3, with the statement that the events which we see going on around us spring from things that do not appear, but from the fact that God rules and over-rules, and that He has prepared and ordered the ages.

The word rendered "worlds" is not used of the created world, which is κόσμος (cosmos), or of the inhabited world, which is οἰκουμένη (oikoumenē); or of the ploughed and trodden earth, which is γῆ (gē), but it is αἰών (aiōn) age, which is here in the plural, and means ages, or dispensations. This is its proper rendering.* It is by faith we perceive (νοοῦμεν, nooumen) that the events we see happening around us do not happen by chance.

Even worldly wisdom can see this and say that "there is a hand that shapes our destinies;" that "things are not what they seem;" and that "we cannot judge by appearances."

We see Babylon replacing Israel, Medo-Persia rising up in the place of Babylon; Greece succeeding Persia; Rome succeeding Greece. To the human eye, all these things are seen merely as historical events, but faith can see beneath the surface. It can perceive what the human eye cannot see. It can see the things that are invisible. It can see the "things not seen." How? By "hearing," i.e., "by the word of God." And here, note that the word rendered "word" is not

---

* This is the sense in which αἰών is used in this Epistle (as elsewhere). See Heb. i. 3, where the verb ποιέω (poieō) is used in the sense of appoint, as in chap. iii. 2. See also Heb. vi. 5, where it is used of "the age to come"; and Heb. ix. 26, where the first word "world" is κόσμος (cosmos) and means the created world, and the second is this word αἰών (aiōn) age.

Logos (as in Psalm xxxiii. 6. Sept. xxxii. 6), but *Rhēma ;* i.e., not the creative Word, but the *revealed words.* By believing the prophetic words we grasp the fact that these ages were all foreknown to God, and all perfectly ordered by Him.

This is the force of the word rendered " framed," as may be seen by studying all its occurrences."* It will be at once observed that in no other place is it rendered " framed," while all the other renderings taken to-gether show that the best meaning to give the word in Heb. xi. 3 would be *prepared*, as in the previous chapter (Heb. x. 5). So that the sense of the verse would be, that while the events which we see with our eyes taking place around us do not happen by chance, as judging by appearances, or from the outward phenomena, they seem to do ; but are *prepared*, ruled or over-ruled by God, who has, in His own ordering, " the dispensation of the fulness of times " (Eph. i. 10) ; and orders all " according to the purpose of the ages which He purposed in Christ Jesus our Lord " (Eph. iii. 11. Compare R.V).

It is by faith in what God has revealed in the "faith-ful sayings " of the prophetic word that we perceive and "understand " this great fact which, to the out-ward eye of mortal man, is neither seen, nor understood, nor even acknowledged.

The rendering of the third verse, according to this, would be as follows :—

---

* καταρτίζω *(katartizō)* occurs in the following passages, and is rendered *mend* in Matt. iv. 21. Mark i. 19. *Perfect (perfected, made perfect, be perfect*, &c.), in Matt. xxi. 16. Luke vi. 40. 2 Cor. xiii. 11. 1 Thess. iii. 10. Heb. xiii. 21. 1 Peter v. 10 ; *fitted*, Rom. ix. 22; *restore*, Gal. vi. 1 ; *framed*, Heb. xi. 3 ; and *perfectly joined together*, in 1 Cor. i. 10 ; *prepared*, Heb. x. 5.

"By faith we perceive (by the word of God) that the ages were prepared, so that, the things we see, come to pass not from things that appear." That is, as we said above, as we walk by faith and not by sight, we understand that we cannot and must not judge by the outward appearances, because in one of His weighty "words" God has told us that He "seeth not as man seeth; for man looketh on the outward appearance, but the LORD looketh on the heart" (1 Sam. xvi. 7).

It was by such a faith as this that these elders knew that things were not what they seemed, and therefore did not judge by sight of the outward eye.

Though the Flood *appeared* to be delayed, and the unbelief of others seemed to be encouraged by it, Noah did not judge by those appearances, but believed the words of God as to "things not seen as yet."

It was by such faith as this that Abraham and Sarah, though at first staggered by the words of the angel, yet as soon as they "understood" that they were "the words of God" they considered not the outward appearances of their natural physical condition, but waxed "strong in faith," and believed God as to what they could not see.

It was by "such a faith as this" that Joseph did not consider the circumstances as they appeared to him in Egypt, but believed God as to their going up thence at the set time that He had prepared, even to the very year.

It was by "such a faith as this" that Moses was not deceived by the outward splendour of his royal surroundings in the Court of Egypt, but voluntarily surrendered all; *refusing* the treasures; *choosing* the sufferings; and *esteeming* reproach for Christ as better than all. For he judged and "endured as seeing Him who is invisible " (*v.* 27).

But we must not anticipate.

The whole chapter and all its parts must be studied in the light of this third verse.

It does not carry us back to Creation, and divert our thoughts into such a totally different channel; but, it lays the foundation in no uncertain way for all that is to follow.

This foundation has been hidden from the readers of the Word

(1). By rendering αἰῶνες (*aiōnes*) " worlds " instead of *ages.*

(2). By rendering καταρτίζω (*katartizō*) "framed" instead of *prepared* as in Heb. x. 5 ; " framed " being a rendering which is not given it in any other of the thirteen passages where it occurs.

(3). By rendering γεγονέναι (*gegonenai*) "made" instead of *happened,* or *came to pass,* which is its usual meaning. There are words for *creating* and *making,* but this is not one of them.

It will be seen that verse 3 is not written to teach that there are "more worlds than one;" or that they were created out of nothing; but it is written to give us, at the outset, the secret of the elders' wondrous witness, which consisted in this ; that they walked "by faith and not by sight"; and that, therefore, they did not look on the outward appearance or judge by outward phenomena; but, understanding that the ages and dispensations were all prepared by God, they rested on the prophetic Word, and believed that He was overruling all for the accomplishment of His own counsels in them and through them.

3. Faith (cometh) by Hearing

In our last paper on this chapter we saw that the third verse was not a digression from the subject which the chapter had introduced, but it laid the foundation still deeper.

In verse 1 we have the definition of faith—as to its nature.

In verse 2 we have fact that it was by the exhibition of such a faith as this that the elders obtained a good report. Having borne such witness themselves, they obtained witness from God, and thus became a great cloud of witnesses (ch. xii. 1) for our example and encouragement.

In verse 3 we are told that faith, in its nature, always has regard to the things which are not seen : and that those who exercise such a faith as this do not walk by sight ; they do not judge by outward appearance, and they "understand" that the things we see do not happen from chance or from things of which the outward human eye takes cognisance.

But this to a certain extent is negative.

Before we pass on to the first example of these elders—to the faith of Abel—we must go deeper, and seek for some positive information as to the origin of "such a faith as this."

This is something beyond the definition of faith or its nature, characteristics, results, and manifestations.

Whence does it come ?

To this question there is only one answer,

IT COMES FROM GOD

We read in Eph. ii. 8 : " For by grace ye are saved through (*i.e.,* by means of) faith : and this not of yourselves. [It is] God's gift : not of works, in order that not any one might boast."

This language is unmistakable, and will be thankfully received by those who do not stumble at the freeness of that grace (Matt. xi. 6).

If we go further, and seek to know how this gift comes from God, then we find the answer in Romans x. 17, and here we have no verb. The A. V. and R. V. both supply the verb "*cometh*" in italics; and probably no better could be supplied.

To see the argument of the context of Rom. x. 17 we must go back to *v.* 13.

13. " Whosoever shall call on the name of the Lord shall be saved.

14. How then shall they call on him whom they have not believed ?

And how shall they believe on Him of whom they have not heard ?

And how shall they hear apart from one proclaiming ?

15. And how shall they preach if they be not sent ?

According as it standeth written " How seasonable [are] the feet of those announcing glad tidings of good things " ! (Isa. lii. 7).

16. But not all obeyed the glad tidings. For Isaiah saith (ch. liii. 1) 'Lord, who hath believed our report ?'

17. So then, faith [cometh] by hearing [the report], and the hearing [cometh] by means of the word of God."

Thus the manner in which faith cometh is graphically explained and illustrated. It believes that which comes from God. Hence it comes as "the gift of God."

In this seventeenth verse (of Rom. xi.) there are three words which call for further notice.

The word rendered "hearing" is not the *sense* of hearing, or the *act* of hearing, but it is the *matter* which is heard. Hence in verse 16 it is rendered "report." "Who hath believed our report?" *i.e.*, what they have *heard* from us.

The word is ἀκοή (*akoē*). And what they had heard was concerning Christ, as is clear from the concluding words of the previous chapter (Is. lii. 15).

> "That which they had not been told them shall they see (or perceive).
>
> And that which they had not heard shall they consider."

That which they had been "told" was about Christ,* and it came from God.

In Hab. iii. 2, we have the same word : "O LORD, I have heard Thy speech ;" *i e.*, what Thou hast said. The Heb. is *Thy hearing.* (See margin).

In Gal. iii. 2., the Apostle asks, "Received ye the spirit ? (*i.e.*, the New nature) by the works of the law, or by the hearing of faith ?" *i.e.*, by believing what ye heard from God through me (compare *v.* 5).

---

* Hence the various reading in Rom. x. 17, which the Revisers have adopted, "and hearing [cometh] by the word concerning Christ." This reading is supported by Lachmann, Tischendorf, Tregeller, and Alford.

The next sentence tells us that, that which faith ("such a faith as this," Heb. xi. 2) believes cometh by hearing "the word of God."

The word rendered "word" here is not λόγος (*logos*) but ῥῆμα (*rhēma*). This is important, and significant: for these words must be distinguished from each other.

The former means a *word* which is made up of letters; while the latter is an utterance which is made up of *words*. Hence it means *saying*, and includes the whole of *what is spoken.**

Finally the word "by" in Rom. x. 17 is not the same in both parts of the verse: "Faith [cometh] *out of* hearing." Here the word is ἐκ (*ek*) *from*, or *out of* denoting *the source* whence it comes. But when it says: "Hearing [cometh] by means of what God has said," the word is διά (*dia*) with the Genitive case, which denotes the *cause*, or *instrumentality*. We have no need to alter the translation so long as we understand and remember the significance of the two words, thus rendered "by."

From all this we learn that the faith that saves comes from God, because there can be no such faith at all apart from what He has spoken.

He is the first great cause of faith. Unless He had spoken there could have been no place for faith.

Now from Heb. i. 1 we learn further that God has spoken "at sundry times, and in divers manners." Or, according to the R. V. "by divers portions and in divers manners."

We may render the opening words of Hebrews thus: the Epistle begins: "In many parts and in many ways, of old, God, having spoken to the fathers by the

---

* See Luke i. 38; ii. 29; iii. 2; v. 5. John iii. 34; v. 47; vi. 63. 68. Acts v. 20. 2 Peter iii. 2.

prophets, at the end of these days He spoke by His Son."*

This statement finds its illustration and explanation in our chapter.

God spoke to Abel, to Enoch, to Moses's parents, to Rahab and others, of which speaking we have no historic record given. We know that He must have spoken, or there would have been nothing for them to believe.

Furthermore, what He spoke to each was not the same ; God spoke *of many matters*, as well as at many times and in many parts, and many ways.

What God spoke to Noah He spoke not to Abraham. He did not tell Noah to get him out of his own country and go into another. Nor did He tell Abraham to prepare an ark.

God spoke on many subjects, and each one who heard His words, and believed what He said, exercised saving faith and pleased God. For "without faith it is impossible to please Him."

We all love to be believed in what we say ; and there is no surer way of giving offence to others than by disbelieving their word.

Now had we been called to make a list of the elders of old who had "such a faith as this," it is certain that we should not have selected the names as given to us in this chapter. We should probably have left out some whose names are here given ; and we should have included others which the Spirit of God has omitted.

---

* The Article not being necessary after the Preposition ἐν (*en*) *by*.

Our list would differ, because our object in forming the list would not be the same as the Divine object.

God, in His infinite wisdom, has caused the *Chronological* order to coincide with the *Experimental* order.

The Chronological or Historical order in which these elders lived, coincides with the Experimental order in which they are presented to us, because that is the order in which we are to learn the great lessons thus set before us.

Abel's faith is put first, not merely because he lived before the others, but because he believed God as to the first great fundamental truth that comes before all others: peace with God; access to God; worship of God; and all this through the blood of an accepted substitute.

We will not anticipate what we have to say on this; but mention the great salient points which distinguish this first group of three.

Enoch's faith comes next, not because he lived next (for other of the Patriarchs must have had "like precious faith"), but because we are to learn the experimental truth that "two cannot walk together except they be agreed" (Amos iii. 3); and that we cannot *walk* with God unless we can *worship* Him. We must know what it is to have "peace with God" before we can enjoy "the peace of God." Hence Atonement comes before Communion. Worship comes before Walk.

Noah's faith comes next, not because no others after Enoch believed God, but because we are to learn, experimentally, that we cannot *witness* for God, unless we know what it is to *walk* with God.

It was because of this great eternal principle that

we read of the Lord Jesus, that " He ordained twelve that they should BE WITH HIM—and—that he might send them forth to preach " (Mark iii. 14).

None can be "sent forth" by Him till they have been "with Him." We must know what it is to *walk* with God, before we can *witness* for God.

Thus, this first group of three elders lays down for us these three eternal principles. They are " written for our learning."

In Abel we have faith's WORSHIP.

In Enoch we have faith's WALK.

In Noah we have faith's WITNESS.

This order cannot be reversed or changed without disaster. Many try to *walk* with God who do not know what it is to enjoy peace with God : hence they try to be saved by their walk, instead of by faith through God's grace. Many try to *witness* for God who do not know what it is to enjoy a " walk with God."

But all this is doing ; and it ends in death.

It is works, and not grace.

It is sight, and not faith.

Let us learn these great lessons which lie at the threshold of Hebrews xi. so that we may better understand the examples and illustrations that are given.

Before we consider these we have to look at the second part of Romans x. 17.

We have learned that " faith [cometh] by hearing." We have yet to learn that hearing [cometh] by means of what God hath spoken.

4. Hearing (cometh) by the Word of God

In speaking of old time to the fathers by the Prophets, God spoke in many parts and in many ways. He spoke in command, in warning, in expostulation, in reproach, in encouragement, in judgment, in prophecy, in promise, and in grace.

Of those who heard, " some believed the things that were spoken, and some believed not," some obeyed and some were disobedient.

God also spoke at many times and on many subjects: and the faith of each one who believed what He said was exercised in a different direction.

In the case of Enoch we are not told what God said to him. From the remote context, the last Epistle of the New Testament (Jude 14), it would seem that it was about the coming of the Lord with all His saints. Whatever it was, Enoch believed God; and from the still remoter context, the first book of the Old Testament, we learn that His faith in this blessed fact resulted in His walk with God (Gen. v. 24).

In the case of Abraham, God spoke in command and in promise. The command was to leave his own country; and the promise was that he should have a son.

In the case of the Parents of Moses, God must also have promised a son; and must have so described him, that, when the child was born, they knew that it corresponded with what God had said.

In this way each speaking of God was the occasion of hearing, the hearing of faith.

The responsibility of each was to believe what was heard. The record concerning Abraham "the father of the faithful" is that, "by the hearing of faith . . . Abraham believed God, and it was accounted (or, imputed) to him for righteousness" (Gal. iii. 5, 6).

This must be the experience of all true believers. They must "believe God," and not man. They must believe what God says and has said; and not the traditions of men.

To "believe God" is not necessarily to believe or rehearse a "Belief."

The popular question, "Do we believe?" is thus seen to be as absurd as it is meaningless.

If we answer this by asking, "Believe what? Believe whom?" the emptiness of the question is at once exposed.

These are the questions for us to-day.

"ABRAHAM BELIEVED GOD."

Do we believe God?

God has told us that there is "no good thing" in man (Rom. vii. 18). Pulpit, Platform and Press, with one voice declare that there is some good thing in man.* Whom do we believe?

God has told us that He created the heavens and the earth and all that is therein (Gen. i., Isa. xlv. 18). Man tells that it was all evolved, apart from God. Whom do we believe?

The Lord Jesus said "no man can come unto Me, except it were given unto him of My Father" (John vi. 65). Man says every man can come. Whom do we believe?

---

* At a convention of "The Alpha Union" for the development of the New Theology, held at Penmaenmaur on August 3rd, 1907. The founder described it as being "a re-asserting of the essential divinity in man."

The Lord Jesus said, " God is spirit : and they that worship Him MUST worship Him in spirit " (John iv. 24). Man says that worship must be by " acts of worship " which the flesh can perform. Whom do we believe ?

The Holy Spirit declares that " there is one Body " (Eph. iv. 2-4). Man makes and insists of having many bodies. Whom do we believe ?

The Holy Spirit gives the solemn charge by Paul, " Preach the word . . . for the time will come when they will not endure sound doctrine " (2 Tim. iv. 2, 3). That time has come, and man says that " Preachers must find something that man will endure," and " must preach something other than ' the Word.' " " We can afford to pay for it, why should we not have it ? " Whom do we believe ?

God declares that these last times are " perilous times " when " evil men and deceivers shall wax worse and worse " (2 Tim. iii. 1, 13). Man says the times were never more full of promise for good; and are getting better and better every year. Whom do we believe ?

" The spirit speaketh expressly that in the latter times some shall depart from the faith, giving heed to deceiving spirits and teachings of demons " (1 Tim. iv. 1). Man, in these " latter times " tells us on every hand that these are not " spirits " (i.e. evil angels) or " demons," but the " departed spirits " of human beings and we are exhorted and invited on every hand to " give heed " to them. Whom do we believe ?

God said to our first parents " ye shall surely die " (Gen. ii. 16). The old serpent said " ye shall not surely die " (Gen. iii. 4). And all his " ministers " to-day with one voice repeat that lie, and teach it as God's truth. Their creed is expressed for them in the words—

> " There is no death,
> What seems so is transition."

Whom do we believe ?

The Prophetic word declares concerning the resurrection of " the rest of the dead " that they " lived not again until the thousand years were finished " (Rev. xx. 5). Man declares they are alive all the time *without any resurrection*. Whom do we believe ?

The Holy Spirit declares that this world is a dark place, and that, the prophetic word being the only light in it we " do well that we take heed " to it (2 Pet. i. 19).

The vast majority of preachers declare that the prophetic word is the " dark place " and we do well to avoid it. Whom do we believe ?

God declares that " If we confess our sins, He is faithful and just to forgive us our sins " (1 John i. 9). The majority of Christians, though they habitually say with their lips, " I believe in the forgiveness of sins," yet refuse to believe God, and tell us that " no one can ever know that he is forgiven." Thus, they " make God a liar," and say, practically, " Lord, I am not going to believe what Thou sayest in 1 John i. 9, until I have some evidence in my own feelings, that what Thou sayest is true ! "

They thus believe their own feelings, but refuse to believe God's pledged Word.

Which are we believing ?

These examples might well be extended, and other illustrations might be found.* For, inasmuch as

---

* Notably 1 John v. 12.

Isaiah lv. 8 is true, and man's thoughts and ways are the opposite of God's, we may always ask : Whom do we believe ?

This was the question for Israel at Kadesh-Barnea. Moses had told the people how God had said : "Go up and possess the land which I have given you, but ye rebelled against the commandment of the LORD, and ye believed him not, nor hearkened to his voice " (Deu. ix. 23).

We seldom think of the awe-inspiring solemnity of the words : " So we see that they entered not in because of unbelief " (Heb. iii. 19).

God spoke to Israel and said : " Go up and possess the Land. Go up over the hill-country of the Amorites." It was a solemn moment ; ever to be remembered.

"TO-DAY, IF YE WILL HEAR HIS VOICE "

They heard His voice that day. He said: "Go up. Enter into My rest. Yet, in this thing ye did not believe the LORD your God " (Deu. i. 32).

As those words of Psalm xcv. (called the *Venite*) are sung week by week (generally as rapidly as the words can be got out of the mouth) how few stop to think of the solemnity of their meaning ! " Forty years long was I grieved with that generation ! "

Yes ! Forty years of wandering. And why ? Because they believed the evil report of ten men, instead of two who witnessed to the truth of God's good report which HE HAD ALREADY GIVEN OF THAT LAND.

True, they did enter at last. After long years of wandering they crossed the Jordan on the East when they might have entered by the hill-country of the Amorites from the South 37½ years before !

And when Peter made the proclamation in Acts iii. 19-21 and called on the nation to " Repent ; " and gave God's promise that He would send Jesus Christ, and times of refreshing should come from the presence of the Lord ; the people were *at another Kadesh-Barnea !* They were, again, face to face with another command, and promise of the Lord. And a way was open over (as it were) " the hill-country of the Amorites." This was the Parousia or Coming of the Lord, made known to faith in the first and earliest of all the Epistles of Paul, and made known by a special revelation in 1 Thess. iv. 13—v. 11.

This was something better than " the hill country of the Amorites," and it was far, far better than crossing by Jordan. For, this would have been a going up indeed ! It was entering the heavenly Canaan without going through Jordan, " the grave and gate of death " to resurrection. This was a hope for those who were alive and remained.

That is why the Apostle could say : " WE, which are alive and remain " : for, how was he to know but what the nation would Repent ; and that he would really be among those who were alive, and would go up over the hill-country, yea, in the clouds of heaven, without dying, or crossing Jordan ?

As 1 Thess. iv. was the Kadesh-Barnea of believers in that day, and Israel as a people did not thus " go up." So is Phil. iii. 10, 14, 20, 21, our Kadesh-Barnea " to-day, if we will hear His voice."

Thousands of Christians refuse to believe His voice. They agree in affirming that the only way of entering Canaan is by crossing the Jordan, the river of death. Some few of them go on to believe that it is by death *and resurrection.* But how few believe that " God has prepared some better thing for us."

In writing to the believers in Thessalonica in A.D. 52, while Peter's offer of the kingdom, made in Acts iii. 19-21, was still before the nation, and before its formal withdrawal, in Acts xxviii. 23-28, nothing could be added to the revelation then made in 1 Thess. iv.

But after that withdrawal of the offer from Israel, and the sending of the Salvation of God to the Gentiles, the question is, was any further revelation to be made? Had God exhausted the riches of His grace and of His glory? Had He nothing more to make known to His children?

May we not gather our answer to these questions from our Lord's words in John xvi. 12, " I have many things to say unto you, but ye cannot bear them now."

Why could the disciples not bear them at that time? Because He was still alive. The corn of wheat had not yet fallen into the ground and died (John xii. 24). Because He had not yet risen again from the dead. On those facts rested important doctrines. Until therefore the events had taken place, *those doctrines could not be made known.*

Was it not even so in the case of 1 Thess. iv? Had not certain events to take place before any fresh revelation of truth would be made known? Had not the formal withdrawal of Peter's offer to take place? and then, would not the way be open for further revelations to be made? Ought we not, reasoning from John xvi. 12, *to look for something fresh* from the treasures of God's grace and glory? Surely we ought. And, if we do, we find that, when the Apostle was in prison in Rome, *those revelations were given* to him; secrets hidden from men for generations, and "hid in God," were made known : The great mystery or secret concerning Christ and the Church.

In that Roman Prison precious secrets were revealed for the Apostle's, and for our own comfort and faith and hope.   And the question again arises :

Do We Believe God?

Shall we be like Israel at Kadesh-Barnea ? Shall we believe God speaking through Paul as He spoke through Caleb and Joshua ? Or shall we believe the majority, as Israel believed the majority of the spies?

Shall we say that when Paul wrote 1 Thess. iv. God had nothing fresh to reveal, in the face of the fact that up to that time we have not a breath of the mystery ? Not a word as to the revelation and teaching given to us in Ephesians ?

Did Paul himself know anything about it until he was inspired to inscribe it in his book and his parchments (2 Tim. iv. 13)?

Does not this tell us that the objects of our faith are WRITTEN DOWN in the Scriptures of truth, and not *handed down* by the traditions of men ?

And did the Epistle to the Ephesians contain all that God had to reveal ?

Is there nothing new in Philippians ?

What is the ἐξανάστασις (*exanastasis*) or *resurrection* and *translation* in Phil. iii. 10, at which the Apostle so desired to arrive ?

What is the " prize " of the " calling on high " (τῆς ἄνω κλήσεως (*tēs anō klēsiōs ?*) *v.* 14.

The A.V. and R.V. have obscured this by translating it " high " as though it were an adjective ; whereas it is an adverb, and should be rendered *upward* (as R.V.

margin) or *on high*.   Was not the Apostle's goal *conformity to Christ in glory ?*

Is this the same as 1 Thess. iv. ? or, Is it something additional ?   The whole context seems to show that the Apostle was reaching forth to something set before him, and forgetting the things behind him.   He did not reckon that he had laid hold of it ; but he pressed toward the goal. He had not already reached it, but he was following on so that he might lay hold of that, for which he was himself laid hold of by Christ Jesus.

If we read carefully verses 10-15, may we gather that we have some fresh revelation of glory hinted at ? and, Is it because we have been trying to identify it with 1 Thess. iv. that the passage (Phil. iii.) has always been more or less of a difficulty with all of us ?

If, then, Faith cometh by hearing what God hath spoken, let us " to-day hear His voice," that we may enter into His rest.

Abel: Faith's Worship of God

1. The Two Ways of Access

"*By faith Abel offered unto God a more excellent sacrifice than Cain by which he obtained witness that he was righteous, God Himself bearing witness to his gifts: and by it* [*i.e.*, by means of his faith which led to his martyrdom] *he, having died, yet speaketh.*"

As "faith [cometh] by hearing" (Rom. x. 17), Abel and Cain must both have heard what sacrifice they were to bring.

As hearing [cometh] by, and consists of, what we hear through the Word of God, Abel and Cain must both have heard *from God*.

Otherwise it would have been by *fancy*, and not by *faith;* and there would not have been room, either for obedience on the one hand, or for disobedience on the other.

We find further particulars on this matter in the history, as recorded in Gen. iv.

But first we have to notice the place where the history is written.

In the *first* chapter of Genesis we have the creation of man.

In the *second* chapter we have man in communion with God.

In the *third* chapter we have the Fall of man ; and, at the end (*v.* 24), we see man driven out from the presence of the LORD God.

In the *fourth* chapter we have *the way back to God* made known.   This is the first thing that is revealed after the

Fall. It stands on the forefront of revelation. It is no mere fragment of Hebrew folk-lore to be dismissed as an " old-wives'-fable." But it takes its place here, in God's revelation, as being the first and earliest event, not only in Chronological or Historical order, but as being the first in Experimental order also. It is the first great lesson that is written down in the Scriptures of truth—" for our learning."

God must have spoken (as we have said) to Cain and Abel, concerning the manner in which He would be approached. He must have spoken of the way in which those who had been driven out might return back, and have access to Himself.

The lesson which is taught us by this first example of faith is that, Abel believed that which he had heard from God on this all important subject, and Cain did not believe God.

It is worthy of remark that in the *Historical* order in Gen. iv. 3, 4, Cain is mentioned first, and in the *Experimental* order in Heb. xi. 4, Abel is mentioned first.

Cain is mentioned first, in the history, for he was the elder. He brought his " offering unto the LORD." He was not godless, as is often represented. On the contrary he was most " religious," and the offering which he brought cost him much more than Abel's did. He sought access to the same LORD and looked for the same blessing as Abel did.

But the point is, that the way back which he took, *was his own way :* while the way which Abel took was *God's way,* which He had revealed and laid down.

Cain had heard the "report" as well as Abel, but he did not believe God. He invented what he must have supposed to be a better, or more excellent way.

"Cain brought of the fruit of the ground, an offering unto Jehovah" (Gen. iv. 3). But, that ground the LORD God had just before put under the curse for man's sin, and had said to Adam "cursed is the ground for thy sake" (Gen. iii. 17).

Cain, therefore, brought, as his offering to the LORD that which He had pronounced to be "cursed."

Abel, on the contrary, brought of the firstlings* of his flock, and the fat thereof.

What was it that made Abel's a more excellent † sacrifice than Cain's?

Commentators have speculated much, and differed widely as to this. A variety of causes has been assigned.

But there is no room for more than one interpretation the moment we remember what the words "by faith" mean.

They mean that God had spoken; that Cain and Abel had heard; that Abel obeyed God and Cain did not!

The whole matter is perfectly simple. And the lesson it brings home to our hearts to-day is just as simple and clear.

It was a question, as we have seen, of believing what had been spoken as to

THE WAY BACK TO GOD

God's way back (which Abel took) was by sacrifice, by the death of a substitute, by the blood of Atonement.

---

* This was the law of redemption, which was afterwards laid down in the Israel's legislation. See Exod. xiii. 12 ; xxxiv. 18-20. Num. iii. 46, 47 ; xviii. 15, 16, etc.

† See Heb. iii. 3, and compare Matt. v. 20; vi. 25; xii. 41, 42. Mark xii. 33   Luke xi. 31, 32 ; xii. 23.

Man's way back (which Cain invented) was "without blood"; and a way which he had devised out of his own heart. But, "without the shedding of blood is no remission of sin" (Heb. ix. 22).

Cain might have brought his sin-offering just as easily as Abel. It lay at his door (Gen. iv. 7). (See R.V. margin); it was ready to his hand. If he "did well" he needed no sin-offering; and he would have been "accepted." If he did not well, and sinned, then God would have had respect to his offering as He had to Abel's.

No! it was the "New Theology" of his day: and it consisted. in *not believing what God had spoken;* and in inventing a "New" way of his own.

In this lay his sin.

This is why God "had not respect" to his offering, however much Cain may have worked to produce it. The "sweat of his brow" could be no substitute for the "blood of the lamb."

In all this we are shown the great fact that there never have been but these "two ways" in the world's history.

However many and however various may be the religions of the world, all may be reduced to these two. Whatever may be the excrescences and excentricities of man's imagination, there is always this "reversion to type" (as Evolutionists say).

Here we have the typical embryo of all the subsequent "History of Religions."

Man may hold his "Parliament of Religions,"* but when all his talking is done, there is a reversion to

---

* And considering the hostilities which exist between them and the conflicts which have raged, they will soon require to hold, not a "Parliament of Religions" at Chicago, but a "Conference" at the Hague, to regulate their warfare.

type, and we come back to these two primal facts, and to these two ways.

> One is God's way, the other is man's,
> One is by faith, the other is by fancy,
> One is of grace, the other is of merit,
> One is of faith, the other is of works,
> One is Christianity, the other is Religion.

The one rests on what God has said, the other rests on what man thinks.

The one rests on what Christ has done, the other rests on what man can do.

These two words sum up and embody the two ways—" DONE " and " DO."

As to what man is to "do" there is no end to the variety. In no sphere is evolution seen to such a remarkable extent.

Evolution is a solemn fact, but it is seen *only in human affairs*, because man has departed from God.*

Nowhere else is evolution seen. *Outside human affairs the evidences of evolution are non-existent :* but it is, undeniably, the order of this present evil world where evil is found ; for evil, like evolution, *is not found outside man's world.* There is no escape for man but God's appointment for him, and that is death. This is why it is Christ's work to " deliver us from *this present evil world* according to the will of God, our Father " (Gal. i. 4).

Evolution consists in unbelief and *in departure* from God. Hence it is that we see its germ first exhibiting itself specially *in the religious sphere of human affairs.* In

---

* See " *The Truth on Evolution*," by Philip Mauro, in *Things to Come*, January and February, 1908.

the Divine sphere, whether in the animal or vegetable kingdoms, we look in vain for any trace of its action.

We see it working in the medical, legal, military, naval, artistic, and in every department of the scientific spheres, but it is in the religious sphere that it was first seen ; and it is in Genesis iv., in the history of Cain and Abel that God shows us its beginning. Jabal and Jubal, and Tubal-Cain and a generation of artificers soon followed in " the way of Cain " (Gen. iv. 20-22).

" The way of Cain " was the first step in the evolution of Religion. Its developments and ramifications are to-day innumerable.

But in the way of Abel there has never been any evolution. *Substitution* and *the shedding of blood* remain the only way for " the remission of sins " to this present moment ; and will remain the same to the end.

These are the Two Ways which are set before us here in Cain and Abel.

In the one no change has ever taken place ; it is the only way back to God. Christ suffered " the just for the unjust that He might bring us to God " (1 Pet. iii. 19). This is its end, and it is headed up in Christ. In the other, there has been nothing but change. *Evolution* has run its constant and persistent course, and will continue so to do until it reaches its end in the deification of man, and is headed up in Antichrist.

All who are in " the way of Cain " are labouring on behalf of man, and for man's improvement. They are ready with their own ideas as to what man must DO to be saved.

Whatever may be the varieties evolved from man's imagination they are all one in asserting that man MUST do something. Whatever their differences or their controversies, they all agree in that. **Man must DO SOMETHING.**

Man must be something, feel something, experience something, give something, pay something, produce something. He must be called and "registered" something.* He must DO something.

They all insist on the last however they may differ about the others. Where they do differ is only in what the "something" is to be. It is this which accounts for the vast number of different systems of religion which have been evolved in the world's history. All these are rightly called "Religions." Even "the Christian Religion" is only one of them; and has as many Sects and Divisions as any of the others.

However many may be these differing forms, they are *all one in Doing*, while in true Christianity they are "all one in Christ" only.

Christianity is of God; and consists in a Person— Christ; Religion is of man, and is carried on for man, and in his interests. It consists of men's Forms, and Rites, and Ceremonies, Articles, Creeds, Confessions, Doctrines, and Traditions, Churches and Chapels, and Synagogues, Halls, and Rooms.

If your something does not agree with that of others, then be careful, or you may be killed, as Abel was, by one of these Cains. For, there is nothing in the world so cruel as Religion.

It was Religion that murdered Abel. It was

---

* This is according to English Civil Law, and it is carried out except when a census is made. Then, Religious enmity and hatred step in, and will not allow it lest it should be shown that one predominated over the other. Without a census, each may make its own boast.

Religion that killed the Prophets, Crucified Christ,* and produced the noble army of Martyrs.

It was Religion and the strife of religious sects that delivered Jerusalem to the sword and power of Rome.

It was Religion that afterward wrested Jerusalem from Rome, and terrified Europe by the threatened advance of the Saracen's sword.

It was Religion that deluged the Holy Land with the blood of the Crusades.

It was the Religion of Pagan Rome that cried " the Christians to the Lions."

It was the Religion of Papal Rome that gave Christians to the Stake; that invented all the tortures of the Inquisition ; that sent forth Armadas with its in-struments of torture, and has ever since been engaged in foul Conspiracies, Plots, and " Knavish Tricks " in order to obtain and secure its ascendency.

It is Religion to-day that lies at the root of, and per-vades the world's political strife: and it is in the struggle for Religious supremacy in " Rome Rule " and " Education" that the greatest bitterness, " envy, hatred and malice, and all uncharitableness," are mani-fested and exhibited in the political controversies in the present day.

The question of 1 John iii. 11,12, brings out the con-trast between Christian love and Religious hate.

" This is the message that ye heard from the begin-ning, that we should love one another. Not as Cain [who was] of that Evil one, and slew his own brother. And on what account slew he him ? Because his own works were evil, and his brother's righteous."

---

* It was not the ungodly rabble, but the Chief Priests and the leaders of the religious party.

Cain's works were evil, because they were his own, and of the Evil one, who (in the previous chapter) had ruined his parents by the same unbelief in God's words. Abel's works were righteous, because they were " by faith," and according to what God required.

Hence Cain's hatred, and hence Cain's murder.

It will be found that Religion has shed more blood, and produced more sorrow and crying than all the wars and desolations caused by the politics and dynasties of the world put together. There have been, and still are, the wars of Creeds, as well as of Races.

There is more in the Margin of Gen. iv. 10, than appears on the surface. The words of the LORD to Cain are full of significance : " What hast thou done ? the voice of thy brother's bloods crieth unto me from the ground." We must need explain this plural, " bloods."

In the ancient Jewish Commentary,* we read : " He says not *blood*, but *thy brother's bloods*, *i.e.*, his blood, and the blood of his posterities, his seeds."

The Targum of Onkelos explains it as " the voice of the blood of the generations which were to come from thy brother."

The Jerusalem Targum says " the voice of the blood of the multitude of the righteous who were to arise from Abel thy brother."

It seems, almost, as though the Lord Jesus meant the same when He said : " That upon you might come all the righteous blood shed upon the earth from the blood of righteous Abel unto the blood of Zacharias."

Whether these interpretations be correct or not, the fact remains most solemnly true that all these various

---

* The *Mishna. Sanhedr.* Cap. iv., 5.

Religions are one, in origin, in character, and outcome, and also in cruelty.

In the vital matter of Salvation they unite, and are
ONE, in saying with one voice :—

SOMETHING in my hand I bring.

Whereas, in true Christianity, which is Christ, the
convicted sinner proclaims the existence of the great
dividing gulf, and says :—

"NOTHING in my hand I bring,
Simply to Thy Cross I cling."

This puts nothing between the sinner and the
Saviour ; whereas it is the essence of all Religions to
put something, whether it be a Priest, or Sacraments,
or Creeds, or Ceremonies of some kind or other. Something has to be said, or done, or believed, or felt, without
which, they, as one Creed puts it,

" Cannot be saved."

This is the first great lesson which we learn from
Abel's faith :—" *The Two Ways of Access.*"

In one of those two ways, each one who reads these
lines, stands, to-day.

Either he is trusting to something *instead* of Christ,
or to something in *addition* to Christ ; or, he is trust-
ing wholly in the merits of that Substitute whom
God has provided, even the precious blood of that
Lamb which "speaketh better things than that of Abel "
(Heb. xii. 24).

2. The Two Ways of Worship

The Faith of Abel shows that, beside the Two Ways of Access to God, there are Two Ways in the Worship of God.

Both are " by Faith;" In both, we see that faith cometh by hearing, and the hearing cometh from what God hath spoken.

As there are only Two Ways of Access, one the true way, and the other the false way, with many varieties, so there are only Two Ways of Worship ; and the False way with as many varieties and differences, each claiming to be the right way.

It is as important for us therefore to learn the true Way of *Worship*, taught us by this aspect of Abel's Faith, as it was to learn the lesson of the True Way of *Access*; especially in the present day when Ritual occupies such a large place in public opinion, and in the conflicts and controversies which rage between the opposing Religions, and clamouring Sects.

In both cases, believing, or not believing what God has spoken lies at the foundation of all.

As to the only way of Access, and the only offering that was to be brought, the command of God must have been the same for Abel and Cain then, as it was for Israel afterward when the law was put into writing by the inspiration of the Holy Spirit, and the pen of Moses.

The Book of Leviticus (which is the book of worship) opens with the words, which give it its name in the Hebrew Canon.

"AND JEHOVAH CALLED

and spake unto Moses out of the Tabernacle of the Congregation saying, Speak unto the children of Israel, and say unto them, IF ANY MAN of you bring an OFFERING UNTO JEHOVAH ye shall bring your offering of the cattle, even of the herd and of the flock."

Observe, that the command was not that they should bring an offering, but that, *if any man brought one*, the command was as to what he should bring.

This agrees with, and explains Jer. vii. 22-24 :

" I spake not unto your fathers nor commanded them in the day that I brought them out of the land of Egypt, concerning burnt offerings and sacrifices ;

" But this thing commanded I them, saying

OBEY MY VOICE

and I will be your God, and ye shall be my People; and walk ye in all the ways that I have commanded you, that it may be well unto you.   But

"THEY HEARKENED NOT

nor inclined their ear, but *walked in the counsels and in the imagination of their evil heart*, and went backward and not forward."

This is precisely what took place at the gates of Eden.   There the LORD God spoke.   Cain and Abel heard.   Abel believed what he heard.   Cain (like Israel afterward) *hearkened not nor inclined his ear, but walked in the counsel and imagination of his own evil heart.*

This is the essence of the whole matter.

God spoke.   He spoke to Israel "out of the Tabernacle," to all who would approach Him there ; and laid down, as He had a right to do, how he would be worshipped.

It is the same principle which prevails to day.

Man himself acts on this principle. If any seek him, it is he who appoints the time and place and determines as to when and where he will be seen.

So, God laid it down from the first that, if any man would bring an offering to Him, it must be such and such an one, and it must be offered in such and such a way.

"And he (the offerer) shall put his hand upon the burnt offering: and IT SHALL BE ACCEPTED FOR HIM to make atonement for him," (Lev. i. 4).

But Cain hearkened not to the voice of God; and, instead of bringing what God had appointed, he brought an offering out of "the counsel and imagination" of his own evil heart (Jer. vii. 24).

And, not only so. Not only was it something, *other* than what God had approved, but it was the product of that which God had laid under a curse: "cursed be the ground for thy sake" (Gen. iii. 17).

So that there was a double affront in Cain's offering: and being not "of faith," it was "sin" (Rom. xiv. 23).

Hence, it standeth written:

"Jehovah had respect
Unto Abel and his offering;
But unto Cain and his offering
He had not respect."

And to day, the Question comes to us:—

To what will Jehovah have respect?
What offering will He accept?

Not the blood of bulls and goats; for all these types have been fulfilled in the antitype. Now, Christ's blood is that which speaketh better things than that of Abel; no one can be accepted but through its merits.

And as to worship: What is it that Jehovah now

accepts? What voice do we hear coming from Him who tabernacled among men? What does the voice say which we are to obey? What are the words to which we are to hearken?

They come from the true Tabernacle which the Lord pitched and not man. And God, who in times past spake unto the fathers by the prophets, hath in these last days spoken unto us by HIS SON : and the Son hath said :

> **'God is spirit**
> **and they that worship Him**
> **MUST**
> **worship Him in spirit**
> **and in truth.'**

These are the words to which we are to hearken, as written down for us from the lips of the Son, in the Scriptures of Truth.

We have no liberty; no choice in this matter. It is useless to follow the counsels and imaginations of our own hearts. That one short word

> "MUST"

settles every thing.

It tells us that God will not "have respect" to anything but what is *spiritual* in our worship of Himself.

The SON, who hath spoken from heaven has declared that "the flesh profiteth nothing" (John vi. 63).

It is useless therefore for us to bring unto the Lord anything that is of the flesh ; or anything that the flesh can do.

It must all be 'spirit'!

The flesh is under the curse. "The mind of the flesh is death" (Rom. viii. 6).

To bring anything, therefore, of the flesh, or that the

flesh can do, is to be exactly like Cain, when he brought the fruit of the ground, of which God had said : " cursed be the ground."

All the senses are of the flesh.

The mind of the flesh is sensual.

" The works of the flesh " are the opposite of " the fruit of the Spirit " (Gal. v. 19-25).

" They that are Christ's have crucified the flesh, with its affections and desires."

Acceptable worship therefore, MUST be the " fruit of the Spirit " and not " the fruit of the ground ": or in other words, not the works of that flesh, which is under the curse.

We cannot worship God, Who is spirit, with our *eyes*, by gazing on a sacrament or anything else.

We cannot worship God, Who is spirit, with our *ears*, by listening to music, however beautiful it may be, or whether " rendered " by ourselves or others.

We cannot worship God, Who is spirit, with our *noses*, by smelling incense, or anything else.

We cannot worship God, Who is spirit, with our *throats* by singing Hymns or Anthems, Solos, Quartets, or Choruses.

The only singing that goes beyond the ceiling or roof and enters heaven " MUST " be of the spirit, and from the heart.

The command is " singing and making melody
                    IN YOUR HEART
to the Lord."

Singing, not to one another, not to an audience, not to a congregation, but
                    " To THE LORD."

What is needed in true worship is not " an ear for music," but a *heart* for music.

If we are "filled BY the Spirit," our singing will be of the Spirit, from the heart.   For "that which is born (or produced) by the Spirit, is spirit."   (John iii. 6).

We shall say with Mary,

"My SOUL doth magnify the Lord
My SPIRIT hath rejoiced in God my Saviour."

Nothing short of this is the worship to which God will have respect.

All else is waste of time, waste of trouble, waste of money, waste of strength, waste of breath ; and,

"IT PROFITETH NOTHING"

It is useless for any one to say ' I like such and such a service.'   ' I like to hear, or to do, this or that.'   ' It creates such nice feelings in me.'   Or, ' I dislike this or that in Divine Service.'

It matters nothing whatever what any one may like or dislike, think, or feel.   It is not a question of what I may like or dislike : The question is

WHAT does GOD LIKE?

What does God require ?

To what will God "HAVE RESPECT" ?

Divine Service is supposed to be, on the face of it, service or worship rendered to God.

It is for Him to say therefore what He desires.

Public Worship is not a Service offered to or for the public, but by the public, for or to God.

It does not matter, therefore, how beautifully a Solo, or an Anthem or a Hymn may be "rendered" (that is the correct expression); but it does matter whether God will "have respect" to it.

It does not matter how beautiful the voice may be to which we hearken, but it *does* matter whether we hearken to God's voice, and whether we obey HIS voice.

The SON of God hath spoken (John iv. 24). We have heard His words.

The one question is Do we believe Him? Do we remember that "whatsoever is not of faith, is sin" (Rom. xiv. 23).

Will We Obey?

Will we worship " by faith," as Abel did? or will we worship by works as Cain did?

Do we desire to obtain God's approval with Abel? or, do we desire to hear God's words to Cain "cursed art thou from the earth" (Gen. iv. 11).

When Cain saw that God "had not respect" to his offering, he was "very wroth." And there will be many who read these words, who will be also "very wroth"; and wroth with us for writing them.

For this cuts at the root all man's accepted traditions, his cherished practices, and his boasted capabilities.

It cuts off from him the praise and applause of man. It writes folly on his vain counsels and imaginations. It makes an end of his attainments and ambitions.

He may, and doubtless will, go on in "the way of Cain," just the same. But it all counts for nothing. 'It profiteth nothing' It is 'labour in vain.'

God has no respect to it.

It would be folly for us to dwell on the faith of Abel, without seeking to learn this great lesson which is thus "written for our learning" and stands on the very forefront of God's revelation, in Gen. iv.

If we learn not the "obedience of faith" in this

matter, it is vain for us to go further with our studies of
this subject of Faith.   For it all turns on this :

Do We Believe God ?

He hath " in these last days spoken unto us by His
Son ?

His Son hath said : " They that worship Him MUST
worship Him truly in spirit."

Do we believe what He has said ?

This is the one final question, the true answer to
which does away with all that passes as " current
money with the Ishmaelite merchantmen," who make a
gain out of so-called, " public worship," to day, just as
the Ephesian silversmiths made theirs out of the
shrines of their goddess Diana.

It puts an end to all the tricks and contrivances of
the Christian " Religion," all the new fashions, and
modern methods, bands and songs and solos, and
orchestral services, cantatas, which are all to do with
the " Flesh," and are all for the praise and glory of
the choir ; and no longer, as the simple worship of
our fathers was—" to the praise and glory of God."

This is the lesson of Abel's faith, as it touches on the
one and only true way in the worship of God.

3. Abel's Faith: the Witness God Bore

"*By which* [faith] *he obtained witness that he was righteous, God bearing witness to his offering*" (Heb. xi. 4).

HERE we have two statements in one, for it is the same verb in each clause. The A.V. renders the first "witness" and the second "testimony."

The R.V. renders it: "Through which he had witness borne to him that he was righteous, God bearing witness in respect of his gifts." On this, there is a marginal note: "*over his gifts.* The Greek Text in this clause is somewhat uncertain."

The uncertainty referred to is about the word "God": as to whether it should be the Genitive case, or the Dative: *i.e.*, whether it should be as it stands in both Versions, or whether it should be "bearing witness by his gifts to God." (Lachmann, & Tregelles).

But the scope of *both* the clauses is the same. It is the witness that Abel obtained and that God gave. God gave it ἐπί (*epi*) *upon* or *over.* Not Abel obtained it "by."

In other words, Abel obtained the witness, because God gave it. He received what God gave.

How this was done is not explained in the history of Gen. iv. There, the whole act is condensed and summed up in the words "God had respect to" his offering: but we are not told how God manifested this respect.

It must have been shown in such a way that there could be no mistake about it; and that Cain could just as evidently see it, as Abel; and knew that the opposite was true in his case ; and that to his offering, which he brought, God " had not respect."

It is the word ἐπί (*epi*), *upon*, (which the R.V. margin renders *over*), which gives us the key to the solution, by reminding us of the subsequent fact revealed in connection with all Sacrifices : viz., that those which God accepted were never consumed by fire emanating from this earth, or kindled by fire " made with hands " ; but by God-made *fire descending from heaven.*

In Gen. xv., 17, Abram, in his deep sleep, saw a smoking furnace; which, beside being typical of Israel's affliction in the " iron furnace " of Egypt, was doubtless the material agency by which the sacrifices, which Abram had so carefully prepared and arranged, were consumed.

In Gen. xxii., 6, 7, when Abram " took the fire in his hand " we have the Figure *Metonymy*, by which the " fire " is put for that which would set light to the wood which was consumed ; as when we say we " light the fire " we do not light the fire but we set fire to the wood. If the fire is literal then the "hand" is literal, and Abraham "took the fire in his natural hand " : which is absurd.

In Lev. ix., 24, on the occasion of the first formal offering on the Altar of burnt-offering, we read : "There came a fire out from before the LORD,* and consumed

---

* Compare chap. x., where Nadab and Abihu used, not this fire from the brazen altar to kindle the incense in their censers, but took *other* fire: *i.e.*, emanating from this earth, or kindled by man's hand. This was called "strange fire," and the consequence was that, " there went out a fire from the LORD *and devoured them,* and they died before the LORD " (Lev. x., 2).

When we reflect that the incense of worship on the golden altar must be kindled with fire taken from the brazen altar of atonement, we can understand the sin of offering in worship to-day the " strange fire " of that which is produced by the flesh, and not by the Spirit of God."

upon the altar the burnt ·offering, and the fat, which when all the people saw, they fell on their faces."

When Gideon prepared his offering in Ophra " the angel of the Lord put forth the end of the staff that was in his hand, and touched the flesh and the un-leavened cakes; and there rose up a fire out of the rock and consumed the flesh and the unleavened cakes " (Judg. vi., 21).

This was no fire kindled by Gideon, or "made with hands" of man. It was supernatural fire produced by the miracle wrought by Jehovah's messenger, to show that He had accepted Gideon's offering.

When Manoah made his offering "and offered it upon a rock unto the Lord, the angel did wondrously; and Manoah and his wife looked on. For it came to pass, when the flame went up toward heaven from off the altar, that the angel of the Lord ascended in the flame of the altar. And Manoah and his wife looked on it, and fell on their faces to the ground " (Judg. xiii., 19, 20).

Here again was miraculous fire from the Lord, con-suming and accepting their offering. It was no fire kindled by human hands.

When David offered his offering on the altar which he built on the site purchased from Ornan the Jebusite, "The Lord answered him by fire upon the altar of burnt offering " (1 Chron. xxi., 26).

At the dedication of the Temple, when Solomon had ended his prayer, we read that "the fire came down from heaven, and consumed the burnt-offering and the sacrifices; and the glory of the Lord filled the house . . . and when all the children of Israel saw how the fire came down, and the glory of the Lord upon the nouse, that they bowed themselves with their faces to the ground, upon the pavement, and worshipped" (2 Chron. vii., 1—3).

When Elijah would offer a sacrifice away from the Temple where Jehovah had caused His name to be placed, and where the fire which had fallen from heaven was kept continually burning,* fire had to fall from heaven specially for the occasion.   After the prophets of Baal had in vain tried to produce the phenomenon by appeals to their god, and after Elijah had soaked the wood and the offering with water we read: "Then the fire of the LORD fell and consumed the burnt sacrifice, and the wood, and the stones, and the dust, and licked up the water that was in the trench.   And when all the people saw it, they fell on their faces, and said: The LORD, He is the God; The LORD, He is the God" (1 Kings xviii., 38, 39).

Add to all these examples the words of Psalm xx., 3, "The LORD remember all thy offerings and accept thy burnt sacrifice."

Here, in the margin of the A.V. we read, against the word "accept," that the Hebrew means TURN TO ASHES.

Why?   Because this was always the way that Jehovah did accept offerings made to Him.   By "fire from heaven" He *turned them to ashes*, and thus showed that He "had respect" unto them, and accepted them as the substitute of him who offered them.

How else did Abel "obtain witness that he was righteous"?

---

* It is in imitation of this that the Church of Rome pretends to keep the perpetual light before their altars, in spite of the fact that it is kindled by man's hands and consumes nothing but their own pretensions.

How else did God testify of his gifts ?

How else did Cain know that God "had not respect unto his offering " ?

Surely there can be no doubt whatever as to the force of the word ἐπί (*epi*), *upon*, for it was the fire that descended *upon* the sinner's substitute *instead of upon the sinner*; upon Abel's lamb instead of upon Abel.

Thus the doctrine of substitution was the very first doctrine taught to mankind; the first that is recorded in the Scriptures of truth; the first with regard to which man was required to believe what he had heard from God.

God had spoken. What he had said may be summed up in the words afterwards recited to Israel, "Without shedding of blood is no remission" (Heb. ix., 22). "It is the blood that maketh atonement for the soul" (Lev. xvii., 11). "The wages of sin is death" (Rom. vi., 23)

This was the pronouncement for the sinner in Gen. iii., 17. And it is in Gen. iv. that we have the further revelation that God provided a substitute whose death He would accept in the sinner's stead.

That is why the acceptance must be God's own act.

All that the sinner could do was in faith to bring his offering and lay his hand upon it and confess it as his substitute. (Lev. i, 4.) *It was for God to give His testimony that He had accepted it.*

It is even so to-day.

It is ignorance of this great first lesson that is the source of much of the quite modern evangelistic phraseology of the present day.

Man's conventional talk of this twentieth century (of the present era) is about the sinner's acceptance of

Christ. God's Word, for nearly sixty centuries has been about the sinner *believing what He had said.*

God has spoken. He has told us that He cannot and will not accept the fallen sons of men in their sins. In ourselves we are not only ruined sinners because of what we have *done,* or *not done*; but we are ruined creatures because of what we ARE. The question is, Do we believe God as to this solemn fact?

What God accepted was Abel's "gifts" (Heb. xi. 4); Abel was accepted only in his gifts (Gen. iv. 4).

So, God has told us that He can accept us, as such, only in the merits and Person of that perfect Substitute—His Christ—whom He has provided. Do we believe Him as to this?

If we do we shall by faith lay our hand on Him, confess our belief in God as to our own lost and ruined nature, and as to Christ as God's provided Salvation; knowing that, by this faith, God pronounces us righteous, *accepts us in the person of our Substitute*; and declares us as "accepted in the Beloved," because God accepted His one offering when He raised Him from the dead.

Christ's resurrection is the proof and evidence that God has accepted Christ. Christ risen is the sinner's receipt which God has given to show that He has accepted Christ's payment of the sinner's debt.

There is no other receipt.

Christ's blood is not the receipt. That is the payment.

The sinner's faith is not the receipt. It is no use for a man to go to his creditor and say he *believes* he has paid what he owes. He must produce the receipt.

What is the receipt which we can produce to God which will prove that our debt is paid ?

Nothing but the blessed fact that God's Word assures us that He has *accepted payment on our behalf* in the person of our Substitute, when He raised Christ from the dead.

We are to believe what He says when He assures us of this, and He is pleased to accept us in Him.

It is always the Creditor who accepts the payment which the debtor makes. And, when payment has been once accepted, no further demand can be made upon the debtor.

This is how Abel was accepted ; and this is how the sinner is saved to this day.

By the same faith in what God has said, we lay our hand on that Lamb of God as our substitute ; and we obtain God's witness that we are righteous. God bears His testimony to this in that He raised Christ from the dead, and has accepted the believing sinner IN HIM.

It is not a question of whether the sinner *accepts Christ*, but *whether* he believes *God* when he says that He *has accepted Christ.*

It may be said that, the same thing is meant, in modern phraseology ; then, Why not say so ? Why not keep to Scripture language ? Why alter it ? Why make it all to stand on what man can DO, instead of believing what God has SAID. Why make it all turn on man's accepting, instead of man's believing ?

God has shut up the sinner as to the uselessness of his bringing any thing of his own by way of merit.

It is useless for him to bring or plead any substitute

other than that one whom God hath appointed. It would be the same as saying it is *not necessary.*

It is useless to bring anything in addition thereto, for it would be the same as saying that it is *not sufficient.*

In either case it would be a proof that God's command had been unheeded; that His word had not been believed; and that His provision had been slighted and rejected.

All are to-day either in Abel's way, or Cain's: in God's way, or man's.

All are trusting either to that Substitute whom God has provided, or they are labouring to provide one for themselves.

This is why such stress is laid on this matter of faith, in Rom. x. "The righteousness which is of faith speaketh on this wise . . . But what saith it? The word is nigh thee, even in thy mouth and in thine heart: that is, the word of faith, which we preach [is nigh thee]: that, if thou shalt confess with thy mouth the Lord Jesus [as thy Substitute] and shalt believe in thine heart that

GOD HATH RAISED HIM FROM THE DEAD

thou shalt be saved."

Thus it is that "Faith cometh by hearing, and nearing [cometh] by the Word of God" (Rom. x., 6—11, 17).

But instead of believing the report of what God has said, sinners are taught to-day to believe in what they can do. As though they were the Creditor, and would fain make God their Debtor!

And all this, because they do not see or understand that "all is of God"; and all is of

GOD'S FREE GRACE

There is no merit in faith, of itself. It is not considered as merit among men, when one man believes what another man has said. How then can there be any merit in believing what God has said? It is our first bounden duty, without which all is " sin."

But, instead of this, the sinner tries *to make God believe in him;* and that it is possible for him to DO SOMETHING.

In his blind ignorance he practically tells God that he, the sinner, is pleased to accept the payment which Christ has made to God!

But all this is only salvation " by works " in its most subtle form. So subtle that thousands are misled on the very threshold of their way back to God.

Hence it is that while the multitude are still taught to do something, many would shrink from doing certain things as " works "; and would be ready to confess, and say: " not the labour of my hands." Yet they do not see that this acceptance of Christ is a work, after all: when it is thus put in the place of believing God.

True, it is " not the labour of my hands." Nothing "made with hands " can obtain a footing in God's new creation, where " all things are of God ": for new creation ground is the ground of resurrection.

Though they would shrink from making a god with their hands, they make their god out of their own heads, and out of the imagination of their own hearts.

But " the God of our Salvation " is the God who hath spoken unto us by His Son, and left to us the simple duty of pointing the sinner to what He hath said.

This is why we are to " Preach the Word." This is the first great lesson of Holy Writ.

It is the oldest lesson in the world.

And, it is to show us that to believe God in this matter of substitution is the only way of salvation, the only way for man to be just with God ; for " The just. by faith, shall live."

4. The Witness Abel Obtained

Though rendered "obtained witness" and "testifying," the verb is the same in both clauses.

"*By means of which* [faith] *he was borne witness to as being righteous* ; *God bearing witness to his gifts.*"

We have spoken of the witness which God gave; we have now to speak of the witness that Abel obtained : *viz.*, that he was righteous.

We have already emphasised the fact that both Abel and Cain had heard what God had spoken, as to what both men were, by nature, in His sight. Both were exactly the same; both were equally begotten by Adam " in his own likeness " (Gen. v. 3).

They were "sons of men" and not (as Adam had been) sons of God : that is to say, sons of Adam, and Eve, as *fallen*. There was "no difference" (Rom. iii. 21).

It is true that Adam had stood in a different category. He had been *created* (not begotten) in " the likeness of Elohim ; " and created in Paradise : but these had both alike been begotten in *Adam's own likeness* ; and were begotten outside Paradise.

From this point therefore our object-lesson begins. This is why it is the first great lesson set before us. This is why it stands on the forefront of God's revelation.

There had been "some good thing" in Adam, though he was human. But there was "no good thing" in Cain, or Abel. "That which is begotten of the flesh

IS (and remains) flesh." And even Paul in later days had to learn the all-important lesson, and confessed " I know (as a solemn reality*) that there does not† (as a matter of fact) dwell in me, that is, in my flesh, good " (or with A.V. " any good thing ").

Thus, boldly and plainly is man's *gospel of humanity*, and the " Divine immanence " in man, set aside as having no part or place in God's sight.

All who are born in the fallen likeness of our first fallen parents, are born with " no good thing abiding in them."

It is not a question here, or indeed elsewhere, about what man has *done*. It is wholly and altogether a question only of what man IS.

The most ungodly man that ever lived will regret, and repent, and be very sorry for many things he has *done*, or left *undone*. The vast majority, to-day, will own that they are sinners.

But, this is only a very small part of the whole matter ; so small as to be hardly a part at all.

It is an ancient Pagan confession to say " *humanum est errare*," " it is human to err." It is equally human to regret it.

But, here, it is a question NOT of what man had *done*. Very probably both Cain and Abel had sinned, but it was a question of what they WERE, by nature.

---

* The verb is οἶδα (*oida*) and it means *to know*, as a matter of absolute knowledge. Not γινώσκω (*ginōskō*) *to get to know*, by effort or experience.

† The negative is οὐκ (*ouk*) and denies objectively and absolutely, as a matter of fact. It is not μή (*mē*) which denies subjectively, and hypothetically. Moreover, the negative οὐκ (*ouk*) here, is connected with the verb "dwell," and not with the noun " good ": " There does not DWELL any good "; not " there dwells not good (or any) good."

As it was with Isaiah, when he saw himself in the presence of God, and in the presence of all that was thrice "Holy"; so it will ever be with all who thus become acquainted with the true character of their human nature.

Isaiah's words were

"I AM

undone." It was not like our "general confession": "We have left *undone* those things we ought to have *done,* and we have *done* those things which we ought *not to have done.*"

There may be all this and more; but there is something behind, and something beneath, and something far beyond all this, and that is:

"THERE IS NO HEALTH IN US."

This is the confession that, we are not only lost *sinners;* but that we are fallen *creatures.*

We are not only "sons of men," begotten by Adam, but we are *born of Eve.* She it was who was in the Transgression. Adam was not (1 Tim. ii. 13, 14).

So that we are doubly ruined: ruined *sinners,* and ruined *creatures.* Ruined, not because of what we have DONE, but because of what we ARE.

If we had never *done anything,* good, bad, or indifferent, we should still have no right to re-enter the garden, or to go into the presence of God. We should have no "right to the tree of life," but should be subject to death. We should still need at least a forensic righteousness: that is to say, we should need to be *acquitted;* to be pronounced "not guilty;" and to be put into a position where our sins would not be imputed to us (Ps. xxxii. 1, 2).

But this is, surely, very different from having a Divine righteousness imputed to us!

The one is negative, and the other is positive.

What we have to ask is: Was the righteousness of Abel the same as that of Abraham's? We read that Lot was "a righteous man" (Pet. ii. 7, 8), and yet he is not included in this chapter.

Abraham himself, from the time of his call in Gen. xii., was surely, as righteous as Lot who left him and went toward Sodom. Surely he was, like Abel, forensically, that is, judicially acquitted. In Gen. xiii. God made him further promises, and in Gen. xiv. God had been with him, prospered him, and sent Melchisedek to bless him. But it is not till Gen. xv., that we read of a very different righteousness, which was imputed to him.

This was no mere negative blessing of *non imputation of sin*. It was no mere pronouncement of "not guilty," but it was the positive reckoning to Abraham, as actually having righteousness imputed to him.

It was on the occasion of God making a further promise of a son, in his old age, and under very special circumstances which were all contrary not only to reason, or to sight, but to all the laws of nature.

THEN, it is written, "Abraham believed God, and it was imputed to him for righteousness." What this meant for Abraham in the way of blessing in God's sight we are not told. But it must have been a distinct advance in Divine favour; and it accounts for much that we read of Abraham which we do not find in the case of others who are mentioned in this chapter.

This positive reckoning of righteousness is revealed only in connection with Christ in the Gospel. This is why Paul announces his readiness to preach this good news in Rome.

For this readiness to announce this good news he adduces *four* reasons: each introduced by the word γάρ *(gar) for* :

1. For I am not ashamed of the Gospel.
2. For this reason: It is the power of God unto salvation to every one who believes God.
3. For this further reason: viz, that in this Gospel a righteousness is revealed "from faith to faith": *i.e.,* God has made fresh revelations for the objects of man's faith; and has revealed how man may not only be acquitted but justified.
4. For, the conclusive reason which constitutes this as being such good news: that, not only is a righteousness from God revealed, but wrath from God is revealed also, from which this gospel brings the good news of complete deliverance.

This is a* righteousness revealed in the Gospel. It is more than a forensic righteousness. It is something given and received by imputation on the principle of faith. And it is this righteousness, which is imputed to believers now. It is not God's *attribute* of righteousness ; nor is it His acting in conformity with that attribute; but, it is something which He imputes or reckons to the believer. In other words, it is *imputed righteousness.*

In Rom. iii. 25, 26, we find both aspects of the word righteousness, with reference (1) to the time past (in the Old Testament), and (2) now "at this time" (in the Gospel.)

(1). As to the *time past,* God was acting righteously in

---

* There is no article here, in the Greek.

passing over sins, in His forbearing grace, *i.e.*, in judicially *acquitting* those who believed Him when He spoke "at sundry times and in divers manners."

(2). As to *the present*, "at this time." He declares that He is equally just in justifying: *i.e.*, in actually imputing righteousness " to him who believeth in Jesus ;" who believeth what He has made known about the Saviour.

Hence in 2 Cor. v. 21, we advance to a further revelation, viz., that those who believe God now in what He has revealed of Christ are made Divinely righteous in Him.

Therefore to believe God in what He says *now*, in His Gospel, concerning His Son, is not only to be saved from wrath by His power, not only to be *acquitted* as " not guilty " but to be *accounted* as positively righteous, by His grace.

Romans iv. is therefore a distinct advance in the argument and treats of this imputed righteousness.

But all is by faith ; *i.e.*, by believing what God has revealed.

Abel believed God, and he was judicially acquitted. God bore witness to his gifts by accepting the death of the substituted lamb, instead of the death which Abel deserved as a sinner. Hence Abel was righteous; and stood judicially acquitted before God.

But this brings us to a further question, as interesting as it is important. Why is this righteousness, whether forensic or imputed, all made to depend on our *believing what God* says?

Why was not some other condition laid down by God?

Out of all the many things which God might have required of man, why is "faith" singled out as the one and only ground of justification, and this, for all time, from that day till now?

Is not this question worth asking?

From Gen. iv. we see the condition in action; and in the Epistle to the Romans we see it *stated* and defined. Moreover a reason is given that "it is of faith that it might be by grace," but nowhere is any *explanation* given as to why it should be so, and why *faith* should be the reason why man should be either judicially acquitted of his sin; or why Divine righteousness should be imputed and reckoned to him.

THE EXPLANATION

is not given in so many words; but it is placed very clearly before us on the opening pages of the second, third and fourth chapters of Genesis.

Faith is made the condition, because unbelief was the cause of Man's Fall, of Sin's entrance, and of Death's appointment for man.

This lies on the surface of the history.

Eve fell by *not believing* what God had said. She tampered with the words which God had spoken.

She dealt with those words in the only three ways in which man can deal deceitfully with them.

(1) She *omitted* the word "freely" in Gen. iii. 1. (See Gen ii, 16).

(2) She *added* the sentence "neither shall ye touch it" in Gen iii. 3. (See Gen. ii. 17).

(3) She *altered* the certainty "thou shalt surely die," (Gen. ii. 17), into the contingency "lest ye die" (Gen. iii. 3).

Satan's two assurances,

> " Ye shall not surely die,"
> " Ye shall be as God,"

were believed; and God's words, having been omitted, added to and altered, were in the end *not believed*.

Thus, by believing Satan's words, was sin brought into the world, "and death by sin." Hence, *only by believing God, can man regain life, and sin be put away*.

(1) Only by believing God in what He has thus revealed *about man himself*, can the sinner be acquitted, and pronounced "not guilty," and, in this sense (forensically) righteous.

(2) Only by believing God in what He has revealed *concerning Christ*, can man be reckoned as being actually righteous, in Christ, and as having a Divine righteousness actually imputed to him.

This is

THE REASON WHY

believing what God says is made to be one necessary condition of justification.

Man MUST BELIEVE GOD in what He says in His Word; and he must believe ALL that God says.

In what sharp contrast does this set all that goes to make up *religion* ! Religion occupies man entirely with himself: with what he has *done*, with what he *can* do, and with what he must *do*. God would occupy man with HIMSELF, and with what He has *said*.

This it is which gives its character to all "religion" in the present day; "Man's Day." Man is exalted, and God set aside. Man's doings are substituted for man's believing. This is why, on all hands, man's *works* are substituted for God's words. And as the importance of man's works increases in his estimation, so God's Word decreases.

This is why, in the religious world the two great

questions which occupy man are : (1) what he must do to be righteous, and (2) what he must do to be holy. It is all "DOING," from first to last, instead of believing God.

But the modern, social gospel of humanity is the gospel of the Old Serpent. It is based on faith indeed; but it is faith in the devil's two lies

"Ye shall be as God"

"Ye shall not surely die."

So subtle is the poison of the Old Serpent, that not only does man, to day, in this his "new theology" not believe God's words ; but he does not believe in God's Word. This is why he puts forth his utmost efforts to get rid of all that is supernatural in the Scriptures of truth.

Here God steps in with His irreversible decree. He lays down the one indispensable condition on which He will ever have any respect to man's doings : or alter His sentence of death on account of man's own self-undoing

MAN MUST BELIEVE GOD

Here, in Abel's faith, we have *the way back to God's favour* unalterably laid down at the fountain-head of God's revelation of Himself, and of humanity.

The only way of access to God is "by faith," *i.e , by believing what He has said.*

Whosoever does that ; and takes that first simple step, stands judicially acquitted, as Abel stood.

Whosoever believes what God has further promised, in, by, and through Christ, "his faith is counted (reckoned, and imputed) to him for righteousness," as it was to Abraham. "Now, it was not written for his sake alone, that it was imputed to him ; but FOR US

ALSO, to whom it shall be imputed *if we believe in Him that raised up Jesus our Lord from the dead*, who was delivered on account of our offences, and raised on account of our justifying." (Rom. iv. 22-25).

Abraham and David believed God concerning His promises in Christ. Hence it is written that righteousness was *imputed* to *them* (Gen. xv. 6 and Rom. iv 3); Ps. xxxii. 2 and Rom. iv. 6). God preached, before, the Gospel unto Abraham (Gal. iii. 8), David spake of Christ (Acts ii. 31); and both believed God.

DO WE?

Do we believe what God has said about ourselves as ruined creatures; and, are we thus pronounced righteous being judicially acquitted?

And, do we go on to believe all that God has said about His promises in Christ, as risen from the dead? and are we thus justified on that account, our faith being reckoned to us for righteousness, yea, a *Divine* righteousness which is *imputed* and reckoned to us, so that we are made Divinely righteous in Christ?

These are the questions which are solved by the consideration of Abel's faith.

It leads us on from " *non-imputation of sin*," to the *imputation of righteousness*.

It takes us beyond the doctrine of *substitution*; beyond the sacrifice of an animal for man's sin; and leads the sinner, into the far higher doctrine of his *identification*, as a saint with Christ.

The one remaining question is: Do we go on " from faith to faith "? (Rom. i. 16, 17).

Abraham went on. In Gen. xii., xiii., and xiv. he believed God in many things about *himself*. But in Gen. xv. he went on from faith to faith. He believed

God, in another thing : *viz.*, about *the promised Seed* ! It was this faith that was imputed to him for righteousness.

Do we thus go on to believe God ?

We may believe what He has revealed of Christ in Romans, Corinthians, and Galatians : but, do we go on "from faith to faith," and believe God in what He afterwards revealed concerning Christ in Ephesians, Philippians and Colossians. and thus "give glory to God " ?

Is not all this something far beyond mere theological reasonings and scholastic arguments as to what is " the righteousness of God ? " * and about the " law-keeping righteousness of Christ," which were very rife among Brethren a few years ago ?   Those controversies created much bitterness, and left much confusion behind.   But, our subject takes us far beyond all this, and reveals to us the blessed fact that Christ Himself, in all that He IS, and HAS, and HAS DONE, is, of God, made unto us who believe Him,

" RIGHTEOUSNESS "

Instead of rejoicing in this blessed fact, and praising God for all the great things He has done for us, many of His children are engaged in a kind of *post mortem* controversy; and are *dissecting* Christ's life and sufferings. Hence, instead of " holding the Head " and living in the "bond of peace," they are biting, rending and devouring each other, the " members."

Oh that we may go on "from faith to faith," and believe God in all that He reveals to us as to our identification with Christ, in having His righteousness, His holiness, His perfections, reckoned to us; and all of His boundless grace !

---

* As though the definite Article were used in the Greek of Rom. i. 17, and 2 Cor. v. 21.

5. "The Blood of Abel" and "The Way of Cain"

WE have seen, in our last chapter, why Faith, *i.e.*, believing what is heard from God, is the only ground of acceptance with God, and the only ground of being judicially acquitted in His sight.

The blood of Abel yet speaks to us.

This is the last of these Divine words written for our learning concerning Abel.

"HIS BLOOD YET SPEAKETH"

This is not the crying of his blood to God. This is the speaking of his faith to us. "By it (*i.e.*, by this faith) though he is dead he continues to speak " (*v.* 4).

The *cry* of his blood from the ground was for vengeance on Cain (mentioned in Gen. iv. 10).

This, is a speaking, in the Scriptures, for our learning

His faith speaks to us to-day. "It" tells us that it is not something else as a *substitute* for faith : "it" tells us that it is not something in *addition* to faith.

It is not *works*. It is not *feelings*. It is not *experiences*. It is not *repentance*. It is not *love*. But it is faith and faith only.

It is not reasoning, or intellectual assent to something about God. But it is believing *what He has told* me about myself, not only as a ruined sinner but as a ruined creature ; not only about what I have done, but what *I am*. It is believing what He has told me about Christ, the Saviour Whom He has provided, and anointed, and given and sent ; and that this Saviour is able to save.

Faith has to do with what we *hear* from God; not with what we *feel* in ourselves. Our feelings do not connect us with God, but *only with ourselves*. Whatever they may be, they do not affect our relation with God, or alter our standing before Him.

They are only human at the best. But, Faith is Divine, and has to do with God.

Faith, of course, produces its own feelings, but only as its own precious fruit; but feelings will never produce faith. "Being justified by faith we have peace with God" (Rom. v. 1).

This "peace" is felt. It is the blessed feeling of "peace with God." But it comes from faith in what God has said; and not from any feeling that originates in ourselves.

Thus, the blood of Abel continues to speak to us, though Abel is dead.

But the blood of Christ speaks also. It speaks of "a better thing * than that of Abel" (Heb. xii. 24).

If Abel's blood cried for *vengeance*, Christ's blood speaks of *peace*.

If Abel's blood speaks of non-imputation of sin, Christ's blood speaks of the imputation of righteousness.

If Abel's blood speaks of judicial acquittal, Christ's blood speaks of a Divine justifying.

This, surely, is "a better thing."

Abel had to do only with a good thing—the type, but we have to do with the "better thing"—the antitype; we have that which the type prefigured, even the precious blood of Christ. If the former was able to

---

* All the Critical Greek Texts and R.V. read the Singular: "thing" instead of the Plural "things."

procure a forensic righteousness, the latter is surely able to procure a righteousness which is Divine.

Thus the faith of Abel continues to speak to us.

But Cain also speaks. He spoke to Abel. What he actually said seems to have dropped out of the primitive Hebrew Text. The Hebrew verb in Gen. iv. 8 is not "talked with" but "said," and ought to be followed by what he said. But the words having dropped out, the rendering "talked with" is only a make-shift due to the accident. Correctly rendered the printed Hebrew Text reads, " Cain said unto Abel his brother, and it came to pass, etc." In the A.V. there is a colon after the word "brother." In some of the MSS. there is a break; in others there are asterisks * * * indicating the omission.

But the Samaritan Pentateuch, the Jerusalem Targum, the Septuagint, Syriac, and Vulgate Versions contain the actual words, which originally stood in the primitive Text.

What Cain " said unto Abel" was " Let us go into the field."*

It was part of Cain's plot, to get Abel to go alone with him into the field ; and when there, together, "he rose up against him, and slew him." His words, and actions, show the deliberateness of his plans.

The carnal mind of a ruined creature at once displayed its enmity. " He was very wroth " when he

---

* The Jewish Commentators, of course, enlarge on this, and tell us a great deal more. Some indeed give us the whole conversation, which, strange to say, is largely imbued with later errors about the future state, and smacks of Babylonish tradition. With all this we have nothing to do: we only note the correction needed, and which is supplied by some of the Documentary evidence.

saw that God did not accept his offering by consuming it with fire from heaven.

While Abel's faith filled Abel with peace, Cain's unbelief filled Cain with "wrath."

Here we have part of "the way of Cain." Here we have, on the forefront of the Bible, the manifestation of what "religion" really is.

Cain was a religious man. He came to worship Jehovah. He brought his gifts and his offering. He brought it "unto Jehovah." But his works were evil; and he slew his brother (1 John iii. 12).

This is the essence of all "religion" from that day to this.

This is "the way of Cain:" and all who possess religion instead of Christ (Who is, in His own blessed Person, the essence and centre of true Christianity) are treading in that "way" to-day.

All religions are alike in this. And the "Christian Religion," as such, is no different in its spirit, and manifestations.

Speak of Christ, to anyone who has only "Religion," and at once his countenance will fall, as Cain's did (Gen. iv. 5).

But, with Cain, the LORD at once put the matter on its true ground "If thou doest well shalt thou not be accepted?" (Gen. iv. 7). This is rendered in the Septuagint Translation "if thou offer correctly."

This is what it means. "If Cain offered correctly; ' *i.e.*, what God had told him, he would have done "well," and his offering would have been accepted.

There was "no difference" between the two men. All the difference lay in their offerings, which proved that the one believed God, and that the other did not.

Abel "did well" because he believed, and hence, obeyed God. Cain did "not well;" because he did not offer correctly, though a sin-offering lay at the door ready to his hand.

He was without excuse.

Oh! how many millions have since trodden "the way of Cain."

They are like Paul himself, who at the very time when he was most religious was all the while "a blasphemer, and a persecutor, and injurious" (1 Tim. i. 13): at the very time when he was as "touching the righteousness which is in the law blameless" he was "persecuting the Church." If any one ever had a standing in the flesh, and in religion, Paul could say "I more" (Phil. iii. 4-7).

All such are like the Athenians who were "very religious" (Acts xvii. 22 R.V. margin).

It is not a question of earnestness, or zeal, or even of sincerity. Sincerity will not help us, unless, what we sincerely believe, is what God has spoken.

Man, with all his religious zeal, loves to offer God something. As one once remarked, "It seems so mean" not to do so!

Hence it is that so many strive to present to God, the labour of their hands;" and, being ignorant of what God has said, or not believing it, their one great effort is not only to improve themselves but to improve the world.

They see that all is not what they would have it to be; but, instead of believing God as to His remedy for it, they seek to substitute their own.

Even where their religion includes a belief that Christ is coming again, they think the world is not yet good enough for that, being ignorant that God has said it is not yet bad enough for His judgment (2 Thess. ii. 3).

Hence, man still treads to-day "the way of Cain," and follows him when he "went out from the presence of the LORD" (Gen. iv. 16). Man cannot endure that presence. He seeks to get as "far off" from God as he possibly can (Eph. ii. 13).

His one effort is to make that "far country" as delightful, and himself as happy, as possible. Like Cain, he builds his cities, and multiplies his luxuries.

The busy labours of "artificers in brass and iron" drown the cries of Abel's blood (Gen. iv. 22).

The noisy handlers of "the harp and organ" stifle spiritual worship and drown the voice of Abel's faith (Gen. iv. 21). So that man, to-day, is surfeited with music not only while he eats and drinks, but even while he worships!

Such is "the way of Cain." It is the way of persecution, but not of peace. It is "the way of religion" but not of Christ. It is the way of death, and not of life.

Yes, man, like Cain, is "very religious." But notwithstanding all, the earth which Cain sought to beautify was stained with his brother's blood.

And, as then, so it is to-day, the world which the Churches are seeking to improve, is stained with the blood of Christ.

As the blood of Christ speaks of a better thing than that of Abel for the believer; so it speaks also of a more terrible vengeance for the unbeliever.

It is in the last Epistle in the Canon of the New Testament that we read of "the way of Cain," and it is there associated with "the error of Balaam," and "the gainsaying of Korah" (Jude 11).

This connection is full of significance. These three downward steps are thus put together for our comparison and contrast; and they speak to us, if we have ears to hear.

Unbelief characterises all three.

The first is unbelief as to the WAY of access which God revealed: "the way of Cain."

The second is unbelief as to the WORKS of our lives which God requires: "the error of Balaam."

The third is unbelief as to the WORD which God has given: "the contradiction of Korah."

The first is necessarily followed by the second, and these are consummated by the third.

"The way of Cain" was not believing God's Word as to the way in which He would be worshipped (Gen. iv.).

"The error of Balaam" was despising God's Word, and following the counsel which Balaam gave, as to the idolatrous licentiousness of life, and the sin which brought down the plague and judgment of Baal-peor (Num. xxv. and xxxi. 16).

"The gainsaying of Korah" was the contradiction of God's Word (Num. xvi.) The Word rendered "gain-saying" ἀντιλόγια (antilogia) means *contradiction*. And though connected with "the way of Cain" in Jude 11, it occurs three times in this Epistle to the Hebrews: (viz., in Heb. vi. 16; vii. 7, and Heb. xii. 3). It is "the *contradiction* of sinners against Christ."

So the third and last of these three stages amounts to the contradiction of the Living and the written Word of God. It is exactly what we see to-day in the contradictions of the " Higher " Criticism, and in the blasphemies of the " New Theology."

The entrance on " the way of Cain " is a *deliberate going.*   " They have gone " (R.V. they went).

Into " the error of Balaam " they *rush* (A.V. " they ran."   R.V. " they ran riotously ").

In " the contradiction of Korah " they *perish* !

This is the end !

Though they pursue their own separate courses, to a certain stage, there is an evolution from one into the other, and they end alike in judgment.

Cain's was a *punishment* greater than he could bear (Gen. iv. 13).

Balaam's was a *plague* from the fierce anger of the Lord (Num. xxv.).

Korah's was the *pit* which opened its mouth and shut them up in the blackness of darkness for ever (Jude 13).

What a solemn lesson for all who refuse to believe God.

What an end to " the way of Cain."

What a contrast between the two ways.

The one is God's revelation ; the other is man's imagination.

The one begins with God ; gives peace ; and ends in glory.

The other begins with man ; goes on to persecution ; and ends in the pit !

Enoch: Faith's Walk with God

1. "The Seventh from Adam"

It is not without the greatest significance and importance, we may be perfectly sure, that Enoch is specially designated, in the Epistle of Jude, as being "the seventh from Adam."

There is, and must be something for our learning; some finger-post pointing us to a Divine lesson, in this expression, which has attracted the attention of most Bible readers.

"Seven," we know, is the number of *spiritual perfection*.* And therefore it points to some spiritual lesson in the person and faith of Enoch, which is distinctly additional to what we have learned from Abel.

In Jude 14 it is associated with prophesying. And this is by the Spirit of Jehovah; so that the first thing we see is the connection of seven with the Holy Spirit: for a prophet is defined as one on whom the Spirit of God is (Num. xii.). He alone gives the words of God, and enables the prophet to utter them as God's "spokesman."†

The expression tells us also that Enoch lived and prophesied in a day of declension and apostasy. For there were no prophets or prophecy until there was departure from God.

There was no need in Eden; for Elohim communed Himself with our first parents.

It is in the midst of the Fall, that we have the first

---

* See *Number in Scripture*, by the Editor.

† Compare Ex. vii. 1 with iv. 16, and see *The Man of God*, a pamphlet by the Editor.

prophecy. The prophecy of the coming seed of the woman was to remove the effects of sin and death : and to crush the head of the old Serpent was named as part of the very sentence of Judgment.

When God provided and ordered the ritual and ordinances in connection with His worship He ordained everything, and appointed every office and duty from that of the High Priest down to the hewers of wood and drawers of water.

But there was no provision for a prophet !

A prophet was not necessary while the priests attended to their duty of teaching the knowledge of God, and while men continued in obedience to God's laws.

Not until the Priests departed from their first duties, to teach the people the word of God, and became absorbed in their Ritual, were prophets sent to supply the deficiency; and to be spokesmen for God.

The very fact therefore that Enoch *prophesied* is sufficient, of itself, to tell us that he lived in days when men departed from God's ways.

The very fact that he "walked with God" implies that others did not.

And this is borne out by other evidence.

It has been objected by some commentators, as being very strange that, after Abel, no one is mentioned until we come to Enoch, "the seventh from Adam." No example of faith is given in Heb. xi., though we read of Enos (Gen. iv. 26) "then began men to call upon the name of the Lord."*

This has sounded strangely in the ears of many, who remember how Adam, and Abel and Seth must all

---

* See Michaelis, *Introd. to N. T.* (Marsh's translation), pp. 225, 226.

have called on the name of Jehovah in truest worship. These are universally regarded as godly men.

These two facts then: the prophesying of Enoch, and the omission of Enos, lead us to suspect that we have not yet rightly understood Gen. iv. 26.

It is a matter of fact that the words have been understood by those who ought to know what Hebrew is, in exactly the opposite sense.

The Targum (or Paraphrastic Commentary) of Onkelos (about the second century B.C. in Hebrew) says: "Then, in his days, the sons of men desisted from praying (or became profane so that they prayed not) in the name of the Lord."

The Targum of Jonathan (or Palestine) says: "That was the generation in whose days they began to err, and to make themselves idols, and surnamed their idols by the name of the Word of the Lord."

Kimchi and Rashi agree with this. The latter says: "Then was there profanation in calling on the name of the Lord."

Jerome also says, (*Quaest,*) that this was the opinion of many Jews in his days.

Without doubt these interpretations arose from a well-known signification of the verb חָלַל (*chālal*) *to call,* but also, *to profane,*† and the information, given in the note below, shows that there is good ground for this view.

---

† It is in the *Hophal* conjugation which is used only once (in Gen. iv. 26), so that we have no means of determining its exact sense. In the *Hiphil* it is rendered *begin* 52 times, pollute 1, *sorrow* 1, break 1, first 1. In the *Pual*, it is rendered *to be profaned* 1, *to be slain* 1. In the *Poel, to wound* 1, *to be wounded* 1. In the *Piel*, it is rendered *to defile* 8 times, *to pollute* 18 times, *to profane* 30 times, cast as profane 1, &c.

The margin of the A.V. shows that an object after the verb *to call*, must be supplied, and the word "themselves" is suggested. But there is better reason for supplying *their gods*:—"Then it was begun to call upon [their gods] by the name of Jehovah."

That corruption began at a very early date is evidenced by the whole analogy of Scripture.

If it was with Enos the grandson of Adam that idolatry commenced it would correspond with his name *Enos*, which means, *weak, mortal, miserable*; and it would correspond also with the fact that it was Jonathan the grandson of Moses, who became the first idolatrous priest in Israel (Judges xviii. 30.)

His name was "Jonathan the son of Gershom, the son of MOSES," for the word Manasseh is one of four words in the primitive Hebrew Text which has what is called a "suspended *Nun*": *i.e.*, the letter *Nun* (נ) is written in a smaller character, in, or over the word to show that it originally formed no part of the word, and was inserted there more by way of suggestion, or for pronunciation.

The word is מֹשֶׁה, and a small " N " is put between the " M " (מ) the " S " (שׁ) not in a line with the other letters—but standing out a little above them; thus making it read *Manasseh* instead of *Moses*.*

In the *Niphal* it is rendered *to be defiled* 1, *to be polluted* 4, profane one's self 2, *to be profaned* 2.

It may be added that there is no other word beside this rendered " profane " in the Old Testament (except חָנֵף (*chānēph*), compare Lev. xxiv. 11, 16. Jer. xxiii. 11, 15). All the other 34 occurrences of " profane " are the renderings of *chalal.*

* Every Hebrew MS. and printed Text presents the word thus :—

The letter נ (*nun*) is seen to be inserted, half in the word and half out. In some cases it is placed above the " S," but never as actually forming a part of the word, or as the true primitive Text.

This was doubtless done in very ancient times to spare the susceptibilities of those who should hear the scriptures read ; and to conceal, or at least to mitigate the terrible fact that, Jonathan, the grandson of Moses, was *the first to become an Idolatrous Priest in Israel*

That Jonathan was the grandson of Moses is also evident from Judges xx. 28, where his contemporary and second cousin Phineas is stated to be the grandson of Aaron.

It is significant that the name of " Jonathan " is omitted in the Genealogy of 1 Chron. xxiii. 15, 16 ; xxvi. 24, where we read " The sons of Moses, were Gershom, and Eliezer. Of the sons of Gershom, *Shebuel* was the chief." And it is equally significant that *Shebuel* must either have been another son of Moses substituted for Jonathan ; or, it may be that another name was taken by Jonathan himself, later in life, for it means " *he returned to God.*"

It may be of course (as the Chaldee paraphrase suggests) that Jonathan did return to God ; and took *Shebuel* as a new name after his conversion.

If Jonathan, the grandson of Moses, could thus profane the name of the Lord, it is no less strange that Enos, the grandson of Adam, should have done the same.

Enos was born 130 years after the death of Abel, and it would be no wonder, if idolatry began within some few years after that ; all the Patriarchs being still alive, except Adam.[*]

---

[*] From the following table the particulars as to " the Generations of Adam " will be at once seen : (See page 84).

By the time Enoch was born (in 622 A.M.) there would be need for a prophet to speak for God, and utter His warning words.

For of what did he prophesy but the coming of the Lord in judgment! And what could that judgment be for but on account of the fast-spreading corruption, and idolatry, and profanation of Jehovah!

If men began to worship the true God aright in the days of Enos, and continued to do so, why should such burning denunciation have been necessary in the days of Enoch?

But, if corruption and ungodliness then began, we can well understand why Enoch should have been raised up to prophesy of these, saying :—

> "Behold the Lord cometh with myriads of His holy ones (*i.e.*, angels), to execute judgment upon all, and to convict all the ungodly concerning all their works of ungodliness which they did ungodlily, and concerning all the hard things which ungodly sinners spoke against Him." (Jude 14, 15).

	LIVED.			
	FROM A.M.	TO A.M.	AGE AT DEATH.	CAIN'S DESCENDANTS.
1. Adam	1	930	930	
[Abel]				Cain
2. Seth	130	1041	912	Enoch
3. Enos	235	1139	905	Irad
4. Kenan	325	1234	910	Mehujael
5. Mahaleel	395	1289	895	Methusael
6. Jared	460	1421	962	Lamech
7. Enoch	622	986	365	Jabel, Jubal, and Tubal-Cain.

The repetition of the word "ungodly" is most emphatic; and it is done to call our attention to the one
subject of Enoch's prophecy, so that we may learn at
once what must have been the existing condition of
things in his days.

His mysterious removal may have given a check to
the flood of ungodliness, but the effect must have
soon worn off. For within another hundred years
Noah was raised up as " the preacher of righteousness "
being warned of God of the then impending judgment; and, moved with godly fear, condemned the
world, by his preaching of righteousness; and the preparation of the Ark.

Here, then, we have our first insight into the nature
of Enoch's faith, and what it was, in respect of which,
he believed God. He was " the seventh from Adam,"
and this carries our thoughts back to Adam, and causes
them to dwell on the character of the days in which the
six who preceded him (five of whom with their
descendants) were all living.

If Enoch prophesied, as God's " spokesman," then
God must have spoken to him and told him what to
say : God's Spirit must have been upon him. (Num. xi.
29 ; xii. 6.)*

But our point is that Enoch " believed God."

It must have been a special revelation to Enoch.
For, How could he otherwise have known of coming
judgment?

---

* We cannot believe that " Jude, the servant of Jesus Christ and
brother of James " who wrote " to them that are sanctified by God
the Father, and preserved in Jesus Christ and called " was quoting
the Apocryphal so-called *Book of Enoch* !

It is much more likely that, some one who read these words of
Jude concocted that " Book " out of his own vain imagination.

He knew from Adam, the great fact that "the seed of the woman" was coming into the world, first to suffer from the assaults of the old serpent, and finally to crush his head; and the coming of the Lord, from that moment, was always the hope of His people.

But, the coming, revealed to Enoch, was a new thing. It was a coming in judgment.

Would men believe God? It appears not. But Enoch believed: and gave forth the solemn warning of his message.

That is the question to-day. The corruption is spreading apace. Idolatry of the worst kind is the characteristic of "religion." In the so-called "Christian religion," men, to-day, do not make their gods out of wood, or metal, or stone; but of something far worse than these: they make him out of their own heads. These materials, at any rate, are pure as God created them; but man's mind is fallen and corrupt; and the imaginations of his heart are only evil continually.

Instead of the "smith with the tongs" (Isa. xliv. 12) working in the coals, we have the Theologian working with his brains in his study. Instead of the carpenter stretching out his rule making it "after the figure of a man, according to the beauty of a man" (Isa. xliv. 13), we have the Preacher stretching out his vain imagination, making his god after the ideas of corruptible man, and belching forth his "new theology." God is man, and man is God, he says.

The corruption in the days of Enos was "new." It was a "new theology."

But where are the Enochs to-day? Where are those who "walk with God," and who witness for God, by testifying: "Behold the Lord cometh to execute judgment on all this abounding religious corruption?"

As Abel's blood yet speaketh, so Enoch's prophecy yet gives forth its warning voice.

Jude, by the Holy Ghost, applies Enoch's words to those in his day, who were going in " the way of Cain." He says " And Enoch, the seventh from Adam, prophesied of THESE ALSO." Jude does not mean that Enoch prophesied as well as others; but that he prophesied of these ungodly ones, of whom Jude wrote, as well as those in his own day.

So he prophesies to the same in our day. He "yet speaketh."

It is remarkable that the word rendered "smith" and "carpenter" in Isa. xliv. 12, 13; xlv. 16, is חָרָשׁ (charash) and is specially connected with the making of idols; and it is the same in meaning as חֹרֵשׁ (chorēsh) rendered "artificer" in Gen. iv. 22.

It is also remarkable that Lamech's sons, Jabal, Jubal, and Tubal-Cain should be the *sixth* in descent from Cain.

These three traders, and inventors, were also the instructors of "artificers" in their respective arts.

How true it is that God "made man upright but they have sought out many inventions." (Ecc. vii. 29.)

This word, rendered "inventions" here, is in two other places connected with man's inventions in departure from God. In 2 Chron. xxvi. 15, it is connected with instruments of war; and in Amos vi. 5, with instruments of music. Thus, four things are allied in Cain's descendants: Commerce, Music, War, and Idolatry: Jabal, Jubal, Tubal-Cain and the "artificers" or workers in wood and iron.

All their names are connected with a common root, *to flow* ; and mark the onward flowing and increasing of Cain's descendants.

They flowed on prosperously till they were swept away by the over-flowing flood,*

They were "carried away" in the judgment; but "the way of Cain" in which they trod is filled to over-flowing with their moral descendants to-day.

"The harp, and the viol, the tabret and pipe, and wine are in their feasts; but *they regard not the work of the Lord, neither consider the operation of His hands*" (Isa. v. 12.)

On all hands we see the "smiths" and the "carpenters" at work, calling themselves and their works by "the name of the LORD" though they regard not the Work or the Word of the LORD. They call their buildings "the house of the Lord," but He has small place in them. All is done for the praise and glory of man.

Man is busy framing new fashions in Religion, new modes of worship, new theologies, new gospels of humanity and socialism; and side by side with these, the same handling of the harp and the organ.

Musical Performances, and "Festivals" turn, for the time being, our Cathedrals and Churches into Concert Halls: and from "solos and singers" we have advanced to the establishment of Institutions for the avowed purpose of the artificial instruction and training of those who rank equally with the Preachers in the announce ments and advertisements of Public Worship.

No announcement to-day is complete without

> "PREACHER, the Rev.————
>
> SOLOIST, Miss————."

---

* The word is from the same root, *Yabal: to flow.*

The "chancels" regarded by many as the most sacred spot, are profaned by being turned into "Orchestras:" and all in "the name of the Lord."

All is for man!

Man's pleasure is sought in the churches; man's achievements are eulogized in the pulpits; man's compositions are "rendered" in the choir; man's criticisms of the Bible are treated as general literature, and his new theologies are blazoned in the Press. It is "man" from beginning to end. No announcement to day, is complete unless the portrait of the Author, or the Preacher, or even the Evangelist, forms part of it.

It is solemn indeed, to find this very feature, which characterises the present day, so closely connected in the Epistle of Jude with "the way of Cain," and the prophesying of Enoch: where men are described as "walking after their own lusts," and "*having men's persons in admiration*" (Jude, 16.)

Oh! where are the Enochs, to-day! Where are those who really believe God in His judgment of all these things now, and in His coming to execute that judgment ere long!

God has warned man of "judgment to come," and all man does, is to *set it to music*, and sing it in the churches which are called by His name; boldly and profanely advertising it as the performance of

"The Last Judgment:"

and all this is engineered by the very man who should be preaching it as a warning; and is carried out by the Jubals who "handle the harp and the organ."

Is not this to repeat the days of Enos, and to " profane the name of the Lord?"

These are the men who are specially designated as

"ungodly" in Jude's Epistle: that is to say "without, or apart from God."

For, as Science has already banished God, from His Creation, so Religion has politely bowed Him out of the Churches; while, as in the days of Enos, they do all "in the name of God." Even this very formula has taken the place, and thus usurped the use, of *prayer* in the pulpit, before the preacher puts forth his profanity.

Oh! for Enoch's faith! To believe God with reference to what we have heard from Him as to His coming judgment, and to warn the "ungodly" of their coming doom.

May we not well heed the Divine exhortation founded on this very fact (in Jude 17-21).

"But, beloved, remember ye the words which were spoken before of the apostles of our Lord Jesus Christ; How that they told you there should be mockers in the last time, who should walk after their own ungodly lusts.

"These be they who separate themselves, sensual, having not the Spirit.

"But ye, beloved, building up yourselves in your most holy faith, praying in the Holy Ghost, keep yourselves in the love of God, looking for the mercy of our Lord Jesus Christ, unto eternal life."

Thus, in this Epistle, while we see angels falling (*v.* 6) and cities falling (*v.* 7) we are commended "unto Him that is able to KEEP YOU FROM FALLING, and to present you before the presence of His glory with exceeding joy" (*v.* 24).

2. "Before His Translation"

Two things are spoken of Enoch's faith: his translation, and " before his translation."

The latter, though mentioned last, must be considered first.

It was " by faith he was translated." It was by faith that, "before his translation, he was well-pleasing to God."

In Gen. v. 21-24, there is nothing said about his faith, but only about its results: " Enoch walked with God."

This it is that connects him with the faith of Abel.

" Can two walk together except they be agreed?" This is God's question by the prophet Amos (ch. iii. 3).

The answer is supplied in the fact, that, experimentally as well as historically, Abel's faith must precede the faith of Enoch.

Abel believed God as to the way in which He would be approached in worship; and Enoch had the same faith, for he who cometh to God in worship must believe that He IS,* and that He BECOMES* a rewarder of them that seek after Him."

The number *two* (in Amos iii. 3), speaks of division or unity, peace or war, opposition or agreement.†

Its first occurrence in Gen. i. 6 is in connection with *division*, and *separation*. But it is also used of *confirmation* of testimony, by the mouth of " two witnesses."

---

* The two verbs both rendered " is " in this verse, must be carefully distinguished. The former is ἐστίν (this is the verb *to be*). The latter is γίνομαι *ginomai* (this is the verb *to become*).

† See Number in Scripture, by the Editor.

Cain and Abel illustrate the former; Abel and Enoch illustrate the latter.

Abel's faith, chronologically, precedes Enoch's faith, and it precedes it experimentally also. For there can be no "walk with God," until there is "peace with God;" and there can be no peace with God before there is the Divinely accepted sacrifice. In other words justification must come before peace. Hence in Rom. v. 1 we read: "Being justified by faith, we have peace with God."

Enoch had Abel's faith which witnessed to his agreement with God; and he had Abel's righteousness, which enabled him to walk with God.

So that we get here, an advance in experimental teaching.

Sin cut off man from communion and intercourse with God. God came down and walked with Adam before the entrance of sin (Gen. iii. 8). Adam and his wife heard the sound of Jehovah Elohim walking in the garden, in the cool of the day."

But sin entered: "so Jehovah Elohim drove out the man" (Gen. iii. 24); and all communing, communicating, walking, talking and revealing were at an end.

Abel's faith shows the first step in the way back to God. The shedding of blood gave remission of sin (Heb. ix. 22). The substitute was accepted in the stead of the sinner.

The blood of Abel's lamb effected what the sweat of Cain's brow could never have accomplished. It gave "peace with God" and restored communion with God. It enabled man once more to walk with God, but on Redemption ground, and no longer on Creation ground.

Hence, the experimental advance was that, God,

who had spoken to Abel and made known, to and through him, how men must come to God in grace, spoke again to Enoch, and revealed how He would come to the earth in judgment.

For it was Amos who says again: "Surely Adonai Jehovah will do nothing, but He revealeth His secret unto His servants the prophets" (Amos iii. 7), and David adds the Divine testimony—

"The secret of Jehovah is with them that fear Him :
And His covenant to make them know it"
(Ps. xxv. 14, margin).

This blessed fellowship with God is based on blood; for, when we enjoy fellowship with God, then it is (and not in connection with sin), that we are reminded that "the blood of Jesus Christ His son cleanseth us from all sin." It is this which gives us boldness of access into the Divine light (the true *shechina*) of that presence, and preserves us alive when there.

"God is light" (1 John i. 5).
We "walk in the light" (Eph. v. 8).
"God is love" (1 John iv. 16).
We "walk in love" (Eph. v. 2).
"God is truth" (1 John v. 20).
We "walk in truth" (2 John 4, 3 John 3).

In fellowship with God, which is the result of His peace which He gives, our ears are opened to hear and receive the truth which He reveals.

To those "friends" God makes known what He doeth (John xv. 13-15). For He said "shall I hide from Abraham that thing which I do? . . . For I know him . . ."

So here, to Enoch, God made known His secret, and

revealed the solemn fact, unknown to all beside; and unknown to Enoch until God revealed it to him.

Enoch "heard" God; and faith cometh by hearing.

Enoch "believed God," and this it was that made him well-pleasing to God, while he walked with God; and this it was that ended in his Translation.

God had spoken about His coming to execute judgment on the ungodly; but, it is equally true that God did not leave Enoch in ignorance of the fact that judgment would not come upon him; for he was godly.

When God warned Noah, and Divinely instructed him as to the coming judgment (v. 7), He at the same time revealed the blessed fact that He would deliver him and bring him safely through it. Surely He must have given the same Divine instruction to Enoch that he also would be translated before it came.

Otherwise, How could it be said that it was "by faith Enoch was translated," if he had not *heard* the word of the Lord, and believed what he had heard? (Rom. x. 17).

Enoch must have *heard* the blessed, welcome, good and glorious news, that he "should not see death," but should be "translated" to heaven.

It is a perversion of the truth of God, to hold from Genesis v. (apart from Heb. xi.) that Enoch's translation merely means "conversion from worldly life and carnal pursuits,"* or to say that it means an early death, and thus a transition from this "mortal life to the immortal."

Heb. xi. is doubtless a Divine addition to Gen. v. The same Holy Spirit, who inspired Moses, inspired Paul, and gave us, by him, His own explanation.

---

* Philo, *De Abrahamo*, and elsewhere, thus allegorises the translation of Enoch.

When He explains that, "*God took him,*" and "*he was not found,*" He means that Enoch did "NOT SEE DEATH" at all, but that he was translated without dying, and was taken bodily from the earth.

It is equally a perversion to take the words "He is not here" used of a Risen Christ, and place them on a tomb-stone (as we have seen them) of one who is dead, and not risen.

Even in Gen. v. there is not the whole of the Divine revelation; for elsewhere we learn that Enoch's body must have been "changed" when he was "translated;" for "flesh and blood cannot inherit the kingdom of God; neither doth corruption inherit incorruption" (1 Cor. xv. 50).

At death, "the spirit returns to God who gave it," but "the body returns to earth as it was" (Ecc. xii. 7. Gen. iii. 19). At death, therefore, the body (the dust) remains on and in the earth. But, in Enoch's case, his body "was not found:" because "God took him," and he did not die at all.

How wrong it is therefore for any to use those words, spoken of one who did *not die*, and use them to-day of any one who *has died !*

Yet, how common it is for us to hear it said of one who has died, "God has taken him," or "God has taken her"!

It is not true. It is not the truth. It is not only non-scriptural, but it is an *unscriptural* expression.

In this case it would have been just as true for the Holy Spirit to have written "By faith Enoch died," instead of "By faith Enoch was translated."

But, people do not die "by faith." Most of them believe the teaching of demons that

" There is no death,
   What seems so, is transition."

They believe the Devil's lie rather than what they
" *hear* " from the word of God.

That word reveals the opposite of all the traditions
of men. It teaches that

   There IS death;
   What is not so, is TRANSLATION.

It required no faith on the part of Enoch to believe
that he would die. It does not say Enoch died by
faith. That would have been a matter of "sight." He
saw death on every hand.

Of each of the six patriarchs before him, it is
recorded "and he died" (Gen. v. 5, 8, 11, 14, 17, 20).
But of Enoch it is written, that he did " not see death,"
and the reason given is that "God, took him," and
" he was not found."

This implies that men looked everywhere for him,
but the search parties could not find him dead or alive.

They could not find Enoch, for God had translated
him. They could not find his corpse, for he had
not died.

Doubtless there was much excitement, if not con-
sternation. It was quite a new thing on the earth.
If they searched, they did not search in silence; but
must have wondered and speculated as to what had
become of Enoch.

Even so will it be in the coming day of the translation of those who believe God, as to His promise to
send Jesus Christ, and "take" them to "meet Him in
the air," and "call them up on high" (Phil. iii. 14).

God has revealed for "the hearing of faith," what He
has in store for His saints.

He knoweth how to execute judgment on the ungodly ; and He knoweth also how to "deliver" those whom He has justified (2 Pet. ii. 4).

As He delivered Enoch by translating him before the coming of the judgment by the Flood of waters, so will He deliver His saints from "the wrath to come."

Alas! how few of us are like Enoch and believe what God has written for our faith.

How few are, *in consequence of this unbelief,* walking with God. The many are walking with themselves, and engrossed with their own walk, instead of being occupied with what God has revealed!

How many there are who believe that they will go through the judgments of the great Tribulation! They must not be surprised if they find they are dealt with "according to their faith!"

If some (as many hold) are *not* caught away before it, as Enoch was, who will they be but "those who believe not!"

Who, of Israel, entered not into God's rest when He bade them go up "by the hill-country of the Amorites," but wandered in the wilderness for forty years, and finally entered by the fords of Jordan? Those who provoked God with their "evil heart of unbelief" (Heb. iii. 12).

To whom did God "swear in His wrath that they should not enter into His rest?" but to "them that believed not" (Heb. iii. 11, 18).

Why could they not enter in ? "Because of unbelief" (Heb. iii. 19).

So we see the full solemnity of the lesson to be learned from Israel's unbelief, and Enoch's faith.

Enoch was "not in darkness" as were the ungodly

to whom he prophesied as to the coming judgment: nor are we (1 Thess. v. 4).

Enoch heard " by the word of the Lord " that the coming judgment would "not overtake him as a thief:" and he believed what he heard.

We read the same blessed hope for ourselves in the same " Word of truth " (1 Thess. v. 1-4 ; Phil. iii. 14).

Do *we* believe it ?

That is the question that must remain with us ; and do its own blessed work in our hearts.

In 1 Cor. x. 11 these things are specially declared to have " happened unto them by way of ensample (or type), and are written for our admonition, upon whom the ends of the ages are come." And in verse 5 it speaks of those who did not believe God, and says that "with many of them God was NOT WELL-PLEASED."

But it is the very opposite that is declared concerning Enoch : for, " before his translation he had this witness borne of him that he had been WELL-PLEASING UNTO GOD."

Why ?

" By faith Enoch was translated."

That is the reason.

He believed what God had revealed to him about it : and this faith was well-pleasing to God.

Do *we* believe what He has told us about our coming Translation ?

Do *we* look for our calling on high (Phil. iii. 14) and walk with God while we witness and wait for that translation ?

If we do, it will prove, like Enoch's and Caleb's and Joshua's, a lonely walk, so far as man is concerned ;

but it will be "with Him" *here*, and soon "with Him" *there*; and, meanwhile, we shall have abounding happiness in the knowledge that we are even now, in the midst of all the confusion and corruption

" WELL-PLEASING TO GOD "

3. "He Well-pleased God"

IT is a remarkable fact that, in this chapter, every verb is, what is called in the Greek, in the *Aorist* Tense, except three, which are in the *Perfect* Tense.

That is to say, all these historical facts and events are described as having been done, and done with, as completed, and hence, are in the *simple Past* Tense, except in three places, where the *Perfect* Tense is used. The Perfect Tense denotes that the thing was done but that its effect remains. When it says, for example, that Pilate " wrote a Title and put it on the Cross," it is in the *Aorist* Tense, because it records a simple passing act that was completed, and a fact that took place, once; but when it says of the Scripture " it is written " it is the Perfect Tense, and means " it has been, or was written, and that what was written remains. So that a good rendering of the Perfect Tense in this case would be: *it standeth written.*"

We have, in the verse we are considering (Heb. xi. 5), the first of the three Perfects in this chapter. We shall come to the others in their places.*

Unfortunately, in the A.V., these three Perfects are not distinguished. In the R.V. the first is noted in the Text, but, in the case of the latter two, the note is relegated to the margin.

It devolves on us therefore, now, and here, to give the full force of the Perfect Tense in this fifth verse

---

* One of the other two is in connection with Abraham's offering of Isaac (*v.* 17); and the third is in connection with Moses instituting the Passover (*v.* 28).

for these are the "words which the Holy Ghost teacheth," and they are "written for our learning."

The Verb in question is rendered in the A.V. "For before his translation *he had* this testimony." In the R.V. it is rendered: "*he hath had* witness borne to him." If this third Person of the Verb refers to Enoch, and means "he," then it might be rendered, *he hath been borne witness to.*

But there is nothing in the Greek to compel us to understand Enoch, or to render it "he." There is no occasion to introduce Enoch at all. It is quite clear without doing this.

What the Greek says is "IT HAS BEEN [and still is] WITNESSED THAT HE WELL-PLEASED GOD."

What was the witness that was thus borne, *and still is borne* concerning Enoch? Surely it is what is witnessed of him in the Scriptures of truth: viz., that in believing what God had revealed for his faith he well-pleased God.

As the witness which Abel obtained was in the fire which descended from heaven, so, Enoch's witness which he obtained, was in his own ascension to heaven.

And thus these first two illustrations of faith are linked together. But the link is closer than this.

The great point in connection with Abel's faith is that his offering was

ACCEPTED BY GOD

The great point in connection with Enoch's faith is that his walk was

ACCEPTABLE TO GOD

We have these two distinguished in Eph. i. 6, and 2 Cor. v. 9, though in the A.V. both are rendered by the same word ("accepted"):

Eph. i. 6 is " He hath made us accepted in the Beloved : " and

2 Cor. v. 9, is " we labour, that . . . we may be accepted of Him."

The distinction between "in " and "of" is not sufficient, because the two words are totally different.

In Eph. i. 6 it is the Verb χαριτόω (*charitoō*) *to make one an object of favour.*

In 2 Cor. v. 9, it is the Adjective εὐάρεστος (*euarestos*) *well-pleasing.*

This latter is the very word used of Enoch in Heb. xi. 5, 6. His faith was well-pleasing or acceptable *to* God. Abel's offering was accepted *by* God.

This is the link between these first two men.

The former has to do with God, and the latter with man.

The former was the act of God's grace in accepting Abel's offering : the latter was the fact of Enoch's faith and walk being acceptable to God.

Thus Enoch's "walk" and Enoch's "faith" are united. He

" WALKED BY FAITH

and not by sight " (2 Cor. v. 7).

It is this walk which is so " well-pleasing to God." For in the immediate context (*v.* 9) the one follows on the other :—

"We walk by faith, not by sight . . . *Wherefore we make it our aim to be well-pleasing unto Him* " (2 Cor. v. 7, 9).

Walking with God ; and walking by faith, and not walking by sight, Enoch did not judge according to the things that he saw.

He was not deceived by any outward appearances or material prosperity ; he was not deluded by any schemes for dealing with social evils, or for improving the corrupt state of things around him.

But he showed that it is possible to "walk with God" even in the darkest days; and to witness for God in the most "perilous times."

He, doubtless, did not please men, or seek to please them. It was enough for him that he was well-pleasing to God.

This is why his translation was not merely a passing historical event, but remains as a standing witness which he obtained; a witness which remains to this day for us, to show us that a "walk by faith and not by sight" is, of all things, "well-pleasing to God."

The blood which tells of Abel's death, continues to speak to us of the only way of being *accepted* by God. So Enoch's translation which tells of his entrance to eternal life without dying, continues to witness of the only way of being *acceptable* to God.

For he that approacheth to God, in worship (as Abel and Enoch did) it is necessary for him

To Believe God;

to believe that He IS; for, "apart from faith it is impossible to well-please [Him]." It is a matter of necessity for him "to believe that He IS and that He BECOMES a rewarder of those who seek Him out."

For we who "seek Him" as Abel sought, will find Him as Enoch found Him; if not by being, while we are "alive and remain," called on high (Phil. iii. 14), and thus "clothed upon" with a spiritual body by translation (2 Cor. v. 2, 4); yet, we shall surely find Him in a glorious resurrection when "absent from these mortal bodies" we shall be for ever "at home with the Lord" in resurrection bodies, made like unto Christ's glorious body, and presented faultless in Him before God with exceeding joy (2 Cor. iv. 14, Phil. iii. 20, 21, Jude 24).

But the abiding lesson still standing before us in Enoch's faith is that, "it is well-pleasing to God " to believe Him, as to this our own " translation."

Abel believed what God had told him about the accepted sacrifice and acceptable worship.

Enoch believed what God had revealed concerning the coming judgment on the ungodly and his own prior translation to glory.

His faith, as well as Abel's blood, continues to speak to us ; and it tells us that if we would be well-pleasing to God the one thing necessary is to believe what He has revealed as the blessed object of our faith.

Our responsibility is far greater than theirs. For God, who spoke to those elders, spoke in sundry portions and in divers manners. We have what He said to them in the Old Testament. But He has since spoken by His Son ; and we have what He said in the Gospels.

But since then He has spoken unto us by His Spirit in the Epistles, and in the rest of the New Testament.

We have more to believe than those who lived in the former Dispensations.

Enoch and Noah had to believe in " the seed of the woman," and in the coming Judgment (Jude 14), others had to believe concerning "the seed of Abraham" and the coming nation of Israel (Gen. xv.), others had to believe concerning " the seed of David " and the coming Kingdom (2 Sam. vii.), others were called to believe on the Lord Jesus Christ as still to come as " the heir of all things " (Heb. i.)

When He was rejected and crucified by His own

People, others were then called on to believe that, on the repentance of the nation, God would send Jesus Christ with the times of refreshing for Israel and the world. (Acts iii. 20, 21).

When this Testimony was refused (Acts xxviii. 25, 26), then further additions were made to the revelation of God's "counsels:" and, His "purposes" which He had purposed "before the foundation of the world" were vouchsafed in the Epistles to the Ephesians, Philippians and Colossians.

Each generation of faithful ones, was in its turn, called on to believe God in what He had revealed for the faith of His people; and they were well-pleasing to Him in proportion as they did so.

But, as of old, the multitude to-day, refuse to believe Him. They still "provoke" Him, as Israel did of old.

It is as though Enoch believed what had been revealed to Abel as to approaching God, but refused to believe what had been revealed to him as to translation by God.

It is as though Abraham believed all that had been made known to Abel, Enoch and Noah, and refused to believe God that in his seed Israel shall be made a nation, and all other nations be blessed.

This is the condition of thousands to-day who call themselves "believers."

They persist in calling Israel "the Jewish persuasion," when of all others, they would not and will not be persuaded, though that blessed One did rise from the dead. (Luke xvi. 31).

They persist in calling themselves "believers" though they steadfastly refuse to believe what God has revealed in the Epistles written after the "casting aside" of Israel in Acts xxviii. 25, 26.

For all that they care, the Holy Spirit might as well have never made any subsequent revelation at all.

Though the Lord Jesus told His disciples that He had many things to say to them, which they could not then understand ; and that He would send the Holy Spirit, who would glorify Him, and guide them into all the truth yet to be revealed, His professed disciples of the present day practically tell Him that there was no occasion to send Him to do this ; and that the truth into which He guides them in the Pauline Epistles can be dispensed with.

They are content with the Old Testament revelation, and the "Teaching of Jesus." They confess their belief that Jesus Christ will " come to judge the quick and the dead," but as for any blessed hope of their translation, ascension or even of resurrection, they can do without it. They practically tell Christ, that He need not come again for *them* : *they* are going to die and go to Him ! Thus, the " traditions of men " are believed, and greedily swallowed, while the *subsequent revelations* of God are unheeded ; and those who do believe them are treated as eccentric expositors, and fanciful faddists.

How can those who thus judge be well-pleasing to God ? Is it not as true to-day as it was of Israel : that " with many of them God was not well-pleased " ?

Why ? " Because of their unbelief." God was " grieved," and " provoked," and " sware in His wrath that they should not enter into His rest."

May it not be the same in the case of thousands to-day who do not believe Him as to the way of entering

into His rest, which He has revealed in Resurrection
(1 Cor. xv.), Ascension (1 Thess. iv.), and Translation
(Phil. iii.) ?

If they persist in believing the " evil report " of the
ten spies, and refuse to enter into His rest by " the hill
country of the Amorites," they must not be surprised
if they have to wander in a wilderness all their lives,
and enter it by crossing the Jordan, the river of death.

Oh ! the blessedness of believing God !

Those who would enter into His rest and be well-
pleasing unto Him, must believe that He IS and that
He will BECOME a rewarder of their faith.

Of this first fresh revelation made after that given to
Abel, Enoch is the blessed example of one who
believed God, and was well-pleasing in His sight.

May we know what it is to enjoy peace with God as
Abel did, and to know the peace of God, and to enter
into His rest, as Enoch did.

Noah: Faith's Witness for God

1. "The Eighth Person"

In dealing with the "Elders," "the great cloud of witnesses" named in this chapter and in xii. 1, we are not writing their Lives or Biographies from the Old Testament standpoint, but we are confining ourselves to this chapter (Hebrews xi.) and other Divine Comments made by the Holy Spirit in the New Testament. These comments help us to understand better the nature of, and reasons for, "the good report" which they obtained and the witness thus borne to them by God.

Moreover, these comments, being Divine, point us to the special aspect of their faith on which we are to dwell, to the exclusion of other events recorded in the Old Testament history.

Noah is the last of the first group of three; for all the Elders named are arranged in perfect order, symmetry and beauty.

This order we shall set out in connection with Abraham's faith, and exhibit it to the eye of our readers that they may admire the Divine workmanship of the Holy Spirit, and marvel at the perfection of His work.

Noah follows Enoch, not merely Historically and Chronologically, but because the special aspect of his faith follows, *Experimentally*, the aspects of faith exhibited by Abel and Enoch.

We have seen in the former two that there can be no *walk* with God (as with Enoch), until there is *peace* with God (as with Abel); and Noah's faith goes on to tell us that there can be no *witness* for God, until there is a *walk* with God.

In other words *Agreement* with God must precede a *walk* with God (Amos iii. 3); and our *walk* with God must precede our *witness* for God.

This is the Experimental order of this first group; and it is Divine.

It cannot be altered without courting disaster in our service. The many failures, which we witness all around us, may be generally traced up to an attempt to reverse this Divine order.

Noah had Abel's faith, and he had Enoch's also. But, he had something more. He was called to believe God in matters of which God had never before spoken; and of which they had never heard anything from God.

They also had their own special aspects, but all were alike in that they each believed what God said to them.

Noah was not murdered, as Abel was; nor was he translated, as Enoch was; but he was called to occupy a special position and to believe God in matters of which they knew nothing; though he offered Abel's sacrifice, and enjoyed Enoch's walk.

The expression in 2 Peter ii. 5,

" THE EIGHTH PERSON,"

points us to the character of his days; and therefore to the nature of his faith, and the need of his witness.

" The days of Noah " became a significant expression on the lips of our Lord, and was used to convey a solemn and important lesson.

Noah was " the eighth person " not in the same sense as Enoch was " the seventh from Adam." Enoch was the " seventh " in genealogical descent from Adam; Noah was the eighth, in numerical reckoning, of eight persons saved and brought through the flood. This expression points us to the fact that, out of all the vast multitudes destroyed by the Flood, only eight persons were saved. This fact is emphasised in 1 Pet. iii. 20, and 2 Pet. ii. 5).

This is what we also are called to emphasise in our consideration of Noah's faith.

There are certain facts which we must take as being settled; for we have given the evidence more than once :* viz., that, some time before "the days of Noah" certain angels fell from their high estate. They are called "sons of God" (Gen. vi. 2, 4; Job. i. 6, ii. 1, xxxviii. 7; Ps. xxix. 1, lxxxix. 6—sons of El.—Dan. iii. 25.) They are called "spirits" (1 Pet. iii. 19). They are called "angels" (2 Pet. ii. 4; Jude 6).

At some time in the history of the world these angels fell. They were "disobedient" (1 Pet. iii. 20). They "sinned" (2 Pet. ii. 4). They "kept not their first estate," or principality (Jude 6, margin). But they "left their own habitation," their οἰκητήριον (oikētērion) their *spiritual body*.† Whatever this was, these angels "left" it.‡ Whatever this may mean or imply, we do not know, nor can any one tell us. We do not always *understand* God, but happy are we if we "*believe God*,"

---

* See our Pamphlets : *The Spirits in prison*, and *The Sons of God*, also *Things to Come*, Vol. xi. 110-112, 137-140; xii. 61-63; *How to enjoy the Bible*, pp. 144, 188-195, and 216-219.

† This word is used only in 2 Cor. v. 2, and Jude 6; both times in this sense : one of the resurrection body of men, and the other of the spirit body of angels.

‡ The word rendered "left" is peculiar. It is not merely the usual word λείπω (leipō) to leave but it is ἀπολείπω (apoleipo) and means *to desert, to forsake, to leave behind*. Compare 2 Tim. iv. 13, 20.

as we most certainly do here. We will not allow our reason to cause us to disbelieve His Word.

The nature of their sin is described with sufficient detail in Gen. vi. 2, 4 and Jude 7, where the cities of Sodom and Gomorrah are stated to have sinned "in like manner" as these angels, in "going after strange flesh." The word for "strange," here, is ἕτερος (*heteros*) and means *different* in kind (marg. *other*).

These angels are "reserved" in everlasting chains, "unto the judgment of the great day" (Jude 6, 2 Pet. ii. 4), and are now, therefore, said to be "in prison" (1 Pet. iii. 19).

Their progeny are not reserved for any future judgment of any kind. They had to be utterly destroyed. They were abnormal, super-human, uncanny: and were the reality, of which the later Greek mythology only retained a vague tradition. That mythology was not an invention or fabrication of the human brain; but it was a remnant of primitive truth the true origin of which the Greeks did not and could not know, apart from the Divine revelation in the Scriptures of truth.

They were called *nephīlīm* or *fallen ones* (from their origin). They were doubtless "giants" in form, as in wickedness. The word the Holy Spirit uses of them is ἀδεβής (*asebēs*) *ungodly, i.e., without God* (2 Pet. ii. 5, Jude 15).

We can, within narrow limits, tell when this Fall took place.

We find Enoch prophesying of the judgment which God was going to execute on these "ungodly" (Jude 14). But we do not read of its having been executed in his day. He was "translated" before it came. We find Noah again proclaiming the imminence of that coming judgment. For he proclaimed a righteousness: not a Divine righteousness revealed in grace (Rom. i. 16, 17), but a Divine righteousness revealed in "wrath" from heaven. For the next verse (18) goes on to reveal this additional fact concerning Divine righteousness.

If the Flood was the execution of the judgment, which Enoch had prophesied, then the fall of the angels must have taken place before the days of Enoch.

Adam was contemporary with Enoch until within fifty-six years of Enoch's translation ;* and, before his death in 930, it was revealed to him that he should live 120 years longer. That is what God said to Adam in Gen. vi. 3. There can be no doubt about this, for it is " *Ha-Adām* " *the man Adam,*† otherwise the words "he ALSO is flesh" are without sense. Adam had become like the rest.

In this case Adam must have been 810 years of age, when that revelation was made in Gen. vi. 3, and the corruption must have begun some time before, for it to have become so wide-spread in the days of Enoch. Adam "also" had become like the rest, and when God made known His intention to destroy, and "take them all away," Noah's family was the only family which had kept itself pure, and " without blemish: "‡ for such is the meaning of the word rendered " perfect " in Gen. vi. 9.

---

* Adam died aged 930 years, and Enoch was translated in 986 A.M., aged 365 years.

† See, *How to enjoy the Bible*, pp. 374-6.

‡ The word תָּמִים (*tāmīm*) is continually rendered *without blemish*, and is used of the perfection of the animals for sacrifice.

" All flesh had corrupted his way upon the earth"
(*v.* 12).

No judgment would do but that of a flood to sweep
them all away from off the face of the earth.*

The angels themselves were " reserved unto the judgment of the great day : " but, their progeny had to be
destroyed utterly, if only in " mercy" to the human
race (see Ps. cxxxvi. 17-22, Num. xxi.). For them, there
can be neither resurrection nor judgment.

It is a great pity that in Isa. xxvi. their later name,
Rephaim, should be translated, instead of transferred.
In *v.* 14 it is rendered *deceased,* and it is said "they
shall not rise," and in *v.* 19, it is rendered " dead," the
earth shall cast out her dead.†

This gives us some little insight into the character
of " the days of Noah," and explains why only " eight

---

* We learn from Gen. vi. 4 that there was another irruption of
fallen angels after " those days ;" not only one in the days of Enoch
and Noah, but another "ALSO, AFTER THAT."

The consequences were the same and the progeny were called by
the same name *Nephilim* (Num. xiii. 33). They were also known as
Emim (Deut. ii. 10); but as *Anakim,* from one of great renown (Deut.
ii. 10). *Horim* (*v.* 11), and *Zamzummim* (*v.* 20). They were indeed
the seven nations of Canaan—so that the results were more limited,
and localised ; and the sword of Israel was sufficient to cut them all
off. Israel we know was not wholly obedient in this matter (Josh.
xiii. 13). If any escaped, it would account for several races of beings
which to-day can scarcely be called human, and are the perplexity
of all Anthropologists. It is true that in 2 Sam. xxi. 16-22 and
1 Chron. xx. 4-8, we are told that David slew the *Rephaim* and it is
implied that these were the last. But even so, these were in the
Land of the Philistines ; and there was ample time between the days
of Joshua and David for others to be alive and migrate. Moreover we know that Israel did not destroy them all. See Josh.
xiii. 13 ; xv. 63 ; xvi. 10 ; xvii. 12-18. Judges i. 19, 21, 28, 29, 30-36 ;
ii. 1-5 ; iii. 1-7. 2 Sam. v. 6. 1 Kings ix. 16.

† There is another word " dead " in both verses, but it is מוּת
(*mūth*) which is the ordinary word, and is quite different. The
R.V. renders *vv.* 14 and 19 the same as in the A.V. but puts in the
margin " or *the shades.* Heb. *Rephaim.*"

souls were saved," and why Noah was "the eighth person." The word rendered "saved" here (1 Pet. iii. 20), is peculiar. It is διασώζω *(diasōzō)* and means *to bring safely through* (with emphasis on the word *through*.)*

The Lord in Matt. xxix. 37-39, Luke xvii. 26, 27, refers to these days, and connects them with "the days of Lot," which were similar in character. They are connected again in 2 Pet. ii. 6, 9, and still more closely in Jude 7. So that the second irruption of these evil angels could not have been long before it took place. The cities of the plain were destroyed in Gen. xix., some 240 years after the flood. Abram's Call, therefore could have been only a very few years before, and this synchronises his call, with God's purpose to use his seed as His sword to destroy the nations of Canaan.

From the Call of Abraham, Satan's enmity, and effort to destroy the human race, as such, would be, henceforth to destroy Abraham's seed, so that the promise in Gen. iii. 15, should be frustrated, and his doom averted. This is why Abraham received the first assault immediately after his Call (Gen. xii. 10-20) ; and, why Israel became the great object of Satan's enmity.

When Abraham enters Canaan Gen. xii. 13. "The Canaanite was then (*i.e.* already) in the Land."

The great enemy, as soon as Abraham was called to possess the Land, directed his assault against him ; and took steps to occupy, in advance, the territory which had been assigned to Israel when God divided the earth among the nations. (Deut. xxxii. 8, 9).

But this we must leave, until we come to consider the faith of Abraham.

---

* See its only occurrences, Matt. xiv. 36 ; Luke vii. 3 ; Acts xxiii. 24, xxvii. 43, 44, xxviii. 1, 4.

In approaching the faith of Noah, connected as it is with his witness for God, it is necessary that we should have a clear insight into the facts which the expression "the eighth person" introduces us; and into the character of "the days of Noah," which explains to us the nature, and necessity, for the witness which he was called to give; and the matters in respect of which he was called to believe God.

For, as Enoch, who, as God's prophet, prophesied the coming judgment. So Noah, as God's herald, proclaimed its near approach.

Enoch walked with God in the midst of the growing corruption; and Noah witnessed for God when that corruption was reaching its height.

This shows us that it is possible for those who believe God to walk with Him, and witness for Him in the darkest days.

Oh that we might all so believe God as to what He has revealed for our faith, and be translated before the coming judgment is executed; and thus escape, not merely the judgment itself, but even the need of being "saved through" it, as Noah was, and as Israel will yet be.

2. "Warned of God"

WE have seen, in the cases of Abel and Enoch, that, according to Rom. x. 17, God must have spoken to them, though the fact of His making known His will to them, is not actually recorded.

But in the case of Noah, the fact is distinctly stated : and the word employed to inform us of this is somewhat unusual.

It is χρηματίξω *(chrēmatizō) to be Divinely instructed.** Its meaning may best be gathered from its usage. It is first used of the wise men being " warned of God " to return another way (Matt. ii., 12) ; then, of Joseph being warned to turn aside to Galilee (Matt. ii., 22) ; of the revelation to Simeon that he should not die until he had seen the Lord's Messiah (Lu. ii. 26) ; of Cornelius being instructed to send for Peter (Acts x. 22) ; of Moses's Divine instruction as to the making of the Tabernacle (Heb. viii. 5). It is used also of those who refused to hear Christ's Divine instruction when on earth. (Heb. xii. 25).

Twice it is used *Intransitively* of the giving of a name or an appellation ; and the implication is (from all the other cases) that the name so given was given by Divine instruction : the one is the name " adultress " of her who marries again while her husband liveth (Rom. vii. 3) ; the other is the name " Christians " given to the believers at Antioch. (Acts xi. 26)†

---

* Here, in the Passive Mood.

† This disposes of the supposition that the name was given by their enemies, by way of derision.

116

We thus learn how the "report," which Noah believed, was heard.

Noah's faith came by "hearing" this report; and the report came to him "by the Word of God." For, he was *Divinely instructed.*

There was no other way by which he could have heard of the coming judgment of the Flood. There was no other way by which he could have known he was to be delivered out of it; or how he was to be saved through it.

There was nothing in what he saw to give him any indication of what was coming. If he had reckoned from the outward "appearance" he could never have concluded what would be the end of the "things that were seen." But he was Divinely instructed concerning them, and these he reckoned according to the fundamental definition of faith as laid down in verse 3.

He "heard" the Divine instruction. He believed it. Hence, he knew what others did not know: for what he knew was "not seen as yet."

If he looked on things as they appeared, he would have seen building, and planting, and marriage and giving in marriage going on, on all hands. He would have seen outward progress and advancement. Others, thought the progress was upward, and the advancement was onward, but Noah knew that it was downward to destruction and onward to judgment. "As it was in the days of Noah . . . . . SO shall the coming of the Son of man be." (Matt. xxiv. 39; Lu. xvii. 27).

Men look around to-day and see progress in the spheres of invention, science and civilization; they see the advancement in outward things; they discuss " social problems;" but they judge by the outward "appearance." Those who are Divinely instructed by the Divine Word, do not thus judge all these " things that are seen." They know what is to be the end of it all. They are Divinely instructed that it will end in a Flood—not of Water, but of Fire.

They too believe God and have a blessed hope.

Those who believe what God has promised concerning translation or the " calling on high " (Phil. iii. 14) will be caught up, as Enoch was, without dying. But those who refuse to believe God* respecting this, and believe that, like Noah, they will be saved through that judgment flood, must not be surprised if God deals with them according to their faith ; and saves them " so as by fire."

Oh! what a privilege to be *Divinely instructed* concerning the "things not seen as yet." How blessed to believe God and thus be " well-pleasing unto Him."

If, like Enoch, we " walk with God," we " walk by faith, and not by sight " (2 Cor. v. 7), we shall not judge the course of events as they appear outwardly, in the eyes of the natural man ; we shall not be deceived by things that man calls " progress." We shall not be misled into fellowship with man in what he mis-calls " good works," for we know that only those are " good works which God hath before prepared for us to walk in." (Eph. ii. 10, marg.)

God's Divine instruction is specially with regard to " things not seen as yet ; " and, if we believe what He teaches us concerning them, we shall be " moved with godly fear " (Heb. xi. 7 R.V.), as Noah was, and shall obey Him as Noah did.

---

* Like those in Heb. xii. 25.

Noah's faith led to obedience. Hence, true obedience is "the obedience of faith:" he prepared an ark to the saving of his house: through which "he condemned the world."

3. "A Preacher of Righteousness"

In 2 Pet. ii. 5, Noah is specially singled out and called "a preacher of righteousness."

But it was what Noah did that "condemned the world," not what he said.

It is a well-worn proverb that "actions speak louder than words."

Lot's preaching to his sons and their wives was unheeded by them ; for his deeds belied his words.

When he proclaimed concerning the coming judgment of Sodom "he seemed like one that talked nonsense unto his sons-in-law."

Why ?

Because he had first "lifted up his own eyes," and chosen all the plain of Jordan (Gen. xiii. 10, 11). Then he "pitched his tent toward Sodom" (v. 12). Then he "dwelt in Sodom" (Gen. xiv. 12). Then he "sat in the gate of Sodom" (Gen. xix. 1), which means that he took part in the government of Sodom and fulfilled the duties of "citizenship."

No wonder that "he seemed like one that mocked" when he warned the men to whom he had given his daughters in marriage, and told them of the imminent judgment of Sodom.

What Lot *did*, condemned himself. What Noah did, condemned the world, because though he was in it, he was not of it. He did not spend his time in improving it, for he knew it was soon to be destroyed.

He did not waste his energies in entertaining its inhabitants, for he knew that the Flood was coming which "took them all away." His seat of government was not on earth: for he believed his God who was in heaven.

"The days of Lot" are coupled by our Lord with "the days of Noah" in Luke xvii. 26, 28, and also with the future "coming of the Son of Man in His day" (*vv.* 25, 26).

Our reference to those days is, therefore, not irrelevant.

Lot was "a righteous man" (2 Pet. ii. 7, 8). He believed God in some things but evidently not all. He was judicially acquitted before God, and *his sin was not imputed* unto him. Nor was righteousness imputed to him, as with Abraham (Gen. xv. 6). Hence, though *forensically* righteous, he is not included in this great cloud of witnesses, though he was Abraham's nephew.

But Noah's faith was evidenced by his obedience. Hence, his preaching is mentioned as being very special. He is the only one of all these elders who is singled out (in 2 Pet. ii. 5) as A PREACHER OF RIGHTEOUSNESS.

The word translated "preacher" is significant. It is not the word for an Evangelist or a preacher of the good-news of the gospel. It is κήρυξ (*kērux*) *a herald*, one *who makes a proclamation*.

Noah was not a preacher of the present grace of God, but a herald of the coming judgment of God.*

---

* This is the word used of Christ's going in his resurrection body and making proclamation to the spirits (the fallen angels) in prison (1 Pet. iii. 19, 20). It was not the preaching of present grace, but the heralding of coming judgment.

He was a herald of righteous judgment. For this is a true side of Divine righteousness.

We have already called attention to the word "For" repeated four times in Rom. i. 16-18, each one giving an additional fact explaining what God's righteousness is. It shows us that, not only does the Gospel reveal a righteousness of God from faith to faith (*v.* 17), but there is another aspect:—"FOR, the wrath of God is revealed from heaven against all ungodliness, and unrighteousness of men" (*v.* 18).

The word rendered "ungodliness" is the very word used of those to whom Enoch prophesied (Jude 15), and to whom Noah proclaimed (2 Pet. ii. 5, 6).† This shows the nature of Noah's proclamation. It was like Enoch's prophesying, and had the same object as well as the same subject.

It was a proclamation of God's wrath against the ungodly, and against all ungodliness. But, as we have said; it was what he *did* that condemned and judged the world. What he proclaimed was only the execution of that judgment.

This is the *Interpretation* of the record of Noah's Faith, but there remains the *application* of it for our own admonition.

It is easy for expositors to wander into the repetition of platitudes which have little to do with the Spirit's design in inspiring these words in this place.

Those Hebrews who were tried, persecuted and wavering, who were tempted to draw back unto perdition (Heb. x. 39) were being warned, helped, comforted, encouraged and quieted. Nothing that man may

---

† ἀσεβής (*asebēs*) meaning *ungodly, i.e., without God*, having nothing to do with Him.

say should divert our attention from the first interpreta
tion of these words to those Hebrews to whom they
were written; or from the lesson which is thus taught
us, by the setting, in which we find these Jewels.
Digressions, however interesting, must not be allowed
to hide the great lesson which is being conveyed to
those whom the Apostle was addressing. We must
ask : *How did these things bear upon them ?* What lesson
were they to learn ?

The key is found in the context; yea, in the Text,
which is Hab. ii. 4. *"His soul which is lifted up in him
is not upright in him : but the just shall live by his faith."*

This is the very Text on which the teaching of this
member (Heb. x. 32-37) is based.

What were the actual conditions of the Apostle's
immediate readers ? We must go back to this passage
(Ch. x. 32-37) and read these verses carefully. "Ye
have need of patience, that, after ye have done the
will of God, ye might receive the promise. For yet
a little while, and He that shall come, will come, and
will not tarry."

ABEL believed God and did His will, and received
the tokens of Divine acceptance with God.

ENOCH believed God; believed that He would come
to execute judgement; but would, before that, translate
him so that his walk with God would end in eternal
life, for " the just shall live (for ever) through faith."

NOAH believed God : and, being Divinely instructed by
Him, he was proof against all the sneers and jibes which,
we may be sure, were levelled at his madness. But,
Noah was preserved, while "the flood came and took
them all away."

The one thing common to all this great cloud of

witnesses was that each one STOOD ALONE with God, and for God; and that, nothing but believing what God has said will enable any one to stand alone here, and live again with Him there.

The Apostle reminds them of his own bonds in the immediate context (Heb. x. 34); He takes them to the time when, he says, "no man stood with me, but all forsook me" (2 Tim. iv. 16), when those to whom he had preached the word of the Lord Jesus, "turned away from me" (2 Tim. i. 15). He stood alone, but he could say: "I am not ashamed" for "I know Whom I have believed [and still believe]" (2 Tim. i. 12). I know HIM. I have believed HIM.

Though the Temple might be among the things "shaken" and be "moved" (Heb. xii. 26—28), yet there are better things that will "remain." Therefore the concluding exhortation is "See that ye refuse not Him that gave Divine instruction* concerning these things, when on earth."

Abel, Enoch, and Noah "suffered the loss of all things" but were all delivered. They stood alone, but God was with them to instruct them as to "things not seen as yet."

Hence, these believing Hebrews were "not in darkness" as to the future. They were not to judge eternal realities by the outward appearance (ch. xi. 3).

This is the immediate interpretation of Noah's faith as it concerned them; but there is an *application* for us.

And it is this: Noah was the "only one in all the Old Testament who is called the "preacher;" yet, judged by outward results and appearances, his preaching was a failure. This tells us that, in all our

---

* The same word as in Ch. xi. 7. *See* above.

witness for God, *faithfulness* is the one great requisite, and the one great measure as to success. We are not commissioned to accomplish this or that, but we are commanded to be faithful in our testimony.

We are commissioned to " preach the Word," whether men will "hear" it, or " whether they will forbear "; whether they will "endure" it or whether they will not. (Ezk. ii. 5, 7. 2 Tim. iv. 3.)

If men will not " endure " or " hear," we are not to seek for something else which they will endure, but simply to " preach the Word."

Looked at from this point of view, Noah's faith exhibits the greatest example of " Witness for God " that the world has ever seen.

People, to-day, look for " results," and unless we are able to show some, or to make up some "report," our work is considered on all hands as a failure. But we have nothing whatever to do with *results*. What we have to do with is our *faithfulness*. Results are in the hands of the Lord; but, for our faithfulness, we are alone responsible.

And what is it that we look upon and regard as " results." Something that *we* have laid down for ourselves? Some ends that *we* have set before ourselves to accomplish?

For whom are we witnessing, if not for the Lord? For whom are we working, if not for the Master? If so, then, surely, it is for Him to know what His purposes and counsels are. It is for Him to decide what the results are to be.

He knew what the result of Noah's "preaching" was to be. Yet He commissioned Noah to continue.

The Master does not always explain what His

servant is to do, or what ends are to be obtained. He need not make known why He wishes this or that to be done. He simply gives His command. And it is for the servant to obey.

Truly, this is Faith's own sphere. There is no room for "sight" in this department of service. If we walk by sight and judge by outward appearances, or by the things that are seen (v. 3) we shall most assuredly fail; even as Moses and Elijah and Jeremiah and other of the most eminent servants of God failed. But the "author and finisher of faith" was perfect, in this, as in all beside.

In Matthew xi. we see the perfect Servant of Jehovah. In verses 1-6, He was doubted by John: in verses 16-19, He was rejected by common people who said that John was possessed by the devil, and Christ was a glutton and a drunkard; in vv. 20-24, He was rejected by the cities wherein most of His mighty works had been done: then, we read, "AT THAT TIME Jesus prayed and said, I thank Thee O Father . . . Even so, Father, for so it seemed good in Thy sight" (vv. 25-27).

Is this what we see around us to-day? Is this the spirit manifested by the Lord's servants? Truly, we may say it is the very opposite spirit which is exhibited. Whence comes all the sadness and sorrow and disappointment, and complaining? Is it not because we have made our own plans, and laid out our own work; or because some one has laid out our work for us, and we have failed in doing that work?

Is it not because we have regarded even the Lord's work as our own?

When a meeting has been arranged and only

a few persons are present, we regard that as a failure: but there may be one there, "whose heart the Lord has prepared."

What does it matter to us how many are present so long as there has been faithfulness in making that meeting known. It matters *who* is there; or, whether that one is there; but not how many others.

It mattered not to the true servant whether he ministered to crowds in Samaria (Acts viii. 5, 8), or, whether he was to leave that work at its height and be sent on a long journey to minister to one lone sheep bleating in "Gaza, which is desert" (*v.* 26). How many servants, to-day, are ready for service after this sort; or to preach to any except a *large* audience!

Oh! to learn the lesson of Noah's faith, and Noah's faithfulness. It would revolutionize much that we see around us.

We should not see one servant being used of God, and then, regarding it as his own work, to be perpetuated by his family, or by a society.

There is not always an Elisha, where there has been an Elijah. That was a remarkable exception.

The rule is all the other way. Noah was a great "preacher," but the Flood was his successor. Paul, though in his own sight "less than the least," was the chiefest of the Apostles, but "grievous wolves" were to be his "Apostolic successors" (Acts xx. 29).

If the Lord raises up a servant to do an important work, we must not jump to the conclusion that He wishes that work to be perpetuated. He may have other servants, and other work for them to do.

May the lesson of Noah's faith be written on our hearts, and bear precious fruit in our service; and may we remember, and apply another lesson which, though the interpretation may belong to others, has a solemn application for us, and reminds us that it will be one day said of certain servants,

" Well done, good and FAITHFUL servant," not good and successful.

Many will speak of what they have done, and of all their wonderful works, but it is only Faith in God's Word, and *faithfulness* in testimony for Him that will find an entrance into

" THE JOY OF THE LORD "

Abraham: Faith's Obedience

1. "He Was Called" "He Went Out"

THE one point common to all that is said of Abraham, is that, like Abel, Enoch, and Noah, he stood alone with God.

Not all the events of Abraham's life are brought forward in this chapter, but only three: and these are specially chosen with a view to serving the Apostle's argument, and to give point, exhortation, example, and encouragement to those whom he was exhorting to stand fast in the midst of trials and difficulties.

Abraham was called to a life of dependence on God; a renunciation of family ties, social position, and all worldly endearments. Instead of a life of ease and security in his own country, and among his own people, he was called to a life of pilgrimage among the lawless inhabitants of Canaan, on the forbearance of whom his life and possessions were dependent.

Living in the world, he was not of the world.

Hence, only those points of Abraham's history are singled out which showed those Hebrew believers, to whom the Apostle was writing, why they should take joyfully the spoiling of their goods, knowing that, like Abraham, they had in heaven, a better and enduring substance. (Heb. x. 34).

This is why only three things are stated in connection with Abraham's faith in Heb. xi. :—

1. HIS CALL: "by faith when he was called he went out " (*v*. 8).

2. HIS SOJOURNING : " by faith he sojourned in a strange country " (*v* 9).

3. HIS TRIAL: "by faith . . . . when he was tried he offered up his only begotten son (*v* 17).

In the example of Abraham we are leaving the first group of three, and passing on to the first of four pairs. Here then will be the place to consider more closely the order in which these " Elders " are set before us.

It may be well, therefore, at this stage, to set out the Structure according to which this "great cloud of witnesses " is arranged.

This is the place, and this is the time to see and observe that all the words as well as the works of God are perfect; perfect in their truth, perfect also in their place, and perfect in their order.

We have already seen something of the correspondence between the Chronological and Experimental order.

We can now add to this the correspondence between the various subjects and persons in this chapter.

It will be observed that, in the first member, marked A, we have more than two. This corresponds with *A*, where again we have more than two. This first group is followed by four pairs: *viz.*, B and C, corresponding with *B* and *C*.

In B and *B* we have a double correspondence ; for, not only is the second of each pair a woman, but the things said of each pair correspond also ; while in C and *C* there are four things which all have to do with over-coming, and with *man ;* just as in the two larger groups, all has to do with God.

Finally, in D and *D* we have one single person in each ; and the correspondence is between Joseph and the Lord Jesus, patiently waiting God's time.

" *The Elders* " (xi. 2), or

" *The Great Cloud of Witnesses* " (xii. 1)

A | ABEL : Faith's worship OF God
   ENOCH : Faith's walk WITH God
   NOAH : Faith's witness FOR God

   B | ABRAHAM : Faith's obedience : (" Get thee out ")
      SARAH : Faith's conclusion : "she judged,&c." (*v.* 11.)

      C | ISAAC : Faith overcoming "the will of the flesh "
         JACOB : Faith overcoming "the will of man "

         D | JOSEPH : Faith waiting God's time.

      C | MOSES' PARENTS : Faith overcoming "the fear of Man "
         MOSES HIMSELF : Faith overcoming "the praise of Man

   B | ISRAEL : Faith's obedience : (" Go forward " Ex. xiv. 15)
      RAHAB : Faith's conclusion : (" I know," &c., Josh. ii. 9)

A | 1ST GROUP : Faith conquering THROUGH God
   "OTHERS" : Faith suffering FOR God

         D | "JESUS" : Faith waiting God's time (Ch. x. 13. 2 Thess. iii. 5, marg.)

In passing from the first group (A) to the first pair (B), it is necessary, as well as helpful, that we should understand why this is so; and where we are being led; and into what lines of truth and teaching the Holy Spirit is Himself guiding us (John xvi. 13).*

We are now in a position to take up the Faith of Abraham.

The first of the three things mentioned concerning him is

      (1). " He was CALLED."

" *By faith, Abraham obeyed when he was called to go forth unto a place which he was to receive for a heritage : yea, he went forth not having any understanding* [as to]† *whither he was going.*" (*v.* 8.)

There is much confusion as to this " Call of Abraham." It is generally taken as being recorded in Gen. xii. 1, which is the reference given against Heb. xi. 8 in the A.V.

But it is remarkable that, while we have " no generations of Abraham" we have "the generations of Terah."

That Abraham, " the father of the faithful," and the founder of the Hebrew race, the depositary of all the promises of blessing for Israel and the world, should not have his own " generations" or family history, is remarkable. It is also remarkable that we have no "generations" of Joseph.

---

* In the above, we have the Structure which should now be compared with the Table of Contents, where we have further details.

† The verb here rendered " knowing" in A.V. and R.V. means more than this. It is used with οἶδα (*oida*), *to know*, in Mark xiv. 68, and with γινώσκω (*ginōskō*) *to get to know* in Acts xix. 15. (So also Euripides (*Hipp.* 382 and *Iph. in Tauris*, 491).

The verb is ἐπίσταμαι (*epistamai*), and means *to have knowledge of, to know with understanding.* See 1 Tim. vi. 4. Acts x. 28. Jude 10.

But the generations *(*or *Toledōth)* of the Bible have both supernatural design and spiritual significance.

There are *fourteen* in the whole Bible: Eleven in Genesis, one in Numbers (xii. 1, Aaron and Moses,) one in Ruth (iv. 18, Pharez and David) and one in Matt. (i. 1 of " Jesus ").

They divide the book of Genesis (with its Introduction) into twelve parts. And we thus have to do with God's twelve divisions instead of with man's fifty chapters. We have the

Introduction (Gen. i. 1—ii. 3)

1. The generations of heaven and the earth (ii. 4— iv. 26)
2. The generations of Adam (v. 1—vi. 8)
3. The generations of Noah (vi. 9—ix. 29)
4. The generations of Sons of Noah (xi. 1—xi. 9)
5. The generations of Shem (xi. 10-26)
6. Terah (xi. 27—xxv. 11) *

So that as Enoch was the seventh Patriarch from Adam, so Abraham begins the Seventh Division of Genesis.

The Holy Spirit by Stephen, in Acts vii. 2, gives additional details of the Call of Abraham; and shows us that Gen. xii. 1, is not to be taken as recording that call in Haran. He says:—

" The God of glory appeared unto our father Abraham when he was in Mesopotamia, *before he dwelt in Haran.*"

God is called " the God of glory " (*i.e.*, the glorious God) in contrast to the idols which were worshipped by Abram and his family.

---

* Our readers can easily complete the remaining *five Toledōth* for themselves.

He appeared to Abraham, there, " on the other side of the flood " (*i.e.*, the Euphrates). This agrees with Josh. xxiv. 2, 14, where it is distinctly stated that Abraham and all his kindred were idolators. So that Abraham was not called for any merit of his own. Indeed in Neh. ix. 7 we see that God chose Abraham simply because He willed to do so :—

" Thou art the LORD God, who didst choose Abram, and broughtest him forth out of the Chaldees, and gavest him the name of Abraham."

Moreover, we are told what the glorious God said to Abraham : but there is nothing said about Abraham's faith, only about his *obedience :* " Then came he." Hence, he was not *called* because he had believed.

In Joshua xxiv. 3 God says, " I took your father Abraham. I led, . . . and I gave." All was of grace.

In Gen. xi. 31 we have the historical record of the instrumental act. " Terah took Abraham." In Josh. xxiv. 3 we have the gracious record of the Divine purpose ; while in Acts vii. 4 we have the inspired comment on Abraham's obedience of faith.

For Terah to have taken Abraham, Abraham must have told him of the vision he had seen of "the glorious God ; " and Terah must have *believed Abraham*. But how much he believed we are not told. He must have believed enough to make him leave Ur of the Chaldees, and take Abraham with all his family, and go into Haran, but not enough to make him give up all his idols, or to go on into Canaan ; for we find these idols still lingering in the family of his great-grandson, Laban (Gen. xxxi. 19, 30, 32).

From whatever reason, whether from age, health, or unbelief, Terah never got further than Haran ;

for, it is emphatically recorded that "they came to Haran *and dwelt there*" (Gen. xi. 31). Whereas it is as emphatically stated that when Abraham "left Haran to go into the land of Canaan, *into the land of Canaan they came*" (Gen. xii. 5).

Abraham's ancestors "*dwelt*" in Haran; and his descendants "*dwelt*" in Egypt; but Abraham himself "*sojourned*" in Canaan.

God has given us a sufficient explanation of the delay of five years in Haran in Acts vii. 4, where, of these two migrations of Abraham we read: "Then came he out of the land of the Chaldeans, and dwelt in Haran: and from thence, *when his father was dead*, he removed him into this land, wherein ye now dwell."

Whatever it was that hindered Abraham's complete obedience, Terah's death ended it.

In Hebrews xi. 8, both these calls (Gen. xi. 31 and xii. 1) are merged, and the Spirit concentrates our attention on the fact that he "*obeyed*."

This is why we have, in our structure of this chapter, specialized Abraham's faith, as "Faith's obedience," obedience being that which distinguished his faith from all the others. We say "distinguished" not because others who believed did not obey; for they all obeyed, they all *acted* on their faith; but, in the case of Abraham, this is the *special* characteristic of it; and therefore stress is laid upon it, by not mixing up anything else with it in this eighth verse.

Abraham's faith, in respect to his *obedience*, is thus emphasised, and has its correspondence with Israel's *obedience* in crossing the Red Sea (*B*).

"Get thee forth" is God's word which came to

Abraham. "Get thee forth" is the command which God said Israel would hear from Pharaoh (Ex. xi. 8).

Abraham's obedience is the more marked, because God did not, at the time of the call, tell him what or where the land was. The words are "unto a land that I will show thee" (Gen. xii. 1). So it was clearly faith, and not sight. God did not say, "a land *I do tell thee of*, but to a land I *will* tell thee thereof." It was the same with the "inheritance. He was to go to the place which he should *after*, receive."

Moreover, the Greek is very emphatic. In the English, the verb "obeyed" is put at the end of the sentence; but in the Greek, it is, by the Figure *Hyperbaton*, put almost at the beginning: "By faith, Abraham being called, *obeyed to go out, &c.*"

Later on, he learned that his "seed" should sojourn for 400 years before they should enter the land (Gen. xv. 7, 13-21), and that the promise would not be ratified till after his death.

Abraham's obedience was further intensified by the words "and he went out." The καί (*kai*) *and*, is peculiar, in this position. It might be rendered, "he even went out not knowing whither he was going." Or, still more emphatically we might say: "Yea, he went forth": the verb *to go out*, being repeated, to impress upon us the great fact, which stamped the characteristic of Abraham's faith, as shown by his obedience.

Thus far, we have the *interpretation* of the Scriptures which speak of Abraham's faith, but what is the *application* of them to ourselves? In what way are we to apply it, so that we may learn the lesson for ourselves to-day, as those to whom Heb. xi. was first written learned the lesson for themselves?

What has Abraham's "obedience of faith" to say to us?

In answer to this we observe that this expression is afterwards specially associated with "the Mystery." This is stated, in Rom. xvi. 26, to be the special object for which it is revealed. It is made known to us "for the obedience of faith," so that, believing it, we may "obey the heavenly vision."

God has "made it known" for this purpose. This word, γνωρίζω (gnōrizō), is another special word, and is associated with the Mystery, not only here, in Rom. xvi. 26, but in Eph. i. 9; iii. 3, 5, 10; vi. 19, Col. i. 27.*

The *application* of Abraham's faith-obedience comes home to us in this connection. Do we exhibit this "obedience of faith" in regard to God having "made known unto us His purpose, in the Mystery"? as He did to Abraham when He was called.

The "Hope of His calling" in Eph. i. 18, is, for us, what the hope of God's call was to Abraham. Abraham obeyed. Do we thus obey? Or, do we act as though God had not made anything known to us that is worthy of our obedience?

If we display Abraham's obedience in connection with what God has made known for *our* faith, we should like him, "go forth" from all human traditions and "doctrines of men." We should "sojourn" in the world as being indeed "a strange land." We should regard our "seat of government" as already *existing*† in

---

* See other examples of the use of the word in Luke ii. 15, John xv. 15; xvii. 26, Rom. ix. 22, 23, 2 Pet. i. 16.

† The verb in Phil. iii. 20, is not the verb "to be," but it is ὑπάρχω (huparchō) to *exist*, *be in being*: *i.e.*, our seat and sphere of government already exist in heaven, and we are subject to that government now and here.

heaven; that heaven from whence we should be looking for the Saviour, and for our "calling on high."
(Phil. iii. 20 and 14.)

"Obedience of faith," is the one thing needful
in connection with the fact of the Mystery having
been made known to us.

It was exactly what Israel lacked when told to go up
into the land. They obeyed to cross the Red Sea; but
they did not obey when told to "go up over the hill-
country of the Amorites" at Kadesh-Barnea.

This command at Kadesh-Barnea exactly corresponded with Abraham's call in Haran (and was indeed
to be the consummation of the call from Egypt, as
Abraham's was the consummation of the call in Ur of
the Chaldees!) :—"Go up and possess it."

But they believed man, instead of God. In spite of
the actual evidence of "the good land," Moses has to say

"YE WOULD NOT GO UP" (Deut. i. 26)

And why? Because

"YE DID NOT BELIEVE JEHOVAH YOUR GOD" (*v.* 32).

The making known of the Mystery is, to us, exactly
what Ur of the Chaldees was to Abraham; and what
Kadesh-Barnea was to Israel. The difference was
that,

"Abraham believed God."

Israel "did not believe,"

They provoked God—(Heb. iii.).

How do we stand in this matter? Do we believe what
God has "made known for the obedience of faith"?
or, do we provoke Him, and grieve Him, with our
unbelief?

Oh, let us go up and possess this "good land" which

is set forth before us in the Epistles to the Ephesians, Philippians, and Colossians, and there discover not only the riches of His grace, but the riches of His glory.

It is a land, not of " grapes, pomegranates, and figs " (Num. xiii. 23), but of all that which they symbolize.

A land of " grapes : " which tell of the Vine, and of Him with whom we are made one Body (Eph. i. 23 ; iv. 4).

A land of " pomegranates : " which tell of our worship being wholly centred in Him, who is the alone object and subject of our spiritual worship.*

A land of " figs : " which were the food of the common people, symbolizing, that He whom we worship is to be the common food of all His people, sanctifying all the common duties of life.†

Oh ! that we may " at once," by faith, go up, and enjoy this " good land," waiting till we shall be called up " on high," exchange our faith for sight, and our spiritual vision for actual possession.

---

* Pomegranates were the chief fruit, used symbolically in worship. See Ex. xxvii.–xxix., and 2 Chron. iii. and iv.

† These three are not "types." They may be used by us by way of "application" as illustrations of truths elsewhere revealed. For Israel they are true *types*, and their Antitypes will all be found in connection with Christ, quite apart from a present application to the Mystery.

2. "He Sojourned, Dwelling in Tents"

IT is not our purpose to go through "the life of Abraham," or to give even a summary of all the events connected with it. We are not writing on Genesis, but on Hebrews xi. Therefore we confine ourselves to the special events which are there mentioned in connection with his faith.

They are three in number :

1. His *Obedience* when called :
2. His *Sojourning* as in a strange land
3. His *Trial* in the offering of Isaac

We have already considered the first of these.

Our next subject in connection with Abraham, is

HIS SOJOURNING

" *By faith he sojourned in the land of the promise, as in a strange [country], taking up his abode in tents together with Isaac, and Jacob, the joint-heirs [with him] of the same [promise.]* (verse 9).

There are several things connected with this sojourning. There is the fact (1) that "the land belonged to strangers," (2) that it was "in tents": for the words "in tents" are very emphatic, being placed before the verb :—"in tents dwelling," to call our attention to this fact. And (3) there is the fact that Isaac and Jacob are linked together with Abraham, as being joint heirs-expectant.

The first point in this sojourning is the first historical event in connection with Abraham's obedience mentioned in the history :

"*And Abram passed through the land unto the place* of Sichem, unto the plain of Moreh.* AND THE CANAANITE WAS THEN IN THE LAND." (Gen. xii. 6)

Here, then, we have the second exhibition of Abraham's faith. First, he *obeyed* and went forth. Next, he *sojourned.*

This sojourning was "by faith." It certainly could not have been "by sight;" for there was nothing for sight but the Canaanite!

What an opportunity for faith!

Faith took his eye off from the Canaanite to "the God of glory" who had appeared unto him in the land of Chaldea; and who appeared again to him as Jehovah in the land of the Canaanite.

The sphere of the stranger is the sphere of Divine communications. The statement that

"*The Canaanite was then in the land*" (*v.* 5), is intended to connect that fact with the subject of God's revelation in *v.* 6.

"*Unto thee will I give this land.* Here was scope for faith. It came "from hearing the word of God," and our attention is directed to this fact by the close connection of these two statements.

Abraham's faith rested on the Word of God; and his thoughts were occupied with the presence of Jehovah, instead of with the presence of the Canaanite. The eye of faith could see Him who is invisible; hence, it saw not the Canaanite who was "then in the land."

How opposite was the case of the spies, who, in a later day went up into this very land with the assurance of Jehovah that it was "a good land."

---

* Or "City," compare ch. xviii. 24; xix. 12; xxix. 23.

They, " believed not." Hence, they saw only the Canaanites; and they said: "the people that WE SAW in it are men of great stature. And there WE SAW the giants and the sons of Anak which come of the giants;* and we were in OUR OWN SIGHT as grasshoppers, and so we were in THEIR SIGHT." (Num. xiii. 32, 33).

Truly they walked by sight, hence they believed not. And, because they believed not, they could neither enjoy the presence of the Lord, nor enter into His rest.

But, as we have said, it is the second of these three points to which our attention is specially directed. The words " IN TENTS " are the emphatic words.

It is not the act of *dwelling* that is emphatic here, but the fact that this dwelling was *"in tents."* The Figure of Speech used calls our attention to this. It is called *Hyperbaton,* which means *Transposition.* By this Figure the words " in tents " are *transposed* or put out of their usual order for the purpose of calling our attention to them, and thus emphasising them. It is in fact the Holy Spirit's own marking, to show us what it is He wishes us to notice, as being important.

If expressed in the ordinary way it would mean " DWELLING in tents with Isaac and Jacob." But, by the Figure *Hyperbaton,* it means " Dwelling IN TENTS with Isaac and Jacob."

The reason for this contrast is given in the next verse, for which our minds are prepared by this emphasis : " FOR he looked for a City."

---

* Heb. *Nephilim.* See Gen. vi. The Canaanitish nations were the same evil progeny as those who had to be destroyed by the Flood " in the days of Noah " They were due to a second irruption of fallen angels " after that " (Gen. vi. 4) ; and that is why they also had to be destroyed. The sword of Israel was to them what the waters of Noah had been to the others.

Here again, there is another contrast. The word "Tents" looks backward as well as forward. The "tents" point us back to the "city" which Abram had left, as well as forward to the "city" which Abram "looked for."

Recent excavations have shown that that city was *Múgeyer*, on the other side of the Euphrates. The modern name, to-day, is given from the *Asphalt* or *Bitumen* used to cement its bricks.

The name "Ur" is found stamped on its bricks, showing it to be a "city" indeed; a centre of learning and civilization and wealth and luxury.

Abram was no mere nomad or wanderer, as some would have us believe. He knew what city life was, for he had been a citizen of "Ur," the excavations of which show was no mean city. He "went out" from this "city" "dwelling IN TENTS" while he "looked for a City which hath foundations, whose builder and maker is God."

It is not merely the fact that they were "strangers;" but that they were "pilgrims" also.

Notice the order of these two words in Heb. xi. 13, and 1 Pet. ii. 11. "Strangers and pilgrims." Not "pilgrims and strangers."* It is possible to be a "pilgrim" without being a "stranger." But once we realise our true strangership we are perforce compelled to be pilgrims.

It is to this point of the sojourning to which the words "in tents" call our attention.

---

* The exigencies of modern poetry may require the non-Scriptural order of these words. The word "danger" may require the word "stranger" for a rhyme in the hymn—

"I'm a pilgrim and a stranger;"

but the difference to which we call attention should be noted.

We may be "pilgrims," and yet, in our pilgrimage, may visit all the cities and churches in the world and include them all in our embrace; but if we are true "sojourners" we shall be "strangers" to them all; and shall be compelled, as Abraham was, to erect our own solitary altar to Jehovah in the midst of them all.

How could Abraham be a worshipper with the Canaanite? Impossible! This is why the "Altar" is so closely connected with the "Tent" in Gen. xii. 8 and in Abraham's sojourney.

"And he removed from thence unto a mountain on the east of Bethel and pitched his TENT on the west and Hai on the east: and there he builded an ALTAR unto Jehovah, and called upon the name of Jehovah."

Here again the Tent comes before the Altar; for as we must be real "strangers" before we can be true "pilgrims," so must we be real "sojourners" before we can be true worshippers.

Hebrews xi. confines our thoughts to Abraham's sojourning "in the land of the promise;" therefore we do not follow him down to Egypt (which the rest of Gen. xii. goes on to narrate). Nor do we turn aside to consider the assault of the old serpent there in order to prevent "the seed of the woman" from coming into the world. But rather we take up the "sojourning" "in the Land of the Promise," after he returns from Egypt; and there we find that he resumes it at the very point where it was broken off.

For "he went on his journeys from the south even to Bethel, unto *the place where his tent had been at the beginning*, between Bethel and Hai; unto *the place of the Altar, which he had made him there at the first:* and

there Abram called on the name of the Lord"
(Gen. xiii. 3, 4).

Here is sojourning indeed! and its reality is soon
manifested in *separation.* "Strangers and pilgrims"
can have no true fellowship with the world's citizens.

Dwellers in Tents can have nothing in common with
Canaanite earth-dwellers.*

Those whose "seat of government exists, now, in
heaven" look for the Saviour, while earth's citizens
have nothing to look for but destruction (Phil. iii. 20, 19).

Hence *separation* is the necessary outcome of true
sojourning. We see it immediately manifested in the
case of Lot.

Lot "walked by sight" and not "by faith." Hence,
"Lot LIFTED UP HIS EYES and BEHELD all
the plain of Jordan that it was well watered everywhere
before the Lord destroyed Sodom and Gomorrah, even
as the garden of the Lord" (Gen. xiii. 10).

It *looked like* "the garden of the Lord," even as
Satan may *look like* "an angel of light" and his
ministers may *look like* "ministers of righteousness"
(2 Cor. xi. 14, 15). But it is not "righteousness," nor
is it "light." Nor was it "the garden of the Lord,"
but it was the plain and "city" of Sodom, and the
end of each will be destruction with fire and brimstone
from heaven.

Notice the steps in a walk by sight when Lot
"lifted up HIS OWN eyes" (Gen. xiii.)

   1. He beheld (*v.* 10)

   2. He chose the plain of Jordan (*v.* 11)

   3. He took the eastward position and journeyed
      east (*v.* 11)

---

* For the deep significance of this title, after the Church shall
have been removed, see Rev. iii. 10; vi. 10; xi. 10; xiii. 8, 14;
xiv. 6; xvii. 8.

4. He dwelled in the cities of the plain (*v.* 12)
5. He pitched his tent toward Sodom (*v.* 12)
6. He dwelt in Sodom (ch. xiv. 12)
7. He sat in the gate (as a Ruler in, and citizen of Sodom (ch. xix. 1)
8. He shared in its calamities (ch. xiv. 12)
9. He was miraculously delivered from its destruction (Gen. xix. 16)

This is the end of a " Walk by Sight."

On the other hand, Abraham who sojourned by faith did not lift up his own eyes ; but " Jehovah said unto Abram (after Lot was separated from him) LIFT UP NOW THINE EYES, and look from the place where thou art Northward, and Southward, and Eastward, and Westward : For all the land which thou seest, to thee will I GIVE it, and to thy seed for ever " (Gen. xiii. 14-16).

Lot made his own choice. Jehovah made choice for Abraham ; and Abraham enjoyed it as God's gift.

Lot's choice was only for a short time. It began in calamity and ended in destruction.

Abraham's gift was " for ever." It began in faith, and will end in glory.

It is significant that these Revelations from Jehovah stand in immediate connection with the three separations of Abraham. The *first* was after he had separated from Haran. The *second* was after he had separated from Egypt. The *third* was after he had separated from Lot.

In each case we have the mention of the " tent " and the " altar." For here again, in connection with his further sojourning, at the end of ch. xiii. we read (*v.* 18) : " Then Abram removed his TENT, and came and dwelt in the plain of Mamre, which is in Hebron, and built there an ALTAR unto Jehovah.

True *separation* is indissolubly connected with true *worship*. In Gen. xiii. 3, 4 it preceded it, in verse 18 it followed. This fact tells us that there can be separation from the world without true worship; but there cannot be true worship without separation.* There can be separation from the world in Monasteries, Convents, and Seclusions and Retreats, but it does not follow that it is separation FROM the world; or that it produces true worship of God; or conduces communion with God.

On the other hand True separation is necessarily followed by true worship. Where it is not true, there may "non-conformity" with other churches, but much conformity with the world. But where we have real non-conformity with the world, then we have real transformation of the mind and the life, and real worship of and service for God.

"Be not conformed to this world, but be ye transformed (or transfigured) by the renewing of your mind, that ye may prove what is that good and acceptable and perfect will of God" (Rom. xii. 2).

This is what Abraham proved; and he soon manifested its *power* in the delivery of Lot from the hands of the four kings who had taken him captive (Gen. xiv.) We stop not to consider that war, but merely note that the effective intervention of Abraham and his 400 men afforded only an opportunity for the evidence of power which came from his true separation with God.

---

* What a search-light this throws upon the religion, and politics and worship of those whose efforts culminate in "Citizen Sunday." How opposite is all this modern earthly citizenship to all that we are here learning in the lesson set us by the Holy Spirit in connection with the sojourning and separation of Abraham.

When "the King of Sodom wished to reward him
with a division of the spoils, his lofty position enabled
him to say "I have lift up mine hand unto Jehovah the
Most High God, the possessor of heaven and earth,
that I will not take from a thread even to a shoe-
latchet that is thine, lest thou shouldest say, 'I have
made Abraham rich '" (Gen. xiv. 22).

No wonder that the visit of "the king of Sodom"
was followed by the visit of "the king of Salem:" and
that the blessing of Melchesidek was bestowed on one
who thus walked in lofty separation "before God."

There is one other point in connection with this
sojourning. There is not only the fact of the "dwelling IN TENTS" but that it was with Isaac and
Jacob "the joint heirs with him of the same promise."

These words are remarkable; for in no other case
are sons called "*joint-heirs with*" *their parents*. Sons are
merely "heirs" of, not "joint-heirs with" their parents.

This is designed to remind us that Isaac was not
indebted to Abraham for the promise; nor was Jacob
indebted to Isaac.

Each received "the same promise" direct from God.
"To thee" was said to Abraham (Gen. xiii. 15; xvii. 8).
To Isaac it was said "to thee" (Gen. xxvi. 3), and to
Jacob, it was also said "to thee" (Gen. xxviii. 13;
xxxv. 12).

They were all three "joint-heirs of the same
promise:" joint heirs "with him," *i.e.*, with Abraham.

They dwelled IN TENTS together because they
"looked for a city which hath foundations." "Tents"
have no foundations. They did not look back at the
city of "UR," from whence Abraham "went out,"
but they looked forward to that "city" of which they
had heard.

Abraham had "heard" all about that "city" from God : for " faith cometh by hearing." If he heard about it, it must have been by the word and report that he had heard from God. No one else could have told him of that coming day of Christ's glory.

But he knew all about it. He saw it from afar, as Christ testifies : " Your father Abraham rejoiced to see my day ; and he saw it, and was glad " (John viii. 56). The Lord does not say " he *sees* it and *is* glad." That is what He ought to have said according to modern theology. But He did not. God revealed the glories of that day to Abraham's faith. He believed God, and saw that day from afar. He died according to that faith, and He must rise again from the dead in order to prove the faithfulness of his God, and to enjoy the promises which had been made to him.

But this division of our theme : " He looked for a city," belongs to, and will form the subject of our next chapter.

3. "He Looked for a City"

WE have already seen the emphasis of the phrase "dwelling IN TENTS," in contrast with dwelling in the city of UR, from whence Abraham "went out."

But there is a second emphasis calling our attention to another city, even the city for which Abraham "looked," that is, a heavenly.

He "looked" for that city because he believed what he had heard about it from God. Hence, he did not build a city on this earth as Cain had done; but was content to "dwell in tents."

There is no record in Genesis as to such a promise having been made by God; but it had surely been made; for the Divine revelation of the fact is given here, by the Holy Spirit, in Hebrews xi.

As the special promise to Abraham was personal, and was not to be enjoyed in this life, it could be entered on only in resurrection, when the kingdom of God should come.

That is why, when He said to Moses, at the bush, "I am the God of Abraham, and the God of Isaac, and the God of Jacob," He meant that they would and must rise from the dead, the reason being that God is not the God of dead people, but of the living, "for all live unto Him" (Luke xx. 38),* and therefore they must rise from the dead. This is the whole scope of the Lord's

---

* J. N. Darby translates this:—" For for Him all live ": *i.e.*, we must be made alive again to perform any service "for Him." Only the living can praise Him (Psalm cxv. 17. Isa. xxxviii. 18, 19).

argument with the Sadducees, who did not believe in resurrection at all. It is distinctly and categorically stated that He used this very argument "touching the resurrection of the dead." (Compare Matt. xxii. 23, 28, 30, 31, 32, and the parallel passages in Mark and Luke.)

Just as we are not told the word which Abel and Enoch and Moses's parents and others heard from God, so we are not told the words which Abraham heard as to this wonderful "city" for which God caused Abraham to hope.

Can this be other than the City of which we read in Rev. xxi. 10-27? There we have a city of which God is the architect and constructor. Can any other city be that for which Abraham looked?

Abraham was left in no doubt whatever that his possession was to be a heavenly one; "the heavenly Jerusalem, the city of the living God" mentioned in the next chapter (Heb. xii. 22).

Believing what God had said about this, he was content to "dwell in tents" : for there is great emphasis on these two words in the Greek of verse 9, as we have seen. Not only did he "sojourn" instead of settling down ; but he sojourned "in tents" instead of building houses, or a city, of his own.

Having thus introduced this great subject of "the sojourning," and mentioned the faith of Sarah in order to introduce the third example of Abraham's faith in the birth of Isaac, there is a digression of a general character on the sojourning of all these elders.

The mention of Sarah, in *vv.* 11 and 12, is in chronological and historical order, because it necessarily preceded the birth of Isaac. But we shall consider the faith of Sarah in its experimental order, as following on the conclusion of the fourth example (viz., the trial) of Abraham's faith.

In our last paper, we gave the Structure of the Examples of Faith, as exhibited in the Elders forming " the great cloud of witnesses."

But there is the Structure of the Text of Heb. xi. yet to be discovered. It may be set forth as follows:—

Verses 2—40

A | 2-12. Particular examples

  B | 13-16. General reflections

A | 17-38. Particular examples

  B | 39, 40. General reflections

These divisions are perfectly clear: the general reflections (B & *B*) both commencing in the same way "these all." In B (*v.* 13) " These all died in faith," and *B* (*v.* 39) " These all having obtained a good report through faith."

The former of these general reflections is given as an appendix to Abraham's sojourning. The latter forms the conclusion to the whole chapter.

So that the correspondence is perfect; and the symmetry, not only supernatural, but Divine.

We must therefore connect verses 13-16 with the sojourning of Abraham, as being at once the expansion and the conclusion of that special aspect of his faith. .

We will give it in full, in our own translation :—

13. All these died according to faith, not having received the things promised* but having seen them from afar, and having been persuaded [of them], and

---

*By *Metonymy (of the Adjunct)* "the promises" are put for *the things promised.*

embraced [them], and confessed (Gen. xxiii. 4) that they
were strangers and sojourners on the earth. For they
who say such things (or, speak after this fashion) plainly
show that they are yet seeking for a home.*

And, if indeed they were remembering that one from
which they came out, they might perchance have had
opportunity to return [thither]. But now, they reach
after a better [home, or city] that is [to say] a
heavenly: wherefore, God is not ashamed† of them, to
be called their God ; for He hath prepared for them a
" city."

Faith was the secret spring of their strength. Faith
supported them in all their sojournings. Faith comforted them in all their sorrows. They believed the
report which they had heard from God. They believed
the promises He had made to them, and though they
all died, they died in this faith, and their faith will be
amply justified.

They could not see that city, except by the eye of
faith. They did thus see it, " afar off." And, in all
their sojournings they " walked by faith."

These are the *general reflections* interposed here (in
verses 13-16) in connection with the sojourning of
Abraham.

We sometimes hear it said that, Israel was an earthly
people, and the church is a heavenly people. But this
is not all, or even half, the truth.

There were always two parties in Israel, as there
are in the so-called " church " to-day.

All through the history of the nation there were

---

*Greek, πατρίς *(patris) an ancestral home, native city.* (Matt.
xiii. 54, Luke iv. 23.)

† The figure *Tapeinosis*, meaning that *He delights in them.*

those who "walked by sight," and those who "walked by faith : " those who believed God and followed Him wholly, and those who did not.

These two may have been symbolically indicated in the two descriptions used by God when he compared them to

    (1) "the *sand* which is upon the sea-shore," which is
           innumerable;

    (2) "the *stars* of the sky," in multitude.

Abraham's seed is compared to "sand" in Gen. xiii. 16; xxviii. 14; xxxii. 12; and to "stars" in Gen. xv. 5 ; xxvi. 3, 4. Exodus xxxii. 13.

But in Heb. xi. 12, *both* are mentioned together, because here, the difference between them is brought out in connection with *faith.*

These two parties in the nation are usually taken as symbolizing Israel and the Church.

But there is much beyond this crude conclusion, and rough and ready reckoning. There is no need to do this violence to the Old Testament Text by introducing the Church, or the Mystery, the secret which has been "hid in God" from the foundation of the world.

These two parties existed in Israel as a nation throughout all its history.

Those who were like the "sand" and "dust" of the earth walked by sight, with their eyes fixed on the earth ; and did not believe God as to what He had prepared to be enjoyed in eternal life. They found their portion on earth, and were satisfied with earthly things.

But those who were like the "stars" were "partakers of a heavenly calling" (Heb. iii. 1). They believed God—and manifested "the obedience of faith."

The general idea is that there is little or nothing in

the Old Testament about a future life; and arguments are brought against the Word of God on this account.

But this mistake has arisen from not understanding that the word "life" is used very frequently in the sense of eternal life—life to be enjoyed in resurrection.

We meet with it at the very outset of Israel's national life, even at Sinai, where Jehovah said: "Ye shall therefore keep My statutes and my judgments: which if a man do, he shall LIVE in them" (Lev. xviii. 5).

What does this word "live in (or, by; or, through) them," mean? The spiritual authorities of the Second Temple interpreted the phrase to mean "eternal life" by faith, as contrasted with "eternal life" by works. Solomon Jarchi, one of the most eminent of Jewish Scholars in the Eleventh Cent. A.D., interpreted the verse to mean "shall live by them to life eternal," and he takes this verb "to live" in the same sense in other passages. Compare Lev. x. 28; Mch. ix. 29; Ezek. xx. 11, 13, 21; Isa. xxvi. 19, xxxviii. 16, lv. 3; Ezek. xviii. 19, xxxiii. 19, xxxvii. 3, 5, 6, 14; Hosea vi. 2; Amos v. 4; Hab. ii. 4; also Gal. iii. 12; Rom. i. 17; Heb. x. 38, &c.* In fact, so far from eternal life in resurrection not being revealed, the Old Testament is full of it, from beginning to end. "The just shall live by faith." Where? How? When? If this were to be only here on earth, in earthly life, every one lived, whether he believed God or not. There surely must be more in the word than this: even the same as in Rev. xx. 5, when, having spoken of resurrection it is added "the rest of the dead lived not until the thousand

---

*So with the word ζάω (zaō) in the New Testament (Matt. ix. 18; Acts ix. 41; Mark xvi. 11; Luke xxiv. 5, 23; John xi. 25, 26; Acts i. 3, xxv. 19; Rom. vi. 10, xiv. 9; 2 Cor. xiii. 4; Rev. i. 4, 18; ii. 8; xiii. 14; xx. 4. 5.)

years were finished" (R.V.) With this agree the words
of Christ "I am the resurrection and the life : he that
believeth in me, though he were dead, yet shall he live"
(John xi. 24). How? When? Where? except in
resurrection?

Those who believed God walked "by faith," and
were accounted righteous. It is in connection with
Abraham's believing God with reference to his seed
being like the stars of heaven, that righteousness was
imputed to him (compare Gen. xv. 3 with verse 4.)

Those who were thus accounted righteous were so
accounted on the principle of "faith"; and these had
the hope of eternal life. This life came not from the
works of the law, but by the obedience of faith.
Hence it was that they were "partakers of a
heavenly calling."

Observe that it does not say "heaven," or "in
heaven," but a country and city which are "heavenly."
When that "city" is seen by John "coming down"
(Rev. xxi. 9-27), it comes "from heaven" and is
therefore "heavenly" in its origin, heavenly in its
foundation, heavenly in its builder and maker, heavenly
in its character, and heavenly "in its glory." Moreover,
it *comes down* from heaven, and cannot be enjoyed in
heaven or until it shall have come down from heaven.

The closing chapters of Ezekiel show how the
changes in that land of the promise will indeed make it
heavenly, yea, heaven upon earth ; when the Temple
shall be rebuilt, and "the Holy Oblation set apart," and
all the heavenly glories displayed by Him who shall
then "sit upon the throne of His glory," and "shall
reign over the house of Jacob for ever " (Lu. i. 32, 33).

It will indeed be "a better country."

It was thus, that the " sojourning " of Abraham **was** **"** by faith."

By faith he left Ur, the city of the Chaldees; he died according to this faith ; and in the blessed hope of that heavenly Jerusalem, which one day will come down from heaven and fulfil all the promises of God.

There is no need therefore to rob Israel of this " heavenly calling " by appropriating it to the Church of God.

Heb. xi. 13-16 is perfectly clear on this point.

If we recognize these distinct spheres of blessing, other things will fall into their proper place.

(1.) Israel on earth will enjoy the earthly blessings.

(2.) " The partakers of a heavenly calling" will embrace those referred to in Heb. iii. 1, and ch. xi., all of whom " died in faith " and were strangers and pilgrims on the earth, and who looked for the heavenly city which God hath prepared for them.

There are the same two corresponding divisions or parties among believers to-day : one may be likened to the " dust " and the " sand," and the other to the " stars of heaven."

As the term " Israel " embraced the whole nation and included both parties, so the term " Believers " or " Christians " embraces two corresponding parties to-day.

(1) There is the party whose members correspond with those of Israel who walked by faith. They look for a kingdom, and their one and only hope is to " go to heaven when they die." They see and know nothing beyond that. To some of them the church is the kingdom, and the kingdom is the church, and they pray for the extension of the kingdom. To others

the kingdom is yet future, so they pray for it to
come; while there are some who are labouring to
realise it on earth now.

(2) But there is another party among believers to-day:
even those who get beyond the " heavenly calling " and
believe God as to what He has revealed for our faith,
and who go on " from faith to faith."

We, and our readers we trust, belong to this second
party (answering to the second or higher party in
Israel). We not only believe the Gospel of the Grace
of God as it is revealed in the earlier Epistles (1 and 2
Thessalonians, Corinthians, Galatians and Romans) but
we go on from this faith to faith in what is revealed
in the later, or Prison Epistles (Ephesians, Philippians
and Colossians).

In other words we believe and embrace "THE
GOSPEL OF THE GLORY" as well as the Gospel
of Grace; and are waiting to be called up on high and
" received up in glory," not needing death and resurrection, but looking for an ever-imminent call, translation,
and change.

Before the revelation of the Mystery, and while it
was "hid in God," no one could believe it, for no one
had "heard" anything about it. It had not yet been
" made known for the obedience of faith."

The "heavenly" portion of the kingdom had been
made known. The good news as to " the kingdom of
God," with its blessed promise of a "first resurrection"
had been " heard "; but the circle of Divine truth had
not been made known and could not be "fully
preached" (Col. 1. 25, margin) till the Mystery, or
Secret, had been revealed.

The Word of God had been heard by all; but, not all who heard, had believed (Rom. x. 16-18).

Thus it was with Israel: and it is the same to-day.

Those who did believe then, and who believe to-day, were, and are, alike, "partakers of a heavenly calling." Those in Israel did not receive the promises on earth, but they will do in heaven, for which they looked. It is the same with their fellow "partakers" to-day. They do not receive the promises here and now; but they look forward to doing so; and, like them, they " die in faith." But, there is a "better thing" in store for both. They will not be made perfect apart from these (Heb. xi. 39, 40). Both alike will share in resurrection, for that is what being *"perfected"* means. The Lord used this word of His own resurrection in Luke xiii. 32 ("the third day I shall be perfected"). This is what it means in Heb. xii. 23 ("the spirits of just men who have been perfected " *i.e.*, reunited with their bodies in resurrection life).

But there is a still " better thing " reserved for those who believe God as to what He has since " made known for the obedience of faith."

And there are the two parties among believers to-day, as there were in Israel of old.

The difference, then, consisted in believing, or not believing, what God had revealed for the obedience of faith : and the same difference exists in respect to what is revealed in the New Testament Scriptures to day ; and in the " prophetic writings " therein referred to.

If all else is " according to faith," surely the measure of our blessing will be.

Abraham's sojourning, and the sojourning of " all these " was by faith. They believed what they had heard of what God had "prepared and foreseen" for them ; and *that* belief influenced their life on earth.

The great question for us now, is, Do we believe God as to what he tells us He has foreseen and "prepared" for us, and has revealed for *our* faith in Ephesians, Philippians, and Colossians? If we do, it will influence the whole of our life in a corresponding manner. We shall be recognized as though we were "dwelling in tents," and all that that implies.

We shall believe, and therefore "reckon," that we died with Christ, and that therefore, though we live in Him (Col. iii. 3), we shall act as though we are dead as regards the "Law" (Rom. vii. 4, 6 marg., Gal. ii. 19), dead as regards the "world" (Gal. vi. 14), dead as regards all forms of false religion (Col. ii. 20), dead as regards "sin" (Rom. vi. 2, 8, 11), and dead as regards "self" (Gal. ii. 20. 2 Cor. v. 15).

If this be a reality in the reckoning of our faith, we shall be persuaded of, and embrace and stretch out towards our goal, *i.e.*, the calling on high (Phil. iii. 14), just as Abraham, and those of his seed who were like "the stars of heaven" looked for what God had "foreseen" and "prepared" for them.

We shall "confess that we are strangers and pilgrims on the earth" in a greater, and more real, and intensified way than they did.

If a home in that city produced their heavenly walk, what will not our heavenly citizenship do for us and our walk ?

If we believe and reckon and recognize our home * as already existing † in heaven itself where Christ

---

* Compare οἰκεῖοι (*oikeioi*), *household* or *home* (Eph. ii. 19).

† This is not the verb "to be," but quite a different word ὑπάρχω (*huparchō*), *to exist in a state of being.* (Compare Phil. ii. 6 and iii. 20.)

is exalted as head over all, we shall surely be constantly looking for the Saviour, the Lord Jesus Christ, to come from thence to change these bodies of our humiliation and make them like His own body of Glory according to the power wherewith He is able to subdue all things to Himself (Phil. iii. 21, 22).

4. "When He Was Tried...Offered Up His Only Son"

In Hebrews xi. 17—19, we have the trial of Abraham's faith.

"*By faith Abraham has offered up Isaac when he was tried* (or put to the test). *Even he, who had accepted* (or waited for) *the promises, was offering up his only-begotten son; with respect to whom it was said that 'In Isaac shall thy seed be called.' Accounting that God was able to raise him up, even from among the dead, from whence, in a figure also, he did receive him back.*"

We stop not to consider the revolting calumnies and profanities of some of the "higher" critics who dare to ascribe this (which the Holy Ghost ascribes to Abraham's faith) to "an incontrollable impulse of Moloch worship!"

The Infidel blasphemies which have been put forth from Porphyry downward are to day repeated from "Christian" pulpits, and professors' chairs in our Universities.*

---

*We refer to the late Dean Stanley, who thus taught (*Lectures on the History of the Jewish Church*) with others in *Essays and Reviews*, and, since then, those who repudiate the whole history.

They say it was *not* "*by faith*" but by a mistaken suggestion of Abraham's own mind, similar to the abominable superstition of the Phœnicians in burning their children; and that Abraham is to be condemned and not commended for it. So far from being proof of his obedience; it was proof of his infirmity and ignorance.

From such blasphemous teachers may God deliver the young men who are sent to sit at their feet!

Even Dr. Torrey (*Hard Problems of Scripture*) suggests that God did not *command* Abraham to sacrifice his son upon the altar.

With these we have nothing to do. We are writing for those who, like Abraham, " believe God," and must leave all such unbelieving critics to that Word which shall itself judge them in that day when the Lord will vindicate His truth.

Our delight shall be to feed in the " green pastures " of the Word, in which we need to be *made* to lie down by the Great Shepherd ; and not to trample it with our feet, which are defiled by the world and its wisdom and its ways.

Thus feeding on the Word, instead of criticising it, we note first the Divine perfection of it in the use of the Tenses in verse 17.

" By faith Abraham when he was tried HAS OFFERED UP Isaac ; and he that had received the promises WAS OFFERING UP his only begotten son."

Both these verbs are important, and loudly call our attention to their peculiarity.

The former is the second of the three times which the Perfect Tense is used in this chapter.*

" Has offered," shows that God reckoned his faith as his act ; and imputed the result to him as though he had actually completed it ; just as He imputes Christ's righteousness to our faith, as our being actually righteous in Him.

The Imperfect Tense, which follows (" was offering,") shows that the act of offering, itself, was not completed ; for it was while in the act of offering, that Jehovah spake, and forbade the consummation.

In verse 16 God regards Abraham as thus having actually done it. He says : " By Myself have I sworn,

---

*The first being in verse 5, and the third in verse 28.

saith the LORD; for because THOU HAST DONE
this thing, and hast not withheld thy son, thine only
son, that in blessing I will bless thee . . . because *thou
hast* obeyed My voice."

This is why the Perfect Tense is used in Heb. xi. 17.
" By faith Abraham HAS offered up Isaac, when he
was tried," &c.

It is this which puts " faith " as being synonymous
with "obedience." This is why we have the expression "the obedience of faith." This is the Genitive
of " Apposition," and means, not only the obedience
which springs from faith, and, which has faith for its
origin and its source; but because faith is put for, and
reckoned as, obedience itself. Obedience, reckoned as
faith: *i e*, "faith-obedience " would be a good rendering.

The two are inseparable. If we believe what God
says we shall necessarily act in accordance with our
faith. If we do not so act, it is proof positive that we
do not believe ; and that there is no faith worthy of the
name.

It is this fact which reconciles what the Holy Spirit
says by Paul, and what He says by James. It is the
same inspiring spirit who " moved " both.

There is no more difference between them than
between different parts of this manuscript, part of
which may have been written with a quill pen, and
another part by a steel pen, or a fountain pen. There
can be no discrepancy except in our own failure to
rightly divide the word of truth, and receive all as
coming from the same Divine Author.

If we really believe God we shall as readily do what
He commands, as we shall rely on what He promises.
And thus faith is translated into obedience, and obedi-

ence is faith translated into action. Any other kind of obedience is not "of faith," and is therefore "sin." There is plenty of obedience and "works" which come from the flesh, and not from faith; but these are called "dead works."

Paul and James spoke and wrote by the same Spirit, and teach the same truth. And we shall see this at once, if we understand this identity of faith and obedience, or faith and works which is contained in the expression "the obedience (that is to say) faith."

But for this identity this Scripture could never have been written. "By faith Abraham HAS offered up Isaac" (Heb. xi. 17), and "Because thou HAST DONE this thing" (Gen. xxii. 17).

It was not "by fact" but "by faith," and this explains everything.

There is another reason why the Perfect Tense is used here. As the whole transaction was a type of the sacrifice of Christ, and, as that has endured through all time, so it could be said that it "*has been offered*," and that its infinite merits are still as perfect and effectual as at the time when the offering was made.

It was the trial of Abraham's faith; and it was the gracious act of God. It was He who said, "Take now thy son, thine only son, Isaac."

God did not try Lot's faith. Sodom was sufficient to try that.

Abraham's obedience here was as ready as when he was called to get out of his own country. It is obedience that is the test of faith; and it is obedience that is in question here, in the case of Abraham.

Hence, in Gen. xxii. 3, we read, "And Abraham rose up early in the morning."

When God " separated " Saul of Tarsus and called him to preach His gospel, we read : " Immediately, I conferred not with flesh and blood, etc " (Gal. i. 15, 16).

Faith never confers with flesh and blood. If it did so it would cease to be " faith," and become " sight " at once.

It was the same faith that said (Gen. xxii. 5), " I and the lad will go yonder and worship." Faith is always occupied with God, whose " word " or " report " it hears. Abraham was not occupied with his faith, or with his obedience, or with himself, in any way whatever, but only with his God. " I and the lad will go yonder AND WORSHIP."

God, and God's Word, filled Abraham's heart, and occupied all his mind and thoughts.

Hence, Abraham added the words, " and come again to you " (*v.* 6).

Was Abraham lying to his young men ? Most assuredly not. It was the language of the most precious faith.

We know not all that passed through Abraham's mind : but we are told that he accounted that "God was able to raise him (Isaac) up even from the dead " (Heb. xi. 17). It is clear from this that Abraham believed that even if he did slay his son God would immediately raise him up again from the dead.

This, surely, must be the force of the words "in a figure " in verse 19. The Greek is ἐν παραβολῇ (*en parabolē*), *in a parable*. But a parable is a *similitude*, in which two things are cast side by side for the purpose of comparison.

Great differences of opinion have been manifested as to the meaning of the words, but there is no room for such differences. Neither view exhausts the meaning. Both are true, and both are needed to bring out the whole truth. Both are needed in order that the comparison may be instituted and the similitude seen.

It is true that Abraham did receive Isaac at the first, as from the dead, according to Romans iv. 19, and Heb. xi. 11, 12.

It is true that Abraham did receive Isaac back again as from the dead ; for, he accounted "that God was able to raise him up from the dead," and his faith being accounted to him for righteousness, it could be truly said, "by faith, Abraham, when he was tried, has offered up Isaac" (v. 17). It was this faith that enabled it to be spoken of as a thing actually done. This is the force (as we have seen) of the Perfect Tense.

Instead of one of these views being true, we may say that both views are true.

Abraham's faith reckoned that, as he had already received Isaac, as it were, from the dead, why not receive him so again ?

This was the reckoning of faith.

Is not all this clearly shown by the words in Genesis xxii. 6 : " I and the lad will go yonder and worship, and COME AGAIN TO YOU."

He knew not how. But he "believed God" and spoke from the assurance of faith, and went forward in "the obedience of faith."

When Isaac enquired about the lamb for the burnt offering, Abraham replied, still in the language of faith, " My son, God will provide for Himself* a lamb for a

---

*Heb ‏לו‎ (lō) *for Himself*, not Himself as some have incorrectly taken it.

burnt offering " (*v.* 8). He was as certain of that as of all beside.

This is why Abraham called the name of the place JEHOVAH JIREH, " Jehovah will provide."

He had said to Isaac, " In the mount of Jehovah it shall be seen " (*v.* 8), and when Abraham had seen, he sealed the answer to his faith in the name he gave to the place.

Similar differences of opinion have been expressed as to the interpretation of the Type as fulfilled in Christ the Antitype. But, here again, there is no room for any difference, no one finite Type can exhaust the Infinite which is contained in the Antitype.

No one offering could set forth all the aspects of Christ's atoning death. No one Gospel could have set forth all the aspects of Christ's earthly life.

Even so, no one Type can contain, in itself, all the perfections and truths and teachings concerning Christ, as the Antitype.

Abraham and Isaac, and the Ram, are all needed to shew forth the intertwinings of the truths which are involved.

Go back to the history in Gen. xxii. and note the several points :

In verses 2, 12 and 16 we are shown Isaac as the only son, " thine only son . . . . thy son, whom thou lovest." Do we not see here, " the only begotten Son," Jesus Christ, of Whom in another parable, it is said : " Having yet one Son, His Well-beloved " (Mark xii. 6) ?

In verse 2 we have the words " I will tell thee of " : and verses 3 and 9, " the place of which God had told him," showing how all had been ordered of the Father concerning Christ, and that in these points Abraham himself appears to be the Type of Christ.

In verses 6 and 8 we have the twice repeated expression used of Abraham and Isaac, "they went both of them together." Here the Type passes to Isaac, and it is he who sets forth the unity of purpose between the Father and the Son (John x. 30). In *v.* 6, the laying of the wood upon Isaac clearly points to John xix. 17.

In verses 9 and 10 the Figure *Polysyndeton* (many "ands") is used to mark off, point out and emphasize the deep significance of every detail. The *seven* "ands" show the deliberate steps, each of which demands our close and earnest consideration :

> " **And** they came to the place .   .
> **And** Abraham built an altar . . .
> **And** laid the wood in order,
> **And** bound Isaac his son,
> **And** laid him on the altar . . .
> **And** Abraham stretched forth his hand,
> **And** took the knife."

Up to this point Isaac is the Type of Christ : and again, in verse 18, as the seed in whom "all nations of the earth shall be blessed."

But, in verse 13 the Ram becomes the Type of Christ, and "we, brethren, as Isaac was, are the children of promise" (Gal. iv. 28), for whom Christ is offered up in our stead.

The Ram was "caught by his horns," the emblems of his strength, to show that the Antitype, Christ, did not succumb to death from weakness, but gave up His life in His strength.

' I lay down my life (He said) that I might take it again. No man taketh it from Me, but I lay it down of Myself. I have power to lay it down, and I have power to take it again. This commandment have I received of My Father '' (John x. 17, 18). Hence it was that, on the holy mount, "they spoke of His decease WHICH HE SHOULD ACCOMPLISH."

Another seven-fold *Polysyndeton* is given in verses 13 and 14, describing Abraham's subsequent action. It is used to set forth and emphasise every act and deed, and to intimate the deep significance of each :

> " **And** Abraham lifted up his eyes,
> **And** looked,
> **And** behold, behind him a ram . . .
> **And** Abraham went
> **And** took the ram,
> **And** offered him up . . .
> **And** Abraham called the name of the place
>   Jehovah-jireh . . . "

Oh, what a volume is contained in those two small words

" BY FAITH "

The whole history is the grand record of *the activities of faith*. It is *faith in action :* Living faith in the Living God.

Every one of these " ands " introduces an *action ;* and yet every action is "by faith."

But this leads us to the conclusion which we must reserve for our last paper on the faith of Abraham.

5. "Abraham Believed God"

THE greatest characteristic of Abraham's faith, and that which distinguished it from all the others, was OBEDIENCE. It stands in correspondence with Israel's obedience in crossing the Red Sea (*v.* 30).

Both are associated with women; Faith's *obedience* in Abraham is connected with Faith's *conclusion* in Sarah (*v.* 11); and Israel's *obedience* is connected with Faith's *conclusion* in Rahab (*v.* 31).

We have seen how Abraham's faith produced his obedience.

1. By faith he obeyed to go out (*v.* 8).
2. By faith he sojourned (*v.* 9).
3. By faith he has offered up Isaac (*v.* 17).

It is important that, in this connection, we should note the expression at the beginning and end of the Epistle to the Romans *Faith-obedience* (ch. 1. 5 and xvi. 26). The Greek is ὑπακοὴς πίστεως *(hupakoēs pisteōs), obedience of faith.* It is the figure *Enallagē*, by which the noun "faith" is changed into, and used as, an emphatic superlative *adjective*, characterising the kind of obedience intended.

There are different kinds of obedience. Some may obey from *fear ;* some from a sense of *duty ;* others from *compulsion ;* others, again, from love or from a desire to please, or from some other second or mixed motive.

When, therefore, the expression " faith-obedience " is used, it shows that the obedience spoken of springs from and is produced by faith—a living faith in the Living God. Apart from this faith all works " have the nature of sin."

We use, and speak of, both these words "faith" and "works," in various senses, each of which, therefore, requires a definition.

Obedience is made up of "works," and the Word of God speaks of three kinds :

"Wicked works" (Col. i. 21)

"Good works" (Eph. ii. 10)

"Dead works" (Heb. vi. 1)

"Wicked works" (Col. i. 21) need no further definition ; we all know too well what they are, and wherein they consist.

"Good works" are defined in Eph. ii. 10 as being the outcome of the creation of the New Nature ; and as consisting of the works "which God hath before ordained (margin, *prepared*) that we should walk in them."

No other than "prepared" works are "good works", all others which appear to be, and are so-called "good works," are works performed by the Old Nature, by the flesh, and are not the product or outcome of the Spirit of God. They may appear to be "good works ;" and may be commonly spoken of as such ; but God calls them "dead works," and the Lord Jesus says they "profit nothing." They are "dead" because they are produced by those who are themselves "dead in trespasses and sins" (Eph. ii. 1) ; they are "dead" because they are not produced by the life-giving Spirit of God.

Man may think and speak very highly of them ; man may laud them to the skies ; he may applaud them and hold them up for imitation ; but God pronounces them to be "dead."

There is a solemn and decisive difference between

death and life; and it is a fundamental axiom of Divine revelation that " the body without the spirit is dead." This is the first thing recorded in the creation of man.

" The Lord God formed man out of the dust of the ground, and breathed into his nostrils the breath of life, and man became a living soul " (Gen. ii. 7).

This is why the body without the spirit (or breath of life) is dead (James ii. 26).

The beauty of 2 Cor. iii. all turns on this fact. The Old Covenant, or Old Testament, is called "the letter," as distinct from *pneuma* which is " spirit "; and, just as the body without spirit is dead, so the Old Covenant without Christ is dead; " The Lord " (Christ) being the *pneuma* which gives life to the Old Testament Scriptures (2 Cor. iii. 17).

The same Holy Ghost inspires James to use the same contrast between " faith " and " works." He says " as the body without works is dead, so is faith dead without works."

There is a dead faith, just the same as there are " dead works." It is the same *pneuma* which gives life to both, and causes them to be, respectively, " living faith " and " good works."

" Living faith " is thus the *pneuma*, or, the life-giving spirit of the works, causing them to be " good works " : for, " whatsoever is not of faith is sin " (Rom. xiv. 25).

Then, in their turn, these " good works " became the spirit-given evidence of the faith which produces them, and thus show that it is a " living faith."

So that it is absolutely impossible to separate the two.

On the one hand, " dead works " are no evidence

of a living faith ; and, on the other hand, lifeless faith is no producer of " good works."

It is all very well to quote the words of James ii. 26, and say " faith without works is dead," but we at once ask, What " faith ? " and What " works ? " not " wicked works," or " dead works," surely. No, but " good works," for these are the evidence of the living faith.

Living faith, is " faith of the operation of God " (Col. ii. 12).

" Good works " are the product of the New Creation, prepared and ordained by God the creator of the New Nature (Eph. ii. 10).

So that, it can be said, with equal truth, that Abraham, who believed God, was " justified by faith " (Rom. iv. 2 ; v. 1),because his " good works " proved it to be Divine faith. And at the same time it could be said that Abraham, who obeyed God, was "justified by works " (James ii. 21), because his works being " good works," proved that they were produced by " living faith " Otherwise they would have been " dead works," and not being of faith, would be sin (Rom. xiv. 25).

When we thus carefully define our terms, Scripture speaks with no " uncertain sound." And we see the full force of the statement in Heb. xi., which distinguishes the faith of Abraham from that of the others : " By faith Abraham, when he was called, obeyed."

It is the same principle of " faith-obedience " by which sinners are saved and justified to-day.

God speaks to us in His Word, as He spoke to these " elders " individually.

They each had a special communication direct from

God Himself, and sinners and saints to-day have the same special communication written down in the Scriptures of Truth.

The question is the same to-day as it was then :

Do we believe God ?

i.e., Do we believe what He says ?

By nature, none of us believe Him. We none of us wish to believe. The carnal mind is enmity against God, and is not subject to the Law and the Word of God. We all seek to evade it by various devices.

Some deny that there is any God to speak to man.

Others believe there is a God, but deny that He has spoken in His Word.

Others believe that he has spoken, and that the Bible contains His Word, but deny that it is His Word.

Others believe that the Bible contains the Word of God, but cannot tell us where to find it or how to distinguish His words, or where to hear His voice.

Others receive it, and receive their emoluments and dignities for so doing, but deny its Divine origin and inspiration, and spend their energies in destroying it ; declaring its histories to be "myths" and "legends," and "old wives' fables," and its prophecies to be the shrewd guesses of mortal men, or the work of those who lived after their fulfilment.

Others receive it, but declare that much of it consists of forgeries, and spend their whole time in criticising it or writing commentaries upon it. No class of men are so busily engaged in writing about the Word of God. They cut it up with their pens, just as Jehoiakim cut it up with his penknife

Others are content to use it as a book to pick to pieces, not to find fault with it, but to find "texts" suitable for sermons or almanacs, or birthday-books, or motto-cards; just as Shakespeare and the poets are used for the same purpose.

Others believe it to be inspired by God, but have their various "schools of thought" as to the kind of inspiration involved, and the nature and the measure of it.

Others believe, as a matter of fact, or as an article of faith, that it is inspired, but hold that no one can really understand it, and thus endeavour to shield themselves from all responsibility to believe it, on the ground of their ignorance.

Others go a step further, and, while holding that, while no one can understand it, the Church (whatever that expression may mean!) can do so. They thus seek to shelter themselves by shifting their responsibility to believe God from themselves to the Church; and thus, while refusing to believe God, they believe man, and swallow down with credulity all that man may say.

Others receive it, as a good book, but are content with setting it to music; and treat it as being useful for making a "libretto" of an oratorio or cantata, or of a song or a solo. Thus, with some it becomes a "book of the words," while the performers are "rendering" the music. They receive the applause of man for singing with great gusto warnings which they ignore; threatenings which they do not fear; commands which they disobey; prophecies to which they do not take heed; and promises by which they are not moved.

Others receive it, and believe it to a certain extent; and value, and even reverence, the Scriptures as the Word of God, but not by a Divine or "living faith," because it has not the evidence of the "good works," which are manifested only in "faith-obedience."

"Faith-obedience" is the obedience which proceeds from, and is produced by, a living faith in the Living God. In other words, it is the acting as *if what we heard were true*

We hear, for example, what God says about our condition by nature; that we are not only ruined *sinners*, on account of what we have *done*, but ruined *creatures*, on account of what we *are*. Do we believe it? If so, we shall act accordingly, and the belief will make us so sad and miserable, that we shall thankfully believe what He says when He declares that He has provided a substitute for the sinner so believing and so convicted; and that He has accepted that perfect One in the sinner's stead.

If we believe this we shall be at peace with God; and have no more concern or trouble about our standing, in His sight; we shall have nothing to do but to get to know more and more of Him, and to be giving Him thanks for what He hath done in making us meet for His glorious presence. We shall not be for ever putting ourselves back into our old place from which we have been delivered. We shall not be always asking for forgiveness of the sins for which He was delivered, because we shall be always rejoicing in Him "in Whom WE HAVE redemption through His blood, even the forgiveness of sins" (Col. i. 14), and while we are giving Him thanks for " HAVING FORGIVEN YOU ALL TRESPASSES" (Col. ii. 13), we shall forget our old occupation of for ever confessing our sins and praying for forgiveness.

We shall be looking and pressing forward to the "CALLING ON HIGH" (Phil. iii. 14).

We shall be free to witness for Him, and to engage in His service, being no longer occupied with ourselves, our walk, or our life. We shall be no longer taken up with judging our brethren, knowing that the same Lord has "made them meet" also; and that they are members of "the same body," and that we shall soon be called on high together. We shall cherish our fellowship with them here (if they will let us) knowing that we shall soon be " together " with them there.

We shall hold not only the precious doctrinal truth connected with Christ the Head of the one Body, but the practical truths connected with the members of that Body.

We shall seek to learn ever more and more of God's purposes connected with " the great mystery concerning Christ and His Church," and to enter into all that concerns its glorious Head.

We shall have such an insight into His wondrous wisdom Who has ordered all these things that we shall thankfully prefer it to our own.

We shall recognise that His " will," manifested in the working out of His eternal purpose, is so perfect, that we shall prefer it to our own, and *desire* it to work out all else that concerns us.

We shall have nothing to " surrender." We shall have done with that new miserable " gospel " of self-occupation; and, all connected with its phraseology will have been left far behind, as being on a lower and different plane of Christian experience altogether.

Christ will be our one object, and we shall count all

things but loss for the excellency of the knowledge of Christ Jesus our Lord (Phil. iii. 8).

If this be not the result of our believing God, it is proof positive that we have not a "living faith," and that all our works for holiness are only "dead works," because we have not this blessed evidence as the result of our "faith-obedience."

We have this simple test in our own hands.

Without the Holy Spirit's Word by the Apostle James we should not possess this test. But now that we have it, and see it, it will be our own fault if we do not profit by it, and use it for our own blessing and peace and rest.

If we do thus use it, we shall find ourselves strangely out of harmony with all that rules in modern Christianity, and all that characterises present-day religion.

We shall realise that its phraseology and its terminology are all based upon a lower plane of experience. We shall find ourselves out of touch with many of our fellow-believers; for we shall have learnt to "cease from man." We shall have lost and given up "religion;" but this will be because we shall have found Christ, and know what it means to be

"FOUND IN HIM."

Sarah: Faith's Conclusion

WE have already remarked on the place which Sarah occupies in the Divine order manifest in this chapter. This is clearly seen from the structure on page 109 (Vol. xiv.), where Sarah is placed in direct correspondence with Rahab.

In these correspondences the same characteristic of faith is obviously emphasised by the Holy Ghost.

In Sarah and Rahab we have FAITH'S CON-CLUSION. This is common to both women. Sarah "judged Him faithful Who had promised" (v. 11). Rahab said, "I know . . . for we have heard" (Josh. ii. 9, 10).

Moreover, both women stand in connection with the two examples of FAITH'S OBEDIENCE, forming two corresponding pairs, with Abraham and Israel respectively.

But we must now give the text in full (verses 11 and 12).

" By faith (A.V., through faith, but the Greek is the same as in the other cases) Sarah herself also received power for [the] foundation of a posterity, and [that], after the ordinary time of life, since she esteemed Him faithful Who gave the promise. Wherefore, even from one,* who was as good as dead as to such things, there sprang [a posterity] even as the stars of heaven for multitude, and as sand which is by the sea-shore, which cannot be numbered."

In this Scripture we have to note one or two

---

* A single individual, in contrast with the multitude afterwards referred to. Not only one, but one as good as dead.

important points which arise out of the words
employed, before we turn to the example given as to
Faith's conclusion.

First, the word rendered "conceive" is so rendered
only here, out of eleven times where it occurs in the
New Testament. This has caused it to be tortured
and twisted, to the offence of every delicate mind, by
certain critics and commentators.

The word is simple enough. There can be no
manner of doubt whatever as to its meaning or usage.

It is καταβολή (kaiabolē). It occurs eleven times, and
is rendered *foundation* in every passage except the one
we are considering. *Seven* times it is used of the
kingdom which is said to be " FROM the foundation of
the world " (Matt. xiii. 35 ; xxv. 34 ; Luke xi. 50 ;
Heb. iv. 3 ; ix. 26 ; Rev. xiii. 8 ; xvii. 8). And *three*
times it is used of Christ as being " *before* the foundation of the world," and of the Church which is His
body as having been so in God's purpose (John xvii. 24 ;
Eph. i. 4 ; 1 Pet. i. 20).

We stop not to enlarge on the significance of the
number of these occurrences, or of their *nature*, but call
attention to our passage (Heb. xi. 11), where the same
noun, *foundation*, is treated as a verb and rendered "to
conceive"!

There surely can be no doubt but that the word
here, can mean only the foundation of that posterity,
the promised "seed of the woman " (Gen. iii. 15), even
Christ, of Whom it was said : "in Isaac shall thy seed
be called " (Heb. xi. 18), " thy seed, Which is Christ "
(Gal. iii. 16).

We are thus lifted completely out of the physiological sphere, out of the letter of the Scripture, and

are directed to Him Who is its object and its end, yea, its *pneuma*, or life.

True, emphasis is laid on the one physiological fact that both Abraham and Sarah were "as good as dead "* (Rom. iv. 19, 20 ; Heb. xi. 12).

In Gen. xvii. 17 we learn that the promise of a son had been given to Abraham a whole year before Isaac was born.

It was repeated in Sarah's hearing some months before.

We may see this by comparing Gen. xvii. 15-19 with xviii. 10 and xxi. 5.

It was on the first occasion that Abraham laughed, and it was on the second that Sarah laughed.

It is evident from Gen. xvii. 15-19 that Abraham considered the promise of a son " out of his own bowels " (Gen. xv. 4) should be fulfilled in Ishmael ; for, when his name was changed from Abram to Abraham in token that he should be the father of many nations (Gen. xvii. 5), he said : " O that Ishmael might live before thee " (*v.* 18), " for he said in his heart, Shall a child be born unto him that is an hundred years old ? and, Shall Sarah that is ninety years old bear ? " (*v.* 17).

Abraham, it will be noted, " fell upon his face † and laughed." His laughter was accompanied by the

---

* It is the same word as that rendered " mortify " in Col. iii. 5. It cannot mean to actually *put to death*. It must be used as a figure of a great reality, to teach us that the command is to be carried out, only by *considering* the " members " of our body " as good as dead," and hence, powerless to produce anything for God.

† This was just the difference between Martha and Mary in John xi. Both sisters when they met the Lord made exactly the same remark (which they had doubtless made before to one another) : " Lord, if Thou hadst been here, my brother had not died." But Mary " fell down at His feet " when she said it (*v.* 32).

deepest act of reverence. His question was not asked for information, but it is the Figure *Erotēsis*, an exclamatory question of gladness. " He rejoiced when he saw My day (*i.e.*, the day of the Lord Jesus). He saw it and was glad " (John viii. 56).

But when Sarah laughed (Gen. xviii 12), there was no such act of reverence; but she " laughed *within herself*."

There is no doubt whatever that, when Sarah first heard the promise, it came as a shock, and was sufficient in itself — so unexpected—to produce a momentary or passing surprise. But it is equally clear that as soon as ever they realised that what they *heard* was the promise of God all doubt and hesitation vanished.

We are distinctly told in Rom. iv. 19 that Abraham was not weak in faith with regard to this "hearing," And it is as distinctly affirmed in Heb. xi. 11, that Sarah " received strength."

This is why she said at the feast of rejoicing when Isaac was weaned : " God hath made me to laugh, so that all that hear will laugh with me " (Gen. xxi. 6), and this is why the child's name was called " Isaac," which means laughter.

To laugh " within herself" was one thing ; but it was quite another to be " made to laugh " by God.

There should be no surprise at the momentary shock.

God's saints are never represented as paragons of virtue, but are truthfully set before us with all the same frailties and infirmities which characterise our-

---

Martha did not (*v.* 21). Hence, note the Lord's answer. With Martha He reasoned. But with Mary, who was weeping, He wept, and " groaned in spirit and was troubled."

selves. That is why they are "written for our learning:" that is why we may find " comfort," and have " hope " (Rom. xiv. 4). We look away from the " great cloud of witnesses" unto Him Who is the Author of their faith, the Giver of their strength.

" By faith Sarah herself received strength " (Heb. xi. 11), and so did Abraham (Rom. iv. 20)*; and, by the same faith, our strength comes from our believing Him Who proclaimed to Sarah those faith-inspiring words " Is anything too hard for the LORD ? " (Gen. xviii. 14)†

It was the same LORD Who had said "Sarah shall have a son," "I will certainly return unto thee" (v. 10), " At the time appointed I will return unto thee " (v. 14).

After this, we are quite prepared to read (Gen. xxi. 1), " And the LORD visited Sarah *as He had said*, and the LORD did unto Sarah *as He had spoken*."

That is exactly the point,

"As He had said

As He had spoken.

All turned on that.

That was the word which faith had heard ; that was the hearing by which faith came (Rom. x. 17).

Moreover, it shows that all the planning of Abraham and Sarah was useless in the accomplishment of the LORD's purposes.

Jehovah must " visit,"

Jehovah must " do,"

And faith must rest, and faith must wait.

The next verse (Gen. xxi. 2) goes on accordingly to

---

*Greek " was strengthened."

†This, again, is the Figure *Erotēsis*, by which the question is asked, not by way of seeking information, but by way of com-municating it.

say that all was accomplished "at the set time of which God had spoken to him."

It is remarkable that it is just this very aspect of faith which is the point of Habakkuk's prophecy, which is the text on which the whole chapter (Heb. xi.) is based.

Jehovah said by Habakkuk (ch. ii. 3, 4),

" For the vision is yet *for an appointed time*,
But *at the end* it shall speak, and not lie.
Though it tarry, wait for it ;
Because it will surely come,
It will not tarry .   .   .
But the just shall live by his faith."

This is exactly what Sarah did as soon as she under_stood the meaning of what God had spoken.

This is the point singled out for emphasis by the Holy Spirit in Heb. xi. 11.

" SHE JUDGED HIM FAITHFUL WHO HAD
PROMISED."

That is the point.

This it is that gives Sarah her place in this " great cloud of witnesses," and places her in correspondence with Rahab, who, in like manner, is the other example of

FAITH'S CONCLUSION

God had spoken. Sarah had "heard." And, in spite of all that appeared to make it impossible, she "judged Him faithful who had promised."

This, then, is the point for us to seize upon as specially " written for our learning."

What is to be our conclusion from what is revealed for our faith ?

The birth of Isaac was the introduction of a new element in Abraham's household.

It corresponds with the introduction of the New nature in the believer to-day. Ishmael corresponds with the Old nature, which, when the New nature comes, it finds in possession.

Its introduction at once brings to light, and rouses to greater life and strength, the activities of the Old nature.

There was no conflict in Abraham's house till Isaac was born " not of the will of man, or of the will of the flesh, but of God " (John i. 13).

" But, as then, he that was born according to flesh persecuted him [who was born] according to spirit, even so it is now" (Gal. iv. 29). " The flesh lusteth against the *pneuma* (or New nature) and the spirit against the flesh, and these are contrary the one to the other " (Gal. v. 17).

" The mind of the flesh is enmity against God : for it is not subject to the law of God, neither indeed can be " (Rom. viii. 7).

In Abraham's house this enmity was at once manifested.

The birth of Isaac did not improve Ishmael, or change his character, or his activities.

There was only one remedy, and that was "cast out this bond-woman and her son ; for the son of this bond-woman shall not be heir with MY SON, even with Isaac " (Gen. xxi. 10). The bond-woman was an Egyptian, and savoured of Egyptian bondage; and the only remedy was to " cast out " both her and her son.

But what was possible in the allegory or type is impossible in the antitype.

The Old nature cannot be " cast out " from believers now, but we have to reckon it to be so, by faith.

This is to be for us

FAITH'S CONCLUSION,

Faith's reckoning (Rom. vi. 11), Faith's judgment (Heb. xi. 11).

This was what Abraham considered in Rom. iv. 19. " He considered* his own body as already having become dead, and the deadness of Sarah's womb ; but staggered not at the promise of God, through unbelief, but was strengthened by [his] faith, giving glory to God " (Rom. iv. 20).

This is to find its exact counterpart in us who believe God, as Abraham did.

This is to be faith's *consideration*, faith's *judgment*, faith's *conclusion* for us.

All that we are called on to do now, is to believe God ; to consider our Old nature to be dead, and unable to conceive, beget, or to bring forth, or produce anything for God.

It requires great faith to do this ; because, all the time we are conscious of its presence and its power. Our faith, therefore, has to be " against hope," as Abraham's was.

All the while they were believing God's promise, he and Sarah were faced with the undeniable fact that all was " against hope."

It is even so with us. We are faced with the ever-present fact of the workings of the Old nature ; and,

---

* Lachmann, Tischendorf, Tregelles omit the " not," Alford puts it in brackets. It comes to the same thing. For in the one sense he did not consider his own body ; and in another sense he *did* consider it, but as now dead.

therefore, we must, "against hope," "reckon ourselves to be dead [persons] to sin, but alive to God, through (or in) Christ Jesus."*

To attempt to *improve* the Old nature is to give a flat denial to Rom. vi. 11.

To attempt to *change* Ishmael is direct disobedience to God (Gal. iv. 30).

To "consider" our Old nature as being alive and able to produce anything for God is a refusal to reckon it as being dead.

To "mortify" its members, in the popular sense, is to consider them as *not* being "already dead," but to recognise them as being very much alive. But to "mortify" in the Scriptural sense is to *consider them as good as dead !* This is the meaning of the word in this connection, as is clear from our context, Heb. xi. 12 and Rom. iv. 19.

Abraham could not have considered his own body as already actually dead, or that he could mortify it by any activities which he could put forth ; but, only by considering it "as good as dead."

That is what we are called on to do in exercising

Faith's Conclusion

We are not to seek to improve our members by mortifying them by any process or rules for daily living. This is only to treat them as though they were *alive.* But we are to treat them "as good as dead," and as being as *incapable* of doing good, as they are capable of doing evil.

But this can be done only by believing God ; and, by faith-obedience, *reckoning* ourselves as already dead

---

* All the critical Greek texts and R.V. omit the added words "our Lord."

in ourselves. Until this is done, there can be no peace. For it is as being "justified by faith, we have peace with God." This is the conclusion of the whole argument of Rom. iv. as continued in ch. v. 1.

Until this is done, there can be no joy, no happiness, no " laughter."

As long as Ishmael was in Abraham's house there was only grief (Gen. xxi. 11). But when God's faithfulness was realised, then Sarah could say "God hath made me to laugh " (Gen. xxi. 6).

Yes, it is the same God Who hath " made us meet for the inheritance of the saints in light," Who makes us thus to laugh.

But if we stagger through unbelief, and do not come to FAITH'S CONCLUSION, and believe Him, "against hope," and in spite of all our feelings and experiences, then there is only one alternative for us: we shall go on our way in grief and unhappiness, mourning for what we have done or not done, instead of " giving thanks unto the Father " for what HE HATH DONE (Col. i. 12). We shall sink under the burden of the incessant confession of our trespasses, because we steadfastly refuse to believe what we hear from God, that " you, being dead in your sins . . . hath He quickened together with Him (Christ) HAVING FORGIVEN YOU ALL TRESPASSES" (Col. ii. 13).

Oh, that we may have Sarah's faith, and "against hope" be strengthened by faith, and have our mouths filled with God-given laughter, and give glory to God, *because we have judged Him faithful Who hath promised.*

Isaac: Faith Overcoming

"The Will of the Flesh"

By a reference to the Structure of the "Great Cloud
of Witnesses" on page 109 (Vol. xiv.) it will be
seen that we have now before us a pair of witnesses,
Isaac and Jacob : and that these are Divinely set in
correspondence with another pair, Moses's Parents
and Moses Himself.

Both pairs have one subject in common. There
was one thing that animated and governed the Faith
and the witness of all the four.

Each one exhibits that aspect of faith which "overcometh the world" (1 John v. 4); and which giveth
the victory over man; delivering us from "the fear of
man"; and making us regardless of "the praise of man."

They are thus set in correspondence :

The Former Pair

ISAAC. Faith overcoming "the will of the flesh,"
by blessing Jacob, the younger, according to "the will
of God "; instead of blessing Esau, the elder, according
to his own will.

> JACOB. Faith overcoming "the will of man,"
> by blessing Ephraim, the younger, according to
> "the will of God"; instead of blessing Manasseh,
> the elder, according to "the will of man" (Joseph).

The Latter Pair

MOSES'S PARENTS. Faith overcoming "the fear
of man," preserving and hiding their babe, "not fearing
the King's commandment" that every man-child should
be destroyed at the birth.

MOSES HIMSELF. Faith overcoming "the praise of man"; *refusing* his honours; *choosing* affliction; *esteeming* reproach; and *forsaking* Egypt and all its works.

The exquisite setting of these four examples of faith, in two corresponding pairs, will be seen at once; and will be admired by all those who regard the WORD of the Lord as the greatest of His works, "sought out of all them that have pleasure therein" (Ps. cxi. 2),

We have now to consider the first of these two pairs:

THE FAITH OF ISAAC

" By faith Isaac blessed Jacob and Esau concerning things to come" (Greek: concerning things about to come to pass).

Isaac's blessing is a perfect illustration of the definition given of Faith in the first verse.

" FAITH IS THE GROUND OF THINGS HOPED FOR."

God had made definite promises to Abraham.

Isaac had *heard* of them; *i.e.*, he believed what had been told to him by his father, Abraham. This was the "ground" of his hope of "things to come."

Abraham was now dead, and Isaac was expecting soon to be buried in the grave he had purchased in the Land given to him and his seed.

There was nothing to be seen for faith to rest on; nothing that gave the smallest ground for hope; nothing to make it even probable (apart from what he had heard and believed) that his descendants, either Jacob or Esau, would ever possess the land which had been promised to them.

Yet, believing the report, Abraham leaves them the blessing which he had himself received.

It is evident that Isaac felt, both by birth and by right, that Esau, the elder, should receive the blessing. His affection for Esau was great; and "the will of the flesh" was strong within him.

For, Isaac must have "heard" from God that Jacob, the younger, was to receive the blessing; and he must surely have heard from report that Esau had already profanely "despised his birthright" by selling it, with all its precious privileges, for "a mess of pottage."

God's gift, which was of "grace," to Jacob, was confirmed to him by the exercise of the "free will" of Esau.

Those who claim to have a free will are perfectly right; but it is a will, so free, that it is *always* exercised in *despising* the gift of God.

Never h: s it yet been known to choose God, and the things of God; and to walk in the blessed paths of faith instead of sight.

Yes! man has a free will; but, "YE WILL NOT come unto me" proclaims its true nature, and tells us that it is a will perverted by the Fall (Gen. iii.).

Man declares that he "CAN come." In that declaration lies his righteous condemnation; for he does not, and "will not come," in spite of his vaunted claim.

The proclamation goes out to-day in no uncertain form to

" WHOSOEVER WILLETH "

This is the old English verb "to will," which has become almost obsolete, being merged in the sign of the Future Tense of the ordinary verb.

"Ye will not come" is, in the Greek, "Ye do not WILL to come." There are two verbs: the verb "to will" in the Indicative Mood, and the verb "to come" in the Infinitive Mood.

All, who have the will to come, are included in this invitation. But, alas! "the Fall of man" is such a dread reality, that the result can be truly expressed only in the words of Scripture (Rom. iii. 10-13).

> "There is none righteous, no, not one ;
> There is none that understandeth ;
> There is none that seeketh after God.
> They are all gone out of the way ;
> They are together become unprofitable ;
> There is none that doeth good—no, not one."

This is God's description (one of many) of the result of the Fall of man. The New Theology takes no account of this. There is no room for this in the new creed. It is no creed at all; for it is not what they "believe," but only what they think. They deny the fact, as well as the Divine record, of the Fall; and with true "ostrichism" they wilfully shut their eyes to the evidences of it all around them. They ignore the fallen condition of the natural man while they seek to get a Millennium out of such material! and, out of "Christian socialism" they hope to "realise the Kingdom of God upon earth,"* a Millennium without Christ.

This is the condition of man to-day. His will is free; but it is fallen; it is utterly perverted, and wholly alienated from God. Nothing but the Divine record in Gen. iii. can explain this.

---

* As we write, the newspaper lies before us which describes this "Socialist Vision," while on the opposite page it describes the Boyertown (Penn.) Theatre Fire, in which it says: "Men behaved more like wild beasts, trampling down women and children in their frantic efforts to escape!"

Not only is man's free will perverted in its character and nature, but it is incapable of righteous judgment.

For, while claiming the free action of his will for himself, he denies the same right and claim to God, the Creator. Man may have a will, but he will not allow God to claim it.

Alas for man! The word of the Lord stands in spite of all; and those who believe what He has written know full well that God has a will; and that will will be done, in spite of all man's imaginations.

"Jacob have I loved, but Esau have I hated" (Rom. ix. 13). Man may love, and man may hate, but he will not allow God to do either; nevertheless the Word of the Lord shall stand for ever.

If we thus acknowledge the truth of that Word, and believe God, then we can understand how and why men to-day are alone responsible for the exercise of the freedom of the will to which they lay claim. We can understand why Esau was "profane" and responsible for his own action when he "despised his birthright."

The Word of God is true; "Jacob have I loved" is true of the exercise of God's will, in His choice of Jacob. It is also true that Esau was responsible for his own will in the choice that he made.

Indeed, what we see in the whole history is the working of

"THE WILL OF THE FLESH"

Esau could not believe God: hence he was overcome by his fleshly will.

Isaac believed God: hence he overcame it, and got the victory over it "by faith."

Esau sold his birthright for "a mess of pottage." That was the working of "the will of the flesh."

Isaac was about to give him the blessing for a mess of "venison." This, again, was the working of the same "will of the flesh" in Isaac.

Esau loved himself more than his birthright, because he preferred to eat of the pottage. This was "the will of the flesh."

"Isaac loved Esau because he did eat of his venison" (Gen. xxv. 28). It was a question of "savoury meat" throughout; and this was "the will of the flesh."

It overcame Esau, but it did not overcome Isaac, though it came near to do so.

Isaac was about to act in opposition to what he had, without doubt, "*heard*" from God, as to His purpose to bless Jacob. "The will of the flesh" had evidently worked very powerfully within him.

We see it working all through the chapter (Gen. xxvii). Otherwise whence came all the anxiety? Why should he have been suspicious of Jacob?

It is evident that up to verse 23 Isaac had "not discerned" Jacob. Hence when the fact is added "so he blessed him," it means that he did so later on. But before he actually did so, much was said and done in verses 24-26. We know not what went on in Isaac's mind. There must have been enough to make him say, at length, "Come near now, and kiss me, my son" (Gen. xxvii. 26). He must surely by that time have discerned the fact that it was really Jacob, and must have welcomed the relief which the discovery brought to him.

The "now," though it is not here (or in the original)

an adverb of *time*, is yet an expletive in command, marking the conclusion to which "faith" had come.

The trembling of Isaac in verse 33 need not have been caused either by the doubt or discovery. The difficulty into which he had got, with a man of Esau's temperament, was quite sufficient to arouse his fears, and account for all his trembling.

The outcome of Jacob's and Rebekah's strategy was that which (unwittingly to all concerned) enabled him at length to see his way out of his struggle with "the will of the flesh," and he seized it "by faith."

For, it was "by faith that he blessed Jacob." It was Isaac's faith and not Jacob's fraud. Isaac must have known, therefore, that it was really Jacob; or it would not have been "by faith." It would have been by favour, had he thought it was Esau. But it was "by faith"; of this the Holy Spirit expressly assures us in Heb. xi. 20.

And the Holy Spirit puts this on record, in spite of all the sins and failures and infirmities of those who were concerned in the matter.

God's choice was made, God's will had been made known and heard. The tears* of Esau could not alter it. The fears of Isaac could not change it. The trick of Rebekah could not forfeit it. The treachery of Jacob could not affect it.

When all these had passed away, the words of the

---

* Heb. xii. 17, requires to be properly understood: Esau "found no place of repentance though he sought it carefully with tears." The margin renders it that he found no "*way to change his mind*." This is good so far; but the question is, Whose mind? Clearly, his father's mind. Esau's mind *did change;* was changed; "he cried with a great and exceeding bitter cry" (Gen. xxvii., 34). *It was Isaac's mind* that he could not change, though he sought earnestly a place or way by which he could accomplish it.

Spirit of truth survive in all their simplicity and solemnity: "By faith Isaac blessed Jacob concerning things to come."

In this sad business, "the will of the flesh" over-came Rebekah and Esau and Jacob, but it did not overcome Isaac, though his conflict with it was great. Isaac's faith overcame all, and carried out "the will of God."

It is very blessed to note that his faith was directed to what he had *heard* from God; and especially what he had heard "concerning things to come." *It did not direct his thoughts to himself*, or to his weakness, or to his frailties, or to his infirmities. It did not occupy him with himself in any way whatever; with nothing except with the blessing wherewith God had blessed him.

Isaac's faith in what God had said did not throw him back on his weakness of faith shown in the working of his own fleshly will, but it took him forward to the glorious things of which God had spoken.

Hence he was occupied, not with confession, but with thanksgiving.

When the crisis came, Faith rose up triumphant, and gave Isaac all the dignity demanded by the solemnity of the occasion; he remembered God's blessing to his father, Abraham; he remembered how that blessing was passed on to himself, and not to Ishmael; even so, now, he passes it on "by faith" to Jacob, and not to Esau.

It was the "things to come" which filled Isaac's thoughts. The future glories of Israel came into faith's vision. They were "not seen as yet" (Heb. xi. 7), but by faith he "saw them afar off" (*v.* 13), he saw them as things "invisible" (*v.* 27).

And, do we desire to have this faith which overcomes "the will of the flesh" which dwells within us; whose workings make it painfully manifest in our inward conflict with "the carnal mind" (*the mind of the flesh*, margin)? Do we desire victory over the flesh working within us; the profanity and sin and treachery working all around us? Then, this victory can come only "by faith," by believing God, in what He has said as to "things to come."

"This is the victory that overcometh the world, even our faith" (1 John v. 4).

The same "will of the flesh" works within us now; the same desires which are the outcome of the "carnal mind" are *constantly in conflict with the spiritual mind;* the New nature.

By nature we always desire the things which are contrary to God : and make it manifest that our thoughts and ways are not His (Isa. lv. 8).

By nature we are always inclined to follow these desires.

When we speak of *liking* this or that in the things of God : of preferring this or that in the worship of God ; *that* is the working of "the will of the flesh."

It is not to be what we like, or what we prefer. The tastes of nature are no guide in spiritual things. Indeed they will most certainly lead us astray if they are followed and obeyed.

The words of our Lord and Master are clear: the Scripture standeth written : "God is spirit, and they that worship Him MUST worship Him in spirit and in truth" (John iv. 24). The Father seeketh SUCH to worship Him (*v.* 23).

Do we believe what He says? If so, then, "by

faith" we shall overcome the working of "the will of the flesh" in the worship of God.

In no other way can it be overcome.

Faith in His word, Who spoke on earth, in the past : faith in His word, Who speaks now from heaven of "the recompense of reward" for all overcomers.

Not only in worship, but in every department of Christian service "the will of the flesh" is seen in active operation. We undertake certain works, because *we like* them! We join in certain efforts because they accord with *our tastes;* we adopt certain *methods* in our service, or choose certain *spheres* of service, not because of " the will of God " in the matter, but because we are deceived by the working of "the will of the flesh," and we follow our own natural tastes and desires.

If we would overcome the flesh in these matters; if we would not " fulfil the desires of the flesh and of the mind," there is only one way to overcome, and that is "by faith "; by finding out what God has said, and by believing what He says.

Most powerful in this respect is what He has revealed to us " concerning things to come." It was his that gave victory to Isaac.

If we believe all the glorious things which God has revealed concerning "things to come," it will set us far above all that would mislead us, or that would seem to be against us.

It is only " WHILE we look not at the things which are seen, but at the things which are not seen " that " the inward man will be renewed day by day, and that our afflictions will seem " light," and their duration will seem "but for a moment," in comparison with " the eternal weight of glory " of the things to come.

This is the Divine commentary on, and Divine conclusion of, our subject. It is written for us in 2 Cor. iv. 16-18.

This blessed victory of an overcoming faith will be experienced only " WHILE we look. not at the things which are seen" (2 Cor. iv. 18); only while " we walk by faith and not by sight" (2 Cor. v. 7).

It is only occupation with the "things to come" which will give us the victory over all the "things present."

The true " life of faith " is not occupation with ourselves, or our walk, or our experiences, or our consecration, or our holiness. All these belong to the "things present," "the things that are seen" and felt. They all end in failure and disappointment. But if we would rise above these, and occupy our hearts with "the things that are not seen," we should have no time to be troubled and perplexed and grieved and tormented with the workings of "the will of the flesh," but we should find ourselves on a different and higher plane altogether. We shall be taken *out of ourselves ;* and know something of the purifying power of "the blessed hope"—the " things hoped for," of which faith in God's promises are the foundation.

" For every one that hath this hope set upon Him (Christ) purifieth himself, even as He is pure (1 John iii. 3, R.V.).

May it be our happy privilege to have, and to use, Isaac's faith, and to enjoy its blessing connected with " things to come."

Jacob: Faith Overcoming "The Will of Man"

" By faith Jacob, when he was dying, blessed each of the sons of Joseph, and worshipped [bowing himself Gen. xlvii. 31] *upon the top of his staff"* (Heb. xi. 21).

JACOB, as we have seen in our last paper, is set in correspondence with Isaac, in a similar act of blessing : but as overcoming, not "the will of the flesh," but

"THE WILL OF MAN"

The point seized on by the Holy Ghost is that, in Jacob's case, Joseph's desire was that the elder son, Manasseh, should receive the blessing. But God's choice had been already made; and, though Joseph may not have heard of it, or known it, Jacob had heard it and believed it.

It is remarkable that, out of all the many acts of Jacob's life, the Holy Spirit should (in Heb. xi.) pass by the evidently inspired blessing and prediction respecting the future of Jacob's own sons, and single out, as the example of faith, his blessing of the two sons of Joseph.

Expositors have been so taken up with the closing words of this verse that they have overlooked the special point which marked the faith of Jacob.

Two things stand out in the sacred text in spite of all the differences and disagreements of commentators.

There are two acts of Jacob which are singled out. Two verbs define them—

JACOB " BLESSED "
JACOB " WORSHIPPED "

The former is recorded in Gen. xlviii., and the latter in Gen. xlvii. 31.

The latter event (the blessing in Gen. xlviii.) is mentioned first in Hebrews xi., because it is this which stands in contrast and correspondence with the faith of Isaac.

The former historical event in Gen. xlvii. is mentioned last in Heb. xi. in order to show the Divine character and origin of this faith ; and to emphasise the fact that, it was not influenced by "the will of the flesh," on the one hand; or by "the will of man," on the other. It rose far above all such considerations, and rested on the words of that God Whom Jacob believed, and Whom he worshipped.

By confusing these two events, which are quite distinct though connected in the context, commentators have been so eager to display their ingenuity, that they have quite overlooked the one object for which the words are written; and the one reason why Jacob is introduced here at all.

The point is that Jacob was not influenced by "the will of man " in the person of Joseph ; not even though Joseph was the son of his love.

We need not repeat the history here. The great facts stand out in all their distinctness. Jacob was " about to die," and he wished to bless the two sons of Joseph. The emphasis lies in the word ἕκαστον (*hekaston*), *each* : *i.e.*, each son, separately. This is to show us that the blessing was not to be a collective one.

Joseph, however, had his own ideas and wishes on the subject ; and *his desire* and intention was that Manasseh, the first-born, should receive the blessing.

In order to secure this, Joseph placed Manasseh to his left hand, and Ephraim to his right, so that Jacob's right hand should rest on Manasseh's head, and his left on Ephraim's.

All this care shows the strength of Joseph's will in the matter.

But Jacob, though his eyes were dim by reason of age (Gen. xlviii. 10), so that he could not see, was being Divinely guided. This is shown by his action in crossing his hands, so that his right hand rested on Ephraim's head, and his left hand on Manasseh's.

In the Hebrew, the Figure *Prosopopoeia* is used to call our attention to this. This is the Figure which, here, *personifies* the hands, and says " *he made his hands to understand.*"

This Figure is not literally translated, but it is beautifully rendered by the words : "*guiding his hands wittingly* " (*i.e.*, knowingly).

Immediately, " the will of man" asserted itself : Joseph cries out " Not so, my father : for this is the first-born ; put thy right hand on his head " (*v.* 18).

And his father refused ; and said, " I know it, my son ; I know it." *

This emphasis is put on the words here in order to mark the exceeding great strength of Jacob's faith.

When his eyes were " dim with age," as those of his father had been,† it is not said that " he trembled very exceedingly," for it was not " the will of the flesh " with which he was struggling, but " the will of man,'' which his faith was overcoming.

Note the significance of the fact that he is called

---

* This is the Figure *Epizeuxis*, which emphasises what is said by repeating it. It is, in Hebrew, exactly as though Jacob said (in English), " I know it, my son, perfectly well."

† Compare Gen. xxvii. 1, with xlviii. 10.

" Israel" here. It was no longer "Jacob" the sup-
planter and the contender. It was not Jacob the bargain-
maker, occupied with his own will, but "Israel,"
because God was his ruler, ruling all after the
Divine will.

This is forced upon our attention, not only by the
persistent use of his name " Israel" by the Holy Spirit,
all through this chapter (indeed from ch. xlvi. 27), but
by the contrast between the use of his name " Jacob "
when others speak to him or of him.

When the Spirit speaks of his coming to dwell in
Goshen, the portion which Jehovah in His grace had
prepared, and which His blessing had prospered, it
says: "And ISRAEL dwelt in the land of Egypt, *in
the country of Goshen*" (ch. xlvii. 27.)

But when stating the historical and chronological fact
as to how long he was there, and how old he was, as an
ordinary man, it says (in the very next verse): "And
JACOB lived in the land of Egypt seventeen years,
&c." (*v.* 28).

And, again, in the next verse, when he is about to
worship God, and to speak in His name, it says : "And
the time drew nigh that ISRAEL must die, &c." (*v.* 29).

Once more, when someone (an Egyptian servant
probably) told him of Joseph's visit, it says : " And one
told JACOB, and said, thy son Joseph cometh unto
thee, &c." (xlviii. 2).

But when, in the next verse, he refers to the time
when he was indeed " Jacob," when he had left his
father's house a fugitive with nothing but a staff in his
hand, and a stone for his pillow ; and when he remembers
the grace which met him there, then we read : " And
JACOB said unto Joseph, God Almighty appeared unto

me (when I was only Jacob) at Luz, in the land of Canaan, and blessed me, &c." (xlviii. 3). There he is JACOB,* and God is *El Shaddai*, God the Mighty and All-Bountiful.

From this point to the end of the chapter, it is ISRAEL, because he has to do with God and the things of God. "Jacob" is the name connected with his fears and his frailties, when he managed his own affairs, and all he had to do was to work; but "Israel" is the name connected with the blessed fact that God became the Ruler in all his affairs, and all he had to do was to worship. (See further on this point, below.)

"By faith" Jacob blessed each of the sons of Joseph.

He had *heard* from God; he believed God. He was therefore not to be influenced by "the will of man," any more than Isaac was, by "the will of the flesh." "By faith" they overcame both the one and the other.

Yes, it was "by faith," and certainly not "by sight."

To "sight," what could be more unlikely than that these two young Egyptian princes, for such they were, should ever forsake Egypt, the land of their birth, and migrate into Canaan?

What more improbable than that they should "each" become a separate tribe?

What more unlooked for, than that, of these two, the younger should be exalted above the elder, both

---

* This explains the meaning and usage of the title "the God of Jacob." It emphasises the fact that it is the God Who met Jacob at the time when he had nothing, and promised him everything, when he deserved wrath, and showed him grace. "The God of Israel" is the God who became his Ruler and his Guide. Note the use of this expression "the God of Jacob" in Psalm cxlvi. 5, "Happy is the man that hath the God of Jacob for his help." The New Testament title which expresses this is "the God of all grace," and happy indeed is he who has this God for his help (1 Pet. v. 10).

in importance, and number; and should become "a fulness of peoples" (xlviii. 19)?

Israel's faith in what God had said to Abraham, and to Isaac, is shown in the repetition of the original promise renewed to himself, in his formal adoption of Ephraim and Manasseh; separating these two from any other children that might be thereafter born to Joseph in Egypt (xlviii. 5, 6). His faith in believing what God must have subsequently revealed to him is shown in the fact that he transmits the promise specially to Joseph's posterity, through Ephraim; for it was the tribe of Ephraim that became representative of the kingdom of "Israel," as distinct from "Judah." How did Jacob know of this, except by believing what he must have *heard* from God? Who could have foreseen the separation of the two kingdoms, or have known anything of it, except by Divine revelation? For observe, it is as ISRAEL that he says "let MY NAME be named upon them . . . and let them grow* into a multitude in the midst of the earth" (*vv.* 15, 16).

The closing words of Israel's blessing (xlviii. 21, 22) show that he had *heard* more definitely as to the particular portion of the Land of Canaan which should become the inheritance of Ephraim, for he said: "Behold I die; but God shall be with you, and bring you again into the land of your fathers. Moreover, I

---

* The Hebrew idiom for "grow" is Let them increase *as fishes do increase* (compare Num. xxvi. 34, 37). This shows that they were not to increase by becoming Gentiles. Fishes do not increase by becoming birds or beasts, but by becoming many fishes. But this forcing of the literal words is one of the pillars of British-Ephraimism. For our part, we would rather be Anglo-Jews and belong to Judah, than belong to the Tribe whose terrible apostasy and departure from God, and gross idolatry led to their dispersion.

have given to thee one portion above thy brethren, which I took out of the hand of the Amorite with my sword and with my bow."*

What wondrous faith! How grand in its simplicity: " I have given."

Here is a pilgrim, dying in a strange land, who can say, by faith, of a distant land and of a future time, " I have given."

Truly. *" By faith Jacob blessed each of the sons of Joseph."*

But there is a second special mark of Jacob's faith.

And he worshipped [" bowing down " xlvii. 31] *upon the top of his staff."*

This worship of God is quite distinct from the blessing of Joseph's sons. As we have said above, this worship, though taking place before the blessing, is not mentioned till after it, in order to bring the two acts of blessing (in the cases of Isaac and Jacob) into close relation and correspondence.

There was no ground for the worship in the act of the blessing (in ch. xlviii.), but there is a very special reason for it in connection with his burial with his fathers in the land of Canaan (ch. xlvii. 27-31).

There can be no doubt whatever that the word rendered " bowed himself "† in Gen. xlvii. 31 means

---

* This portion was Shechem. (See Gen. xxxiv. 25-29, and Josh. xvii. and xxiv. 32.)

† Heb. *yishtachū* (see Gen. xxii. 5. 1 Sam. i. 3. 2 Kings v. 18). In 1 Kings i. 47 we have the corresponding expression with regard to David, when confined to his bed: " He bowed himself (*i.e.*, he worshipped) upon the bed," where we have a different word for "bed " from that in Gen. xlvii. 31.

exactly what the Greek word means: "he worshipped "* in Heb. xi. 21.

We have the Holy Spirit's own interpretation of
Gen. xlvii. 31 in Heb. xi. 21, where he says that Jacob
worshipped "upon his staff."

The Hebrew word for "stuff," without the vowel-
points, is MTTH.   If the vowels be supplied thus,
MaTTeH, the word means *a staff*.   If the vowels be
supplied thus, MiTTaH, it means *a bed*.

The Massorites, in later times, put the vowels as
in the latter case.   The Holy Spirit (in Heb. xi. 21)
shows that they made a mistake, and that the vowels
should have been put as in the former case.

Gen. xlvii. 31 would then have read, as in Heb. xi. 21,
"he worshipped [bowing himself] upon his staff."

But why did he worship specially, then and there?

Because he had just secured the promise from Joseph
that he would not bury him in Egypt; but would carry
him up out of Egypt and bury him in the sepulchre of
his fathers.

Thus did he exhibit his faith in God's promise.   It is
not enlarged on or specified as such in Heb. xi. 21,
because it was the same as Joseph's faith, which is to
be dealt with in the next verse (*v.* 22).   Israel's faith is
included in his worship.

But there is something more in this worship.

Israel's character comes out most markedly here, at
the close of his life, as it did in earlier days.

When he was going to meet Esau, and was in fear of
his life, not knowing what vengeance he might take,
he used every precaution to mitigate Esau's wrath.

---

* Greek προσκύνησεν (*proskunēsen*).   What sort of worship
this means may be seen from John iv. 20-24, etc.

He divided his possessions and his family into portions, so that as Esau met one after the other, and found each was a present for himself, his feelings might be changed towards him.

Having done all that, having laid his plans with the utmost care, and arranged everything in his own wisdom and strength, he was left alone.

He had been all his life ordering and arranging and planning all, by himself. But that night he had a different lesson to learn—the great lesson of his life. His "faith," here, shows that he had learnt it at last.

It has all been hidden from the English reader by the renderings of Gen. xxxii. 28 and Hos. xii. 3, 4.

(1) There is nothing about "prayer" or about "power with God" (a rendering which has become popular by giving us the idioms of "religious phraseology"), "power in prayer" and "prevailing prayer." It comes into the English version from the Latin Vulgate.

(2) The meaning of the name "ISRAEL" is given in the R.V. margin as meaning "*He who striveth with God*," or "*God striveth.*" This latter meaning is the correct one, not the former : for names compounded with "El" have that as the nominative, when the other part of the name is a verb, as here.

Then the word rendered "power" is in R.V. "striven." This is better, but not good enough.

If we think for a moment of the origin and meaning of the name "Jacob," we shall find that it arose from the fact that "the children *struggled* together within her " (Gen. xxv. 22). The name *sar* is used of one who *orders* or *arranges* (hence the later usage of "prince"). A good word would be "boss," were its usage more refined.

The " officers " of Pharaoh are so called (Gen. xii. 15). Potiphar is called "captain." Pharaoh's butler had a "chief." The king's cattle had " rulers " (Gen. xlvii. 6). The Hebrews had " taskmasters." All these are the renderings of the same word *sar*.

This gives us an insight into the meaning of the word " prince," and tells us that Jacob was an *arranger*, a commander, struggler and *contender* from the first.

He ordered his own affairs, and, as a rule, generally succeeded in securing his own will and way.

He contended with Esau in the womb, though he failed (Gen. xxv. 22-26).

He contended with Esau for the birthright, and secured it (Gen. xxv. 29-34).

He contended with Esau for the blessing, and succeeded (Gen. xxvii.).

He contended with Laban for his daughters, and obtained them (Gen. xxix.).

He contended with Laban for his cattle, and secured them (Gen. xxx., xxxi.).

But that night all was to be reversed. God was going to be the controller. God was going to command and rule and order and arrange for him.

Jacob had arranged everything for meeting and appeasing his brother Esau. Now, God is going to take him in hand, and order all things for him.

To learn this lesson, and take this low place before God, Jacob must be humbled. He must be lamed as to his own strength, and made to limp. Jacob's new name was to be henceforth the constant reminder to him that he had learned, and was never to forget this lesson, that it was not he who was to order and arrange his affairs, but God; and *his new* name, ISRAEL, henceforth told him that "God commandeth."*

Hence, as we said, "God striveth" (of the R.V.) is not a helpful rendering.

The rendering that brings out the point is: "Thy name shall be called no more Jacob, but Israel, for thou hast commanded with God and with men, and hast prevailed" (*i.e.*, as "Jacob"), implying that, as "Israel," God would henceforth command, and order all his affairs. To this end, in his own ordering of his goings, he would limp; but, in God's ordering he would be blessed indeed, far beyond anything he could arrange for himself.

This it was that gave him his "faith" in blessing

---

* It is God who is the doer of what is in this verb: *e.g.*, Hiel = *God liveth*. Daniel = *God judgeth*. Gabriel = *God is my strength*. Uriel = *God is my light*. Nathaniel = *God giveth*, &c., &c., in about forty places.

This enables us to translate Hos. xii. 4, in harmony with its context, which is all about "controversy" (*v.* 2), and his weeping and supplication (of *v.* 4). Verse 3 in A.V. is entirely out of harmony with the context, and introduces success where we should expect failure. The whole reads:

"Jehovah hath also a controversy with Judah,
  And will punish Jacob (*ya ākob*), according to his ways;
  According to his doings will He recompense him.
  In the womb, his brother he-took-by-the-heel (*ākab*).
  And in his manfulness (R.V. *manhood*), he contended (R.V. marg. *strove*) with God:
  Yea, he contended (same word in Heb.) with the angel;
  And He (the angel) overcame him;
  He (Jacob) wept, and made supplication unto him (the angel).
  He (the angel of Jehovah) found him (Jacob) at Bethel,
  And there He spake with us;
  For Jehovah [is] the God of hosts;
  Jehovah [is] His memorial." (Hos. xii. 2-5).

each of the sons of Joseph. It was no longer contending for his will to be done, much less " the will of man " in
the person of his son Joseph. God had ordered it. God
had arranged it. God commanded it. That was
sufficient ; Jacob believed God, and Jacob's faith carried
out the will of God. All that Jacob had to do now was
to remember his name, " ISRAEL," and worship.

' Jacob worshipped [bowing himself] upon his staff."*
It was a wondrous manifestation of faith, and of his
confidence in God, that He would do all that He had
said ; and perform all that He had promised.

In the blessing of Joseph's sons, his faith rose superior
to " the will of man."

May our faith rise to the same blessed height, so
that when God has shown us His will, and made it
plain to us, as only He can do, we may not be turned
aside by any who may say to us " *Not so, my Brother*, not
so : " but may we be able, in the full assurance of faith,
to say " I know it, I know it." For we are not
ignorant of the workings of the perverted " will of
man." We know how the Lord's servants suffer from
the imposition of the will of their brethren ; often more
so than from the open opposition of their enemies.
We know how workers at home, and especially abroad,
will bear witness to the sorrowful and, at times, almost

---

* It would be wrong to omit to mention the fact that the Latin
Vulgate renders this "*adoravit fastigium virgæ ejus*," "he
worshipped the top of his staff," thence deriving an argument for
the worship of images. The stupidity of Rome is seen (1) in
assuming that it was Joseph's staff, whereas it was Jacob's (*virgæ
suæ*, not *ejus*), and (2) in assuming that there was an image upon it.
And the sin of Protestants is very grievous, in combining to support
the circulation of this, among many other corruptions in the Versions,
made from the Romish Latin Vulgate.

heartbreaking fact, that their greatest hindrances and oppositions come from those who profess to be their brethren, and ought to be their fellow-helpers in Christ.

We may indeed say with Jacob : " *We know it*," " *We know it*." But let us not be cast down. Let us have "faith in God," and that alone will enable us to overcome "the will of man" in all its manifold manifestations.

Joseph: Faith Waiting

" *By faith, Joseph, at the close of his life, made* [prophetic]
mention of the Exodus of the Children of Israel [from
Egypt], *and gave commandment concerning his own bones* "
(Heb. xi. 22).

THAT is all, after his long and eventful life. After
all his sorrows and " afflictions " (Amos vi. 6), and
self-denials and sufferings ; after all his triumphs
and glory in Egypt, this is the greatest and most
wonderful thing that emerges " when he was dying."

What is the one thing that is thus singled out ?

Not God's foreknowledge in sending the dreams in
his youth ; not His grace, manifested, foreshowing his
destiny ; not His wondrous power in overruling all the
enmity of his brethren ; not the marvellous " acts " of
God in ruling and overruling the events of his life ; not
the mysterious ways, by which the " evil " designs of
his brethren were made to accomplish and carry out
the " good " things God had purposed ; not all his
exaltation and glory in Egypt which God had bestowed
upon him ; but one simple act, his dying act, in
remembering and making mention of one thing which
GOD HAD SAID.

This was the greatest thing in Joseph's eventful life.
God had spoken ; Joseph had heard the words he had
uttered ; Joseph believed what he had heard ; faith
came by hearing, and it was " by faith " that he
remembered that word, and made mention of it.

The Holy Spirit, here, does not direct our attention to
all those things which we delight to dwell upon ; all the

213

types foreshadowing the humiliation, rejection, sufferings, death, exaltation, and glory of the true Joseph; but to one simple act of faith; greater, more blessed, and more precious than all the acts of his eventful life.

It is the course and close of this life which is here indicated by the word used for his dying. It is not the word used of Jacob, in the preceding verse. There, it looks forward to a death which is about to take place, for the word is ἀποθνήσκων (apothnēskōn), *about to die and become a corpse.* Here, it is τελευτῶν (teleutōn), a word that looks backward to *a life about to end* and close up all the past dealings of God with him.

The word used of Jacob looks forward to, and has respect to the corruption which was to come in, through, and after his death.

The word used of Joseph looks backward, and has respect to the ending of his long life which had been full of mercies and crowned with blessings.

At such a moment his thoughts are filled, not with the many wonders which God had wrought, but with one thing God had said.

Joseph had been highly exalted in Egypt. It would have been truly according to nature if he had arranged for some grand memorial. It would have been according to the custom of the Egyptians if he had ordered a colossal pyramid to be prepared as his tomb, and a grand monument to be erected to his memory. But what he had heard from God, by "the hearing of faith," had upset all these things which were so "highly esteemed among men," and made them of no account in the reckoning of faith.

" The archers had sorely grieved him, and shot at him and hated him; but his bow abode in strength, and the arms of his hands were made strong by the hands of the mighty God of Jacob" (Gen. xlix. 22-26). God had highly exalted him. He had delivered him from the pit, and brought him forth from prison, and made him ruler over all the land. But none of these things moved him from what he had heard and believed. All the wonderful works which God had *done* were not to be compared to the one thing which He had *said*.

So Joseph rests on his memories; and his thoughts dwell on what God had spoken concerning things yet to come.

And what was it that Joseph had heard?

The answer takes us back to some words which God had spoken to Abraham some 200 years before.

In Gen. xv. 13, 14, Jehovah said unto Abram "Know of a surety that thy seed shall be a stranger in a land that is not theirs (and shall serve them; and they shall afflict them) 400 years. And also that nation whom they shall serve, will I judge; and afterward shall they come out with great substance."

These words were handed down, and were surely believed by Isaac and Jacob. They were passed on to Joseph; and, when he heard them, he believed what God had said.

So far as human sight was concerned, only some of those words had proved to be true; for his people were indeed "strangers in a strange land." But, up to the present, there had been no servitude and no affliction.

As far as sight could go, there was no sign of it. And, had Joseph walked by sight, he must surely have become an unbeliever. For, judging by "the things which are seen" (*v.* 3), the fulfilment of what he had "heard" seemed not only most unlikely, but impossible

He himself was next to the throne; and his brethren dwelt in the land of peace and plenty.

True, he had been sold for a servant; and his feet they hurt with fetters. The great Archer himself had shot at him and wounded him. His brethren had been used to put him in the pit; the Ishmaelites had sold him into bondage; Potiphar's wife had been used to cast him into prison; the chief butler had been used to keep him there:

"Until the time that His word came,
The word of Jehovah tried him."

In spite of all the designs of the enemy,

"The king sent and loosed him;
The ruler of the people let him go free;
He made him lord of his house,
And ruler of all his substance,
To bind his princes at his pleasure,
And teach his senators wisdom."

(Ps. cv. 19-22).

To sight, and judging by the outward appearance what sign was there of the possibility of any servitude and affliction?

There was none.

There was nothing but Jehovah's word,

"KNOW OF A SURETY"

Joseph knew of a surety because he "walked by faith," and believed God.

How else could he have known anything about "the departure of the children of Israel?"

More than two hundred years had passed away since God had spoken of it to Abraham, and more than one hundred years had yet to run.

Joseph knew "of a surety" that the Exodus would

take place 400 years after the birth of Isaac ("thy seed," Gen. xv. 13, Acts vii. 6), and 430 years after "the promise" (Gal. iii. 17, Ex. xii. 40).

See how he emphasises the certainty of his faith, twice over, when his life was drawing to a close. He used the beautiful Figure of Speech called *Polyptōton*, by which the same verb is repeated in a different inflections, "in visiting He will visit you." This is beautifully rendered "God will SURELY * visit you." Joseph was in no doubt whatever about it.

His words are :

" I die : and God will SURELY visit you, and bring you out of this land unto the land which He sware to Abraham, to Isaac, and to Jacob.

" And Joseph took an oath of the children of Israel, saying, 'God will SURELY visit you, and ye shall carry up my bones from hence'" (Gen. l. 24, 25).

Note how the words "ye shall" entirely depend on "God will." Apart from the fact that God had promised, Joseph's assurance would have been merely the expression of a pious opinion. He could only have said, "I think." But he said "*I know*."

In Joseph's heart were "things hoped for." The ground on which his hope was based was on what he had "heard." If he had heard from man that his people would have a mighty deliverance from Egypt, he could not have much ground for his hope. But what he had heard was what God had sworn to his fathers. He believed what he had thus "heard." He had, therefore, good "ground" for his hope: and

---

* The emphasis is variously rendered in the A.V. according to the scope of the context, *e.g* , "dying thou shalt die " (Gen. ii. 17) "thou shall SURELY die."

thus " faith " was to him " the ground of things hoped for " : for, " faith cometh by hearing, and hearing by the Word of God " (Rom. x. 17).

It was not a vague, general promise which he had heard from God, but a definite assurance based on Jehovah's oath.

On such safe ground as this he could surely take an oath of his brethren.

Note the repetition of the word " TO "; individualising the patriarchs, and specialising the promises made to each.

" To Abraham " : " to THEE "

" To Isaac " : " to THEE "

" To Jacob " : " to THEE "

Thus giving each one the blessed certainty of an individual oath that he, in his own person, should POSSESS the Land which God had sworn to give him.

As not one of these three ever did possess it, or receive the promise in his own person, it is certain that they must be raised from the dead, in order to do so; otherwise, Jehovah's oath would be broken, and His promise would fall to the ground.

This is why the Lord Jesus quoted the words of Jehovah to Moses at the bush for the express purpose of proving the doctrine of resurrection.

When the Sadducees, " which say that there is no resurrection," asked Him, concerning the woman who had married seven husbands, " In the resurrection whose wife shall she be of the seven ? " He replied " In the resurrection they neither marry, nor are given in marriage."

Having answered their question as to the particular point raised, the Lord goes on to establish the general fact, and He adds " But, as touching the resurrection of the dead, have ye not read that which was spoken UNTO YOU by God, saying,

I am the God of Abraham,
And the God of Isaac,
And the God of Jacob?

God is not the God of dead people, but of the living " (Matt. xxii. 23-32).

The obvious conclusion of the argument being that, in order to possess the land and realise the promise and oath of God, they must of necessity live again " to Him " in resurrection ; inasmuch as God is not the God of the dead.

If they were alive at the time when the Lord spoke, how would that prove the doctrine of the resurrection ?

If God is not the God of dead people, but of living persons ; and, if this was said " as touching the dead that they rise " (Mark xii. 26), Is it not clear that Abraham, Isaac, and Jacob must rise, in order that God may be their God ?

When it is said that the Old Testament saints knew nothing or little about a future life in resurrection, it is because the word " life " and " live " are not properly understood.

When it was declared in Lev. xviii. 5, concerning the commandments, " which if a man do, he shall live in (or rather, by) them," it means *live again in resurrection or eternal life.*

When it says " the just shall live by faith," it cannot mean merely go on living in this life ; for the unjust go on doing that, without faith. It cannot mean live holily or walk righteously ; for many who do this do not necessarily live long lives ; but it means "shall live again " in resurrection life. Hence the Chaldee paraphrase renders it "shall live by them to life eternal." Or, according to Solomon Jarchi, " live in the world that is to come."

Examine the many other passages where the word "live " is used in this sense (Lev. xviii. 5; Ezek. xx 11, 13, 21 ; Neh. ix. 29; Hab. ii. 4 ; Rom. i 17 ; x. 5 : Gal. iii. 12 ; Heb. x. 38. The Verb " to live " is used in this sense more often than is generally thought. Compare Isa. xxvi. 19 ; xxxviii. 16, lv. 3 ; Ezek. xviii. 19 ; xxxiii. 19; xxxvii. 3, 5, 6, 14 ; Hos. vi. 2 ; Amos. v. 4, &c,

The spiritual authorities of the Second Temple so interpreted this phrase.

Thus, in the Gospel, " eternal life " by faith (*i.e.*, on faith-principle) is set in contrast with eternal life by works.

God is not the God of dead people, but of those of whom He was the God when alive, and He will be their God when they live again in resurrection life.

When Joseph rested his faith on the oath God had made to his fathers, and " gave commandment concerning his bones " that they should be carried up out of Egypt to that land which God had promised, it was in the sure and certain hope of resurrection ; and that he would wake up in the Land which God had promised.

This promise it was which he " remembered : " this blessed hope it was of which he " made mention."

It is often the case that, when we have an alternative rendering suggested in the margin, both are true; and that both, taken together, do not exhaust the fulness of the Divine meaning.

So here, in Heb. xi. 22, Joseph by faith " made

mention" of the Exodus, or, as in the margin, "remembered" it.

What he "remembered" was Jehovah's word to his fathers; and he not only remembered it, but he "made mention" of it.

Both were facts, and both will be manifested in all who possess Joseph's faith.

We do not read that God had spoken directly to Joseph, as He had to Abel, Enoch, Noah and Abraham, but what he had "heard" was what had been spoken to others, and handed down and passed on to him. In Gen. xlviii. 21, 22, we read:

"And Israel [not Jacob] said unto Joseph, Behold, I die: but God shall be with you, and bring you again unto the land of your fathers; moreover. I have given TO THEE one portion above thy bretnren, whicn I took out of the hand of the Amorite with my sword and with my bow."

Joseph believed what he heard. Yes! He believed he would possess that "one portion" which Israel said "I have given *to thee*." He believed he would possess it and enjoy it "above" his brethren. Hence "ye shall take up my bones with you."

What simple faith! Oh! to possess "like precious faith" as to what we have "heard" and has been handed down to us, not by the teachings of Babylon, or the errors of Rome, or by the traditions of men, but by the inspiration of God in the Scriptures of truth.

We, too, who believe God, have a blessed promise of "a portion above our brethren:" of a going up to our inheritance over the hill-country of the Amorites: of being "called on high" (Phil. iii. 14): of experiencing that wondrous "change" (Phil. iii. 20-21), and that "fashioning like unto the glorious body of the Lord Jesus Christ our Saviour."

Do we "remember" this? Do we "make mention" of it? Are we reaching forth unto those things which are before? Are we pressing "toward the goal, toward the prize of our calling on high, by God, in Christ Jesus?"

Oh! that we, as many as are thus initiated (for this is the meaning of the word "perfect" in Phil. iii. 15; compare 1 Cor. ii. 6), may be of this mind! "And if ye be differently minded in any matter, God will reveal even this [as well as those other matters] unto you."

May He thus reveal more and more to us of this thrice blessed hope, and may we, in our turn, not only "remember" it, but "make mention" of it, for the comfort of our own hearts, and the blessing of many others.

Moses' Parents:

Faith Overcoming the Fear of Man

"*By faith Moses, having been born, was hid three months by his parents, because they saw that the child was goodly, and* [because] *they did not fear the king's commandment* " (Heb. xi. 23).

WE come now to the second pair in this "great cloud of witnesses" whose faith overcame what had to do with man.

The faith of all, except these two pairs, had to do with God.

In the first pair, ISAAC's faith overcame "the will of the flesh" (in himself); and JACOB's faith overcame "the will of man" (in Joseph).

In this second pair, the faith of Moses's parents overcame "the fear of man" (in Pharaoh's commandment); and Moses's faith overcame "the praise of man" (in refusing the offer of Pharaoh's daughter).

It is the former example, in this second pair, with which we have now to deal.

It is strange that most commentators miss the one point which the whole chapter is designed to enforce. On the one hand, they dwell on the beauty of the babe; and on the other hand, they dwell on the faith as being a general conviction that God having called the nation in Abraham, would not now allow the enemy to succeed. But this would make the faith of these parents like the faith of Sarah and Rahab—a general conclusion, judging from what they had heard.

The whole point of the chapter starts from the definition of faith, in the first verse, which, again, is based on Rom. x. 17, that " faith cometh by hearing "; and that our *hope* rests on believing what we have heard from God.

This at once tells us that Moses's parents must have had a direct communication from God, telling them exactly what would happen, and what they were to do.

If their action had been based on the beauty of the child, it would have been by affection, or by fancy, or by infatuation. But it is written that it was " BY FAITH."

This excludes all other and lower reasons.

Affection would not have driven away their fear; it would have increased it. The more they admired and loved the child, the more would they fear lest any evil should happen to it. But it was not so. It was " by faith "; and the more they loved, the less they feared.

They must have *heard* from God a description of the babe; so that, when they saw it, they would see also the truth of what they had heard; and would believe God, like their father Abraham. It was " by faith," and it was because of this faith that they hid the child, and had no fear as to the consequences of obeying God rather than men.

It is necessary that we should now go back to the first chapter of Exodus, and see what else the same Spirit of Truth has recorded there, so that we may the better understand what we are reading here.

After the death of Joseph, in Gen. l. 26, the first recorded fact in connection with the sons of Israel is their marvellous increase. To impress this upon us, the Figure of Speech, called *Synonymia* is used, by which words and expressions of similar meaning are heaped together for emphasis, as well as the Figure called *Polysyndeton* (or many "ands") which singles out and marks each item.

This Figure is in verse 7, which reads—

 " And the sons of Israel were fruitful,
 And increased abundantly,
 And multiplied,
 And waxed exceeding mighty ;
 And the land was filled with them."

We are left in no doubt as to the impression intended to be created in our minds by these words.

And this is stated in order to explain the conclusion the king came to, and the commandment he gave.

He was "a new king." A new king in every sense of the word. Not merely the nominal successor of the king before him ; but altogether new—even a new dynasty.

This is the force of the word so rendered here ; as may be seen by its usage in Deut. xxxii. 17 : " They sacrificed unto devils, not to God (Eloah) ; to gods (*elohim*) whom they knew not ; to NEW gods that CAME NEWLY UP, whom your fathers feared not."

This is borne out by the word rendered " AROSE UP a new king " (*v.* 8). In Daniel ii. this same word is used of the standing up of one world-power in the place of another. See verses 31, 39, 44.

It is also witnessed to in the words of the Holy Spirit by Stephen when he said : " The people grew and multiplied in Egypt till ANOTHER king arose, which knew not Joseph " (Acts vii. 17, 18).

The word rendered " another " here is ἕτερος (*heteros*),

and means, not "another" of the *same* kind * but, "another" of a *different* kind. Here, it means "a different king"; another king of a *different* dynasty.

This proves the truth of the discoveries of the Egyptologists, who say that at this time there was a new and different (Assyrian) dynasty.

This agrees with Isa. lii. 4, where Adonai Jehovah says :

> "My People went down aforetime into Egypt to sojourn there,
>
> And the Assyrian oppressed them without cause."

Commentators on this verse have *created* a difficulty which they find it hard to solve. They first assume that it refers to the captivity of Israel by and in Assyria ; and then they feel unable to explain why two events, in two lines, separated only by a comma, should be mentioned thus in immediate connection with each other, when they were separated by many centuries.

The difficulty is (we have said) *created ;* as most so-called "discrepancies" are ; the fact being that, there was no interval at all, and that the "Assyrian" who oppressed them was the "new" and "different" king, who "stood up" in the place of the previous dynasty ; and who oppressed the People of Israel then sojourning there.

This confirms also the statement of Josephus, when he speaks of "the crown being come into another family" (Ant. ii. 9).

Thus from all these sources comes the explanation why this "new" Pharaoh did "not know Joseph"; and why, so soon after his accession, he should be in

---

* Which would be ἄλλος (*allos*).

fear of enemies rising up, with whom the Israelites could take sides, and so " get up out of the land."*

The " commandment " of this king was given in consequence of his fear, aroused by the marvellous increase recorded in verse 7. When he saw it, his fear was that " when there falleth out any war, they join also unto our enemies, and fight against us, and so get them up out of the land " (Ex. i. 10).

So he said to his people: " Come on, let us deal wisely with them."

This wisdom was shown: First, in their oppression, and in their affliction with heavy burdens under cruel task-masters; second, in " the king's commandment " to the midwives to kill every male child at the birth, and to let the female children live (v. 16).

This was Pharaoh's " wisdom "; and by this wisdom he hoped to keep down the number of the children of Israel, and put an end to their phenomenal increase.

But we read : " The more they afflicted them, the more they multiplied and grew " (v. 12).

But there was a power behind the throne. There was " the Jews' enemy " using Pharaoh here, as he afterwards used Athaliah, to " destroy all the seed royal of the house of Judah " (2 Chron. xxii. 10); and Haman, to destroy the whole nation (Est. ii. 6, 8); and Herod, to compass the death of " the seed of the woman," who had, according to Jehovah's word, at length come into the world (Matt. ii.).

---

* We had thought of giving the names and even the portraits of these Pharaohs ; but there are still differences between the Egypto-logists, and they are not yet agreed as to the dynasties. So, like true scientists, we prefer to wait until the whole of the data are available. Conclusions drawn from partial information must necessarily be incomplete, if not incorrect ; but this is exactly what is done in most branches of science. Hence their constant changes and modifications.

Pharaoh had *his* purpose to serve in the preservation of himself and his people ; but Satan had *his* purpose to serve in preventing " the seed of the woman " from coming into the world, and thus averting his own doom, and causing Jehovah's word to fall to the ground.

None but Jehovah could know of this fell design of Satan. Therefore He had to interfere, directly, Himself, here, as in all the other attempts of Satan to carry out his purpose.

Pharaoh was only his tool ; and thought only of his own danger ; but behind him, and instigating him, was " the Jews' enemy."

Pharaoh's wisdom has got to be thwarted ; and it standeth written (probably before those very days) in Job v. 13 :

> " He taketh the wise in their own craftiness ;
> And the counsel of the froward is carried headlong."

Pharaoh might say : " Come on, let us deal wisely " ; but " there are many devices in a man's heart ; nevertheless, the counsel of the LORD, that shall stand " (Prov. xix. 21).

The highest " wisdom of Egypt " might be relied upon by man ; but " there is no wisdom, nor understanding, nor counsel against Jehovah " (Prov. xxi. 30).

> " Jehovah bringeth the counsel of the heathen to nought :
> He maketh the devices of the people of none effect.
> The counsel of Jehovah standeth for ever,
> The thoughts of His heart to all generations "
>
> (Ps. xxxiii. 10, 11).

It was so here. Pharaoh's wisdom for preventing the people of Israel getting up out of Egypt was brought to nought ; and his counsel made of none effect ; for, it ended in his having to give board and lodging and education to the very man who accomplished the very thing thing that Pharaoh was trying to prevent. "This same Moses" it was, who " led forth Jehovah's people, whom He had redeemed " (Ex. xv. 13).

> " He sent Moses His servant, and Aaron whom He
>   had chosen ;
>   They shewed His signs among them and wonders
>   in the land of Ham. . . .
>   Egypt was glad when they departed ;
>   For the fear of them fell upon them "
>   (Ps. cv. 26, 38).

Thus was Pharaoh's wisdom turned to foolishness, and Satan's devices defeated.

But how was this wonderful result brought about ? By what means were the counsels of the enemy thus turned upside down ?

It is all told in a few words. A few sentences suffice to tell the wondrous story.

It was here with the king of Egypt just as it was in Persia in a later day, when Haman's plot was ripening for the destruction of the whole nation, and we read : " On that night could not the king sleep " (Est. vi. 1). On that night there was another mighty king—the king over the Medes and Persians, whose law " altereth not " (Est. 1. 19 ; Dan. vi. 8), and which " no man may reverse " (Est. viii. 8).

Ah ! Quite true ; "*Man*" might not be able to " reverse " it. But God could bring it to naught. And by very simple means too. All that we need to be told is : " On that night could not the king sleep." That is all. We know the rest ; or we can find it recorded in the Scriptures of truth, written in the book of Esther " for our learning."

It was just as simple here in the case of the king of Egypt.

The words of ch. ii. 1 are introduced here in connection with the concluding verse of the first chapter ; not that the marriage then took place (for Miriam and Aaron were already born and were growing up) ; but, to introduce the birth of Moses, which took place *after* "the king's commandment" had gone forth.

The mention of the fact in this connection shows that the commandment made no difference in their ordinary family life. If there was no "fear" on the one hand, there was no presumption on the other. All went on in their home just as before. Indeed, the conception and birth of Moses at this juncture is mentioned to magnify the " faith " of Moses's parents.

It looks as though it were almost *defiance*; but it was not : it was "faith." It looks like recklessness, but it was "the obedience of faith," for they must have *heard* from God what He was about to do.

" By faith . . . . they feared not the king's commandment."

The midwives mentioned in Ex. i. 15, were actuated by a similar faith, for (it says) they " feared God " and not man. The Targum of Jonathan and the Targum of Jerusalem (two ancient Jewish Commentaries) say that Shiphira was Jochebed, and Puah was Miriam. But this is only imagination. What we are *sure of* is that they were Hebrew women, and that they " feared God."

It looked as though their efforts to disregard the king's commandment would be futile, for no secret was made of the object behind the command. The avowed purpose was the extinction of the sons of Israel. But in spite of this, and in due time, the woman conceived, and bare a son; and when she saw he was a goodly child, she must have remembered what she had " heard " from God; and, just as each step following Esther vi. 1 was ordered by God, so here each step that the mother took must have been by the same Divine ordering. The preservation of the child; the hiding it; and, when secrecy was no longer possible, the making of the ark of bulrushes; and the covering it with pitch (as Noah had pitched his ark by the same faith); the laying it in the waters, just in the place where He, Who was ordering all, knew Pharaoh's daughter would be walking,* and would be doing on that eventful day. All this corresponds with king Ahasuerus's sleepless night. The reading of the record; the asking for Mordecai; the appearance of Haman at that very moment; all, all was Divinely ordered.

And here, all was " by faith " in the word of Him Who was ordering all. It was not by foresight, but " by faith." It was not by affection, but " by faith." It was not " by fear "; of this we are assured by the word of God.

The king's commandment to his people was: " Every son that is born ye shall cast into the river " (v. 22). Jochebed committed her son to the waters of the very same river : but he was safe amid those waters of death, by a Divinely devised and ordered protection : and the same Divine ordering ruled and over-ruled all to the

---

* Compare ch. viii. 20.

working out of His own counsels. The standing of his sister Miriam was also ordered : as were all the steps which accomplished Jehovah's purpose.

Pharaoh's daughter came down to the river by the same Divine ordering which brought Haman to the gate of the Persian king ; and it was as small a circumstance as that which would not let the king sleep that caused compassion to fill the heart of Pharaoh's daughter.

In this case it was only a baby's tear. So small, and so weak in itself, but mighty enough to upset the craft of Satan, the wisdom of Egypt, and the commandment of the king.

So small, and yet large enough to waken "compassion" in the woman's heart. For, it is written : "When she had opened it, she saw the child; and behold, *the babe wept,** and she had compassion on him.*"

In that tear lay the deliverance of Israel, and the defeat of Satan.

God ever uses the small things of this world to accomplish his own purposes; yea, the "base things . . . and things that are despised, hath God chosen . . . that no flesh should glory in His presence" (1 Cor. i. 28, 29).

For this same reason God puts His "treasure in earthen vessels, that the excellency of the power may be of God, and not of us" (2 Cor. iv. 7).

It is well to note, in our reading of Scripture, the

---

* Man, with his usual indifference to accuracy (where the Bible is concerned), always, in his pictures, represents this babe as happy and smiling instead of crying and sobbing ! Just as he always represents *angels* as women ; and puts the *Saviour's* heart on the wrong side !

small things that God has ever thus used, that there may be room for faith in Him, and in His word. Let us note them, in the deliverances He brought to His people, as shown in the deliverers whom He raised up. We shall find a "left-handed" man (Judges iii. 21); "an ox-goad" (Judges iii. 31); "a piece of a millstone" (Judges ix. 53); "a woman" (Judges iv. 4); a tent-peg (Judges iv. 21); "pitchers and trumpets" (Judges vi. 20); "the jawbone of an ass" (Judges xv. 16).

Let us note them in the deliverances of His people from the errors and tortures of Rome in later days; and we see Luther, a miner's son; Calvin, a cooper's son in Picardy; Zwingle, a shepherd's son in the Alps; Melancthon, an armourer's son; John Knox, the son of a plain burgess of a Scottish provincial town.

There is a question somewhere in the Talmud :— "Why did God create man last?" and the answer given is : "Because if He had not done so, man would have claimed to have had some share in the work."

However that might have been in the old creation, we know that *it is true of man* that he does make that claim in the new creation ! His claim is that "God must do His part, and that *man must do his.*" These are the oft-repeated words. Man does make this claim in this highest and most Divine of all His works.

No, wonder, then, that God puts man down; and uses the weakest things for the accomplishment of His greatest works.

It was this baby's tear which was over-ruled to bring about the redemption of Israel; yea, the redemption of His Church and People, by preserving the line by which the seed of the woman at length, and in due time, was to be born into the world, to do the Father's will in the accomplishment of our salvation.

And all this is included in the words "By faith, Moses, when he was born, was hid three months by his parents . . . . not fearing the king's commandment."

May it be ours to have a "like precious faith," which overcomes all fear of man. We should then have no fear of what the world or our "Brethren" may do. We should not be affected by what they might think, or what they might say. We should have no fear of the enemy; or be moved by what he might threaten or do; we should have no fear of a church, or an assembly; and be without care for its persecutions and excommunications.

"By faith" in what God has revealed, and which others may refuse to receive, we shall no longer have any regard or fear as to all "the commandments and doctrines of men" to which we have been so long in cruel bondage and subjection.

Moses: Faith Overcoming the Praise of Man

1. He Refused. . .He Chose. . .He Esteemed

" *By faith Moses, when he had grown up, REFUSED to be called the son of Pharaoh's daughter, CHOOSING rather to suffer affliction with the People of God, than to have a temporary enjoyment of sin; ESTEEMING the reproach for Christ greater riches than the treasures of Egypt : for he looked away from* [them] *unto the recompense of reward* " (Heb. xi. 24-26).

In connection with Moses we have three acts of faith mentioned.

1. By faith he refused . . . he chose . . . and he esteemed (*vv.* 24-26).

2. By faith he forsook Egypt (*v.* 27).

3. By faith he kept the Passover (*v.* 28).

It is with the first of these that we now have to do. And three things are predicated of his first act of faith.

1. He *refused* to be called the son of Pharaoh's daughter.

2. Much followed by consequence from this first act. It brought upon him the suffering of affliction or hardship with God's People, and his own people, Israel ; and he deliberately *chose* this.

3. What he chose he *esteemed* also. He was not merely choosing the lesser of two evils; but, he esteemed what it brought upon him. It brought reproach for

Christ's sake, reproach, *i.e.*, obloquy and the derisive ill-will of others, but he *esteemed* this above all the treasures of Egypt.

1. But we must come back to the first step which he took: "He refused to be called the son of Pharaoh's daughter." This, we are distinctly told, was "by faith."

Two things are thus plainly implied :

(1) Moses must have had the *offer*, and the opportunity of thus becoming a member of Egypt's Royal Family; and

(2) He must have *heard* from God that he was not to accept this high privilege. Otherwise it could not have been "by faith." It would have been by folly, or a fanatical love of his people, thus to refuse the opportunity which might be so well used in mitigating their oppression ; and lightening their heavy burdens. But we are distinctly told that it was "by faith."

Inasmuch as "faith cometh by hearing," Moses must have *heard*. And, inasmuch as this "hearing cometh by the Word of God," God must have spoken or communicated His will to Moses ; for Moses heard, Moses believed, Moses obeyed.

God had other counsels and purposes with regard to Moses. Moses must have been told that "God, by his hand, would deliver" Israel from Egypt's bondage.

When he delivered one of his brethren who was smitten, he "supposed they would have understood" this (Acts vii. 25). This word used for "supposed"*

---

* νομιζω *(nomizō)* means *to reckon, and to reckon according to law* (Luke iii. 23); and therefore he had every right to conclude they would have understood.

implies that Moses must have already made God's purpose perfectly clear to his brethren, so that it was well known to them; and he had good grounds for this reckoning.

God had told Moses, and Moses had told them. But he believed God; and they did not.

All this, however, was not till Moses was grown up. The expression in Ex. ii. 11 does denote an increase in stature and years, but the verb גָּדַל *(gadal)* is frequently used to denote growth in dignity and importance.* The expression in Heb. xi. 24, μέγας γενόμενος *(megas genomenos)* means, literally, *having become great*, and is used because it contains both meanings, and includes a Divine comment, both on Ex. ii. 11 and Acts vii. 23.

Pharaoh's daughter had "taken him up, and nourished him for her own son" (Acts vii. 21); and then there must have come a moment when Moses had grown up, that he had to decide whether he would or would not become the heir-apparent (by formal adoption) to the crown of Egypt.

We know, by Divine revelation, that it was "by faith" that he refused that high dignity.

What Moses had heard from God had fallen on prepared ground. His mother was his nurse; and she was the daughter of Levi,† and was therefore in the

---

* Compare Gen. xxvi. 13. 2 Sam. vii. 22. Ps. civ. 1. Ecc. ii. 9. Jer. v. 27. Est. iii. 1; v. 11; x. 2.

† As may be seen from this Genealogy:

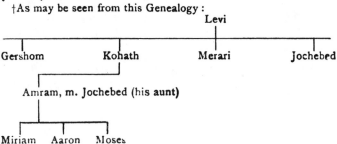

direct line to hear and learn the history of the Divine dealings.

Moses, indeed, was "learned in all the wisdom of Egypt," but he must have been learned also in the wisdom of God and His People, Israel. Indeed, it was possible for Moses to have heard the very history of Abraham at third hand; yea, and even the story of the Flood. For, Adam was for 243 years contemporary with Methuselah, who conversed with Shem for 100 years.

Shem was for fifty years contemporary with Jacob, and Jacob might therefore have conversed with Jochebed, the mother of Moses. The oppression of Israel was physical and would not have pressed all knowledge out of the minds and hearts of the people.

Moses had, without doubt, heard much from his own kindred as to the past, and he was learned in the wisdom of Egypt; but, he had *heard* direct communications as to the future from God Himself. The " things to come " had been revealed to him. The "things of Christ" had been made known "in part." He knew God. He knew that Jehovah had a People, and that they were in sore bondage in Egypt. He knew that they were to be delivered. How, then, could he accept the position of heir to Egypt's throne? Believing what he had heard from God, how could he do other than "refuse to be called the son of Pharaoh's daughter," and, eventually, Egypt's King? But this was only the first step. Moses not only *refused* this honour: he chose the opposite.

2. "He chose rather to endure hardship with the People of God than to have a temporary enjoyment of sin."

This is an extraordinary exhibition of faith.

What he had *heard* from God must have been so good, so great, so wonderful, so glorious, that, believing it to be true, he deliberately chose the hard lot of that people to Egypt's crown.

It is the very word used of God's own electing choice. He did not merely accept it as an inevitable alternative, but he deliberately preferred it.

What must he not have heard to bring about so wondrous a result as to make him prefer "affliction" to "pleasures?" Ah, he had heard of their issue. He had heard of the "eternal weight of glory." Hence, he looked not at the "things that are seen," for "he endured as seeing the Invisible" (*v.* 27). The pleasures themselves were of brief duration—only "for a season"; but, in view of the eternity of the glory, the "affliction" seemed briefer still, "light" and but "for a moment."

Oh, to have "like precious faith"! How it would enable us to endure! There would be no more repinings; no more murmurings. We should look at "affliction," and all that is connected with it, from such a totally different standpoint that it would enable us to *choose* it in preference to the other. But only "WHILE we look not at the things that are seen, but at the things that are not seen" (2 Cor. iv. 18). And only "WHILE" we do that. Not otherwise.

When we are on the top of a high tower, and look down on the scene below, horses and men seem no larger than insects; but when we get down again among them, then they stand out in all their natural size; and we are under the shade of the tower itself.

It is even so in the spiritual sphere. While we look at "affliction" it seems heavy indeed and never ending; but "while" we look at it from the height of His glory of which we have *heard*, and dwell on its eternal weight, then there is not only no difficulty, but the difficulty is the other way; for we *choose* it with a preference which cannot be disturbed.

But there was not only something which Moses *chose*; there was something that Moses *esteemed*.

3. He esteemed "the reproach of Christ" greater riches than the treasures of Egypt, for he looked away from these unto the "recompense of the reward."

We must take the Genitive, "of Christ," as the Genitive of *relation*. It is not the Genitive of possession. It is not the reproach which Christ endured; but it is our reproach which we endure for Christ's sake, viz., "reproach for Christ."*

Christ, in the days of His flesh, suffered reproach; and, all who are His suffer that same reproach. The Apostles knew what it was to endure reproach. After they were imprisoned and beaten, "they departed from the council, rejoicing that they were counted worthy to suffer shame for His name" (Acts v. 41). Here the verb is "to suffer dishonour." In Heb. xi. 26, it is "reproach," *i.e.*, obloquy, derisive ill-will.

And note: it does not say that Moses *put up with* this reproach, or *endured* it, because he could not get away from it; but he *elected* to have this reproach, in preference to the treasures of Egypt, esteeming this reproach as a still "greater treasure," or, like the Apostles, he "counted it all joy"; like Paul, he

---

* Just as in Rom. viii. 36, the Greek, "sheep of slaughter," is correctly rendered "sheep for the slaughter" in A.V. and R.V.

could say, " I take pleasure in my infirmities, in
reproaches, in necessities, in distresses, for Christ's
sake " (2 Cor. xii. 10).

Well might he exhort these suffering Hebrew
believers by the example of Moses, and tell them to
" call to remembrance the former days . . . in which
(he says) ye endured a great fight of afflictions . . .
and were made a gazing-stock both by reproaches
and afflictions. . . . For ye had compassion of me in
my bonds, and took joyfully the spoiling of your
goods." And why? Because they knew that they
" had in heaven a better and an enduring substance "
(Heb. x. 32-34).

And what was it that produced this wondrous
choice? Faith. It was " by faith." It is this
exhortation in chap. x. that leads up to and forms the
basis of these very examples of faith, in chap. xi.

Oh! what exquisite examples they were! And note
how this faith of Moses in overcoming " the praise of
man " speaks to our own hearts.

"Esteeming reproach for Christ." What do we
feel about the reproach which we have for His sake?
Yes, His sake; for in the Greek the word " Christ"
has the definite article. It is "*the* Christ," the Christ
of God. Not the Christ of the New Theology. There
is no reproach to be suffered for that Christ. No!
that brings "the praise of man ": an infidel can accept,
and be thankful for such a Christ as that.

But, it is the Christ of God that man will not have:
the Christ That suffered for sin and was raised from
the dead, and is now exalted, and is coming again with
His recompense. There is reproach for His sake if

we believe what we have heard from God about Him; and especially when that faith makes us independent of "the fear of man" and "the praise of man."

And what do *we* do under this reproach? This is the thing which tests our faith more than any other test that can be used. For the most part, one finds mourning, groaning, murmuring, depression, distress. And why? Because of the absence of Moses' faith. Because we are looking at "the things which are seen." Because we see not "the Invisible." Because we are down below, in the dark shade of the high tower, instead of looking down from its height.

If we *believe* what we have *heard* from God about His Christ, and this brings reproach upon us, it ought to make us the happiest of beings. It ought to act like water to a parched plant. It ought to make our joy to grow exceedingly.

Look at Moses. There we see "first the blade, then the ear, after that the full corn in the ear" (Mark iv. 28).

First there was "the blade," when Moses *refused* to be called the son of Pharaoh's daughter.

"Then the ear," when he *chose* the affliction of God's people to the pleasures of sin.

After that there was "the full corn in the ear," when he *esteemed* reproach for Christ as being greater riches than the treasures of Egypt.

Oh, what a wondrous power there is in those two small words, "BY FAITH," when it comes from, and is based on, what we have heard from God.

This is the faith that overcometh the world and gives us victory over man, and all his "praise" (1 John v. 4).

This is the reason given: FOR "he looked away [from the treasures and from the reproach] unto the recompence."

This recompence is twofold. It has respect to the retribution of the ungodly, and to the rewards of the righteous.

The whole life of Moses was based on and governed by faith in what God had declared concerning both. Both would surely come, and he preferred, yea, he esteemed, present and temporary reproach to all the treasures of Egypt, and hence looked unto the promised and future treasure, which will be eternal.

Gentile self-esteem limits all true understanding of Resurrection and eternal life to the Church, and to the so-called "Christian dispensation." This would be amusing were it not for the ignorance from which it springs, and the evil consequences to which it leads. It is assumed that it matters *what* we believe in this Dispensation which is so far in advance of what those believed in past dispensations.

But it is not *what* we believe, but WHOM we believe.

"Abraham believed God" (Gen. xv. 6. Rom. iv. 3); Paul said, "I know Whom I have believed" (2 Tim. i. 12).

They each believed what they had heard, and this was saving faith to them, just as it is to us to-day.

There is no new way of salvation to eternal life. It has *always* been "by faith." Right back in Deut. viii. 3 we find the Scripture quoted by the Lord in Matt. iv. 4, "By every word that proceedeth out of the mouth of the LORD, doth man live"; *i.e.*, live again in resurrection and eternal life.

The actual words which Jehovah had spoken for the hearing of faith were immaterial compared with the blessed fact of believing them, *whatever they were*.

We can gather what they believed from what is written of them :

" Abraham rejoiced to see My day.

And he saw it

And was glad " (John viii. 56).

The same Lord Jesus declares that Moses and the prophets wrote "concerning Me" (Luke xxiv. 44), and that Moses "wrote of Me."

To Abraham, Christ said : " I am thy exceeding great reward" (Gen. xv. 1). Moses was inspired to write those words. Was not this the same Christ, *his* "exceeding great reward " ? And, What more could He say to us ? True, more is revealed, greater and more blessed truths are recorded for our faith ; but it is " like precious faith "; it is the same act of faith which " sets to its seal that God is true," and that His words are truth.

In Psalm xc. 12, Moses prays : "so teach us to number our days that we may apply our hearts unto wisdom."

Yes ! all the adults of that generation *knew* they were to die within the forty years ; well might they pray to "number their days" aright; for the days were numbered for them. They had heard that from God ; and those who believed what He said did apply their hearts unto wisdom. By the same faith, in the same "living God," we know that we are *not to number* our days. Indeed, we cannot do so, for none of us know whether we shall have another day to number ; we are waiting and looking for HIM, and not numbering our days. We know that " we shall not all sleep " (1 Cor xv. 51). We know that there will be those that are "alive and remain" (1 Thess. iv. 17). " We look for the Saviour, the Lord Jesus Christ, Who shall change our body of humiliation, that it may be fashioned like unto His glorious body " (Phil. iii. 20, 21).

Do we believe God ? This is the one great question for us.

Do we believe what God has revealed for our faith ?

Moses believed what he had heard from God. Do we ?

Abraham abandoned the tradition which he had received from his fathers. Have we ?

They were idolators ; they believed in " familiar spirits," and that there was " no death," and hence, no resurrection." But Abraham gave up all these tradi- tions, and believed God.

Moses gave up all the traditions embodied in the " wisdom of Egypt,"* and which he knew from Egypt's "book of the dead," because he had believed God's revelation.

Even so are we exhorted with the believers among this dispersion, and reminded that we have been re- deemed . . . " from all that we have received by tradition from our fathers."

Let us receive all, from God Himself, through His Word. His Word is truth ; and if we believe what we hear from that, it will enable us to *refuse* the praise of man, to *choose* the afflictions of God's people, and to *esteem* reproach for Christ greater riches than the treasures and wisdom which the world can offer us.

---

* Israel, alas ! did not. The pertinacious devotion of the Israelites to necromancy, etc., which they had learnt in Egypt first, and afterward from the nations of Canaan, shows what a hold on them tradition had obtained. See Deut. xviii. 11, and many other passages throughout the Old Testament Modern spiritism is in direct descent from the ' wisdom of Egypt,' and the corruptions of Babylon ; and the traditions of the so-called Christian " Religion," are all permeated with its teachings.

2. "He Forsook Egypt"

" By faith he forsook Egypt, not fearing the wrath of the king " (verse 27).

THE forsaking of Egypt, alluded to here, has been generally understood as referring to Exodus ii. 15, when " Moses fled from the face of Pharaoh." But, notwithstanding the many commentators ancient* and modern who have so considered it, we venture to say that this is not the case; and this, from the reason given. In Heb. xi. he forsook, *"not fearing* the wrath of the king," whereas in Ex. ii. 14, 15 it is distinctly stated that *" Moses feared* . . . and fled from the face of Pharaoh."

Moses left Egypt on two occasions; and it is to the latter of these (Ex. xiij., xiv.) that Hebrews xi. 27 refers, when it states that Moses feared not the wrath of Pharaoh; and could even exhort Israel " Fear ye not, stand still, and see the salvation of Jehovah."

In Ex. xiii. Moses' act was " by faith." In Ex. ii. 14 it was "by fear"; and there was room for his fear. For " it came to pass in those days (when he had become great) that he went out unto his brethren, and looked on their burdens : and he spied an Egyptian smiting an Hebrew, one of his brethren." The word rendered " smiting " is נָכָה (*nākah*), and, when in the *Hiphil* form (as here), it is used, not in the sense of merely giving a blow, but of smiting so as to

---

* Among whom are Chrysostom, Theodoret, Theophylact, and Œcumenius.

246

inflict mortal injury. It is used of *killing* and *extirpating* in war; and, even of inanimate things, it is used of destroying them (Ex. ix. 31, 32).

In the face of this, critics (as the late Dean Stanley) can write that "seeing an Israelite suffering the bastinado from an Egyptian, and thinking that they were alone, he slew the Egyptian."*

These are Dean Stanley's words; not the words God has given us in the Scriptures of Truth. There is nothing about the "bastinado" in the Hebrew. It is evolved from human brains.

And further: Why should the very worst construction be put on the words in verse 12 : "He looked this way and that way, and when he saw that there was no man"?

Why should we assume that he was looking to see if there would be any eye-witnesses of a pre-meditated act?

Why should we not put a good motive on his act, seeing that we have the very same expression used in a good sense in Isa. lix. 16, "and he saw that there was no man"? Here it is used of looking for some one to help as in Isa. lxiii. 5. "I looked, and there was none to help . . . therefore my own arm brought salvation." Hence, Isa. lix. 16, goes on to say, he "wondered that there was no intercessor, therefore His arm brought salvation."

Why may we not conclude that the words are used in the same sense in Ex. ii. 12?

Moses evidently looked this way and that way, not that he might commit a crime without being detected; but to see whether any "*help*" was coming from any other quarter. The figure of speech used to empha-

---

* Smith's *Dictionary of the Bible*. Article, "Moses."

sise this very point, is *Epizeuxis ; i.e.*, the repetition of a word to show the earnestness and eagerness of his looking,* and that he did not act *until he had looked everywhere for help, but in vain*. So that he was driven to decide that his own arm must bring deliverance to one of his own brethren.

We make this digression to expose the *animus* which moves the minds of the self-constituted critics of God's Word ; and to show how ready they are to put the most atrocious construction on an action that was humane in itself, dictated by *the very highest motives*, and necessitated by the exigency of the circumstances : and this, not until every resource was exhausted in his looking for help to come from some other source.

This, however, in no way removed the ground for Moses' "fear" and subsequent alarm which he would naturally feel when the excitement of the occasion was over.

That fear was why he fled. But, when he "forsook Egypt" (Heb. xi. 27), there was no such fear. There was no *fleeing* then. By fear he fled ; "by faith he forsook." The word in Hebrews means simply that he left Egypt behind. He "*forsook*" it. He relinquished all its honours, all its treasures. And this was "by faith." This was because he "had respect unto the recompence of the reward." Moses had heard of this reward from God Himself, and he believed it. He saw the face of Pharaoh "no more," but he saw "the face of God." All that he forsook was more than made up to him.

---

* The Heb. is *kō, kō*, this and this, *i.e.*, this way and that way, implying that *he looked every way*. Just as in Isa. the Heb. " e, peace " is beautifully rendered " perfect peace " (Isa. xxvi. 3 and margin).

Moses is remembered to day. But Pharaoh, king of Egypt, is but a noise—a noise which passes away and is lost.

We should never have heard about Pharaoh but for Moses! No one would have taken the slightest interest in him, or in his mummy, or in the " noise " he made. Yet, to day, many of the men who are making so much of Egypt and the Pharaohs are the very men who are be-littling and discrediting Moses. They too will have the recompence of their reward.

" By faith Moses forsook, or relinquished, Egypt." This is the central point of our subject. And our thoughts are turned, as we have said, not to Ex. ii., but to Ex. xiii., xiv.

In the former we have Moses' "·fear" and " flight."

In the later Moses' " faith " and " forsaking."

There was no fear where there was faith. Indeed, his faith in what he had *heard* from God enabled him to give the blessed exhortation to the people " Fear ye not, stand still and see the salvation of Jehovah." (Ex. xiv. 13).

Moses had heard from Jehovah of His salvation. He believed what he had heard; and, in the strength of this faith, he could say " fear ye not."

" By faith Moses endured as seeing Him Who is invisible."

This is the prerogative of faith. It is the opposite of sight ; and yet it sees things that are invisible to human sight, and to the natural eye.

"Stand still and SEE " was his memorable language of faith. Jehovah's salvation can be seen, and it can be enjoyed.

The fact that it is His shows that it is perfect and

complete, because it is His own, in which man can have no part, except to enjoy it.

It is "Jehovah's salvation." Not partly His, and partly man's. But wrought out and revealed by God, to be believed and enjoyed by those who are the subjects of it.

If man had any share in it, it could not be called "Jehovah's salvation."

The people were "sore afraid" (Ex. xiv. 10). Why? Because they believed not. But, by faith, Moses feared not "the wrath of the king."

He endured, as though he saw Him Who is invisible. He remained steadfast (as the word means). With inflexible firmness he insisted on Jehovah's demand "Let My people go." He held out, in spite of Pharaoh's continued prevarications and changes of mind.

When Pharaoh urged that they should worship God "in the land" (Ex. viii. 25), Moses declared "it is not meet so to do:" that it must be in the wilderness (viii. 27).

When Pharaoh agreed to the wilderness, but urged that it might not be "very far away" (viii. 28), Moses "endured," insisting that it must be "three days' journey" (viii. 27).

When Pharaoh agreed, but urged that only the "men" should go (x. 11), Moses "endured," and insisted "we will go, with our young and with our old" (x. 9).

When Pharaoh agreed, but urged that the flocks and the herds should be stayed (Ex. x. 24). Moses "endured" and affirmed "our cattle also shall go with us" (x. 26).

We must put ourselves on resurrection ground, and insist on all that God included in Israel's "three days' journey."

When we are urged to leave our little ones in Egypt, with a secular education, may we endure, and insist on bringing them up "in the nurture and admonition of the Lord" (Eph. vi. 4).

When we are urged to leave a shred of property or possessions behind, in Egypt, may we endure and say, "we know not with what we must serve Jehovah until we come thither." We can never get to know, or learn this, while in Egypt. We must be clean out of Egypt and all its snares, "If any man willeth to do His will, he shall know of the doctrine" (John vii. 17).

We can know neither God's claims, nor our own privileges "till we come thither." We must know all that redemption has done for us. Then, and only when we believe what we *hear* from Him, can we endure as though we could see Him Who is invisible to the natural eye.

Moses had *heard* what God had said to him. He believed what he had heard. Hence he "endured" as if he could really see Him.

Precious faith!

May it be ours when we have to do with our Pharaoh. Nothing but unfeigned faith in what we have *heard from God* will enable us to endure.

When we are urged to worship God in Egypt, let us endure, and say that it is impossible for us to combine spiritual light with Egypt's darkness; and worship in spirit among Egypt's "fleshpots."

When we are urged to go "not very far away," may we endure and maintain that we must put a clear space between ourselves and Egypt's boundaries. There must be no border-land temptations.

The *endurance* of Moses was called for and necessitated by the devices of the enemy which would prevent complete severance from Egypt, and thwart the demand of Jehovah—" Let My People go."

Nothing would do but complete separation from Egypt and all its maxims, and all its worship, and all its ways.

Our separation from the world to-day needs the *same endurance*, for we have the same enemy, and the same snares. "We are not ignorant of his devices" (2 Cor. ii. 11).

Nothing but the Red Sea would do to complete the separation of Israel, and nothing but what answers to that will do for us to-day. Nothing but the knowledge that we have "died with Christ" and "risen with Christ" will enable us to endure as Moses did; and "not fear" the wrath of those who hinder that separation.

"If ye died with Christ from the rudiments (*i.e.*, the religious teachings) of the world, why, as though living in the world, are ye subject to ordinances?" (Col. ii. 20).

"If ye then be risen with Christ, seek those things which are above, where Christ sitteth on the right hand of God" (Col. iii. 1).

Here is the secret of true separation. This takes us "out." This takes us "very far away," where the enemy cannot reach us.

It takes us "into the wilderness," but it takes us to "the Mount of God," to the tent of His assembly, to the guidance of His Pillar of Cloud and Fire, to a worship and a Tabernacle "not made with hands" (Heb ix. 11), where "carnal ordinances" (Heb. ix. 10) find no place ; where all is of the Spirit, and where " all things are of God."

Blessed are our ears, which have heard these "deep things of God"; and happier still if we believe what we have heard, for so only shall we endure "as seeing Him Who is invisible."

3. He Kept the Passover

" By faith he kept the Passover, and the sprinkling of blood,
lest he that destroyed the first-born should not touch
them " (verse 28).

WE have before remarked that all the verbs in
this chapter are in the Aorist, or simple past Tense,
except three, which are in the Perfect Tense.
We have considered two of these.* The verse before us
is the third. So that it reads : " he (Moses) hath
instituted the Passover." Moses did not do this as he
did the other acts of his faith. They were all *personal* to
himself ; they are past and over ; and there is nothing left
of them but their record, their example, and their
lessons.

But, here is something that affected not merely
Moses, but the People of Israel ; and not merely that had
regard to that particular time, but to all time ; yea to
eternity.

" He hath instituted the Passover," because, like the
sacrifice of Isaac (*v.* 17), the reality (of which it was
the type), continues for ever. Even though the annual
observance of the Feast was never properly carried
out ; and has for centuries been impossible, yet, the
institution of it is an abiding fact.

It was done not only for " that night," but it has been
ever since telling of " Christ our Passover " ; and of that
Lamb of God, fore-ordained before the foundation of
the world, but manifest in these last times for us
(1 Pet. i. 18-20).

---

* Verses 5 and 17.

Even to this day, it has been telling, and is telling, of the same blessed fact; and teaching its abiding lesson to all who are included in that word "our."

The institution of the Passover was an act of faith, similar to that of Noah's preparation of the ark (*v. 7*).

To realise what this faith must have been, we have to go back to "that night," and note the special circumstances, which can alone explain the meaning of the words: "by faith."

God's judgments had been poured out on Egypt and its king, and its people. A crisis had arrived: for, after nine plagues had been sent, Pharaoh and the Egyptians still remained obdurate. Indeed, Moses had been threatened with death if he ever came into Pharaoh's presence again. (Ex. x. 28, 29).

On the other hand, the Hebrews were in more evil case than ever; and Moses, who was to have delivered them, had not made good his promises.

It was at such a moment that Moses *heard* from God what he was to do. To sense and to sight it must have seemed most inadequate, and quite unlikely to accomplish the desired result.

Why should this last plague be expected to accomplish what the nine had failed to do, with all their cumulative terrors?

Why should the mere sprinkling of the blood have such a remarkable effect?

And if they were indeed to leave Egypt "that same night" why should the People be burdened with all those minute ceremonial observances at the very moment when they ought to be making preparation for their departure.

Nothing but "faith" could be of any avail here.

Everything was opposed to human understanding, and human reasoning.

With all the consciousness of ill-success upon him, nothing but unfeigned faith in the living God, and what he had heard from Him, could have enabled Moses to go to the people and rehearse all the intricacies of the Paschal observances, and tell them to exercise the greatest care in the selection of a lamb on the tenth day of the month, to be slain on the fourteenth day, and eaten with (to them) an unmeaning ceremonial.

It called for no ordinary confidence in what Moses had *heard* from God to enable him to go to his brethren who, in their deep distress, must have been ill-disposed to listen ; for, hitherto, his efforts had only increased the hatred of their oppressors, and their own miseries as bondmen.

It would, to human sight, be a difficult if not impossible task to persuade the people, and convince them of the absolute necessity of complying with all the minute details of the observance of the Paschal ordinance.

But this is just where " faith " came in. This was just the field on which it could obtain its greatest victory. Hence we read that " By faith " every difficulty was overcome ; the Feast was observed, and the Exodus accomplished.

All was based on " the hearing of faith." The words of Jehovah produced the faith ; and were at once the cause and effect of all the blessing.

We need not go into all the details of Exodus xii. The two things important for us are selected and presented by the Holy Spirit in this one verse (Heb. xi. 28)—

The Sprinkling of the Blood,
and its Eternal Efficacy.

For, the verb must be repeated in the second clause:
"he (Moses) hath instituted the Passover and [he hath
instituted] the sprinkling of the blood."

That type, the sprinkled blood, told of the eternal
merits of the Antitype—"manifested in these last
times for us."

All is summed up in two sentences,

" When I see the Blood
I will Pass over you " (Ex. xii. 13).

Much has been said in explanation of the term
"Pass-over." But no explanation is needed. Jehovah
Himself gave it that name in order to explain it to
us. It is written for our faith, not for our reasoning.

The sprinkling of the blood may have seemed, to
some, " foolishness "; and may have been to others, a
"stumbling-block."

It would require no ordinary persistence on the
part of Moses to impress the people with the truth of
what he had heard from God. His own faith must
have carried such conviction that the thing was done;
and, "he that destroyed the firstborn did not touch
them."

As students of God's Word, desiring to know and
understand what He has caused to be written for our
learning we must discover the *interpretation* of our
verse, before we proceed to make our *application* of it.

The immediate *interpretation* of this last clause of
v. 28, belongs specially to those to whom the Apostle
was writing at the time. The great argument was, not
merely that these Hebrew believers should come out

and make a bold avowal of Christ, but that they should
believe God in what He had further revealed for their
faith; and, in spite of all their surroundings and
traditions, should "go on to perfection," and should
go forth "without the camp," as their fathers had
gone forth from Egypt.

We may not take these words away from their
context. They come between chap. vi. 1-3 and xiii. 13.
They carry out the argument of the former passage,
and lead up to the conclusion of the latter.

Here was a reason why they should *leave* what they
had heard concerning the beginning of the teaching of
Christ (which related to the kingdom); and not lay
again the foundation truths of repentance from dead
works, and their other beliefs—but "go on unto
perfection," whither the Apostle was seeking to lead
all believers, at that time.

The sprinkling of the blood told of other things far
beyond deliverance from "eternal judgment." It was
"*foreordained before* the foundation of the world," but
its results pass on into eternity. It went beyond the
"teaching of Christ" in the Gospels; for it culminated
in the "words which the Holy Ghost teacheth," when
He tells not merely of non-imputation of iniquity, but
of a Divine righteousness imputed and reckoned to us;
of our Identification with Christ, and not merely of
the substitution of Christ, of a "better covenant"
(viii. 6); a "better substance" (x. 34); "a better
sacrifice" (ix. 23); a "better hope" (vii. 19); a
"better resurrection" (xi. 35); a "better thing"
(xi. 40); and "better promises" (viii. 6), because all
these were now centered in Christ.

Yes, this sprinkling of the blood "spoke of better

things than the blood of Abel " and of the Passover
lamb. It tells of wondrous truths which cannot be
learned until we go forth " without the camp " of the
churches and their traditions ; for, it tells how " the
Father hath made us meet to be partakers (not of
Canaan but) of the inheritance of the saints in light,
Who hath delivered us (not from Egypt; but) from the
power of darkness, and hath translated us (not to
Sinai and the wilderness and to Canaan but), into the
kingdom of His beloved Son. In Whom we have
redemption through His blood even the forgiveness of
sins " (Col. i. 12-14).

The Apostle, at the close of the Pentecostal Dispensation of the Acts, was found a "prisoner,"
indeed ;—a prisoner of the Romans, and bound with
their " chain," " for the hope of Israel " (Acts xxviii. 20).
But when that Dispensation was closed, he became a
" prisoner " again, but, of quite another kind, and for
quite another reason. He became "the prisoner of
Jesus Christ," and this (he says) was "for you Gentiles."
And there, in that prison in Rome he, as " the Lord's
prisoner " in view of this very purpose, wrote of these
" better things."

He would lead them on " to perfection ": not to any
moral or spiritual perfection *in themselves;* but to the
perfection of the truth and teaching of " the Spirit of
truth " as He guided him and them "into all the truth "
according to the promise of Christ in John xvi. 13. In
the Epistle to the Ephesians he had spoken of the
Father " Who hath blessed us with all (not some)
spiritual (not temporal) blessings in the heavenly
sphere (not in Canaan), in Christ (not in connection
with Israel but), according as He hath chosen us in

Him (not in connection with any one Dispensation, but before them all—even) before the foundation of the world" (Eph. i. 3, 4).

This shows us what is the *interpretation* of our verse in connection with the context, and with the time and occasion of the Apostle's writing. Here was an argument for the faith of these Hebrew believers to go forward and take in all that was to be learned " without the camp" and to believe what another Moses was now telling them for their " hearing"—things as hard for us to believe as those which Moses rehearsed to the people when instituting the Passover.

But this leads us on to the *application* for us to day.

Tradition, to day, makes it as difficult for us to believe the further teachings of the Holy Spirit; to leave the beginning of the teaching of Christ, not to lay again the foundation, but to "go on to perfection" (Heb. vi. 1); just as the fears and miseries of Israel made it difficult for them to believe what they heard from Moses.

Nevertheless, our resolve shall be the same as that of the Apostle :

"THIS WILL WE DO, IF GOD PERMIT "

We will say " this one thing I do" (Phil. iii. 13). We will "go on " and not stand still ; we will "go forth " from the camp, and not remain in it with all its bickerings and controversies, its "hatred, envy and malice, and all uncharitableness." We will " go forth UNTO HIM," and leave others to themselves and their camps. We will " go on" to the perfection of truth and teaching into which the Holy Spirit has guided us. We will, as " full grown," delight ourselves in the meat, yea the strong meat, of the Word. We will leave our milk, and our feeding-bottles. Others may say that we have "gone wrong" and "got off the lines." These things are easily said; anyone can say them; but we will bear with them, knowing full well what it is that makes us all "dull of hearing" (Heb. v. 11, vi. 1), and why so many of us are "not able to bear" the "meat of the Word" (1 Cor. iii. 1, 2).

All such are spoken of as "carnal" in 1 Cor. iii. 3; and, as seeking to *make* a unity of the body, which ends in "strifes and divisions." But we will endeavour to "*keep* the unity of the Spirit, which is the bond of peace."

All such are still in the camp, occupied with "carnal ordinances" (margin, *rites* or *ceremonies*), "imposed until the time of reformation" (Heb. ix. 10).

But Christ has been offered "without the gate" (Heb. xiii. 12), and "UNTO HIM" we would "go forth," (not unto some other "camp," but "unto Him"), believing what we have heard from Him, and rejoicing in the "better promises" which He has given us—not of an Exodus through death and resurrection, but of an Ascension, and a glorious change when He shall call us on high (Phil. iii. 14).

The application of our verse (Heb. xi. 28) abides. The lesson is for us, what it was for Israel, and more. The same faith in the same word of the same God, can alone give us the same deliverance from all bondage, and bring to us the same security, and enable us to enjoy the fulfilment of all the promises of God and of all the blessings which He has given us "in Christ."

> "When I see the blood,
> I will pass over you."

This was all that the Israelites had to rest on. They needed nothing more, and we need nothing less.

In the heavenly and spiritual sphere we cannot trust to our feelings, or rest in our experiences. These are all carnal, and have to do with the flesh, and the mind. It is not a question of our thoughts or views, or opinions, it is a question of fact.

Jehovah said "when I see," not "when you feel." There is no foundation in such things as "feelings or experiences." Our thoughts may be wise, or otherwise; but they have no place in the sphere where Jehovah speaks, and we have only to hearken and believe.

It is a question of what He sees, not what *we* feel. Here, and here only, is rest and peace.

It is not the question " Do we believe ? " But it is the one great question

WHOM DO WE BELIEVE?

If a firstborn son in a certain house had asked his father whether he had sprinkled the blood, and he believed the answer when his father said he had done so, the firstborn's peace and enjoyment would have been " according to his faith." But his *security* would not ! For, if the father, from failure or infirmity, had omitted to do so : though the son might have peace, he would not be secure from the work of the destroying angel !

But, if on the other hand the father answered yes, and the blood had really been sprinkled on the lintel and door-posts, but the son *doubted the father's word*, he would know no peace. His doubt would surely cause him to be in fear and misery the whole night through ! But *he would be secure !* The destroyer's hand would be averted !

The faith of the one who believed what was not

true would not have made him secure. The doubt of the other who did not believe what was true would not have affected his security.

The former would have had a false peace and died a violent death.

But the latter, who doubted, would have had no peace, but would have partaken of Jehovah's redemption.

And why? Because security depends on GOD'S WORD, while our enjoyment of it rests on OUR OWN FAITH, and in believing the word which God has spoken.

This is why man's words and our feelings are of no avail in the sphere where all is spiritual.

"WHEN I SEE THE BLOOD!"

are the words of Jehovah. Not when I see your faith, or your doubts, or your fear or your feelings.

How many are practically saying, "Lord, I cannot believe what Thou sayest unless I have some evidence within me that what Thou sayest is true!" How sad! How solemn! How serious! For what can be the result but misery. Misery is ever the result of looking within, and of being occupied with one's own thoughts and feelings. Well might Asaph say in similar circumstances, "This is my infirmity" (Ps. lxxvii., 10). It is the "infirmity" of many a true child of God. But, whatever the miseries may be, they all come from the same source—unbelief!

"WHEN I SEE" . . . "I WILL."

These are the words of Jehovah's greatest promise. Jehovah's work and Jehovah's word are the only true bases of rest and peace.

And it is the sprinkling of the blood which "hath

been instituted" that is the abiding ground of the atoning work. The Passover and the Exodus are over, but "the sprinkling of the blood" remains in its eternal efficacy. Neither on the lintel, door-posts nor mercy-seat could anything be added to it; still less substituted for it.

So with "the precious blood of Christ." It spoke not of life lived, but of life given up: the life of another, "without blemish and without spot." Hence the life—yea, the eternal life—of all for whom He was substituted is secure.

All the religious movements of the day, from Rome to Keswick, aim at bringing their respective adherents up to some standard of good or holy living. "Touch not, taste not, handle not," brings all alike under the yoke of man. Abstinence from "leaven," and the partaking of "bitter herbs," and "rules for daily living" are all based on the same principle, and are all used and designed to influence the heart and life.

But very different are the means employed by God the Holy Spirit. His work is not finished, and will not be complete till we are "called up on high." But Christ's work "IS FINISHED." To this the Spirit ever points us and leads us.

He never occupies our thoughts with His own works and acts, though human teachers do little else. His one great unceasing work is to glorify Christ (John xvi., 14), and the measure in which He fills us with His graces and gifts, is the measure in which we are occupied with Christ, and glorify Christ. "He shall receive of Mine" (said Christ) "and shall show it unto you." (John xvi., 13, 14.)

What He shows is that Christ's finished work is the

alone foundation of salvation, and faith's rest on it is the alone foundation of our real enjoyment of it. " He (Christ) is our peace." This peace is not the Spirit's work ; His work is seen in bringing us into the know-ledge and enjoyment of all that God has made Christ to be unto us, and all that He has made us to be in Christ.

Oh that we may enter into the verity and truth of Jehovah's words, and, believing what we have heard from Him, live in the fullest enjoyment of His grace and peace.

Israel: Faith's Obedience

1. They Passed Through the Red Sea

CORRESPONDING with ABRAHAM, in the Structure of this chapter* we have here, as in his case,

"THE OBEDIENCE OF FAITH."

In verse 8 we read: " By faith, Abraham, when he was called to GO OUT . . . obeyed."

So, here, " By faith, [the Israelites when commanded to GO FORWARD] passed through the Red Sea as on dry land; which the Egyptians assaying to do, were drowned."

The character of the faith is the same in each case. Both are followed by the faith of a woman. Abraham's faith, by Sarah's; and Israel's faith, by Rahab's. Moreover, the faith of each woman was shown in a corresponding manner, viz.: *the conclusion drawn from what they had respectively heard.*

The faith of Abraham and Israel was shown in obedience to a command: "GO"! To Abraham, it was GO "OUT"; to Israel, "GO FORWARD."

Abraham's faith we have already referred to. It now remains for us to consider the faith of Israel.

For our purpose here, it matters not about the Red Sea, or how it got this name, or where the passage took place†. Neither are we concerned with Pharaoh,

---

*See Vol. xiv. p. 109 (Oct. 1908).

† The Scriptures of the Pentateuch describe and agree with the Egypt *of that day*, as shown by the monuments and records of those times. The Egypt of to-day is very different.

whether he was Thothmes II., or Menephta, the son of Rameses II., or any other.

When the Egyptologists have settled this question, and obtained *all* the data necessary for their conclusion, it will be quite time enough for us to give our attention to them.

If it were necessary for our learning, the Holy Spirit would surely have told us.

As He has not done so, it shows that our attention is to be directed to Jehovah and Israel, and not to Pharaoh.

We have the inspired record in Exodus xiii. and xiv.

The fact is again and again emphasised, that Jehovah "brought them out of Egypt." This fact they knew. They had heard Jehovah's word, that He would do so. They *believed* what they had heard, and had kept the Passover, by the same faith. Now, they heard another revelation—that He Who had brought them out would *bring them in*. This promise had been made at the Bush (Ex. iii., 8, 17) and it is recorded again and again, for their faith and ours. (Ex. iii. 17 ; vi. 6, 8; vii. 4; xii. 51 ; xiii. 3, 5, 14, 16; Deut. vi. 23, etc.).

The acknowledgment of this was to be ever remembered, and was to be confessed every year in the presentation of the first fruits (Deut. xxvi. 8-10).

This promise they had *heard*. This word they *believed*.

The crisis which called for this faith is recorded in Ex. xiv.

When the hosts of Pharaoh approached, the Israelites "lifted up their eyes."

What could be the effect of this "sight" but doubt and fear? These are the invariable fruits of sense and sight. They were sore afraid in themselves; and they chided Moses, in words of grossest unbelief (*vv.* 10-12).

Shut in between the great fortress " Migdol," which was on the "Shur" or wall (built to protect Egypt from Asia), and the sea, with Pharaoh's hosts behind, and shut in on the other side by the wilderness (Ex. xiv. 2, 3), it was indeed a crisis.

But it was a crisis designed for their good, and for a lasting lesson.

They were being guided by the " pillar of a cloud" given them for leading and for light.

It was Jehovah's command that they should "turn and encamp between Migdol and the sea"; and not yet "go forward."

Jehovah had His own purposes to carry out, and His own glory to secure. He knew what Pharaoh would say when he saw them, as he thought, " entangled in the land " and " shut in by the wilderness " (Ex. xiv. 3).

While Jehovah was arranging events for being "honoured upon Pharaoh and all his host," and while the Egyptians were learning their lesson that He was Jehovah, Israel must be left to learn their lessons also, which should manifest their faith, and Jehovah's sovereign grace.

Just as He had ordained and foreseen, so it was ; and we have the inspired record, in the short sentence: "*and they did so.*" (*v.* 4.)

All Jehovah's works and ways are perfect : and *one* act accomplishes manifold ends. When *we* do one thing, it may accomplish one end, but, at the same time it may upset, and turn out wrong, in conflicting with many others.

Not so with Jehovah's perfect way : for while He was arranging His ends with regard to His own glory and Pharaoh's overthrow, Moses was teaching Israel their great and needed lesson.

Moses heeded not their chiding, and made no reply thereto. He turned their thoughts to Jehovah. They had seen the hosts of Pharaoh, but there was something else for them to see ; viz.—"the salvation of Jehovah." Enemies they "had seen," but they should "see them again no more for ever."

But that "salvation" could not be seen by the natural eye. The eye of faith must first see it, before it could be seen by the eye of sense.

That salvation must first be revealed for the hearing of faith. "He will show you to-day," were the words they heard.

Here was the ground of their faith. Jehovah's word, and this alone, could give them the faith to obey Jehovah's command, and "Go forward."

When the promise had been heard, then the command was given : not before.

Their obedience was not based on the *Command* which was given, but on the *Promise*.

It was produced by, and flowed from, this promise, "Jehovah said unto Moses . . . Speak unto the children of Israel that they Go forward." (Ex. xiv. 15.)

Faith must be based on the hearing of Jehovah's word* and obedience to the command must spring from the faith thus produced by it.

---

* Hence the importance of noticing how many times this formula "Jehovah said" and "Jehovah spake" are used in the books of the Pentateuch. In this book of Exodus, "Jehovah said" occurs 45 "sundry times," and in 10 "divers manners."

I Absolutely iii. 7 ; xxxiii. 21.

"Go forward" was Jehovah's Command. "Stand still" was Moses' injunction.

Both were perfect: for when Moses spoke, Jehovah had not yet commanded.

Moses waited for that command. There is no reproach in Jehovah's word, "Wherefore criest thou unto me?" It is not a question asked for information; but it is the Figure of speech, called *Erotēsis*, which puts a *statement* in the *form of a question* in order to emphasise here, the word "ME" and "the children

---

2 To Moses (or " to him ") iv. 2, 4, 6, 11, 19; vi. 1; vii. 1, 14; ix. 22; x. 1, 12, 21; xi. 1, 9; xiv. 26; xvi. 4, 28; xvii. 5; xix. 9, 10, 24; xxiv. 12; xxxii. 7, 9, 33; xxxiii. 1, 17; xxxiv. 1, 27.

3 To Moses to say to Aaron, viii. 16.

4 To Moses to say unto Pharaoh, iv. 21 (cp. 22); viii. 20; ix. 1, 13.

5 To Moses to rehearse to Joshua, xvii. 14.

6 To Moses to charge the People, xix. 21.

7 To Moses to speak to the People, xi. 1 (cp. 2).

8 To Moses to say to the children of Israel, xiv. 15; xx. 22; xxxiii. 5.

9 To Moses and unto Aaron, ix. 8; xii. 43.

10 To Aaron, iv. 27.

The importance of this note will be seen when we think of the solemnity of the fact here recorded.

Jehovah either *did speak*, and the Book of Exodus is inspired by the Holy Spirit; or He *did not speak*, and we have an impious fraud which has no claim whatever on our further attention; and which we had better leave altogether and turn to something that we can feel sure about. The position of those who do not believe in Inspiration is inconceivable. They are confronted by the above dilemma. May the Holy Spirit lead them to the true conclusion.

We may also add that the expression "Jehovah spake" occurs 20 "sundry times" in Exodus, and in 7 "divers manners"; the first being Ex. vi. 10. Our readers can find them for themselves, and base on them the same powerful argument.

of Israel" as though He said "Thou criest to Me but, speak thou to the people."

It was a true word which Moses spoke in verse 13. For he spoke *before* the command was given. Moses had no right to say "Go forward till then." And even when this command *was* given, obedience had to be preceded by another command : "lift thou up thy rod, and stretch forth thine hand over the sea and divide it."

In the crisis in which the Israelites found themselves, it required as much faith to "Stand still" as it did to "Go forward;" and not until we have learnt the lesson of the former can we obey the latter. We can "go forward" only when faith has *seen* that which is invisible : in other words only when faith sees "the salvation of God," before it is wrought for us

As Abraham "went out, not knowing whither he should go": so it was here. Whither should Israel go but into the sea? Probably not until their feet touched the water did the dividing thereof begin. Here, then, was their faith.

They had thought they would be destroyed by Pharaoh's hosts. The very last thought would have been to look to the sea as a means of escape! And yet it is added:

> "The children of Israel went into the midst of the
> sea upon the dry ground; and the waters were a wall
> unto them on their right hand and on their left."

And now, let us ask: (1) What was the immediate *interpretation* for those to whom the Apostle was writing?

(2) What is the remoter *application* for our own selves to-day?

We must find the answer to the former question before we can correctly answer the latter.

How did the Apostle intend these Hebrew believers to apply that act of Israel's faith, to their own position as professed believers?

He was giving a similar command, or rather a weighty exhortation:

"LET US GO FORTH UNTO HIM,"

(Heb. xiii., 13).

Jesus Christ had suffered, and His sin offering sufficed to set them free. Many "divers and strange teachings" were aflcat (*v.* 9) They were not to be "occupied" with meats: "Touch not, taste not, handle not" (Col. ii., 20, 22), "which have not profited them that have been occupied therein." We have a great sacrifice*—a sin-offering which was offered "without the gate" (just as the sin-offerings were burned up "without the camp,") "that He might sanctify the People with His own blood. "Let us GO FORTH UNTO HIM without the camp, bearing His reproach" (Heb. xiii., 13).

This is the *interpretation* of this passage. This was the lesson which believing Israelites at that juncture were to learn. They were to "GO FORWARD" like their fathers, once again, into the midst of the sea. Not the Red Sea, with Pharaoh and his hosts behind them, but into a sea of trouble which they saw before them if they left all the traditions of their fathers, and all the shreds of Judaism, and rested only and solely upon "HIM."

---

*By the Figure *Metonymy* (of the Subject), "altar" is put for the Sacrifice upon it. It cannot mean the "altar" of stone itself; for "altars" are not eaten. They are not articles of food; hence the apostle adds: "of which [sacrifices] they have no right to eat which serve the Tabernacle." "They which eat of the sacrifices are partakers of the altar." (I Cor., x., 18.)

They were to leave the "Camp" for a Person. They were to leave "Religion" for Christ: (for He alone is true "Christ-ianity.")

In Phil. iii. Paul had shown the great difference between the Jews' Religion and Christianity. But he had given up all for Christ. Once, he counted them as his "gains"; but he had learned that they were "loss" for Christ.

His new standing before God was to be

"FOUND IN HIM' (*v.* 9)

His new *object* in life was to

"GET TO KNOW Him"

and his new *hope* was to be

"LIKE HIM"

It was all "HIM."

He had given up all for Christ. He had "gone forth" without the camp "of Israel," knowing that the city, of which he was henceforth a citizen, already and really existed* in heaven.

Jerusalem was to be shaken, but he looked for a city "in the heavenlies," a city which hath foundations which no shaking could remove.

His exhortation was: Leave the earthly city with all its religion, "knowing for yourselves (margin) that ye have, in heaven, a better substance, yea, an enduring substance† (Heb. x. 34).

This was the very basis of all that follows in the next chapter (ch. xi). This is the reason why they should follow the great cloud of witnesses. They all went

---

*This is the meaning of the word rendered "is," in Phil. iii., 2o. It is not the verb "to be," (ἐστί, *esti)* "it is," but it is ὑπάρχει (*huparchei*) "it exists."

† The Figure, *Ellipsis* may be thus well supplied.

forth " by faith " to something that was contrary to
their surroundings, and unseen by the natural eye.

The promise was " eternal life " for " the just shall
live [for ever] by faith." Let them believe therefore all
that God had revealed for faith-obedience (Rom. xvi
26, 1 Tim. iii. 16).

Let them " Go forth unto Him " and find " in Him,"
not only acceptance (Eph. i. 6), but holiness (Heb. xiii.
12), completeness (Col. ii. 10), and perfection (Eph.
iv. 13).

" Go forward " had been the word to their fathers·
and " by faith " they obeyed.

" Go forth " was the word to them; and only by the
same faith could they " obey."

And, what is the *application* for us to day ?

We, too, are to " go forward " and " go forth." But
it must be " unto Him." We are to leave, each one,
his " camp," and find our all in " Him."

We yield, at the best, only a partial obedience. Some
" go forth " ; but, it is only unto another camp, and not
" unto Him." Some go from camp to camp. They
find varying " commandments and doctrines of men,"
and " ordinances " to which they are required to submit
and be " subject " (Col. ii. 20-22) : they find varying
conditions of entrance into the different camps ; and
varying forms of admission to "fellowship" therein. But
all this falls short of " HIM." *Another* " camp " is put
in the place of His glorious person, and a Heavenly
citizenship.

Ah ! it is only " by faith " that we can " go forth unto
Him." And alas, how difficult !

It is easy to " go forth " unto another camp. Only
sight is required for this. It is done constantly by

those who " walk by sight ;" but, to go forth from all camps unto Him we must " walk by faith."

There may be a sea before us, and persecuting Pharaohs behind us ; there may be Egyptians pursuing us, with their Migdol fortresses on our right hand and on our left ; but faith will see only "the salvation of God," and hear only Jehovah's word.

May it be ours to find our all in " HIM." He will be better to us than all our fears. His city in the heavenly sphere will prove better than all camps. And it *exists*, there ; it exists, *now*. It is to be enjoyed *now*. But it is on the " other side " of the sea, which must be crossed " by faith." It is on the other side, where there is only praise, and giving of thanks unto the Father Who hath made us meet to be partakers of the inheritance of the saints in light " (Col. i. 12).

Only when " by faith " we have crossed that sea, and are beyond the confusion of " the commandments and doctrines of men," can we truly live a life of " giving thanks " for having found our completeness in " Him."

" THEN sang !" (Ex. xv. 1). When did they thus sing ?

Not until they were on the wilderness side of that sea.

Before that, while in Egypt, there was only sighing, and crying, and groaning (Ex. ii. 23). Not until they "SAW that great work which Jehovah did " and reverenced Jehovah, and " believed His word," could they truly sing.

And what did they sing of ? Ah ! it was all concerning Him. Nothing about themselves. Oh how different from Modern Hymnology. How opposite to it. It was all about " HIM."

"WHO IS LIKE UNTO THEE?"

was the burden of their song of praise.* It was ever thus. His Saints always sang of HIM. They made melody IN THEIR HEARTS, and it was always "UNTO THE LORD" (Eph. v. 19).

Until we are on the other side, we sing about ourselves, and our present experiences, and our hopes, and our fears, and we may sing about happiness as a future thing; but once we believe God as to our completeness in Christ, we shall have done with ourselves, and rejoice that we are already on the other side "in HIM," and our one theme will be "Who is like unto Thee?"

May it be ever thus with us, "GIVING THANKS UNTO THE FATHER" for what HE hath made us to be IN CHRIST; and then there will be no more sighing and crying, and groaning on account of what WE have NOT DONE.

"THEN SANG"

---

* It is emphasised by the Figure *Erotēsis*, read Deut. xxxiii. 26, 27; 1 Sam. ii. 2; 1 Ch. xvii. 20. Ps. xxxv. 10; lxxi. 19; lxxiii. 25; lxxxvi. 8; lxxxix. 6, 8; cxiii. 5.

2. "The Walls of Jericho Fell Down"

" By faith the walls of Jericho fell down, after they had been compassed about seven days " (v. 30).

THE second example of the obedience of Israel's faith is the taking of Jericho

The taking of Jericho is placed out of its *chronological* order, in order that it may be coupled with Israel's first act of faith, in the passage of the Red Sea.

Rahab's faith, which follows it here, came earlier in time. But it is placed later (*canonically*) (*v.* 31), so that it may correspond with Sarah's faith which is similarly transposed (*v.* 11), for the like purpose.

This is because the faith of Abraham was manifested in the same way as that of Israel, viz., *obedience :* and, because the faith of Sarah was shown to be of like character with that of Rahab, in the right *conclusion* which their faith drew from what they had, respectively, *heard*.

Israel, here, had *heard* from Joshua (Josh. vi. 6; 7), what Joshua had *heard* from Jehovah (*vv.* 2-5).

Joshua's faith was strengthened by the vision he had just previously seen, and by the words he had just heard from "the Captain of Jehovah's host" (Josh. v. 13-15).

The obedience of Israel's faith is emphasised by this fact. It is not *recorded* that Joshua had repeated to the people the words of Jehovah : though doubtless he must have done so, or it could not have been said to be "by faith." This silence is intended to call our attention to the special *character* of their faith :—*obedience.*

He simply gave the command to the priests: "Take up the ark," &c.; and, to the armed men—"Pass on before the ark of Jehovah." That is all.

"And it came to pass, that the seven priests . . . . passed on . . . . and the ark of Jehovah followed them. And the armed men went before the priests . . . . and the rereward came after the ark" (*vv.* 8, 9).

Thus the essence of Israel's faith was *obedience* to a command.

Truly, it required faith, great faith; for, such a command was entirely contrary to *reason*. Never had such an effect been produced by such a cause. There was every ground for doubt, yea, for unbelief. But, here, in this case, there was not a question prompted by "*sight*." Only prompt and unquestioning obedience.

It was unheard of, that, by merely marching round a city, and by the blowing of trumpets, the fortified walls should fall down and be crumpled up.*

Those who witnessed such a procedure must have laughed at its apparent innocence and impotence.

Some commentators actually do this very thing; and in order to get rid of the miraculous, say that it merely means "circumvallation," or the laying siege to the city by surrounding it.

They do not see their own folly, which implies that according to verse 15 *seven sieges* must have been laid to the city *in one day !*

It is astonishing to what shifts commentators are compelled to resort, and what pains they will take to shut out Jehovah from His own Word, and get rid of all that is supernatural in it.

---

*Heb. "Fall down under it." (A.V., margin).

To accomplish this they do not hesitate to assert that the city was "stormed" by Joshua's troops on the seventh day! They thus substitute their own words for the words of the Holy Spirit, instead of believing them.

Oh! for Israel's faith, in this narration of fact and truth; for, even in those who believe it, there is seen an *effort* to *prove* its truth.

Most of our readers have doubtless seen during the present year the newspaper headings "The Walls of Jericho," "Discovery of Remains of the Ancient City," and other striking headings of similar character.

In all the discoveries which are to day being constantly brought under our notice, the one aim on all hands seems to be to prove the truth of God's Word.

We use them in quite an opposite way. We conclude that the discoveries are true if, and when the Scriptures corroborate them.

Hence, in this case, we know that the interpretation of these discoveries is not true.

It is said that the walls are still standing and ancient houses are still there, built up against them, a great breach in the walls being found in one particular part.

The Scripture statement shows that there must be something wrong about the discovery, because the words of the plain and simple record tell us that the walls "fell down flat."

This Scripture bids us "try" the discovery.

It is made at the instance of the German Oriental Society, under Professors Sellin and Watzinger, who are employing upwards of 200 men.

History tells us that Jericho was twice rebuilt and twice destroyed after the taking of it by Joshua.

It remained under Jehovah's curse, until it was first

rebuilt by Hiel in the reign of Ahab, in B.C. 918
(1 Kings xvi. 34).

Hiel's Jericho was captured and looted by one,
Simon, under Herod the Great. Archelaus, the son
of Herod rebuilt it again, and founded a new city,
which was the Jericho of our Lord's day. He planted
it with palm trees, which gave it its more modern name
—" the City of Palms."

This again was destroyed by the Roman commander,
Vespasian, in A.D. 68, and his work was complete; for
since that day the ruins have been buried, and, over
them, all that tourists have seen, is a wretched little
hamlet bearing the same name.

When the explorers have gone deeper, and completed
their work, they will find no walls with breaches in them,
or houses leaning against them, for they " fell down flat,"
and the stones of which they were built were utilised in
rebuilding the successive cities of Hiel and Archelaus.

We come back, therefore, to " the Scriptures of
truth," not waiting for corroboration which any discoveries of spade or pen may produce, in order to have
our faith confirmed, and not disturbed by the vapourings
of sceptics of the earlier nineteenth century, like
Voltaire, who held that the Jews were mere ignorant
bandits down to comparatively late times, and that
they evolved their historical books out of their own
imagination.

We leave the unbelief of such men to be dealt with
by others, while we turn back to the Word of God,
which, in the simplicity of language which claims to
be the truth, records the fact; " By faith the walls of
Jericho fell down after they had been compassed about
seven days."

These words are written here (Heb. xi. 30) to show us the nature and character of true faith, which is the basis of all that we hope for; and to show how the Hebrew believers to whom they were addressed might use them in their then present and critical position.

Surely this example of Israel's faith was intended to have its blessed effect in inciting them to personal obedience based on the word of the same God.

The Apostle is not dealing in vague generalities; but, is using well chosen and pertinent illustrations indited by the Spirit of God.

Out of a multitude of examples which any other writer would find ready to hand, he selects a few instances of faith exactly suited to the then circumstances of those who would be the first readers of his words. This will be their *interpretation*, whatever the *application* may be to ourselves.

Israel's obedience to God's command, by Moses, had carried them forward, and delivered them out of the hand of Pharaoh. Israel's obedience to God's command, by Joshua, had carried them across the Jordan, and delivered their enemies into their hand.

What were the commands now being given by the same God, by another of His chosen vessels—the Apostle Paul ?

Were they not exactly similar in character ? Had he not just charged his readers to *leave* the traditions of their fathers, and the teaching which belonged to a Dispensation which was passing away ?

Everything around them was being " shaken." The destruction of their City and Temple was drawing near. All this signified " the removal of those things that are shaken, as of things that are made "—yes ' made with hands."

But they were reminded that there were "things which cannot be shaken" and that these will "remain" (ch. xii. 27). The earthly kingdom was being shaken, and removed; but "we"—himself and those who believe his "revelation" were "receiving a kingdom which cannot be removed" (v. 28). This was in heaven. This was the new truth he was setting before them.

This was the very exhortation at the end of chapter x. on which the exhortations of chapter xi. are based, They could "take joyfully the spoiling of their goods" which were being "shaken" and "removed," "knowing (he says) in yourselves that ye have in heaven, a better [substance] even an enduring substance" (x. 34).

This is the "substance" which in Phil. iii. 20 the Apostle had already revealed as "*existing* (even then), in heaven." A glorious reality which will "remain" after all earthly things have been shaken and removed.

Earthly walls and defences may be shaken and fall down flat, but "by faith" they were to go forward, and go up and take the spoil; and never to lay those foundations again.

They had heard and believed what Christ had taught in the Gospels; and what had been proclaimed and made known by His Apostles in the Pentecostal Dispensation. But further revelations of precious truths had been made known for faith-obedience. A great secret had been revealed and written down; and now they were to leave the old foundations; they were to forget the things that were "behind," and reach forth unto those that were "before" (Phil. iii. 13).

It may be, and indeed has been objected, that we are bringing the great Secret, or Mystery, into the Epistle to the Hebrews, while the word is not mentioned in this Epistle; and it is not specifically referred to. But we must remember that it had been revealed and made known and committed to writing for at least six years before this Epistle was written to these Hebrews. Are we to suppose that they had heard nothing about it?

They were exhorted to *leave* that six-fold foundation (Heb. vi. 1-3); but, for what? if not for the seven-fold spiritual foundation revealed in the Epistle to the Ephesians? Can it mean that they were to leave them altogether, and give them up, and have nothing to put in their place? Impossible! They were to "go on," not to go back. They were to "go on unto perfection." But what were they to "go on" to? and to what "perfection," if not the perfection of doctrine and truth which already had been revealed, according to the promise 1 Cor. xiii. 10? Surely it cannot refer to moral perfection?

Certain things were to be "done away." "Prophecies," "knowledge," partial truth, and things pertaining to childhood, all these were to give place to a promised "perfection" of truth. Before this they had seen only dimly as in a mirror; and what they had seen was only imperfectly and partially perceived. It was indistinct and undefined. But they were to see now "face to face"; they were to see precious things not reflected as in a mirror, but to see the result themselves: not as in a mirror, but as "face to face." They were to see clearly as they were seen, and to know as they were known. Hence they were to be not as children, but as full grown; and were to feed on them, as men upon meat; and no longer upon milk which was suited for babes (1 Cor. xiii.).

They had heard and believed and hoped for the Descension of the Lord into the air, and of a resurrection (*anastasis*) FROM among the dead (1 Thess. iv.) That, in itself, was a special revelation for them during the Pentecostal Dispensation ; and it was a marvellous advance on the beginning of Christ's teaching in the Gospels, which did not go beyond a "resurrection OF the dead."

But now, seeing that the King and the Kingdom had been alike rejected (Acts xxviii. 25, 26), and notwithstanding the witness borne "by signs and wonders, and divers miracles and gifts of the Holy Ghost according to His own will " (Heb. ii. 4), a still further revelation had been made for their faith. It was not the Descent of Christ unto the air, and of a meeting with Him there, but an ASCENSION even a " calling on high " (Phil. iii. 14) to a portion and a place already existing there (*v.* 20) ; for those who should be alive and remain, while for those who should fall asleep, an " OUT-resurrection FROM among the dead " (*v.* 11).

Here are three resurrections plainly and clearly distinguished.

(1) *Anastasis*, a resurrection OF the dead, as revealed in the Old Testament and Gospels.

(2) *Anastasis ek*, a resurrection FROM among the dead, as revealed in the earlier Pauline Epistles ; and now

(3) *Ex-anastasis ek*, an OUT-resurrection FROM among the dead (Phil. iii. 14).

Traditional theologians have no place for this last. They have not obeyed the command of Heb. vi. 1-3. They have not *left* the doctrine of a " general resurrection." They have not "gone on " to the " perfection."

When for the time they ought to be " teachers " there is need for them to be taught. And the humblest believer, who believes "all" that the Scriptures have revealed can teach those who are still like children feeding on milk.

What is this " *ex-anastasis ek* " ? What can it be but a further revelation ? It is an *advance* on 1 Thess. iv. That will remain true for all who do not have part in that of Phil. iii.

After we shall have been *called on high* Phil. iii. will have been fulfilled (and filled full) ; but 1 Thess. iv. will remain true for all who shall thereafter believe, and be waiting for Him, and who will then say : " Lo This is our God ; we have waited for Him " !

We shall not rob them of their hope of being caught up to have their joy as set forth in Rev. vii.

So that, while the Mystery is not brought into the Epistle to the Hebrews, and while we do not bring it in, we may and must *bring it out*, if we are to understand the *interpretation* which the Hebrew readers of Paul's words would put upon them.

While there was much for them to *leave*, there was nothing for them to " go on to " but the " perfection " of truth which had been for some years already written down for their faith.

They were exhorted, to " go forward " as Israel of old had been ; they were to " go on," in learning ; they were to " go forth unto HIM."

How were they to understand these exhortations addressed primarily to them, if not in this way ?

Faith in God's revealings could alone enable them to obey. No effort on their part was necessary. They had, like Israel of old, only to hear and obey. They must forget the things which were behind; they must reach forth unto those things which are before. They must "not lay again those foundations" of former beliefs—even as the foundations of Jericho were not to be re-laid. They must leave them, and go forward; yea they must "go forth" from their camp UNTO HIM! In Him they had a "better substance," a better covenant (vii. 22), better promises (viii. 6), a better hope (vii. 19), better sacrifices (ix. 23), a better country (xi. 16), a better resurrection (xi. 35).

Yes, in Him, and by faith in His word, they could leave their belief in things which were being shaken because their hopes were being directed to things which "cannot be shaken," and to "an enduring substance," which can never be removed.

That substance already *existed* in heaven; it was and IS already there; but, in HIM. That was why they could, and were to, look for the Saviour, the Lord Jesus Christ (Phil. iii. 20).

Surely the *application* for ourselves has already been made by our readers. It lies on the surface. It needs no labour to dig it out.

We are in a similar position. The same mistake has been made by believers in this Dispensation. We have gone on to believe the same truths which have been revealed for our faith. The Prison Epistles contain a record of our "better things," our "enduring substance"—"in heaven," and not on earth.

Other Hiels and Herods have arisen who have *laia again the foundations of another Jericho;* and in days o. idolatry, like those of Ahab of old.

We too are to leave these foundations, and look foi "a city which hath foundations" which God has laid,

" in heaven," from whence we·look for the Saviour to translate us thither.

We are to go forward, and "go forth unto Him," " forgetting the things which are behind, and reaching forth unto those things which are before," and "press towards the mark for the prize of the calling on high, of God, in Christ Jesus."

"Let us, therefore, as many as be perfect, be thus minded; and if in anything ye be otherwise minded, God shall reveal even this unto you" (Phil. iii. 14, 15).

Rehab: Faith's Conclusion

"*By faith the harlot Rahab perished not with them that believed not, when she had received the spies with peace.*"— (Heb. xi. 31.)

WE have now to consider the faith of the woman who is linked on to Israel's obedience, and to the City of Jericho's foundations which fell down flat; just as Sarah's faith is linked on to Abraham's obedience, and to his city which hath foundations which can never be moved.

If "by faith," then, Rahab must have *heard* (Rom. x. 17).

This is exactly what she says: "WE HAVE HEARD how Jehovah dried up the water of the Red Sea for you, when ye came out of Egypt; and what ye did unto the two kings of the Amorites, that were on the other side Jordan, Sihon and Og, whom ye utterly destroyed. And as soon as WE HAD HEARD these things our hearts did melt, neither did there remain any more courage in any man because of you; for Jehovah your God, He is God in heaven above, and in the earth beneath." (Josh. ii. 10, 11; Cp. v. 1).

The prophetic utterance of the Song of Moses in Ex. xv., had, in part, been fulfilled, which said:

"The peoples SHALL HEAR, and be afraid:
Sorrow shall take hold on the inhabitants of Palestine.
Then the dukes of Edom shall be amazed;
The mighty men of Moab, trembling shall take hold of them;

All the inhabitants of Canaan shall melt **away ;**
Fear and dread shall fall upon them ;
By the greatness of Thine arm they shall be still
    as a stone." (*vv.* 14—16).

The nations had heard and were afraid. Trembling
had taken hold of them. Their hearts had melted.

It is proverbial that news travels with mysterious
swiftness in the East. Jethro had heard the news long
before Rahab.*

The Amorites who had defeated Moab were defeated
by Israel.

Sihon, and Og the giant king of Bashan, had shared
the same fate. And the nations had " heard " of these
great events.

Unlike the Atheists of our own day, the heathen
believed in the existence of a God. The only question
with them was, whether Jehovah, the God of Israel,
was mightier than other gods. All the other gods with
which they were acquainted were " made with hands,"
but Israel's God was invisible, and His worship was
totally different from the worship of all other gods.

Was He more powerful?

Rahab's faith was strong. Her *conclusion* was certain.
She said " Jehovah your God, He is God in heaven
above, and in the earth beneath." (Josh. ii. 11).

" I KNOW

that Jehovah hath given you the Land, and that **your**
terror is fallen upon us, and that all the inhabitants **of**
the land, faint because of you." (*v.* 9).

How did she " *know* "? Only from the certainty
which faith gave ; only from the conclusion which faith
drew from what she had heard.

---

* Ex. xviii. 1., &c.

Others also had " heard " the same reports. They must have heard, or it could not have been written they " believed not."

But her faith was Divinely wrought, because God would have one vessel to magnify His grace, and His truth. He had also other purposes, in the riches of His grace, to bring her into the sacred line of genealogy.

With her description, as being a harlot, we are not concerned. It is parenthetical, but not without its importance. We have no sympathy with those who from Josephus downwards have striven to show that she was an ordinary " Inn-keeper," though we respect their motive. Etymology and usage are alike against it, (which we may see for ourselves by comparing Judg. xi. 1, xvi. 1 ; 1 Kings iii. 16 ; Matt. i. 5 ; Jas. ii. 25).

When this interpretation was first suggested, the christian " conscience " eagerly welcomed it. But now that the suggestion has been abandoned, Rahab is passed over in silence. But the Holy Spirit does not pass her over in silence. On the contrary, He singles her out from all others for special honour in the roll-call of faith.

The " higher " critics do not know what to do with her.

Professor Harnack says "the mention of Sarah is an astonishment to the expositor," and he thinks the Epistle must have been written by a woman, which would account for what he calls " the vagaries of grammar." He does not see that the thoughts and idioms are Hebrew, while the language is Greek. This theory is from a German higher critic.

But English expositors also are astonished, and some seek to find support for Professor Harnack's idea. Dr. Rendal Harris* sees a proof of feminine authorship in the reference to other " women " in verse 35 ; while among those who were " made strong " in verse 34, he suggests Esther and Judith.

Unfortunately for all this display of human wisdom and ingenuity, the adjective " strong " (*v.* 34) is in the *Masculine* gender, and must refer to men ; while the suggestion that the " me " (in verse 32) refers to a feminine authorship is fatal also, for it must be masculine, because the verb " to tell " is a participle· and is masculine also.†

The Text would have to be altered to suit the " vagaries " of the critics. We therefore thankfully fall back on the inspired words given by the Holy Spirit, and we are satisfied, with reason, for the introduction of Sarah and Rahab, when we look at the Structure and see how and where their names are placed.‡

It was "the work of faith" which characterised Rahab; and this is the great fact on which the Holy Spirit would have us fix our minds.

This explains the words of the same Spirit by James, (Jas. ii. 25). Her justifying work was the "work of faith": *i.e.,* faith, divinely "worked in," that it might be effectually worked out (Phil. ii. 12, 13). "This is the work of God, that ye believe what He hath said." (Compare John vi. 29).

* *Side-lights on New Test research.*

†ἐπιλείψει γὰρ με διηγούμενον (*epileipsei gar me diēgoumenon*) —for the time would fail me in discoursing.

‡We might also see why *only* these two are mentioned; and why Deborah is omitted though Barak is included.

"The work of faith" which is mentioned in 1 Thess. i. 3, is defined in verse 9 as turning from idols.

This is exactly "the work of faith" which we see in Rahab. She had "turned" from all the gods of the Amorites, and Moabites and Canaanites.

She had "heard" how Balak and Balaam had failed by all the arts of divination that could be resorted to against the God of Israel, and she had turned from them to serve the living and true God (1 Thess. i. 9).

But the great point of the whole is that she "perished not with them that believed not."

Why? Because she was "justified" and "saved" by faith's gracious and glorious "work." (Jas. ii. 25).

How was she saved? Why did she not perish? "Her house was upon the town wall, and she dwelt upon the wall" (Josh. ii. 15). Her window looked out from it! The spies were let down out of it into the open country. The scarlet cord by which she let them down was to hang out of the window as the "sign."

How then was she saved when the walls "fell down flat"? (Josh. vi. 20).

Her house must have fallen down with the walls upon which it was built. And so it did!

But, before that judgment fell on Jericho, "Joshua HAD said unto the two men that had spied out the country, go into the harlot's house, and bring OUT THENCE the woman and all that she hath, as ye sware unto her." (Josh. vi. 22). And the young men that were spies WENT IN and BROUGHT OUT Rahab AND* her father, AND her mother, AND her bretheren, AND all that she had: AND they

---

* Note the Fig. *Polysyndeton* (many "ands"), emphasising each item and each detail.

BROUGHT OUT all her kindred, AND left them WITHOUT THE CAMP of Israel, AND they burnt the city with fire." (Josh. vi. 22, 23).

Is not the *interpretation* forced upon us? We do not have to force it out. It stands forth on the page of Holy Writ.

A greater than Joshua—even Paul—had told these believing Hebrews, that their city (Jerusalem) was devoted to destruction. It was soon to be shaken to its foundations. And not only so, but a greater shaking was to shake, not Jerusalem only, "but also heaven." (Heb. xii. 26).

But another promise had been given by one greater than the two spies, that those who believed God should be saved and "brought out" of it, BEFORE that shaking should come. The words of the promise ran that all who have turned from idols, believed God, and waited for God's Son, should be "caught-up to meet the Lord in the air." This promise which had already been given in 1 Thess. iv. was *still* open and still *true* to all who believed God, that the true Joshua—even Jesus— should deliver them, and BRING them OUT BEFORE that shaking came.

But to know that blessing, they must be brought out as Rahab was, and left "without the camp of Israel." (Josh. vi. 23).

This was the *interpretation* to them. This was another reason why they should at once "go forth unto HIM without the camp" (Heb. xiii. 13); forgetting the things which were behind and reaching forth unto the things which are before.

But there is a further interpretation to be noticed in the words. "When she had received the spies in peace" (Heb. xi. 31).

Rahab had received fellow believers of God, though they were not her own country-men. She had received them in peace.

The Apostle had already, in the previous chapter, alluded to "the former days" in which they were made a gazing-stock both by reproaches and afflictions; and became companions of them which were so used" (Heb. x. 33).

The position of a Hebrew believer in those days was one of peculiar difficulty and distress. He was cast out by his relatives because he was a believer, and despised by Gentiles because he was a Jew.

If then his fellow believers refused their sympathy, where was he to look for fellowship when Christians were few, and their power to succour was circumscribed?

Is not this the reason why, in ch. xiii. 1-3, he exhorts "Let brotherly love continue. Be not forgetful to entertain strangers; for thereby some have entertained angels unawares. Remember them that are in bonds, as bound with them; and them which suffer adversity, as being yourselves also in the body."

The *interpretation* of Rahab's example was therefore full of instruction.

She was a stranger, but yet a fellow-believer in Jehovah, the same Covenant God. What a reproach then, if those who believe the same precious truths should not receive one another in peace!

Alas! for the *application* to day. Instead of receiving one another "in peace," those who have not forgotten so many of the things that are behind, and have not yet attained to so many of the things that are before, are ready to tear the others in pieces.

Instead of "brotherly love" *continuing* we may well ask whether it ever began. If it did it must have long well nigh ceased, for we see and find very little of it !

But, we need not pursue this application ; it is so self-evident, that it is itself an illustration and requires no explanation.

There is however another *application* for us which will be both profitable and helpful. That is the lesson of the scarlet cord.

Where was it to be placed ? It was to be bound in the window, where Joshua could see it from the outside (Josh. ii. 18). It would have been no sign, and no use, if it had been hung within the house, however elaborately cared for, prized, and preserved. It was to be placed where Joshua could see it.

It is the lesson of the Passover blood over again.

"WHEN I SEE THE BLOOD"

I will pass over you." (Ex. xii. 13)

And so here with the scarlet cord. The colour was no chance colour. Rahab may have had no thought about it. It may have been the first piece that came to hand. But, our God, Who over-rules all, so over-ruled here, that it should be the colour of the precious blood which now saveth us.

And note, it was not Rahab's design that it should be the token. It was given, as the sign and token, to her.

In like manner our token is given to us. It is outside us, and not within. It is not our feelings or experiences within, but a risen Christ above. It is His precious blood that is the "token" *there*, that the Father has accepted Him as our Substitute, and that we are accepted in Him.

It might have been a comfort to Rahab and her kindred if they could have seen and handled the scarlet cord. It might have given peace, but it would have been a false peace. It would have given neither safety nor security. Even so with the precious blood of Christ. It is our " token " that we shall be taken out and taken away, and called on high, before the judgment comes ; and the word of our God which we have heard is the alone source of our peace.

We are called on to believe, not the word of two spies, two poor mortal men, but the Spirit and the Word of truth.

We have the assurance of both, that, whether we are alive and remain, or fall on sleep, we shall be "called on high," or have an "out-resurrection from among the dead," and be placed in a place of safety, already prepared for us, before the trumpets of judgment shall be heard on earth.

Rahab was called out before the city was taken and burnt with fire.

We are not told when this was done. Josh. vi. 22 does not tell us the moment when his command was obeyed. It could not have been left till the walls had actually fallen ; for her house was upon the wall. It must have been before that. And if before, the only moment for it was before the siege actually commenced, for verse 1 tells us that even before that, " Jericho was straitly shut up, because of the children of Israel: none went out and none came in."

If none came out after that, and none went in, then Rahab must have been fetched out, and placed "without the camp" before the city was "straitly shut up," and before the trumpets of war were sounded.

Is not the double application clear for us to day?

We shall, as surely, be " fetched out " and called up on high, and placed, in reality, in fact and act " outside the camp," when that happy moment comes.

Let us then even now, in heart, and mind, and spirit " go forth unto Him," looking for the Saviour to take us to that heavenly sphere where nothing can ever be " shaken " and where we shall ever " remain."

Faith Conquering Through God

1. Gideon: Faith Conquering Through God

REFERRING again to the Structure on page 130, we see, next in order, two groups, corresponding with the first group, Abel, Enoch, and Noah.

Those in the first group were all connected directly with GOD.

The others are all directly connected with MAN, except Joseph, who corresponds with the LORD Jesus at the close of the whole list.

These last two groups are in like manner connected wholly with God, as the first group is.

The former of these last two groups contains the names of those who CONQUERED THROUGH God; while the second group consists of " others," who are unnamed, who SUFFERED FOR God.

Our business now is with the former of these two groups, which we give in our translation :

" *And what shall I say more ? For the time would fail me in discoursing concerning Gideon, Barak, Samson, Jephtha, David, and Samuel also, and the prophets,* . . . " we need not go further in this list now.

Passing over the actual circumstances of the individual acts which marked and gave character to the faith of each one, the Apostle leaves it to his readers, and to us, to supply them for ourselves.

In doing this we are to note that there is some doubt about the conjunctions. Most of the Critical Texts, including that of Tregelles, give them as we have rendered the passage above. If this is correct, then the importance of each individual is not so great, and does not admit of the same minute analysis as those cited in the former part of the chapter. There are seven examples in the list, and ten characteristics of their faith ; so that, in distributing the ten over the seven, we must be prepared to assign more than one to some of them.

The names are given neither in their Canonical, nor in their Chronological order. Gideon is named before Barak, Sampson before Jephtha, and David before Samuel. So that there must be some other reason for this order.

The six names are given in three pairs ; the prophets (unnamed) standing out alone as the seventh.

The seven are divided into four and three ; four being all judges, written in the book of Judges; and three being all prophets, written in the later books.

The four form an introversion thus—

    a | Gideon, ch. vi., vii.
       b | Barak, ch. iv., v.
       b | Samson, xiii.—xvi.
    a | Jephtha, xi., xii.

Of these four, the first and fourth stand out as being more important in the character and strength of their independent faith ; while the second and third are associated with women ; the former in his rise (Barak), and the latter in his fall (Samson). BARAK was associated with two women who helped him (Deborah and Jael); SAMSON with two women (his wife and Delilah) who both betrayed him.

The other three are likewise mentioned in the order of an introversion,

c | David, (1 Sam.—1 Chron.)

d | Samuel, (1 Sam.)

c | The Prophets

All these were prophets; but David stands out, corresponding with the prophets—the last in the group—as being a prophet indeed; while Samuel links on the judges with the prophets, and as partaking of the character of both.

So much for the outward literary form which tells us that we have to begin with

I GIDEON

He is introduced to us at a time when Israel was in deep distress. Three judges had preceded him*; and, for the fourth time, Israel had been delivered, on account of their apostasy, into the hand of their enemies.†

The history of those years is summed up in Judges ii., 11—19, to which we must refer our readers. It may be summed up negatively, in their disobedience in not driving out the nations of Canaan; and positively, in their Apostasy in worshipping the gods of the Canaanites, instead of Jehovah. Hence, He delivered them into the hand of their enemies.

From time to time He had raised them up judges "which delivered them out of the hand of those that spoiled them . . . then the LORD was with the judge . . . . and when the judge was dead they returned and corrupted themselves more than their fathers." (Judges ii. 16-19).

---

* Othniel, Ehud, Barak.

† Canaan, Moab, Canaan again, and Midian.

It was toward the close of the fourth of these cycles, when Israel was groaning under the servitude of Midian, that Gideon is first mentioned. (Judges vi. 11).

A prophet had already been sent to admonish the people : and now an Angel of Jehovah came to raise up Gideon and commission him to deliver the people once again out of the hand of their enemies.

His condition and occupation, at the moment of the angel's appearance, show the low estate into which he and his people had been brought.

So great was the number of the Midianites, that they "left no sustenance for Israel" (vi. 4), "and Israe was greatly impoverished because of the Midianites" (vi. 6).

Hence we read "Gideon threshed wheat by the wine-press, to hide it from the Midianites" (vi. 11).

The threshing-floors were in exposed situations that the wind might blow away the chaff; but, as Gideon dared not thresh the wheat there, he had to work under cover, inside the wine-press.

There, the angel of Jehovah appeared to him and spoke to him.

We thus reach the essential point which brings Gideon into the eleventh chapter of Hebrews.

If Gideon believed God, he must have "heard" from God; for faith cometh only "by hearing." And if he heard, Jehovah must have spoken.

This becomes, therefore, the starting point of Gideon's faith, and of our consideration of it.

Twelve times Jehovah spoke to Gideon. Twelve times he heard Jehovah's words. Twelve, because the whole subject had to do with *government* and *rule* ; Jehovah's end being to bring His people out of the rule of the Midianites, and back once again under His own Rule and Government.

But the Instrument must first be prepared for the work it has to do. The servant must be fitted for the service he has to perform.

Hence, the first seven times Jehovah spake were connected with this object ; and, what was said had to do entirely with Gideon's *personal qualification* for the position he was to occupy.

Seven is the number of *spiritual* perfection, and therefore this stands first. There must first be spiritual "power from on high," before there can be effective service.

Hence, when wise men were wanted to carry out a business work, requiring wise business capacities, the Twelve said, "Look you out seven men full of holy spirit (Gr. *pneuma hagion*) and wisdom, whom we may appoint over this business" (Acts vi. 3). They wanted business men, who could pay as well as pray, but they wanted spiritual men as well. They could get the one without the other, but they needed the two together.

Even so here. For the work that was to be done in freeing Israel from the yoke of Midian, "a mighty man of valour" was needed. That, Gideon was already, but he must needs be made a humble "man of God"; and this was the first thing to be done. God must first do His work with Gideon, before Gideon could do his work for God. To accomplish this, God makes this wine-press of Joash to be to Gideon what He made the back-side of the desert to be to Moses.

All must be accomplished by "the word of Jehovah."

To this end Jehovah speaks *seven* times to him ; just as the Messiah did, in a later day, to the woman of Samaria, to bring her first to herself, and then to Himself (see John iv.) *Seven* times Jehovah speaks to Gideon, and it is ours to watch the process and progress and perfection of this Divine work.

(1) " *Jehovah is with thee* " was the first word (Judg. vi. 12). This was to rouse inquiry ; as the request "Give me to drink" roused inquiry in the woman of Samaria's heart. She asked "How ? " and Gideon asks " Why ? " and " Where ? " *His heart is exercised.* That is the first thing that is needful. Jehovah's work is perfect. To have the heart exercised in Divine truth is far more important than to have an intellectual enjoyment of the truth. It is possible to have the latter, and all the time be a stranger to the former. But, if our heart be first exercised with truth, intellectual enjoyment is sure to follow, and be all the more real and satisfying.

This is Jehovah's object here " Jehovah is with thee " was the first word that Gideon heard. He naturally asks : If this be so, " *Why* then is all this befallen us? and *where* be all His miracles which our fathers told us of ?

Jehovah's first words had accomplished their object. The arrow from His bow had gone home to Gideon's heart. All the rest was included in this. The result was assured.

(2) *Jehovah looked upon him and said, Go in this thy might, and thou shalt save Israel from the hand of the Midianites : have not I sent thee ?*

This repeated reference to Gideon's " might " was intended to bring him to himself, and make him conscious of his weakness, and his inability to undertake such a task.

For his real " might " consisted in the very consciousness of this weakness. It was this that forced him to believe Jehovah's word: " thou shalt save Israel." This was what Gideon " heard ; " and, on this his " faith " was grounded.

Gideon naturally asked, " Wherewith shall I save Israel ? " This brought forth the confession of his impotence. He was concerned with *what he was*. " Behold (he says) my family is the meanest in Manasseh, and I am the least in my father's house " (*v.* 15). In this confession consisted his might. This very poverty and impotence compelled him to cast himself on Jehovah's omnipotence. There could be only one reply to this.

(3) " *I will be with thee, and thou shalt smite the Midianites as one man* " (*v.* 16).

From this Gideon knew that he had " found grace " in Jehovah's sight ; and asked for a sign. Not because he doubted, but because he believed; not to prove the truth of Jehovah's word, but because he would prove the truth of Jehovah's grace, in the acceptance of his offering which he proposed to go and fetch (*vv.* 17, 18).

(4) " *I will tarry until thou come again*," was His next utterance (*v.* 18). And then, when the offering was brought, the angel of God said--

(5) " *Take the flesh and the unleavened cakes, and lay them upon this rock, etc.*" (*v.* 20). This was followed by a miracle, by which Gideon " obtained witness " that he had indeed found grace in Jehovah's sight. The

supernatural fire told him of his acceptance with God, and filled him with awe and fear (*vv.* 21, 22).

This prepared the way for Jehovah's blessing.

(6) " *Peace be unto thee ; fear not.*"

In token of this peace, Gideon built an altar there, with which is connected one of the sweetest of the Jehovah titles—"JEHOVAH SHALOM"—*The LORD send peace !*

All that was now needed was the final command, given in the *seventh* utterance of Jehovah, embodying the outcome of this spiritual preparation, and leading up to the five-fold command connected with Gideon's public mission, in which this Divinely perfect grace was contained and accomplished.

7. *Take thy father's young bullock, even the second bullock of seven years old, and throw down the altar of Baal that thy father hath, and cut down thy Askērah that is by it, and build an altar unto Jehovah thy God upon the top of this rock, in the ordered place, and take the second bullock, and offer a burnt sacrifice with the wood of the Askērah which thou shalt cut down* (vi. 25, 26).

This command was obeyed : and, it at once led up to the end.

It told Gideon that it was indeed Jehovah ; and that he had to do with One who knew everything ; how many bullocks his father had, and even their ages. If He knew this, He knew all else. Hence Gideon, like his father Abraham, " believed God," and obeyed the command which he had heard.

Five more times Jehovah spake to Gideon, and all were commands, connected with the work for which Jehovah had prepared him ; and five more times Gideon heard, believed and obeyed.

We need not dwell on each, but will content our-selves with enumerating them, that our readers may study them for themselves.

The first three (vii. 2, 4, 5) were directions to reduce the number to 300 men. Twenty, and two thousand (20 and 2000 = 2020) returned on Gideon's first proclamation, and 10,000 were left.* After a further test 9700 must have " bowed down on their knees " showing that they were Baal-worshippers and had "bowed their knees unto Baal" (compare 1 Kings xix. 18). Only 300 were left.

Jehovah spoke yet twice more, saying 1st, " *By the 300 men that lapped will I save you* " (vii. 7) ; 2nd, " *Arise, get thee down unto the host, for I have delivered it into thine hand* " (vii. 9).

This completes the cycle of Jehovah's words. We at once see the effect of Gideon's faith in what he had heard ; and we know how it is recorded in the next chapter.

All is now clear ; and Gideon's faith stands out in all its fulness. We are told more of what *he* had heard, than we are told of some others in this great cloud of witness-bearing elders.

We may well say "the time would fail " to write and say all that might be said even of Gideon.

The great facts stand clearly out ; God's servants must be all and each *prepared* for their work. and the *work* itself must be also prepared for them. Only such prepared works are " good works " (Eph. ii. 10, margin) ;

---

* Therefore the original number must have been 12020. not 32,000 as stated in the heading of the chapter. Cp. 1 Sam. vi. 19, ch. xii. 6. From Num. xxxi. 5 we learn that 1,000 from each tribe was prescribed, when Israel was directed by Moses in a former war with Midian. See *How to Enjoy the Bible*, p. 365.

and only such servants are "faithful and wise servants" whom their Lord has appointed and prepared. (Matt. xxiv. 45).

Looking at these seven utterances from Gideon's side, we note :—1. That in this work all begins with God. He must reveal Himself. He *comes* to the soul, as He did to Gideon (vi. 11, 12). He *speaks*, by the Spirit and the Word.

2. The next thing is the result of this revelation,— *an exercised conscience* (*v.* 13): a heart which is moved by the truth that is heard and received. To have a spiritual experience of truth is essential ; while a mere *intellectual enjoyment* of truth stands for nothing, except. it may be,—the hardening of the heart against its real power. Intellectual enjoyment belongs to time ; but spiritual enjoyment goes on to, and carries us into, eternity.

Oh ! for a spiritual interest in God's word, written, For the result of that brings to us a third blessing :

3. *A sense of our impotence* for producing or doing anything good.

This is not a mere concern about what I have *done*, but about what *I am*. "My father's family IS the meanest in Manasseh, and I AM the least in my father's house " (*v.* 15, marg.).

This is the next thing with all who have to do directly with Jehovah. "I AM vile " (Job. xl. 4). " I AM undone " (Isa. vi. 5). " I AM a sinful man O Lord " (Luke v. 8).

When this position is taken, there can be worship : not before. People may " set " the Divine communica- tions to music, and " render " such words as " I have sinned " with all a musician's art and skill before an audience; but, not until our hearts have been *exercised* by the Divine word, can we say, from its depths, " I AM a sinful man " before the Lord.

4. Only then can we truly understand the spiritual nature of worship. Only then can we know that our offering has been accepted with a Divine acceptance (*vv.* 20, 21), and

5. Enjoy the Peace which our Divine Substitute has "made" (Col. i. 20), and "preached" (Eph. ii. 17), and "given" (John xiv. 27); and realise that " He IS our peace " (Eph. ii. 14), and that His peace "fills" our hearts (Rom. xv. 13) and "keeps" (Phil. iv. 7) and rules our hearts (Col. iii. 15).

The enjoyment of this peace comes, when He speaks peace to our hearts; and says, as He said to Gideon, " *Peace be unto thee, Fear not* " (vi. 23).

6. Then, Jehovah is worshipped as the One Who has made this peace, and sent it as His gift. Then He is known as Jehovah Shalom (vi. 24); and all follows in perfect order.

Now, and not before, was Gideon's preparation complete. Now, and not before, are we, with a like experience, ready for effective and acceptable service.

7. This comes with the command (vi. 27). A prompt obedience follows, and brings with it the only one thing which is now required to bring Jehovah's design to a successful conclusion. And even this must still come from Himself. It is "power from on high "; and, the end is not merely the defeat of Midian or the deliverance of Israel, but the *fulfilment of His word* which Gideon had heard and believed, and obeyed: " *the Spirit of Jehovah came upon Gideon* " (vi. 34).

If we would complete Gideon's witness by expressing it in harmony with the other witnesses, we should say :

By faith, Gideon, " out of weakness was made strong, waxed valiant in fight, turned to flight the armies of the aliens " (Heb. xi. 34).

Even so will it be with us who believe what we have heard from God.

2. Barak: Faith Conquering Through God

WE have seen that BARAK, who is mentioned next,
in Heb. xi. 32, is not the next in Chronological
or Canonical order, in Judg. iv.; and the reason (with
the Structure) was given in considering the faith of
Gideon.

When Barak was raised up, the twenty years, during
which Jabin king of Canaan " mightily oppressed the
children of Israel," were drawing to a close (Judg. iv. 3).

Deborah was acting as judge; but she was not a
judge in the proper sense of the term. She was "a
prophetess," but " she judged Israel *at that time* . .
and the children of Israel came up to her for judgment"
(Judg. iv. 4, 5).

That she was not a judge whom Jehovah had
"raised up" is shown by the fact that it is written:
" When Jehovah raised them up judges, then Jehovah
was with the judge, and delivered them out of the
hand of their enemies *all the days of the judge*"
(Judg. ii. 18).

But here, the people were under oppression, and
were not delivered; hence, the importance of the
words "she judged Israel *at that time*."

Though not a judge, she was " a prophetess," and
Jehovah spoke to her, and through her. This lies at
the root of BARAK's faith, and here is the reason why
he is included in the " great cloud of witnesses " in
Heb. xi. His faith came "by hearing," and he *heard*
the word of Jehovah through the words of Deborah :—

" Hath not Jehovah, God of Israel, commanded,

saying, Go and draw toward Mount Tabor, and take
with thee ten thousand men of the sons of Naphtali,
and of the sons of Zebulon, and I WILL DRAW
unto thee to the river Kishon Sisera the captain of
Jabin's army, with his chariots and his multitude;
and I WILL DELIVER HIM INTO THINE
HAND."

Here was the grand victory and deliverance from
the oppressor's hand to be hoped for; and faith, in
the word which Barak had heard, was the ground on
which this hope was based. (Heb. xi. 1).

How that faith was justified, and, how Jehovah was
faithful to His word, we all know.

Yet another word of Jehovah came to Barak in
verse 14, when "Deborah said unto Barak, Up; for
this is the day in which the Lord hath delivered
Sisera into thine hand. Is not Jehovah gone out
before thee."

Victory was thus assured; and all the rest followed
in due course.

Barak could not have been surprised when Jael
came out to him and showed him the dead body of
the foe of Israel and of Israel's God.

He had "heard" from God, through Deborah, that
He would "sell Sisera into the hand of a woman,"
and here His word was seen fulfilled.

We have no sympathy with those who endeavour to
apologise for God, and who think they see a difficulty
in His actions here, or in Deborah's song which
celebrates them.

Those who do not rightly divide the word of truth
do not find the truth. They naturally read the present
Dispensation of Grace into the past dispensation of

Law. They thus create their own difficulties; and apologise not only for Deborah's song, but for David's so-called "Imprecatory Psalms."

We see no difficulty whatever in either; but we see how Jehovah's administration of that day, in Law and righteous judgment, was as perfect as His administration of grace in the present day.

The Lord in a later day said: " Blessed is he whosoever shall not be offended in Me."

That is, " Blessed is he who shall not be stumbled [at any thing] in Me " (Matt. xi. 6). Yes, Blessed, indeed, is he who finds nothing to stumble at in His words, in His work, in Himself, in His grace. Many do stumble even at " the *gracious* words of Christ," let alone His judicial words; and many stumble at the righteous words and acts of Jehovah the God of Israel.

They stumble at the latter because they measure by the wrong standard, and judge by the wrong rule.

To those out of Christ Jehovah is " a man of war ;" but only to His own People is He the " God of Love." He is a God " having mercy on whom He will have mercy, and whom He will be hardeneth " (Rom. ix. 18).

He has no need that any should apologise for Him. His command is that we shall hear, believe, and obey. It is written, " Abraham *believed* God." It does not say Abraham *understood* God.

We have only to heed what is written in order to praise Jehovah for His righteous acts.

In our preceding paper on Gideon, we remarked that Barak and Samson are placed (in Heb. xi. 32) out of their Canonical and Chronological order ; Barak, after Gideon, and Samson before Jepthah.

One effect of this is to bring Barak and Samson together; and this, because both were associated with women.

In the case of Samson, he was betrayed by both his wife and Delilah.

In the case of Barak, Deborah commenced his mission, while Jael completed it.

Why this association of these two women? There must be some good reason for it; for all His words are perfect.

We have only to read the history more carefully, to see that the oppression of Jabin had a very special character. It was directed with the object of carrying off the women of Israel. This is clearly shown by the words of the " wise ladies " of the mother of Sisera, the General of Jabin's army, in Judg. v. 30

    " Have they not sped ?

    Have they not divided the prey,

    To every man a damsel or two ? "

And why rehearse the righteous acts of Jehovah at " the places of drawing water ? "

Why does it say " THERE " shall they rehearse His praises ?

Because " there " were the places where the *women* were accustomed to draw the water. It was the women's special work, as may be seen from Gen. xxiv. 11.

" There " Moses betook himself in Ex. ii. 15-20, and rendered signal service to the daughters of Jethro.

It was this special characteristic of the oppression of Jabin, king of Canaan.

The circumstances were so well known that the *Ellipsis* needed no supply of words then, as they do for us to day.

We may well supply " the women " instead of " *the inhabitants* " in Judges v. 7. We may say "[the women of] the villages ceased in Israel," or " The villages in Israel ceased [to be safe] ."

In verse 6 we read " the highways were deserted."

Is not the antithesis clear, when Deborah sang " until I Deborah arose, that I arose, a mother in Israel." Why all this emphasis to call our attention to the fact that it was she, a woman, who was called of God to deliver the women of Israel, and thus to be a mother indeed.

May we not see also, in these things, another attempt of Satan to frustrate Jehovah's purpose to bring in the promised seed of the woman ? In the antediluvian world Satan used his own fallen angels and attempted to destroy the whole human race (Gen. vi.) In Egypt he used Pharaoh and attempted to destroy every man-child at the birth. (Ex. i.) Here, he used Jabin, and attempted to abduct the women in Israel.

No wonder Deborah had reason for her song of deliverance which takes its place with the song of Moses in Ex. xv.

The occasions were similar. Both celebrated a deliverance from a great oppression.

And why is Jael " Blessed above women " while Mary was only " blessed among women ? " Because, there would probably have been no Mary, had there been no Deborah and Jael.

We have no patience with the maudling sentimentality which, instead of believing God, deems it its duty to apologise for Him.

It should be ours to " rehearse the righteous acts of

Jehovah," and to say with Deborah " so let all Thine enemies perish, O Jehovah."

It will be noted how the song ends. The answer of the wise ladies of the mother of Sisera is cut short, by a sudden silence,* to make way for the glorious ending† of the last verse.

All this is because they were Jehovah's enemies, " So perish all THINE enemies O LORD."

Those who hold up their hands in horror at these " righteous acts and judgments " do so because they refuse to rightly divide the Word of truth, as to its Dispensations; and, while they do this, they reverse their principle, and break the hearts of their brethren in Christ by their unrighteous acts and judgments ; and treat us as the enemies of God and His truth, because we are trying to rightly divide that Word.

When we see the evil effects of such inconsistency, we are more than ever convinced that we are right in our effort to obey to the fullest extent the precept of 2 Tim. ii. 15.

Those who thus act are turning things upside down. They first read the principles of this Dispensation of Grace, into Judges v., and create a difficulty which is dishonouring to God's word ; and then they turn round and apply the very principles which they thus condemn, and use them against their brethren in Christ, and, instead of " praying for all saints," are contending with them and condemning them.

Thus we read the history of Deborah's prophecy, Jael's blessing, and Barak's faith ; and believing it, we

---

* The Figure called *Aposiopēsis*.

† Called, the Figure *Epiphonēma*.

desire to profit by the experimental enjoyment of God's truth.

Even so were those to profit whom the Apostle directly addressed.

Barak overcame all difficulties and conquered by his faith ! and they, would be " more than conquerors " by the same faith. Barak's faith was based on what he " heard " from Jehovah by the mouth of a prophetess ; their faith and ours is to be based on what we hear to-day by the mouth of His " Apostle " for us Gentiles.

The messages of old varied with the Divine administrations toward man, and with the duties and circumstances of those who " heard."

And now, the latest messages had been heard from the Apostle Paul in the letters he had written from his prison in Rome. These Hebrew believers had " heard." But, the question was would they believe and obey ? Would they heed the teaching of the Apostle Paul as Barak had believed the prophetess Deborah ? Would they leave behind the things that belonged to an Administration which had passed away, with all its ordinances and legal requirements, and go forth unto a Person—even Christ—and find their all in Him ?

That is the question for us to day. God grant that we may hear, believe, and obey.

3. Samson: Faith Conquering Through God

THOUGH Samson and Jephthah are named together, we have already noticed that SAMSON is connected with BARAK, rather than with Jephthah. This is because, while BARAK was helped by two women (Deborah and Jael), SAMSON on the other hand was betrayed by two women (his wife and Delilah).

But our object in these papers is, not to consider the *history* of these "Elders" as recorded in the Old Testament, but their *faith* as referred to in the New Testament.

Those who read the Old Testament histories without rightly dividing them according to the different Dispensations, and the different principles of the Divine administration which characterised them, are liable to misunderstand the history and misjudge the characters of which they speak.

We have already referred to this in speaking of Barak; but it must also be borne in mind in reading the histories of Samson and Jephthah.

What was appropriate for a Dispensation when God was ruling in Israel among the nations, in righteousness and judgment, is not appropriate for the present Dispensation when He is dealing in grace.

Then, every sin was visited with the judgment it deserved, by the righteous rule of a Righteous God.

But since man has rejected His rule and murdered His Son, God has withdrawn both Himself and His Son; and the world is left to itself and to the rule of "the god of this age."

God is not administering, ordering or ruling its affairs; though He is *over-ruling* all things in order to secure the accomplishment out of His secret counsels and purposes. His Rule, and Dominion is in abeyance; and, while He is silent, He is, by His Spirit whom He has sent, bringing the world in guilty, of sin, and of righteousness, and of judgment (John xvi. 8).

" Of sin (said the Lord) because they believe not on Me."

" Of righteousness, because I go to the Father."

" Of judgment, because the prince of this world is judged."

(1) The world believed not Christ. This is its sin. (2) His " real absence " brings the world in guilty concerning righteousness and manifests that there is no righteousness in it, and (3) that the prince of this world has been judged.

The world waits for nothing but judgment. A judgment-summons has been obtained, and all that is needed now is for " execution " to be put in, and the usurper cast down and cast out.

That is the character of this present Dispensation. God is keeping silence. He is taking out His own people in pure grace; and meanwhile He is dealing with the world on the same principle. His sun rises on the evil and on the good, and His showers descend on the just and on the unjust. (Matt. v. 45).

It was not so in the Dispensation in which Samson and Jephthah lived. God did not keep silence. He ruled among men ; His judgments descended on the evil and his blessings were bestowed on the good. He withheld His rain, and He sent floods.

The standard by which we must judge that Dispensation is wholly different from that by which we must judge this. If we read the present into the past we can have only confusion.

Samson is not to be judged by modern "Church" standards; still less on "Keswick lines."

He was raised up as a "Judge" to act for God in executing His righteous judgment.

He was Divinely set apart and fitted for the work he was appointed to carry out. Even his marriage with a Philistine woman, was "of the LORD" because He sought an occasion against the Philistines (Judg. xiv. 4). If any see a difficulty in this the only answer to it is in Rom. ix. 20.

Let us beware then how we judge Samson in fulfilling this his mission.

One thing marked him out as being worthy of inclusion in this "great cloud of witnesses"; and of mention in this list of "Elders who obtained a good report."

That one thing was *faith*, "He believed God."

Before his birth God had spoken of him to his parents. In Judges xiii. we have the full account of all that was said, and of all that took place.

Of the child that was to be born, Jehovah had said, "he shall begin to deliver Israel out of the hand of the Philistines" (*v.* 5). Manoah and his wife believed these words and obeyed all the instructions given with them.

In a moment of fear, when Manoah knew that he had seen God, his wife, strong in faith, reasoned, as Sarah and Rahab had reasoned before, and came to faith's sure conclusion: "If the LORD were pleased to kill us, He would not have received a burnt offering and a meat offering at our hands, neither would He have shewed us all these things, nor would He at this time have told us such things as these" (*v.* 23).

This was faith's reasoning, and happy shall we be if we remember it for our own peace and blessing.

We shall often find ourselves in circumstances where it will stand us in good stead.

If Manoah's wife could reason thus, how much more can we reason, when we think things are "against us" and say: "He that spared not His Own Son, but delivered Him up for us all, how shall He not, with Him, freely give us all things" (Rom viii. 32). And, if we further feel that we are unworthy of so great a blessing, then, we may recall the fact that the word here rendered "freely," is the same word as that rendered, in John xv. 25, "without a cause"

There was no cause why our Lord and Master should be hated. There was no "cause" why the promise should have been made to Manoah and his wife, rather than any other husband and wife in Israel.

It is precisely for the same reason that we are "justified without a cause by His grace" (Rom. iii. 24). Here, it is the same word as in John xv. 25. So that we can show no cause why we should have the least of His mercies.

Samson was brought up in the strong faith of his parents, and, though no angel had appeared to him, and no Divine voice had spoken in his ears, yet, he had *heard* from his mother's lips the words which had come from God to her.

Samson believed what he had thus heard and grew up in that belief of which we are told in Heb. xi. He wrought the will of God, and fulfilled the word of God.

He "began to deliver Israel." This was the extent of the promise. Nothing was said as to the completion of the work either by him or by another.

When the time for action came "the Spirit of the LORD came mightily upon him." This was another important characteristic of that Dispensation. It differed entirely from the present Dispensation. This was announced by the Lord in John xiv. 17, when He spoke of the then future operation of the Holy Spirit and said : "He dwelleth with you and shall be in you."

Before this, the Spirit "came upon" a person; and "departed" from him again.

Three times do we read that He thus "came upon Samson" (Judg. xiv. 6, 19; xv. 14); and after that, we read in xvi. 20, that "the LORD had departed from Samson."

Hence, it was perfectly correct and appropriate to that dispensation to pray, "take not Thy Holy Spirit from me" (Ps. li. 11). But it is equally wrong to pray that prayer now, in this dispensation, as it was right in that dispensation.

How can one who has been assured by the Lord's word; "He dwelleth with you, and shall be in you," pray that He may not be taken away.

And on the other hand, how can we pray for Him to "come" (as we are made to do in so many of our hymns) when He has already come, and is here.

No one can imagine the havoc that hymns have made in lowering Christian experience; or how terrible has been their effect in creating a false system of theology.

Just as "science" is man's reasoning about God's *works*, so "theology" is man's reasoning about God's

Word. Otherwise no intelligent Christian instructed in that Word would frame his theology for this present dispensation of grace, on the principles which governed the past dispensation of works.

It is the same low condition of Christian standing which makes it possible for any believer to-day, to put the Epistles to the assemblies in Rev. ii. and iii. on the same footing as the Pauline Epistles ; and to imagine that the Epistle to the Assembly at Ephesus (Rev. ii. 1-7) is addressed to " the saints which are at Ephesus, and to the faithful in Christ Jesus . . . blessed with all spiritual blessings in the heavenlies, in Christ, . . . chosen in Him, and accepted in the beloved " (Eph. i., 1-6).

When we read of "the Spirit of the LORD coming UPON Samson," it is a sufficient guide to a right appreciation of the rest of Samson's history.

His morals are not to be judged by the standards of the modern views of "holiness." All that is written is " for our learning," not for our criticism.

But there is another kind of criticism which we must not pass over, and that is the difficulty which some have found in believing the miracle connected with his death, when Samson, after prayer, " took hold of the two middle pillars upon which the house stood, and on which it was borne up, of the one with his right hand and of the other with his left," and putting forth his special Divinely-given strength, fell, with the house and all within it (Judges xvi., 29-31). This scripture is illustrated by the discoveries which have recently been made in the excavations of Gezer, where slabs of stones were found on which pillars, exactly similar to those at Gaza stood. These are to be seen there to-day in a similar Temple of Dagon. The pillars were not *let into* the stones, but stood *upon* them, in the centre while the two beams, with their ends resting on the outer walls, met and were joined together on these two central pillars.

All that Samson had to do was to pull them out of the perpendicular, and his end was attained.

Thus the reports of excavations which we have heard from man are proved to be correct by this Scripture which we have heard from God.

Our faith, like Samson's rests on the same Word: and, though what we have heard differs as to its subject-matter, our duty and our blessing are precisely the same in our case as in his: and it was the same in the case of those Hebrew believers to whom the Apostle was writing.

He includes Samson in his list of witnesses as being an example of God's truth and God's power. How blessed are our ears to hear what God has spoken to us, and to believe what He has written for our learning.

4. Jephthah: Faith Conquering Through God

JEPHTHAH is introduced to us under the same title as Gideon, "a mighty man of valour " * (Judges xi. 1).

Again, we have not to consider his history as a man, but his faith, which was of God.

He was one who feared Jehovah. In his earliest words he calls Jehovah to witness; and he afterwards went and "uttered all his words before Jehovah, in Mizpeh " (v. 11).

His message to the king of Ammon (vv. 14-27) shows that he was well versed in the history of his People, as recorded in "the book of the Law." He must have studied it closely, and to some purpose; for, he not only knew the historical events as facts, but he recognised them as being ordered by Jehovah.

He traced all to Jehovah. It was He Who had "delivered Sihon and all his people into the hand of Israel" (v. 21). It was Jehovah, God of Israel, who had dispossessed the Amorites before His People (v. 23). What Jephthah and Israel would now possess was what God had given to them (v. 24). And it was Jehovah, the Judge, Whom he called on to judge between Israel and Ammon (v. 27).

Jephthah had *heard* the words of Jehovah as written down in the Scriptures of truth; and he believed them.

This is exactly an instance of what the Apostle refers to in Hebrews xi. He, too, knew the history which Jephthah believed, and the faith which conquered

* By the Figure called *Epanadiplosis* (by which the verse begins and ends with the same word) the verse is rounded off for emphasis, and stamped as important.

through God. This it is that gives Jephthah his place in this great " cloud of witnesses."

When he had thus called on God to judge, we read : "Then the Spirit of the Lord came upon Jephthah," and we again note the words which thus describe the action of the Holy Spirit in that dispensation (*v.* 29).

In the power of that Holy Spirit, Jephthah undertook the war with Ammon, and Jehovah crowned his faith by delivering the Ammonites into his hand (*v.* 32).

This is the exceedingly simple account of Jephthah's overcoming faith ; and there is little to be added to it. He had simply read what Jehovah had done ; and thus heard what He had said. He believed what he had thus read and heard, and this is quite sufficient to cause him to be placed among the " elders who received a good report " on account of their faith.

But, in the case of Jephthah, as in no other, we feel compelled to go out of our way to vindicate him from what we shall show to be the unjust judgment of men.

His God-wrought faith must not be tarnished without the sure and certain warrant of the Word of God itself.

Like Moses, Jephthah " spake unadvisedly with his lips," but this does not touch his faith in what he had heard from God ; his vow was made according to his zeal, but not according to knowledge.

That he would sacrifice his daughter, and that God would not reprobate by one word of disapproval a human sacrifice is a theory incredible. It is only a human interpretation, on which Theologians have differed in all ages, and which has been reached without a careful examination of the text.

It is important to remember that the ancient Jewish

Commentator Rabbi David Kimchi (1160—1232) renders the words of the vow (Judges xi. 31) very differently from the A.V. and R.V., and he tells us that his father Rabbi Joseph Kimchi (died 1180) held the same view. Both father and son, together with Rabbi Levi ben Gerson (born 1288), all of them among the most eminent of Hebrew grammarians and commentators, who ought to know better than any Gentile commentator, gave their unqualified approval to the rendering of the words of the vow which, instead of making it relate to *one* object, translate and interpret it as consisting of *two distinct parts.*

This is done by observing the well known rule that the connective particle ׳ (*vau*, our English *v*) is often used as a *disjunctive*, and means " or," when there is a second proposition. Indeed, this rendering is suggested in the margin of the A.V.

The following passages may be consulted :—

Gen. xli. 44 : "Pharaoh said to Joseph, I am Pharaoh, and without thee shall no man lift up hand OR foot, in all the land of Egypt."

Ex. xx. 4 : "Thou shalt not make unto thee any graven image, OR any likeness of anything that is in heaven above, OR that is in the earth beneath, OR that is in the water under the earth."

Ex. xxi. 15 : "He that smiteth his father OR his mother shall surely be put to death."*

Ex. xxi. 17 : "He that curseth his father, OR his mother, shall surely be put to death."

Ex. xxi. 18 : "If men strive together, and one smite another with a stone, OR with his fist, &c."

---

* Gesenius does not admit the force of this reference; though R. David Kimchi relies upon it.

Num. xvi. 14 : " Moreover thou has not brought us into a land that floweth with milk and honey, OR given us inheritance of fields and vineyards," &c.

Num. xxii. 26 : " When there was no way to turn, either to the right hand OR to the left," &c.

Deut. iii. 24 : " What God is there in heaven OR in earth," &c.

2 Sam. iii. 29 : " One that hath an issue, OR that is a leper, OR that leaneth on a staff, OR that falleth on the sword, OR that lacketh bread," &c.

1 Kings xviii. 10 : " There is no nation OR kingdom, whither my lord hath not sent to seek thee."

1 Kings xviii. 27 : " Either he is talking OR he is pursuing, OR he is in a journey."

With a negative, the rendering " NOR " is equally correct and conclusive :—

Ex. xx. 17 : " Thou shalt not covet thy neighbour's wife, NOR his manservant, NOR his maidservant, NOR his ox, NOR his ass, NOR anything that is thy neighbour's.

Deut. vii. 25 : " Thou shall not desire the silver OR gold that is on them, NOR take it unto thee," &c.

2 Sam. i. 21 : " Neither let there be rain upon you, NOR fields of offerings," &c.

Psalm xxvi. 9 : " Gather not my soul with sinners, NOR my life with bloody men."

---

* We have the same in 1 Kings ii. 9, where David is mis-represented in the same manner. David is giving charge to Solomon concerning Shimei. David says "I sware unto him by Jehovah that I would NOT put him to death with the sword. Now therefore hold him NOT guiltless (for thou art a wise man, and knowest what thou oughtest to do unto him) NOR bring thou his hoar head down to the grave with blood." The rendering of the second disjunctive as "but" entirely reverses the meaning of what David said.

Prov. vi. 4 : " Give not sleep to thine eyes, NOR slumber to thine eyelids."

Prov. xxx. 3 : " I neither learned wisdom, NOR have the knowledge of the holy."

We are now in a position to read and understand the words of Jephthah's vow, where we have the same word, or rather the letter which represents it, in the Hebrew.

" Jephthah vowed a vow (*i.e.*, made a solemn vow) unto Jehovah," which he had a perfect right to do. Such a vow was provided for in the Law which prescribed exactly what was to be done in such cases ; and even when the vow affected a person (as it did here) that person could be redeemed if it were so desired See Lev. xxvii. where in verse 1-8 it affected " persons," and verses 9-13 it affects " beasts " ; and verses 14-15 a house.

It thus seems clear that Jephthah's vow consisted of two parts ; one alternative to the other. He would either dedicate it to Jehovah (according to Lev. xxvii.) ; or, if unsuitable for this, he would offer it as a burnt offering.

It should be noted also that, when he said " Whatsoever cometh forth of the doors of my house to meet me," the word " whatsoever " is Masculine. But the issuer from his house was Feminine, and therefore could not come, properly, within the sphere of his vow certainly not according to the literal meaning of his words.

In any case, it would have been unlawful, and repugnant to Jehovah, to offer a human being to Him as a burnt-offering, for His acceptance.

Such offerings were common to heathen nations at

that time, but it is noteworthy that Israel stands out among them with this great peculiarity, that human sacrifices were unknown in Israel.

It is recorded that Jephthah " did with her according to his vow which he had vowed, and she knew no man " (*v*. 39). What has this to do with a burnt offering, one way or the other ? But it has everything to do with the former part of his vow, in dedicating her to Jehovah. This seems to be conclusive. It has nothing to do with a sacrificial death, but it has to do with a dedicated life. She was dedicated to a perpetual virginity.

To what else can the " custom in Israel " refer (*v*. 39, 40) when " the daughters of Israel went yearly to lament the daughter of Jephthah the Gileadite, four days in a year " (*v*. 40).

The word rendered "lament " occurs only in one other passage in the Hebrew Bible, and that happens to be in this very book. So that we could not possibly have a surer guide to its meaning.

The passage is in Judg. v. 11, " There shall they *rehearse* the righteous acts of Jehovah." It means to *talk with others* hence to rehearse together.

This being done annually, the friends of Jephthah's daughter went to rehearse with her, this continued virginity of her life, and not to mourn over the past fact of her death.

We may conclude from the whole tenor of scripture, as well as from Ps. cvi. 35-38. Is. lvii. 5, etc., that human sacrifices were abomination in the sight of God ; and we cannot imagine that God would accept, or that Jephthah would offer, human blood.

To uphold this idea is a libel on Jehovah as well as on Jephthah.

We can understand Voltaire and other infidels doing this, though they reason in a circle, and depend on the two cases of Isaac and Jephthah's daughter (which we dispute) to support their contention. Their object is clear. But what are we to say of the "higher" critics, most of whose conclusions are to be found, in some shape or another, in the writings of French and English Atheists and Deists of the last century?

On the other hand, it is worthy of note to remark how the enemy of God's word has used even innocent persons to perpetuate traditions which bring a slur on Jehovah's works and words.

Milton's words combined with Haydn's music (The Oratorio of " The Creation ") have rivetted the tradition on the minds of all that God created "chaos," whereas "all His works are perfect " in beauty and in order.

Milton's words, again, combined with Handel's music (the Oratorio of " Jephthah ") have perpetuated the tradition that an Israelite father offered his daughter as a burnt-offering to Jehovah.

It is too much to hope that these words of ours can do much to break the tether of tradition with regard to either of the above important subjects.

There is Rutualism to contend with on one hand, but there is *Ritualism* on the other ; and so deep are the ruts, that only the strongest faith (like the strongest axles) can get out of them with success.

We need something of Jephthah's faith in the inspired records of God's Word and words. He believed what Jehovah had caused to be written in "the book of the Law." He had read and pondered over those records of Jehovah's words and works, or he could not have spoken so strongly and so truly of what had been written for his learning.

May it be ours to have a like faith, so that when we have to contend with those who oppose us, we may not depend on our own arguments or our own wisdom, but quote God's Word written, and use "the sword of the Spirit"—the God-breathed words which are so profitable to equip the man of God, and all who would speak for Him, when we meet with those who "resist the truth."

Jephthah had heard,
Jephthah had believed, and
Jephthah was one of that group of overcomers
who conquered through God.

5. David, Samuel, and the Prophets

WE come to the last named in this first of the two groups, which correspond with the first group (Abel, Enoch and Noah), and are connected, as they were, with God.

And here, we have this group of three, followed by ten particulars, and characteristics of faith, which apply in part to them, respectively, but belong to others whose acts are mentioned but not their names.

All is connected with conquering and overcoming ; and all is done THROUGH God.

The former of the last two groups, differs from the latter ; in that those in the latter group, do not conquer, but suffer. They likewise are connected with GOD : and not with themselves, or man, as are the other individual cases named. They are overcome by man, but they suffer FOR God. These latter are simply called "others," and are not even named.

But all is through Faith.

DAVID

is the first named in verses 32-35 :—

" And David, and Samuel, and the prophets. Who, through faith, subdued kingdoms, wrought righteousness, obtained (or realised) promises, stopped the mouths of lions, quenched the violence of fire, escaped the edge of the sword, out of weakness were made strong, were made valiant in war, put to flight the armies of the aliens, women received their dead to life again."

Here we have ten particulars; but it is very difficult to apportion them precisely among those who are included in this first group. So we will take the ten particulars in order.

a. Subdued Kingdoms

If we followed others, we should immediately think of Joshua, and his conquest of Canaan ; and David, and his subjugation of Syria, Moab, Ammon, Amalek, Edom, and the Philistines (2 Sam. viii.); but, the Greek of this passage is remarkable. It does not direct our thoughts so much to warfare, or to the arms and munitions of war, but to conflict which may be moral rather than material, and internal rather than external.

It is natural that these words should be taken in a material rather than a moral sense, in the view of the natural man. When man thinks of evil, he generally associates it with outward evil acts which are more directly connected with man—and not with the moral and spiritual evil which is so abhorrent in the sight of God.

Here, as in all else, " Man looketh on the outward appearance, but Jehovah looketh on the heart." (1 Sam. xvi. 7).

Man makes crusades against outward evils, because he can see them ; and they interfere with his own ease and peace. He can wage war against the " works of the flesh " for these, Scripture says, are " manifest." Man can understand these. Hence, we find him contending against " murders, drunkenness, revellings, and such like," but " idolatry, witchcraft (spiritism), hatred, variance, wrath, strife, seditions," of these he takes little note, except to give them encouragement rather than opposition.

It is the same in things ecclesiastical. The things that are "manifest" engage his attention. Man can see them; and if he abhors them, he protests against the rites and ritual. He can see the masquerading of the Mass, and these things are offensive to his eye. But what of the " Idolatry," which is a sin of the heart, and is the sin for which God has reserved His severest judgments? This can be indulged in and inculcated without any outward practices which are offensive to the eye.

Man might succeed in abolishing all outward practice of ecclesiastical and social evils, but the spiritual and moral evils would remain. Altars might be removed, but the pulpits would remain, and from these all the moral and spiritual evils which are abomination in the sight of God would be used to further the same ends.

The same principle is seen at work in the interpretations of the words before us : "subdued kingdoms." We can think only of actual warfare. But the Greek word (used in Heb. xi. 32), turns our thoughts into another channel.

It is not the word for fighting with weapons, as soldiers, in war ; but it is the word used for contending or wrestling, as athletes in the arena.

There are other words for waging war, either of which would have been more appropriate here, had warfare been intended. Either *strateuomai*, or *polemeō* would be ready to hand, if needed. But the word is *katagonizomai* and occurs nowhere else in the New Testament. It implies the entering into (successful) conflict with kings and kingdoms: not with carnal weapons to obtain material issues; but with moral weapons for the upholding of spiritual truth.

Such conflict as Samuel had with Saul; or Elijah with Ahab; or Elisha and the prophets with other kings of Israel, of which the sacred history furnishes many examples.

Their conflict was for truth; the truth of God. They contended against Royal and national idolatry, and departure from God.

They wrestled mightily against the advancing apostasy, and the encroachments of Royalty on the duties of the priests, the worship of God and the liberties of the people; they fearlessly stood up for the weak against the strong, for the right against the wrong.

Micaiah could proclaim the truth of God against Ahab and the false prophets of Baal; Jeremiah could be strong in his witness against Jehoiakim; and this in the spite of the greatest oppostion.

Micaiah could stand and be smitten in the face. Jeremiah could go into prison; and other faithful prophets could successfully contend against error in spite of neglect and contumely.

The whole matter assumes quite a different complexion when once "look on that which Jehovah looketh;" and take a moral, instead of a material view of it.

This view is not only warranted by the word employed, but is suggested by it.

And how was this conflict with error successfully carried out? The answer is supplied. It was "through faith." Through believing God; believing what He had spoken to them; obeying the voice they had heard, and the command they had received. This faith enabled them to stand, and to stand alone, with God, and for God, and THROUGH God.

They did not merely witness *against* evil, but they contended *for* the truth.

Hence, they were true protestants. The first syllable of this Latin word is *pro*, which means FOR. It is not *con*, which means AGAINST. Everyone knows the difference between "pro and con." But the very mention of this fact condemns much of the protestantism of the present day. Like many other words it has degenerated by use, and has come to have just the meaning which men's acts give it—a purely negative meaning. "Protest" has come to be used only in the sense of protest *against*, instead of witness *for*.

The second part of this Latin word is *testans*, which means "witnessing." So that a true Protestant is one who witnesses FOR : *i.e.*, FOR God, FOR His truth, FOR His Word.

This was exactly the witness and work of the prophets of old.

In this connection 2 Chron. xxiv. 19, is interesting and enlightening. "Yet He (Jehovah) sent prophets to them to bring them again unto Jehovah." They were sent for positive and constructive work, not merely or necessarily for negative and destructive work. And then it is added "And they testified against them." In the Latin Vulgate (*i.e.*, the Translation or Bible of the Church of Rome), these last words are rendered "QUOS PROTESTANTES" meaning, "who [were] witnesses FOR [Jehovah]": in other words "WHO [WERE] PROTESTANTS."

It is strange that this evidence should come from the Church of Rome. That Church, ignorant of its own

Bible, tells us that the word "protestant" was invented at the Reformation, and was used of the Reformers and their followers, for the first time, after the Diet of Spires. But, centuries before this (Rome's own Bible being witness), the word was used of God's faithful servants the prophets.

We may turn the Word, and its lessons, against that church, for it was the Reformers who were the true successors of those prophets of old whom God raised up to be faithful witnesses FOR Him, and His truth.

Alas that so many who call themselves Protestants to-day are witnesses only *against* error, and not *for* truth. They are "Anti-Romanists" instead of witnesses FOR the Word of God which Rome at once both hates and fears.

If this lesson could be written in our hearts, we should soon render more effective service. We should not merely be opposed to the varied and outward forms which Rome's errors take; but we should understand, and be able to witness for the truth which those errors have displaced, and the doctrines of the Word of God which must replace the tradition of men.

If this lesson could be learned we could act upon it in another sphere. We should be found not merely contesting against a brother with the view of putting him in the wrong, or defeating him in argument; but we should have faith in the truth which we hold, and should be content with witnessing FOR that truth, instead of combatting error, or defeating an opponent.

We should depend less on our own words, and more on God's Word; for, if men will not believe His words they will not believe ours.

Let our knowledge of that Word be such, that we may always have some of its words ready for use. Then, if we "believe God" and believe His words we can sow that good seed, and leave it to do its own blessed work. We shall have perfect confidence in the seed of the Word, and go on our way, and sow more. Of the Enemy of the Word, it is written. "He sowed tares among the wheat AND WENT HIS WAY" (Matt. xiii. 25). He had no doubt whatever as to what the result would be: and had no anxiety about it. He "went his way." He knew perfectly well what would spring up. Cannot we have the same confidence in the "good seed" of the Word; and go on our way and sow more; instead of waiting to reap; or remaining behind to argue about it; or to see if it is coming up? Do not we know exactly what the result will be?—even the purpose and pleasure of Jehovah (Isa. lv. 11).

This we shall do if we believe God. Our witnessing will be FOR Him, and not merely against man.

But there is another point which we may consider in connection with this. The second evidence written concerning the overcoming faith of these prophets is, that they

b. "Wrought Righteousness"

This, again, we may take as meaning that they *asserted the right and delivered the messages of God's retributive justice;* and were, in certain cases, the instruments in its accomplishment.

It was Elijah who asserted the right of Jehovah to the worship of His People, and executed His righteous judgment on the prophets of Baal. It was the same Elijah who was sent with the message to Ahab and

Jezebel denouncing their sins and announcing their coming judgment.

It was "the man of God that came from Judah" who brought the messages to Jeroboam, and spoke for and from God as to the future defilement and destruction of the altar he had built; a prophesy which was fulfilled long years after by king Josiah.

Alas! we all know how that man of God failed after his successful conflict with king Jeroboam. And this adds to the importance and significance of his example. As long as he believed and obeyed the word which he had "heard" from Jehovah, all was well; for the path of obedience is ever the place of safety.

He could say to Jeroboam, "If thou wilt give me half thine house, I will not go in with thee; neither will I eat bread nor drink water in this place; for *so was it charged me by the word of Jehovah.*"

When the "old prophet" who lived at Bethel said "Come home with me and eat bread," he got the same answer.

But, when the old prophet alleged that an angel had given him an order (though it was directly opposite to the solemn charge of Jehovah) the man of God that came from Judah believed what the old prophet told him. This is called (1 Kings xiii. 21), disobedience, but the word in Hebrew is the same as that used in Num. xx. 24; xxvii. 14, of the sin of Moses and Aaron at Meribah, where it is spoken of as *rebellion.*

Yes, it is rebellion against God to believe even an angel in a matter on which God has already spoken by His Word.

How much more is it rebellion in the present day

for individuals to profess that they have received *a new revelation.*

What a solemn responsibility rests on us all to reject such a revelation, and to resent such a claim.

Even if made by an angel himself, each one of us is bound not only to reject him and his message, but *to pronounce him accursed.* For the word of Jehovah, by the Holy Spirit in Gal. i. 8, 9, is: "Though we or an angel from heaven preach any other gospel unto you than that which we have preached unto you *let him be accursed.*"

"If any man preach any other gospel unto you THAN THAT YE HAVE RECEIVED *let him be accursed.*"

But if the claim be made by mere mortals of the earth as it is to-day in the cases of several new religions. What are we to say? Is it possible to increase the solemnity of the Divine denunciation so positively asserted and declared above!

In the case of "the old prophet" we are distinctly informed that

"HE LIED UNTO HIM"

The man of God therefore in ceasing to believe God —believed a lie!

And yet we are told on every hand that "it does not matter what a man believes so long as he is sincere."

But *it did matter* to the man of God from Judah. It cost him his life, and caused him to die a violent death. His sincerity did not save him.

And the more sincerely we believe a lie, the worse it will be for us; whether it be an investor who believes a lying Prospectus, or a woman who believes the promises of a lying Impostor. The one loses his property; the other loses what is dearer than life, and gains a living death.

Sincerity is of no avail. The greater the sincerity with which we believe what is not true, the more certain and real will be our ruin.

It is WHOM and WHAT we believe, that matters; and, in the spiritual sphere, safety is found in believing only God, and His truth. Those who continue in their refusal to believe what is the truth, must not be surprised if they are left to believe the lie (2 Thess. ii. 11).

Oh! to believe God! What peace it gives. What happiness it brings! The path of believing Him is the path of safety.

Let us shun, as we would shun the Evil one himself, anything that is put before us which professes to be in any way a new revelation; or an addition to " what we have received " from God.

This, alone, will be sufficient to preserve us from such modern errors as Mormonism, and Eddyism, and all other forms of new religions which rest on an *addition* to the Bible " which we have received" from God.

Let us believe God and work righteousness by asserting the right, and thus warning men of God's retributive justice as " His servants the prophets warned Manasseh " in 2 Kings xxi. 10-16. The passage is worth reading in this connection, though too long to be quoted here.

Such was the commission which Jeremiah received (Jer. i. 10), when according to the Hebrew idiom he was said to do what he was to declare, according to the word of Jehovah, should be done to the nations to whom he was sent by Jehovah Himself.

5. David, Samuel, and the Prophets

c. "Obtained Promises" (vs. 33)

AGAIN we have to see that we do not follow any traditional interpretation; but we have to discover what the Holy Spirit would have us understand from the words He has chosen to use. These are the words which are "inspired," not the words which any English or other Translators may use; though modernism delights in demolishing what no average Bible Student asserts, and seeks, by denying the inspiration of a translation, to get rid of inspiration of the Sacred Text altogether.

Misled by the rendering "obtain," some Bible readers see in this word a trace of human merit; as though we might be able by human effort to deserve and thus "obtain" Divine promises.

But, in its very essence, a "promise" is all of grace; and, moreover, these Elders, referred to, received these promises "through faith."

Therefore, they *must* have *heard* them before their faith could have had anything to do with them at all. The *hearing* came first, then the *promise* which had been heard. And, not till after this, the *faith* which believed the promise, was "persuaded of it, and "embraced" it (*v.* 13).

This is the essence of the word here used, which is not the ordinary word for either obtaining, or, indeed, for receiving.

It is *epitugchanō*, and means to *happen on, to light on,* or *hit on* (as we say) as by good fortune or favour; and this, unexpectedly and undesignedly. There are eight other words which are rendered "obtain," which do include effort. But merit or effort is altogether excluded by the word used in this passage.

This, indeed, would still be the case, even if one or other of the eighteen words rendered "receive;" had been used, as four of them are in verses 8, 11, 13, 17, 19, 31, 35, 39. In verse 17 we read: "Abraham when he was tried offered up Isaac; and he that had received the promises offered up his only begotten son."

How did Abraham "receive" the promises? and why did he receive them? Abraham was an idolater living in Chaldæa, a Gentile, never having even "heard" of "the living and glorious God" who appeared to him there (Acts vii. 2).

Before Abraham had ever heard of "the land of promise," the Blessed Promiser appeared to him; and what he had never expected was revealed to him.

Abraham believed God. He believed the promises God made to him. He did not "obtain" the promises, but he was "persuaded" of them and "embraced" them.

All this is involved in the ordinary word used of Abraham. But there is more in the word used here in our verse (33). This means that, not only did the promises unexpectedly come to them, but that, by faith, they realized them, and proved them true.

Thus it was with all those favoured ones who are included in this group.

We have already referred to Abraham, who stands out above all as the most notable example; and, it may be that all others who are to be included are not merely those who received promises connected with themselves and with their own individual experiences, but more especially the Messianic promises as they were from time to time communicated.

Joshua, Caleb, Gideon, Manoah, and others who might be named, all received personal promises, which had to do with themselves in connection with the work of Jehovah ; but there were other more " precious promises " which concerned the Messiah and the word of Jehovah.

When the very first promise came to Abraham, it came in " the land of the Chaldæans " (Acts vii. 4), and it concerned another land "the land of promise" (Heb. xi. 9).

When the second promise came to Abraham, it came "in the land of Canaan " (Gen. xii. 5), and it concerned " the seed " of Abraham : " Unto thy seed will I give this land " (*v.* 7).

So that the " *seed* " and the " *land* " are thus marked out as the great subjects of the first promises of Jehovah : and both were bound up with Jehovah's faithfulness to His word : for "faithful is He Which promised." (See Psalm cv. 8-12 ; 42-45).

Here, we must remember the difference between a " promise " and a " covenant."

Every covenant is a promise ; but not every promise is a covenant. A promise is made by one party only ; but a covenant consists of two promises made respectively by the two contracting or covenanting parties.

It is this fact that explains that difficult passage, Gal. iii. 20, where all is seen to depend on this distinction.

The land is not the inheritance of Israel according to the law, because the law was confirmed by a covenant, to which there were two parties (Ex. xxiv. 4-8), as was proved by the fact that there was a mediator, in the person of Moses ; for where there is a mediator, there must be two parties.

But Israel broke their promise, and there is a breach in that covenant.

How then does that affect Israel's inheritance ?

The answer is—not at all ! Because that inheritance does not depend on a *covenant*, but on a *promise* ; and that promise was made 430 years before the covenant of the Law was made.

That is why.

God gave the land to Abraham "by promise ;" for there was only one contracting party. "God is one." There was no other, for Abraham was carefully put to sleep, so that he should have no part in it. He was quite ready to "do his part." He had carefully prepared the sacrifices, dividing them in half, putting one piece over against the other, so that he might walk between them when the moment for making the covenant should come (Jer. xxxiv. 18).

Had he been allowed to carry out his intention there would have been a covenant instead of a promise ; and Abraham would as certainly have broken it, as man ever has done.

"Which My covenant they brake " would have had its illustration in Abraham, as it had afterward in Israel.

The Land, and the Seed, depend not on any covenant, but solely on the promise of the one living and true God.

The promised Land is bound up with the promised Seed—which is Christ as the son and heir of Abraham.

As long, therefore, as Israel rejects Christ, so long must the Land reject Israel. Herein lies the key to the " Zionist movement."

But, as the Land and the Seed both depend on the promise of Jehovah, so also the Throne and the Kingdom depend as much on the same promise.

The promise of the former was given to Abraham, the promise of the latter was made to David.

2 Sam. vii. is the counterpart of Gen. xv. David had not been prepared as Abraham had been, and therefore he was occupied with a thought and an object totally opposite to God's. David's thought was how he should build God a house, a house "made with hands." God's thought was how He would build David's house through his spirtual seed—even Jesus the Messiah.

David was not looking for any promise from God. He was rather thinking of how he would make a promise to God. Hence, when he realised the promise through faith, he was overwhelmed with the flood of Divine grace.

Before this, David sat in his own house, and before himself; and his thought was about himself and where he sat. He did not rise above who 1 am. But when the fulness of Divine grace flowed in upon him he " went in and sat before the Lord, and he said, Who am I, O Adonay Jehovah, and what is my house ? " (2 Sam. vii. 18).

He did not " obtain " this promise in any sense of the word ; he had done nothing to merit it ; and he did not deserve it. It was not only entirely unlooked for, but he was thinking of doing exactly the opposite.

But, once the promise had been heard, David believed

it ; ana " through faith " he enjoyed it, and realised it, as though he already possessed it.

This was all that faith had to do with it.

These Messianic promises were successively received and enlarged by the prophets, and were confirmatory and supplementary to those received by Abraham and David.

God, " at sundry times and in divers manners, spake unto the fathers by the prophets," during the old Dispensation of the Law ; and He spake of Christ ; for, His promises for His people Israel, and for the earth, were all and always, from eternity, in and through Christ.

Hence it was that the enmity of Gen. iii. 15 centred in opposing *the purposes of God in Christ.* That enmity may be traced in the Word of God, all through the ages. It is the thread which runs through the Old Testament. It was not so much the person of Christ whom Satan opposed, but Jehovah's *purpose* in Him. As this purpose of God was successively unfolded the enmity of Satan is seen opposing it.

So soon as the promise of the SEED had been made to and through Abraham (Gen. xii. 3), Satan attempted to destroy it by working on Abraham's fears to deny his wife, and thus jeopardise and frustrate the promise (Gen. xii. 10-20). So soon as the promise of the LAND was made (Gen. xi. 31), Satan occupied it, in advance, with the nations of Canaan (Gen. xii. 6) and did a work which eventually ended in the disruption of the kingdom, the dispersion of Israel, and the captivity of Judah.

So soon as the promise was made concerning David (1 Sam. xvi. 1), Saul's javelin was used to accomplish, if possible, his destruction (1 Sam. xviii. 10, 11) ; and so soon as the time through David's seed was announced concerning the Throne and the King, Satan directed his efforts to breaking up the royal line : and, at one time, so nearly accomplished it, that he reduced the succession to the life of an infant (Joash) who had to be hidden six years from his enemy (2 ch. xviii. 1, 31 ; xxi. 4, 17 ; xxii. 10, 12).

So soon as Christ was conceived, Satan worked on Joseph's fears, as he had upon Abraham's, and Mary narrowly escaped being stoned to death (Matt. i. 18, 19, compared with Deut. xxiv., 1).

But the enemy over-reached himself in the death of Christ, for in that lay the purpose of God eventually "by death to destroy him who has the power of death" (Heb. ii. 14 ; 1 John iii. 8).

After the final rejection of Christ by the Dispersion, in Rome (Acts xxviii. 25, 26), the final promise and purpose of God in Christ was revealed for our *faith* through Paul while a prisoner in *bonds*, that we might be delivered from all *bondage* by *receiving the promises* of perfection and completeness in Christ.

And the application for us now is, how do we stand, individually, in relation to these promises? They had been kept secret till then. The purpose of God, as it concerned Christ, had been made known, in the Old Testament in part, but nothing had been revealed about the height of the glory which He was to receive as the result of His humiliation. His " sufferings," and "the glory which was to be revealed," had been made known ; but, the height which that glory was to reach had been kept secret till it was made known in Ephesians i. 19-23 ; Philippians ii. 9-11 ; and Colossians i. 15-20 These secrets were then for the first time revealed for our faith ; and the promise and purpose of God, as to what we are made in Christ and what Christ is made to us, were never known by mortal man, till then. These were the "things of Christ," which He referred to in John xvi. 12-15, as the subject of a then future revelation.

Again, we ask, How do we stand with regard to those "promises" which we have received (not "obtained.") Are we "persuaded of them?" Have we "embraced them?" Have we "confessed" that these promises have made us to be "strangers and pilgrims on the earth" (Heb. xi. 13)? Have we realised them "through faith," and do we rejoice in them as being made our own?

The position of those to whom the apostle was writing, is the position of the vast majority of Christians in the present day.

The promises of God in Christ had been made known, but these Hebrew believers did not embrace them. They were clinging to things made and done with hands ; they would not "leave" the things which were behind. The *sevenfold* foundation of God had been made known in Eph. iv. 1-6, but they preferred the *sixfold* foundation of the new Dispensation which was then passing away.

In former papers we have traced Satan's "enmity" only as far as it related to the PERSON of Christ ; and did not follow it beyond His Ascension ; for we had failed to notice the workings of that enmity as it related to the PURPOSE of God, and as it affects us now, to-day. *That enmity against the purposes of God in Christ has not ceased ;* but our eyes have been veiled, so that we might not see it and its workings.

That Satan is "the god of this age" has been powerfully exposed by others, but chiefly and mainly in the moral, material, religious, and political, spheres. His present activities in *the spiritual sphere have been overlooked*; for the workings of "the god of this age" are to this very end, to-day. It is to veil the minds of them which are without faith, so that the light of THE GOSPEL OF THE GLORY OF CHRIST, who is the image of the invisible God, should not shine forth unto them "(2 Cor. iv. 4). We have not fully seen the preaching of Paul's ministry concerning Christ Jesus as Lord of all (2 Cor. iv. 5), but our eyes have been veiled by Satan's ministers, appearing and working as "ministers of righteousness" (2 Cor. xi. 13-15). These "deceitful workers" preach righteousness; not the righteousness of God, but the righteous living of mankind. They occupy believers with what they can do for God, not with what God has done for us in the promises which we have received and which are in Christ.

This is the outcome of Satan's enmity in this present dispensation. It is manifested to day by "his ministers," and in their ministry.

What they preach *must of necessity appear to be right* and true, or *they would not deceive.* Hence they are called *"deceitful* ministers." When they preach downright error and blasphemy they deceive no one, or but very few. Therefore, the more holy their teaching appears, the more likely is it to "deceive the very elect."

They will preach the sufferings of Christ, but not the glory. They will preach "Christ crucified," but not Christ risen and the power of His resurrection.

They will preach all that concerns man. They will

preach about man and his doings, but not about God's wonderful works ; they will preach about our feelings and experiences, and set us to work at introspection, to our own misery ; they will even occupy us with the attainment of perfection in ourselves, while their minds are veiled to the holiness and perfection which is *already ours in Christ.*

They will even preach " the gospel of the grace of God," but not " the GOSPEL OF THE GLORY OF CHRIST."

For, it is this last which is the object, now, of Satan's enmity.

He did not cease from his labours when Christ ascended into heaven, but he commenced immediately in a new sphere, but with the same object. As the workings of this enmity are manifest throughout the Old Testament dispensation, so are they manifest throughout this present dispensation ; and this is the very form and direction in which we should look for them. How else could he carry out that enmity except by doing his utmost to prevent or hinder God's purposes in Christ from being accomplished ?

We have " obtained promises."

Oh, let us " through faith " cherish these precious promises which we have received, that they may become real to our experience now, as they will one day be seen in all their perfection and all their glory.

Let us indeed go further than that and be occupied not with our gifts, but with the Giver ; not with our blessings but with the Blesser, and with Him to Whose care and keeping all our blessings are now entrusted ; not with the promises, but with the Promiser, and the coming glory of Him in Whom all the promises find their centre and their end.

5. David, Samuel, and the Prophets

d. "Stopped the Mouth of Lions" (vs. 33)

THESE words at once carry our minds back to Samson and Daniel; but, at the same time, they lead us forward to the faith through which those mighty works were effected.

Of one thing we are assured, and that is—that it was "through faith."

We have to remember, that, in all these statements in this whole chapter, it is the same word in the Greek which is rendered "by" and sometimes "through;" and, it is the same faith.

Then, if by faith, SAMSON DAVID and DANIEL must have heard; and it was "through" the faith in what they had heard that they were able to conquer for God.

Samson's parents had already "heard," in converse with "the angel of Jehovah," what they were to do unto the child that should be born, and how they should order the child (Judges xiii. 8, 12). They must have often repeated that promise to Samson, and told of the work for which he had been specially raised up; how he was to be strengthened to carry it out, and, how he, single-handed, was to begin to deliver Israel out of the hand of the Philistines.

Samson knew, without being told, that Divine strength would have to be imparted to him, for he could not even "begin" to deliver Israel in his own strength.

The first thing that we read of him is that he was born, and grew, and that "Jehovah blessed him;" and, "that the Spirit of Jehovah began to move him at times" (Judges xiii. 24, 25).

Thus we see that, though Samson was to "begin to deliver Israel," Jehovah "began" before him; and, the first recorded exploit was that mentioned in Heb. xi. "he shut up the mouth of a lion," for, when he went down with his father and his mother to Timnath, and came to the vineyards of Timnath, a young lion roared on meeting him, and the Spirit of Jehovah came mightily upon him, and he rent him as he would have rent a kid, and he had nothing in his hand" (Judges xiv. 6).

His faith was of "the operation of God;" for He, Whose word Samson had "heard," gave the mighty power through which he overcame the lion.

This faith was still more conspicuous in the case of DAVID; though we are not told exactly what David had heard. That he had heard something is evident from his whole attitude when he got down to the camp of Israel, when the battle was set in array against the Philistines (1 Sam. xvii).

The holy oil had already anointed him, and he was conscious of the Divine presence and power. All that was needed for David was to believe what he had heard.

From Psalm viii. which David wrote, and afterward gave to the director of the Temple-worship, calling it "the death of the champion,"* we learn that David knew of the "strength" which Jehovah had "ordained." (v. 2), and what had been revealed to him of the true David, even of Him who was at once "the Root (from which David had sprung) and also "the offspring" of David (Rev. xxii. 16).

---

*See *The Chief Musician*, and the remarks on the present title of Ps. xxii. A.V.

If David had "heard" about his antitype; and how dominion in the earth had been given to him (Psalm viii. 1, 6, 9): he had surely heard how he (David) was to be the type, and how he should "still the enemy and the avenger" in the person of Goliath (a type also of the yet greater enemy) whom the Messiah is to "destroy with the brightness of His coming" (Isa. xi. 4; 2 Thess. ii. 8).

Even, when relating to Saul, the exploit to which he refers in 1 Sam. xvii., when he stopped the mouth of the lion, he refers all the glory to Him Whom he believed and in Whom he confided. He says "Jehovah Who delivered me out of the hand of the lion . . . He will deliver me out of the hand of this Philistine" (1 Sam. xvii. 37).

While therefore it is said to have been done "through faith," it was not so much faith, as He Whose word faith had heard, that gave the victory to David: "Jehovah That delivered . . . He will deliver."

But it is DANIEL who stands forth as the greatest of these three, and as the one who is particularly referred to in Heb. xi., 33; for, in his case, he did not slay the lions, but God sent His angel to "shut their mouths."

Daniel had heard of Samson and of David, and he believed that the same God could deliver him, if He saw fit to do so.

Even Darius felt sure as to the power of Daniel's God, and said: "Thy God, Whom thou servest continually, He will deliver thee" (Dan. vi. 16); and later, he enquired: "Is thy God, Whom thou servest continually, able to deliver thee from the lions?" (v. 20).

And Daniel replied: "My God hath sent His angel, and hath shut the lions' mouths, that they have not hurt me" (v. 22)

How wonderful! What is here, by Daniel, ascribed to the power and act of God, is ascribed in Heb. xi. 3 by the Holy Spirit, to Daniel's faith.

And this is the way of God; not that we may be puffed up, but that we may be humbled; and, to the heart which is rightly exercised, this will ever be the effect of Divine grace.

It will act with us as it did with David when he "went in and sat before Jehovah and said: ' Who am I, O Adonai Jehovah ? ' "

It is humbling to find that that, which we hardly dared to call faith, is put down to our credit, as though it were our own; while, all the time, we were only working out that which Divine grace had already worked in us (Phil. ii., 12, 13).

It is in the prison Epistles of Paul that we are let into this Divine secret concerning grace and all it contains. There we learn that it is "the gift of God" (Eph. ii., 5, 8). Hence it is that we can be said to do things through grace and "through faith," and through what, ever may be the gift of God to us.

e. "Quenched the Violence of Fire" (vs. 34)

The reference here is, undoubtedly, to Shadrach, Meshach, and Abednego, in the burning fiery furnace, recorded in Dan. iii., 27. They had heard of the oft repeated commands of God that they should not bow down to images. They believed what they had heard, and they obeyed what they believed.

They knew that the present condition of Israel and Judah was due to this very sin of idolatry.

They had heard of God's power to deliver if He saw fit, and, through faith in what they had heard, they were without care, as well as without fear.

" We are not careful to answer thee in this matter" was their reply to the threat which was made to them.

Their faith in the command of God, and in the power of God, gave them perfect rest in His will; for that, after all, is the source of calm peace and rest in the presence of danger, and in the midst of trouble.

This is the point of the Saviour's words in Matt. xi. The chapter is full of that which would bring unrest into the hearts of any of God's servants. John had sent, questioning (*vv.* 2-15); the men of that generation rejected Him. They had charged John with being possessed by a demon (*vv.* 16-18); they accused his Lord of being a glutton and a drunkard (*v.* 19). He had to pronounce His woes over the cities wherein most of His mightiest works were done (*vv.* 20-25); and then we read: "AT THAT TIME Jesus prayed and said: 'I thank Thee, O Father, Lord of heaven and earth . . . . Even so, Father, for so it seemed good in Thy sight.'"

Here was rest indeed! Perfect rest! And it was found in the Father's will.

The whole point of the lesson here conveyed lies in these three words: "AT THAT TIME."

Some Scriptures derive their chief importance from some wondrous revelation of truth made known by them.

Others derive their chief importance from some remarkable word or words employed in them.

Others, again, derive their chief importance from the place where we find them. For every Scripture is perfect and is in the right place, and, to see its perfection, we have to look at what goes before it and what follows it. And we are to examine it closely.

" At that time." What time? The time when the Lord's rejection was determined on: when a council had been held against Him " how they might destroy Him " (Matt. xii. 14).

At the time when John questioned ; when the people calumniated both Himself and His forerunner ; when His mighty works produced no results—" At that time " the Master was *without care ;* and in perfect peace, finding His rest in the Father's will.

This was the result of the faith of these three men in Dan. iii. They said to the king, " we are not careful to answer thee in this matter. *If it be so* our God Whom we serve is able to deliver us from the burning fiery furnace, and He will deliver us out of thine hand O king. *But if not*, be it known unto thee O king, that we will not serve thy gods, nor worship the golden image which thou hast set up " (Dan. iii. 16-18).

Notice the alternatives in these noble words. They were the outcome of a God-wrought faith. " He is able to deliver us from the burning firery furnace." That fact they firmly believed, for they had heard of His almighty power. But, in any case, He would deliver them *out of the king's hand*, for death in that furnace would speedily accomplish that.

Hence they were *without care.*

Oh, that we might learn the same blessed lesson. The Lord has set it for our learning in the most perfect manner. The gem is set in words of infinite beauty in order to impress us with the solemnity of the *lesson* to be learned ; the power of the *command* to learn it ; the perfection of the *promise* conveyed by it ; and the *assured result* in the " perfect " rest which it gives.

Look at the precious gem in its perfect literary setting :—

A | "Come unto me all ye that are weary and heavy-laden." (OUR BURDEN HEAVY.)

  B | "And I will give you rest." (HIS REST GIVEN.)

    C | "Take My yoke upon you, and learn of Me." (HIS LESSON: COMMANDED.)

    C | "For I am meek and lowly in heart." (HIS LESSON: THE REASON FOR IT.)

  B | "And ye shall find rest unto your souls." (OUR REST FOUND.)

A | "For My yoke is easy and My burden is light." (HIS BURDEN LIGHT.)

Note the sparkling of this gem to impress us with its preciousness and its power :—

A | OUR burden HEAVY.

A | HIS burden LIGHT.

B | HIS rest GIVEN.

B | OUR rest FOUND (for we have none to "give")

C | The command to learn the lesson.

C | The reason for learning it.

Can anything be more perfect in its literary beauty ! Can any lesson thus set for us be more blessed in its assured results !

Do we believe what we thus "hear" from His anointed lips ?

If so, we shall exalt the Father's will above all, and, in the face of the fiercest fires which men's hands can kindle, we shall be without care.

Without care as to the "fear of man," and without care as to the "praise of man."

What would we not give to "find" this rest ! Rest in the will of God.

It is to be found only as His own gift, and learnt only in the lesson He has given. We are to learn of Him.

We are not like Shadrach, Meshach, and Abednego, confronted with burning fire and a material furnace ; but we are surrounded with fiery trials which, though they do not consume the flesh, have a more lasting and injurious effect ; for they affect the mind, they wound the feelings, and they break the heart.

The Apostle Paul knew something of these fires when he says he was " in perils by mine own country-men . . . in perils among false brethren."

But we know something of the perils and trials among true brethren ; and nothing can set us perfectly free, and make us *without care*, but a living faith in the living God ; and a blessed assurance that His will is not only best, but is perfect.

Let us hear the words of our Lord and Teacher, and learn of Him. Then, though we shall have no rest to " give," we shall " find " a rest in our most fiery trial ; and we shall be more real and happy than in free-dom from the trial.

We shall find it better to be in the furnace with " the fourth," than outside, alone, concerned about ourselves and occupied with our cares.

We want to be without care at any other time ; but this rest is to be found only " at that time." No other. When the trial is greatest, when the burden is heaviest, when the fire is fiercest, then, " at that time " faith can make us to be without care.

If we " learn " His lesson, and learn it of Him (not from books, or from the experience or exhortation of others) we shall be able to say from the depth of a blessed experience, " I thank Thee, O Father."

"Even so, Father," and find peace, perfect peace; rest, perfect rest.

We shall be "meek," not weak; "lowly," not holy (in ourselves)—no, nothing in or of ourselves; but all *found* in Him, holy in His holiness, lowly in His lowliness; "meek" in His meekness.

This is the application of the example of the faith of Shadrach, Meshach and Abednego, who, through faith, "quenched the violence of fire," and were without care in the presence of the fierceness of the seven-fold heated furnace.

The word rendered "without care" is peculiar. It is one of nine words rendered care or careful, but never so rendered anywhere else, and occurs only in Dan. iii. 16 and Ezra vi. 9. In the latter place it means *to have need of*.

So that what it says to us here is that if we believe what we have heard from God, and have *learned* the lesson set us by our Lord, there is *no need* for us to answer any one who may try us, or oppose us. We are on an altogether different plane, where we have ceased from man; and are with "the fourth," even if it be in a fiery furnace of trial. For we are with One Who can "quench the violence of fire."

5. David, Samuel, and the Prophets

f. Escaped the Edge of the Sword

TIME would indeed fail to tell, in full, how many of those who believed God, proved the truth of His word in this particular manner, and thus overcame through God.

We have already seen how Rahab, through believing the promise made to her by the spies, thus conquered, and thus escaped, when Joshua and his army " utterly destroyed all that was in the city . . . with the edge of the sword " (Josh. vi. 21).

Before the sword fell Rahab and all her house were brought out, and " left without the camp of Israel " (*v.* 23).

Of the many others we may single out

DAVID,

whom Jehovah delivered " from the hurtful sword " (Ps. cxlv. 10).

Here, as in the other examples of faith, we must look beyond their personal escape, as individuals, and see *God's purpose in the escape* ; we must rise above the historical event as ruled by " the will of man " and as seen by the human eye ; and behold, by faith, the unseen design of Jehovah which was over-ruling all for the accomplishment of " His own will."

Hence, in the case of David, we are to see not merely the " escape " of David from the sword of Goliath, but the confirmation of David's faith in the Word of Jehovah.

David had *heard* that word which came to Samuel, as David stood before him : " Arise, anoint him, for this is he " (1 Sam. xvi. 12).

If this was he, who was to become the king over Jehovah's People, and through whom God's purpose in Messiah must be fulfilled, how could he fall beneath Goliath's sword?

David's belief in that word assured him of that " escape ; " and it was emphasised by the fact that, not David, but Goliath himself was slain by the edge of that sword (1 Sam. xvii. 50 51).*

The aim of Satan was at once to get rid of Jehovah's Anointed ; and he hoped to accomplish his end by means of Goliath's sword.

When that failed, then he would use Saul's javelin (1 Sam xviii. 10, 11), and would use it again (1 Sam. xix. 10), when David " escaped that night."

It is not merely David's " escape " that we are to see, but David's faith in Jehovah's Word (1 Sam. xvi.) ; by which word he escaped both Goliath's sword and Saul's javelin.

Another example is furnished in the case of

Elijah

Jezebel's sword was doing its deadly work, engaged in slaying Jehovah's prophets " with the sword " (1 Kings xix. 10, 14) ; and, the word of Jehovah came to Elijah, saying : " Get thee hence and turn eastward and hide thyself by the brook Cherith, that is before Jordan . . . I have commanded the ravens to feed thee there" (1 Kings xvii. 3, 4).

---

* By the Fig. *Hysteresis*, and the consequent structure, 1 Sam. xvi. 14-23 is placed here, *Canonically*, in order to bring together in contrast the Spirit of Jehovah departing from Saul and coming upon David. *Chronologically* and Historically that event comes between verses 9 and 10 of chap. xviii.

This is indicated for us in the words " as at other times " (1 Sam. xvii. 30 as referring to xvi. 14-33). There is no corruption or " misplacement " of the Sacred Text, except to the eye of the " natural " man ; but not to the discernments of the spiritual mind.

The only purpose manifest to the natural eye in this command was the preservation of Elijah's life in the approaching dearth. The same purpose is seen in *v.* 9, "Get thee to Zaraphath . . . and dwell there. Behold, I have commanded a widow woman there to sustain thee."

Not a word is said about any further and deeper Divine purpose in this hiding and nourishing of Elijah. But, there was another, of which Elijah was not informed at the time. It was that he might "escape the edge of the sword."

Elijah heard the command of Jehovah; and, through faith he obeyed. Thus, he was not only sustained in life, but preserved from death, and "escaped the edge of the sword."

The word of Jehovah is like Himself—infinite; it embraces all His will. It contains more than we can see; and the same word accomplishes many different things, includes different designs, and reaches various ends.

It is for us to believe that word, confident that in obeying it we shall accomplish and prosper in many ways, which we may never understand, or be aware of at the time, or ever even hear of.

Elijah learnt later on that he had not only been kept in life during the famine, but that at the same time "escaped the edge of the sword"; for he afterwards reminded Jehovah how Jezebel and the children of Israel had "slain Thy prophets with the sword" (1 Kings xix. 14).

More than one thing will be accomplished if faith acts on the word which it hears from Jehovah.

If we believe God, and know anything of His

infinite wisdom, we shall thankfully depend on Him to direct our way, and we may be sure that it is better than our own way.

We may not see the reason of it at the time ; and we may not even live to discover in what way it was better. But, if we believe Him, we shall be sure of it, and praise Him for it. We shall never be disappointed.

Our trouble and infirmity is this : we think we know better than God does. But oh, what folly, what weakness, what ignorance. Oh, to know more of His infinite wisdom ! and learn more of the blessedness of His will.

If we knew this we should go on our way, and be at perfect rest.

The simplest events in life, will become sources of joy.

The visit that we made to a friend and did not find him at home, instead of being a disappointment, will be turned by faith into a ground of thanksgiving. We shall not be occupied with our ignorance, but with God's infinite wisdom ; not with the failure of our will and purpose, but with the sweetness of His will.

We shall think of how we have "escaped the edge of the sword" in being kept from some accident, preserved from some snare, saved from the germs of some dire disease if we had been or gone elsewhere.

The whole point of Elijah's lesson for us lies in that one word " there."

" I have commanded the ravens to feed thee THERE" (1 Kings xvii. 4) ; and " I have commanded a widow woman THERE, to sustain thee " (*v.* 9).

Had Elijah gone to any other place and not "there, he would neither have been Divinely fed, nor Miraculously sustained ; no, nor would he have " escaped the edge of the sword."

Oh! to be " THERE "; in the place where God would have us to be : for we know not what we "escape" when " there." It may not be a beautiful place, or the easiest place, or the most comfortable. But it will be the *right* place : the place of blessing, the place of rest, because it is the place which He wills. It is " there."

Our trouble comes because we do not know Him ; because we do not realise how infinite is His wisdom ; how infinite is His power ; and how infinite is His love.

If we knew anything of our own impotence, and anything of His omnipotence, we should thankfully cast ourselves upon it, and say, Lord, not my ignorance, but Thy wisdom ; not my weakness, but Thy strength ; not my way, but Thy will ; not here, but "THERE."

We should not be led astray (it may be unwittingly and undesignedly) by those who seek our good ; by those who tell us to " try to be willing for His will ; " or to " be willing to be made willing." Unconsciously, it may be, they are occupying us with ourselves, and thus leading or rather misleading us into further misery and deeper trouble.

There would be no need to be " made " anything, if we knew enough of His wisdom as would make us sick of our own ; and cause us to trust Him and to distrust ourselves.

Elijah *heard* the word of Jehovah, and he believed it.

Hence we have the two terse statements :—" So he went " (1 Kings xvii. 5) and " So he arose " (*v.* 10).

It reminds us of John Wesley, when some one expressed his surprise at his being able to rise so early in the morning : his enquirer wondered how he was able to do it, and asked whether he ever prayed about it ? No, said John Wesley, " *I get up.*"

£ven so with us, if we commit our way to God, and desire His way, preferring it, whatever it may be to our own way, we shall understand Elijah's action ; " So he went . . . " " So he arose."

We shall be " there," where we shall not only be *fed* and *sustained*, but where, at the very same time we shall *escape* evils of which we are wholly unaware.

JEREMIAH

affords another example of those who thus escaped.

But here again, it is not the personal or individual escape which is uppermost ; but *the purpose of God in the escape*.

Jehoiakim had just " cut up the Word of God with his penknife," and " commanded . . . . to take Baruch the scribe, and Jeremiah the prophet ; but Jehovah hid them " (Jer. xxxvi. 26).

That was their escape. It was done by Jehovah Himself. We are not told how it was done, but it was effectually done, for Jehovah had His own purpose to serve.

When we are assailed ; or when the same Word of God is cut up with the pens of those whom the same enemy of that Word is employing to-day, we may not be thus " hid ; " for the LORD may not have an immediate purpose or use for us in this conflict.

Nevertheless, the example holds good, for Baruch and Jeremiah escaped the edge of Jehoiakim's sword.

Jehovah's purpose in all this was accomplished, for Jeremiah was preserved to re-write the words of the scroll which had been burnt by the king, " and there were added unto them many like words " (Jer. xxxvi. 32).

But later on, when this work was done, Jeremiah was no longer hidden ; but " taken " and put in prison and kept there till the reign of Zedekiah (Jer. xxxvii. 11-15).

Zedekiah made Jeremiah's life more endurable until faithfulness to God brought the prophet to the lowest dungeon and like to be "put to death" by the princes of Zedekiah (Jer. xxxviii. 1-6). Again he "escaped the edge of the sword." This time by an Ethiopian Eunuch named Ebed-Melech.

With the king's consent, which he had obtained, he drew up Jeremiah out of the filth of the dungeon (xxxviii. 7-13).

For this act of mercy the word of the Lord came to Jeremiah after he had been quite delivered by Nebuzar-adan, and dwelt among the people.

It came with a message for Ebed-Melech (Jer. xxxix. 15-18). It was as follows: "Go and speak to Ebed-Melech the Ethiopian, saying, 'Thus saith the LORD of hosts, the God of Israel; behold, I will bring My words upon this city for evil, and not for good; and they shall be accomplished in that day before thee. But *I will deliver thee* in that day saith Jehovah: and thou shalt not be given into the hand of the men of whom thou art afraid. For I will surely deliver thee, and thou shalt *not fall by the sword*, but thy life shall be a prey unto thee: *because thou hast put thy trust in Me*, saith Jehovah.'"

Here was an "escape from the edge of the sword," and it was "through faith."

We are not all Jeremiah's or Ebed-Melech's. We are not all called to fill their positions, to have their experiences, or to need their deliverances; and this, because we are not needed in the carrying out of God's purposes, in His rulings and over-rulings.

But He is the same Lord whom we serve ; and it is the same Word which we believe, and in which we trust.

Even worldly wisdom has learnt that it is better to "bear the ills we have, than fly to others that we know not of."

How much more shall not we learn that it is better to be "there" according to the will of God, than anywhere else according to our own will.

5. David, Samuel, and the Prophets

g. "Out of Weakness, Were Made Strong" (vs. 34)

WE have already referred to the suggestion which has been made by certain of the higher critics that these weak ones were women, and to the argument based upon it in favour of the conjectured feminine authorship of the Epistle to the Hebrews.

But in answer to this, it is necessary only to point out that the Greek adjective here rendered "strong" is in the *masculine* gender, and this confines its reference to men.*

Here, again, we have to rise above the common thought of physical weakness and strength which comes first to the mind of the natural man; and to express our belief that we must rise higher in our thoughts, and go deeper into the Word, and remember that we are here in the spiritual sphere, and have to do not with fleshly weakness, but with spiritual strength.

We are led to this conclusion by the fact that the word rendered "made strong" is always used in a spiritual sense in the New Testament.

It occurs first in Acts ix. 22, "But Saul *increased the more in his strength*, and confounded the Jews which dwelt in Damascus, proving this [one] is the Messiah." Here it is spiritual power manifested in the Apostle's words and testimony.

Rom. iv. 20, "He [Abraham] staggered not at the promise of God, through unbelief, but was *strong* (*i.e.*, made strong) in faith, giving glory to God."

---

* The suggestion that the "me" (*v.* 32) refers to woman is shown to be fatal, from the fact that it is masculine also.

Here is a case which serves as our first example (Heb. xi. 33, 34) by asserting that it was "through faith . . . they were made strong out of weakness." Abraham was weak in himself, so weak that "he considered not his own body," because it was "now as good as dead, when he was an hundred years old." It was out of this spiritual weakness that he was "made strong" through faith. He had "no confidence in the flesh," but was "made strong" even in spiritual strength, through faith.

The next occurrence is in Eph. vi. 10. "Finally, my brethren, *be strong* (*i.e.*, be made strong) in the Lord, and in the power of His might."

We cannot be made strong in ourselves ; nor can our natural fleshly strength be converted into spiritual strength. This strength comes from the Lord. Nothing short of this will empower us to stand against "the wiles of the devil" (*v.* 11).

In Phil. iv. 13 the Apostle exclaims "I can do all things through Christ, Who *strengtheneth me*" (*i.e.*, makes me strong).

The next occurrence refers to the Apostle being specially "made strong" for his special ministry connected with the gospel of the glory of the blessed God" (1 Tim. i. 11). In *v.* 12 he says : "I thank Him Who *made me strong*—Christ Jesus our Lord—that He counted me faithful, appointing me to [His] service."

In 2 Tim. ii. 1 he exhorts Timothy to "be made strong in (or by) the grace which is in Christ Jesus." This strength was needed for the same special service. Thou must be "made strong," he says, so that "the things which thou didst hear from me by many witnesses, the same commit thou to faithful men, such as shall be competent to teach others also." It was this special ministry committed to Paul which required special strength, so that he and Timothy and others also had to be *made strong* for it.

The last occurrence is in 2 Tim. iv. 17. And here, this Divine strengthening was specially needed ; for he says in *v.* 16, " At my first defence no one stood with me, but all forsook me." The Figure (*Pleonasm*) is used to greatly emphasise his weakness as to all human aid. It is put two ways, positively and negatively. While only one was necessary for the sense, the other was necessary for the emphasis, to impress us with the terrible loneliness of his position. " Notwithstanding, (he adds), the Lord stood with me, and *made me strong* in order that the proclamation might be fully made, and all the nations should hear." Here again the object of this special strengthening is clearly stated, and is seen to be specially needed in view of the weak support given by others to the proclamation of the mystery (or secret) specially committed to Paul.

But this is not our subject here. We are now merely showing that every one of the occurrences of the word rendered " made strong " in Heb. xi. 34 is used of the spiritual sphere ; and has to do with spiritual strengthening.

The Apostle is not referring, here, to these New Testament occurrences of this word ; but to the examples of Divine strengthening in the Old Testament. But the New Testament use of the word shows us that these Old Testament examples must refer, in the same way, to spiritual strengthening.

Moses affords a good example, and shows how to be weak in faith means to be weak in strength.

Jehovah had said to him, " they shall hearken to thy voice " (Ex. iii. 18), but Moses answered and said, " But, behold, they will not believe me, nor hearken to my voice, for they will say ' Jehovah hath not appeared unto thee'" (Ex. iv. 1). Here was spiritual "weakness " indeed, and the result was great depression.

But this is hardly the "weakness" referred to in Heb. xi. 34. He was not "made strong " out of that " weakness." He had to be made weaker still, and sink into still lower depths of natural weakness before he could be "made strong " in spiritual strength.

It was very different in *v.* 10, when he realised his own insufficiency.

To doubt Jehovah's sufficiency was one thing; but to believe in his own insufficiency was quite another. This, and only this, could become the true source of strength, "O, my Lord, I am not eloquent, neither heretofore nor since Thou hast spoken unto Thy servant ; for I am slow of speech, and of a slow tongue " (Ex. iv. 10). That was having "no confidence in the flesh." That was the weakness which could be turned into strength by the Divine alchemy.

Jehovah said unto him, " Who hath made man's mouth ? . . . now therefore go, and I will. be with thy mouth, and teach thee what thou shalt say . . . Aaron . . . thy brother cometh to meet thee . . . and thou shalt speak unto him, and put words in his mouth : and I will be with thy mouth, and with his mouth, and will teach you what ye shall do. And he shall be thy spokesman unto the people : and he shall be, even he shall be to thee instead of a mouth, and thou shalt be to him instead of God " (Ex. iv. 11-16).

Here was a case of being made strong indeed,

Moses could surely say, as Paul did in a later day. "when I am weak, then am I strong" (2 Cor. xii. 10).

But this process of Divine strengthening must needs be continuous ; for our weakness is continuous.

Moses himself was soon depressed again. At the end of the fifth chapter he is in despair at his want of success. But this was from want of faith, not from want of strength. It was not weakness but wickedness to tell Jehovah that He had not kept His word by delivering the People.

To have "no confidence in the flesh" (Phil. iii. 3) this is true weakness; this is the weakness that can be converted into spiritual strength ; for the very man who used these words could say, in the next chapter, " I can do (or, am strong for) all things through Christ, Which strengtheneth me " (iv. 13).

We have an illustration of an opposite experience n the case of king Uzziah. Of him we read : " he was marvellously helped till he was strong. But when he was strong, his heart was lifted up to his destruction " (2 Chron. xxvi. 15, 16).

Weighty words ! Solemn lesson ! Oh ! that they may be written on our hearts ! They are the counterpart of the Apostle's words, " When I am weak, then am I strong."

Many examples are given by other writers, but they are all cases of physical weakness occasioned by fear of man. The weakness which our subject speaks of is that which comes from believing what God has told us about ourselves.

It is *to know that we are weak*, not because we *feel*

weak, but because God tells us *we are weak* when we act or work in our own strength.

If we judge by feeling, we may feel strong in ourselves, as King Uzziah did. But that is the very weakness, which is our danger. True weakness is (when we *feel strong*), to *believe that we are weak because God tells us so;* because God tells us that the flesh is absolutely powerless to do service for Him. In other words, spiritual work can be done only by spiritual strength. Fleshly strength is entirely out of place in the spiritual sphere. It is weakness itself. To realise this *because God tells us it is so,* and we *believe* what He says, *that* is the secret source of the Divine strengthening which is produced " by faith " *i.e.,* by believing God.

There is an experience of weakness which comes from " the fear of man." There is a strength which comes from the incitement of " the praise of men."

But true weakness and true strength come from believing God. He tells us that *without Him we can do nothing* (John xv. 5); it does not say we can do only a *little* with a little of our own strength, but " nothing " without His strength.

It was when we were " without strength " we were saved (Rom. v. 6). And it is when we are without the same strength that we can do all things.

Hence we cannot cite Elijah's weakness in 1 Kings xix., for that was occasioned by the fear of Jezebel; neither can we cite Hezekiah's weakness, for that was caused by the fear of the King of Assyria (2 Kings xix.) and the King of Terrors (Isa. xxxviii).

But rather, we can turn to Isaiah. He realized true weakness when he saw the majesty of Jehovah's glory. He realized his own uncleanness when he heard the Heavenly beings cry " Holy, Holy, Holy is the LORD of hosts." Then it was that he exclaimed " Woe is me ! for I am undone ; because I am a man of unclean lips." There was no strength left in him. But it was exactly then that " out of weakness he was made strong." For, when he heard the question " whom shall I send and who will go for us ? Then said I, send me " (Isa. vi. 8).

Then it was that Jehovah could say " Go ! " as He had said to Gideon when he realised his poverty and helplessness : " Go in this thy might " (Judges vi. 14). In that weakness lay his strength. " Out of that weakness he was made strong."

It was the same with Jeremiah at his call : " Ah Adonai Jehovah ! behold, I cannot speak, for I am a child " (Jer. i. 6). This was Jeremiah's source of strength ; and it has been ever thus from that day to this.

> " How ready is the man to go,
>   Whom God hath never sent !
> How timid, diffident, and slow,
>   God's chosen instrument."

We see the same in Ezekiel. His own strength was turned to weakness by the vision of Jehovah's glory, as was Isaiah's. (*See* Ezek. i. 28 ; ii. 1, 2 ; iii. 14, 23, 24). We see the same in Daniel (*See* Dan. x. 8), and in John (Rev. i. 17).

Nehemiah was specially conscious of his own weakness and realised his need of entire dependence on Divine strength. (*See* Neh. iv. 4, 5, 9, 14).

All who have taken this low place before God, believing His word, that all work for Him must be done in His strength and not their own, have ever found this to be the place of true strength.

When we are thus weak, then are we indeed strong, and only then; for then it is Divine strength. In such weakness we take hold of His strength (Isa. xxvii. 5).

Our strength is to have "no confidence in the flesh" (Phil. iii. 3), and to put no confidence in man (Ps. cxviii. 8).

This is the very thing that Israel was warned against; and the passage is worth quoting because it is usually taken in the very opposite sense; and used as a false and baseless exhortation; "Their strength is to sit still." It shows the mischief of garbling Scripture when this is put on a picture-card or hung up as an illuminated wall-text.

For, who are they of whom this is said in Isa. xxx. 7? If the context be read, it will at once be seen that these words are a very solemn warning against putting our confidence in man.

Israel is being rebuked for trusting in man instead of Jehovah. "Woe to the rebellious children, saith Jehovah, that take counsel but not of Me . . . . that walk to go down into Egypt, and have not asked at My mouth; to strengthen themselves in the strength of Pharaoh, and to trust (or put confidence) in the shadow of Egypt. Therefore shall the strength of Pharaoh be your shame, and the trust (or confidence) in the shadow of Egypt your confusion . . . . For the Egyptians shall help in vain, and to no purpose; therefore have I cried concerning this *their strength is to sit still*" (Is. xxx. 1-3, 7).

The pronoun "their" refers to the Egyptians; and

the meaning is that, so far from helping you, they will " sit still," and you will be put to shame.

This warning is needed to-day by us, as well as it was by Israel in a by-gone day. For we are told that this was the fact in the case of Israel. " They (Israel) were all ashamed of a people (the Egyptians) that could not profit them, nor be a help, nor profit, but a shame, and also a reproach " (Isa. xxx. 5).

Christians to-day are tempted to go down to Egypt for help !

We see it being done on all hands : the turning to man, instead of to Jehovah ; asking counsel of man, instead of God ; adopting the world's maxims and methods in raising money for the Lord's work; in seeking help of Egypt, instead of God ; in having confidence in the flesh, instead of in Jehovah.

Listen to His words of counsel in the face of Israel's conduct and ours. They are written in *v.* 15.

" For thus saith Adonai Jehovah, the Holy One of Israel :

> " In returning [to Me] and rest, shall ye be saved ;
> In quietness and confidence [in Me] shall be your strength,
> And ye would not."

How solemn is the warning! How needed is the lesson ! Oh ! may we learn it, for our souls' good.

Our strength is Jehovah, and not Egypt ; not in man, not in the flesh. When we are weak as to all these, then alone are we in a position to find that " the joy of the LORD is our strength," and to learn the lesson of the words we are considering ; words written of God's witnesses of old :—" Out of weakness were made strong."

5. David, Samuel, and the Prophets

h. "Waxed Valiant in Fight; Put to Flight
the Armies of the Aliens" (vs. 35)

THIS special example of what faith can do through God is most significant, and full of instruction.

It tells us that the path of faith is, of itself, a path of conflict. This conflict is with fighters. The word rendered " armies," here, means " camps "; and it is put by the Figure, *Metonymy* (of the Adjunct) for *those who live in camps*. It occurs *ten* times in the New Testament. In Acts xxi. 34, 37; xxii. 24; xxiii. 10, 16, 32 it is rendered "castle." In Heb. xi. 35; xiii. 11, 13. Rev. xx. 9, it is rendered "camp" in both A.V. and R.V.

This word is the first key to the instruction we are to get from this example of faith.

It does not refer to a mere warlike operation engaged in by two parties for their own purposes or conquests; or their mere personal aggrandisement.

" Waxed valiant in fight " is followed by another expression telling us the nature of the fighting.

It was not a mere exercise of strategic skill, or victory gained over a mere human foe, but the condition of conflict which rages within the special domain of faith. It is just the word which indicates that conflict which Israel entered upon with the nations of Canaan who were in possession of the Land; warriors living in camps, occupying the ground in advance, and contesting it at every step.

It points therefore to a conflict foretold, *which faith*

had heard of, and believed, and entered on in the obedience which comes of faith.

We see this, first, in Abraham, "the father of the
faithful." Abraham was not a mere soldier, but a
simple believer ; he was not a world-conqueror, but one
who believed what he had heard from God, and acted
upon it.

The moment he took the first step in faith's pathway,
he found it was to be contested step by step by the great
enemy.

The sphere of faith thus became the sphere of conflict.
And that conflict, not personal as between man and
man, but Dispensational as between Satan and the purpose of God.

We have already seen something of this in " the great
conflict of the ages ; " but, having the veil of Tradition
over our eyes, we have regarded it too exclusively as a
conflict between the *person* of Satan and the *person* of
Christ.   Instead of which the conflict was really with

The Purpose of God in Christ

It is this which gives us the key to the whole matter.

Satan's aim was not merely, or only, to prevent the
promised " Seed " coming into the world as the personal
Christ of God ; but to make the word of Jehovah, who
promised it, of none effect and to thwart His *purpose*,
as contained in the promise which revealed it.

All he could know of God's purpose could be only as
it was revealed.   At first it was that Man (Adam) was
the one in whom all dominion in the " heavens and
earth which are now " (Gen. i. 28-30 ; Ps. viii. 4-9) was
vested.   Whether this means that Satan, before his
fall, was supreme in the " world that then was "
(2 Pet. iii. 6), and whether that fall led to the disrup-

tion of that world of Gen. i. 1, 2, we are not plainly told ; though we may confidently infer it ; for, already, in Gen. iii. 1, Satan is introduced to us as having fallen ; and, if his fall did not take place between the 1st and 2nd verses of Gen. i., there is no other place for it between Gen. i. 2 and iii. 1.

Man, therefore, having been set, in the purpose of God, as the head of " the heavens and earth which are now, by the same word " (2 Peter iii. 7), was the object of Satan's first assault.

It was not personal or individual to Adam, but it was against the *purpose* of God in committing dominion in the earth to him.

Man therefore must be attacked so that God's purpose in him might fail.

This is the reason for what is revealed in Gen. iii. " The fall of man " was not a mere historical incident. We are not to look on it in connection with its subsequent effects, whether individual, moral, physical or spiritual ; but in connection with its object, purpose and design, viz., to defeat the expressed *purpose* of Jehovah concerning man.

That was the one prime reason of the great event which lies at the root of human history. We are so taken up with its results, as they affect ourselves personally, that we are tempted to leave out of our account the result as it affected *the purpose of God* in Adam.

We must not dwell further on the course of that conflict here ; but only notice the next and consequent purpose of Jehovah revealed for faith, in Gen. iii. 15.

Man had fallen. Man must die. But, was Jehovah's purpose in man to fall ? That was the one great question which was now raised.

We, as we have said, naturally think of the Fall only as it affects ourselves. Self comes in, and comes first and all the time, as usual.

But in the Word of God, God is first, yea, all in all.

He had given to man universal dominion in the earth ; and now, man is to die. He has forfeited his trust. He has lost his dominion.

Now, it is time for God to work, His first word of prophecy is heard in the midst of the failure, and out of the depth of the ruin.

His purpose is declared, He will not improve man. He has been "marred in the hands of the potter." Jehovah declares His purpose to make a new man, ("the second man") a new Adam ("the last Adam"), "as it pleased the potter to make it " (Jer. xviii. 4).

This is why the coming "seed" of the first man is called " the Son of Man." It is He, " the second man," Who now has all dominion committed unto Him, and not "the first man, Adam." Hence, while it is man alone who received the promise in Gen. i. 28-30, it is " the Son of Man " Who takes up the promise in Psalm viii. 4, and Heb. ii. 6.

The purpose of Jehovah is now declared ; and the one object of Satan's strategy is now clear.

It is not merely the *Person* of the coming One, but *the purpose of Jehovah in Him*, against which Satan's " enmity " is thus manifested.

There was nothing yet to show Satan by what line the Son of Man was to come. Hence his enmity was first directed against the whole race of mankind ; and as early as Gen. vi. his whole plot is revealed.

We need not go through the details of that terrible assault which accomplished the destruction of all earth's inhabitants with the exception of " eight souls." These were saved ; and these alone.

But the next thing we hear of is the call of Abraham, in Gen. xii. 31, and the promise to give him and his seed the Land of Canaan for his inheritance. All blessing for all mankind is henceforth vested in Abraham and his seed for ever.

From the moment that Satan knew of the declared *purpose* of Jehovah concerning Abraham, he evidently realised that there was not a moment to be lost in his attempt to meet it, by occupying the land in advance, in order to contest each step which should be made by Abraham's seed to take it into their possession.

The time must have been very short, but it was long enough. It must have been this moment which is referred to in Gen. vi. 4, and Gen. xii. 6. Not only was there the attempt on the whole human race "in those days " (*i.e.*, "the days of Noah "), but there was another attempt also " after that " affecting the Land. This latter was evidently more limited both in character and extent, and was confined to the Land of Canaan.

A few years later, Abram and Lot take their journey thither. "They went forth to go into the Land of Canaan and (it is added) into the Land of Canaan they came " (Gen. xii. 4). Why, this emphasis on "the Land of Canaan ? " Because when Terah and his family first set forth from Ur to go thither, they did not come into the Land of Canaan, but stopped short and abode some years in Haran (or Mesopotamia). This delay, for aught we know, may have been the work of the enemy, for it gave him the time he was needing to forestall the coming of Abram, and thus delay its approach.

Hence, when we read verse 6, and learn how " Abram passed through the Land unto the place of Sichem unto the place of Moreh," we have the significant parenthetical remark "and the Canaanite was then in the Land." These brief parentheses are often full of teaching calling our attention to them by their position and their brevity.

Modern critics love to read this word "then" in the sense of *still*, and make it refer to the late date of the authorship of Genesis, by meaning that the Canaanites remained still in the land after the exile in Babylon ! Whereas the word means that the Canaanites were already in possession of the land, and had already occupied it in advance.*

We must pass over the assault of Satan in attempting to forestall and destroy the purpose of Jehovah as to Abram's " seed " by the denial of Sarah ; also the separation of Lot and his choice of Sodom, as his dwelling-place. Sodom was already marked out as being associated with the sin of the fallen angels (Jude 6), and the dread results of their irruption.

Gen. xiv. reveals the presence of several branches of the Rephaim, who evidently rebelled against the four kings (Amraphel, Arioch, Chedarlaomer and Tidal). Four branches of them are named, or at any rate four of the names by which they were known by others : for the *Rephaim* we are told were known as *Zamzuzumim* (Deut. ii. 20), and *Emim* (Deut. ii. 10), and *Horim* (Deut. ii. 12).

It looks as though the five kings were closely con-

---

* For a similar significant parenthesis see chap. xiii. 7. The emphasis of this parenthesis is to show the evil of the disputes of brethren in the presence of the enemy.

nected with these, for after the four kings had smitten them, they went out against them and were defeated.

But, alas ! Lot was living in Sodom, and was taken prisoner "with all his goods."

Here we reach the point which furnishes us with our first illustration ; another example of Abraham's faith— its power to conquer through God.

Abram was no warrior. He was no world-conqueror ; or invader of other countries. He was a man avoiding all "strife." · But, through faith, he "waxed valiant in fight, and put to flight the armies of the aliens."

But while his faith could do this to rescue his nephew Lot, the same faith restrained him from using this valour to acquire the land by his sword. If he could do the one, he could surely have done the other ; but he had *heard* of the land ; he had received the promise, and faith would wait God's time for his possession of it.

Not only would he not "take it in possession," but he would not take from the king of Sodom "from a thread even to a shoe-lachet " or anything that was his—lest he should say " I have made Abraham rich " (Gen. xiv. 23).

Abraham was already " rich : " he possessed the Word and promise of God ; and, having this, faith possessed all. He had need of nothing that Sodom could offer. Lot, on the other hand, " walked by sight." He lifted up his own eyes (Gen. xiii. 10). Abram " walked by faith," and lifted up his eyes, only at the command of Jehovah (Gen. xiii. 14).

Abraham by faith could " wax valiant in fight and put to flight the armies of the aliens," in rescuing Lot from the war on Sodom ; but it required the Angels of God to rescue Lot from the destruction of Sodom.

What Abraham had heard from God we are not told. But his action in rescuing Lot stands out as being so unlike every act of his life, and takes on such a special character from the blessing of the King of Salem and the colloquy with the King of Sodom and the intervention of Melchisedek, that faith must have played a large place in the whole event.

The God Who had delivered Abram (*v.* 19) was the God Who had called him, and the God Who must have spoken to him.

He was *Elyōn El,* " the MOST HIGH GOD, the possessor of heaven and earth," the One Who had the right, therefore, to give the Land to whom He would.

Abram admitted this claim, and by faith he upheld and vindicated this right.

He had said to the King of Sodom " I will not take even to a shoe-lachet, and I will not take anything that is thine, lest thou shouldest say ' I have made Abram rich ' " ; and immediately " after these things the Word of Jehovah came unto Abram in a Vision, saying ' Fear not Abram I am thy Shield, and thy exceeding great reward ' " (Gen. xv. 1).   Here was blessing indeed : here was possession in truth ; for as yet it was only through faith, faith in what he had heard from "the Most High God, the possessor of heaven and earth."

Other examples of the faith that " put to flight the armies of the aliens," and of those who were made valiant in fight, must be looked for, not in Israel's wars with neighbouring nations such as Syria, Babylon, Assyria, or Egypt, but in the casting out of the " aliens " who had taken the land in possession.   These are the aliens which are specially referred to here. These are the foes which were to be extirpated. Against these they had the promised presence and blessing of God. His word had been given to Moses, and repeated to Joshua " There shall not any man be able to stand before thee all the days of thy life ; as I was with Moses, so I will be with thee. I will not fail thee nor forsake thee " (Josh. i. 5).

The latter part of this promise had been first given to Jacob (Gen. xxviii. 15). It had been passed on to Moses, and by him to all Israel (Deut. xxxi. 6), then to Joshua (Josh. i. 5). Samuel had claimed it (1 Sam. xii. 22), and Solomon had made it his plea in his prayer at the dedication of the Temple (1 Kings viii. 57) ; while in Heb. xiii. 5 it is passed down to us to-day.

Through faith in that word, Moses had put to flight the armies of Sihon, king of the Amorites, and Og the king of the giant cities of Bashan, for these had been put in their possession by Satan—" the Prince of this world." Hence, we read that Jehovah said to Moses : " Behold I have begun to give Sihon and his land before thee : begin to possess, that thou mayest inherit his land " (Deut. ii. 31).

It was no act of cruelty in thus casting out and cutting off these nations of Canaan. They were usurpers of most evil kind. They were the Nephilim (Num. xiii. 33) and the Anakim, and the Rephaim (Deut. ii. 11, 20). They had gone by other names given by the still earlier inhabitants of the land. They were known as " Emim," " Zamzummim," " Avim," and " Horim " (Deut. ii. 10, 20, 23).

It was because of their nature, and because of their Satanic origin and character, that it was absolutely

necessary they should be destroyed and extermin-
ated.

It was necessary that the sword of Israel should do
for these what the Flood had done for those "in the
days of Noah."

Not long since, a friend declared that she could not
believe in Inspiration, because she thought it so cruel
of God to destroy those nations. "Ah, dear lady," we
replied, "you know nothing whatever about it. Have
you not read of Him

> "Who smote great kings,
> > For His mercy endureth for ever :
> And slew famous kings :
> > For His mercy endureth for ever :
> Sihon, king of the Amorites,
> > For His mercy endureth for ever :
> And Og the king of Bashan,
> > For His mercy endureth for ever :
> And gave their land for an heritage,
> > For His mercy endureth for ever."
>
> (Ps. cxxxvi. 17-21)

Yes, it was "mercy" for His People ; mercy for us.
But there was to be no "mercy for them."

It was disobedience to this command of extermina-
tion that was the direct cause of Israel's apostasy;
Israel's dispersion is traced back entirely to this failure.

Israel, instead of obeying God and exterminating
those aliens, "learned their works" and worshipped
their gods, sacrificing their very children unto devils.
"They shed innocent blood, even the blood of their
sons and of their daughters, whom they sacrificed unto
the idols of Canaan, and the land was defiled with
blood" (Ps. cvi. 37, 38).

They refused to shed the blood of those guilty creatures, and were snared by "him who has the power of death" into shedding the blood of their own innocent sons and daughters.

And all this, in spite of the promise of their God to make them valiant in war, and to put to flight the armies of these aliens.

Not so was David. His first act on becoming king over all Israel was to advance against one branch of them, the Jebusites, which occupied Jebus. There he slew them, and Jebus became "Zion, the city of the great king." This is why Zion acquired such a glorious name, and will yet became the joy of the whole earth. God had "chosen Zion," and it was He Who had made David valiant in war.

It is in these exploits we are to see the illustration of our subject.

It was not in the resistance of Egypt, Assyria or Babylon. These enemies were raised up by God for judgment on Israel, for the very reason that Israel had ming'ed with the heathen instead of cutting them off.

Israel could not stand against the invading armies which came from without; for they had no promise to rest on. Indeed there was a direct command to submit to Babylon. Hezekiah's successful resistance to Assyria showed what could be done by one who destroyed the idols of Canaan and put away the gods of the Canaanites.

Israel, instead of putting to flight the armies of the Canaanites, was put to fight and carried away out of the land by the Assyrian armies, and after a time Judah was carried away to Babylon.

These are not the "aliens" referred to in Heb. xi.

34.   Still less are we to look for our illustrations among the Maccabœans.   Modern critics would fain see in those later times the examples of this faith.   By so doing, they not only bring the sacred records down to a late date B.C., but they miss the whole point of the sacred history : and lose the thread which runs through it from beginning to end.   They do not see the purpose of God ; hence they fail to see the objective of Satan.

And now, we may ask, this being the *interpretation* of the history, what is the *application* for us ?   What is the lesson we are to learn for our own instruction and edification ?

There are two.   One is individual and the other is Dispensational.

The individual application is, that we are to look for our enemy within, rather than without.   Our war is to be waged with our old nature.   Our enemy is firmly intrenched in his citadel.   Like the Canaanites of old, he occupies the ground in advance.   We find him already in possession, and the command has gone forth that we are to hold no parly with our old nature ; we are to give it no quarter.   In God's sight it was crucified when Christ was crucified, and we are to "reckon it as dead."   We are not to have any communication with what is dead.   We cannot improve it, and we may not confer with it.

Our course is clear.

But there is something very important in connection with the other application, which we said is Dispensational.

The command in the history was accompanied by the promise " I will never leave thee nor forsake thee."

We have seen how this was first made to Jacob

(Gen. xxviii. 15); and was handed down through Moses for journeying (Deut. xxxi. 6); passed on to Joshua for conflict (Josh. i. 5); claimed by Samuel (1 Sam. xii. 22); pleaded by Solomon for service (1 Kings viii. 57); and now, once again, for the last time, it comes to us. It is introduced by the words " He hath said." Yes, He hath said; and He will make good His own word.

" He hath said, I will never leave thee nor forsake thee."

Where do we find it? Here, in this very Epistle to the Hebrews; and at the close of an Epistle in which the Apostle had been pleading with them to leave the beginning of the account of Christ's teaching; to leave the things which were behind; to leave the practices, and beliefs, and ordinances, of a Dispensation which had passed away, and to go on unto perfection; for, " that which is perfect had come."

In Heb. xiii. 5, we find the promise : and it stands in connection with the New Dispensation on which their, and our lot is now cast. They were to remember their leaders (not " rulers ") who spoke to them the Word of God (*v.* 9); and, because God hath said " I will never leave thee nor forsake thee " (*v.* 5), they might boldly say " the Lord is my helper," and, " I will not fear what shall man do to me ? "

The promise now comes to us, and it is coupled with a command not to fear man, but to remember the word which as it comes to us, tells us that Jesus Christ remains the same. Though Dispensations may change. He remains the same, " yesterday," in the past, in the Old Dispensation of the Old Testament ; and the same " to-day," in which the gospel of the grace of God, and the gospel of the glory of Christ are proclaimed ; and "for ever," when those glories will be consummated.

And then, following on this, we have the exhortation based upon it ; " Be not carried about with divers and strange doctrines. For it is a good thing that the heart be established with grace ; not with meats, which have not profited them that have been occupied therein," and then, after referring the one sin-offering, so suited to the special needs of those whom the Apostle was addressing, his exhortation becomes general, and includes ourselves to-day ; " Let us go forth therefore unto Him without the camp, bearing His reproach."

Our enemies are within. Not only the old nature within us each, as individuals ; but, *within the camp.* We may not fight or " strive " with these, for they are our brethren, and the Canaanites are in our land (Gen. xiii. 7, 8).

The only course open to us is to separate (*v.* 9) ; and to go "outside the camp" altogether. Not to form another camp of our own among their camps, but to go forth " unto Him." He has gone into the holiest of all, even Heaven itself. That is now our " place of worship," and He Himself is our one object of worship.

Yes, "without the camp," outside the place of fighting and strife ; for, as we have seen, the word " camp " is the same word that is translated " armies " in xi. 35.

" The servant of the Lord must not strive " (2 Tim. ii. 24). The Dispensation has changed. It is now the Dispensation of " the gospel of the glory of Christ " (2 Cor. iv. 4), and we are to go forth from those strive, whether " aliens," or " brethren," outside all camps— " unto Him."

5. David, Samuel, and the Prophets

i. Women Received Their Dead Raised to Life Again (vs. 35)

THIS sentence brings us to the last example belong-ing to the first of the final two groups, which has for its subject " Faith's power to overcome THROUGH God." The second of these last two groups has for its subject the contrast : " Faith's power to suffer FOR God : " the two together forming one group which stands in correspondence with the first group (Abel, Enoch and Noah) which is connected with " God " in a way that speak of the examples of faith's stand.

The division of these 34th and 35th verses, in the A.V. and R.V., completely destroys the great and important distinction between these two groups, by thus merging them together. This affords another instance in which failure to rightly divide the word of truth hides the truth instead of revealing it.

Moreover, the rendering of the A.V. is more or less expansive. The Greek reads " Women received by resurrection their dead [sons]."

Two women are referred to, though they are not named. We (as the Apostle's readers were) are sup-posed to be familiar with the Old Testament histories, as they are written in 1 Kings xvii. 17-24 and 2 Kings iv. 14-37.

Neither, of this widow, nor of the Shunammite, woman, is anything said about *their* faith ; but only about the *prayer* of Elijah and of Elisha.

Those prayers were the evidence of their faith, and

being " by faith " they must either have " heard " from God of His purpose, or have *judged* " by faith " as Manoah's wife had done (Judges xiii. 23) that God would not in the midst of His miraculous dealings make any mistakes, or have said and done so many wondrous things, and then fail His servants who were being guided and ordered by Him.

Elijah had *heard* enough of his God to believe that He would not bring calamity on a poor widow, whose cruse of oil He was at that same time miraculously supplying.

Elisha had *heard* enough from God to believe that the son which he had promised to the Shunammite woman would not be taken away by death, except to subserve some greater purpose. Moreover, it is it is hardly likely that Elisha would have dared to make so direct and positive promise, unless he had *heard* from God that he was to do so.

After what standeth written—" faith cometh by hearing," we are left to conclude that the word of God (by which the " hearing " comes) had come to both Elijah and Elisha.

As to the resurrection itself, all the parties concerned must have *heard* and *believed*.

Now, the word "resurrection" by itself does not denote the additional " secret " (not " the great secret") concerning Christ and His Church (Eph. v. 32) of 1 Cor. xv. 51. This was *a secret*, never before revealed to the sons of men, that there was to be a resurrection which involves a " change."

Resurrections which had before taken place on earth, whether the son of the widow of Sarepta, or of the Shunammite woman, or of the widow of Nain, or the

Ruler's daughter, or Lazarus, or the " many saints " at the resurrection of Christ ; or Dorcas, or Eutychus, all these were merely a *standing up again* (as the word *anastasis* means) on earth, and in this life. But the " change " involves something more, and beyond this.

This " secret " was revealed in 1 Cor. xv. 51, but on explanation is given. The resurrection of those who " are Christ's at His parousia " had been revealed in *v.* 23, and now a further secret is made known concerning the " we " who shall " put on immortality " in that glorious coming day.

In the prison epistles, after " the great secret " had been fully made known by being committed to writing, we have a still further and clearer revelation in Phil. iii. 20, 21. Here there is no mention of resurrection at all (except in *v.* 11, " the out-resurrection out from among the dead "), but we have " the calling on high " in *v.* 14. Either or both of these include the glorious assertion in *vv.* 17, 20, 21 :—

> " Brethren 'be followers together of me and walk as ye have us for an example. . . . For our *politeuma* (or seat of government) EXISTS in heaven from whence, as Saviour also, we are waiting, the Lord Jesus Christ, Who will transform the body of our humiliation for it to become conformed to His GLORIOUS body according to the working of His mighty power, even to subdue all things to Himself " (Phil. iii. 17-20).

This is the resurrection of which *we* have *heard* ; which we have believed, and for which we wait.

Oh, blessed faith, which thus enables us to overcome the world and conquer through God. " A great cloud of witnesses " witness to us of their faith, may we be in their ranks and believe God in each successive revelation which He made to them, and has since made known to us.

Faith Suffering for God

"And Others"

a. "Were Tortured not Accepting Deliverance" (vs. 35)

WITH these two words we are introduced to the latter of the last two groups :—Faith's power to suffer for God :

"*But others were tortured not accepting proferred release in order that they might attain to a resurrection that was better* [than a release from the torture procured by apostasy]."

We must first notice the place that these "others" occupy in the great theme which is the subject of this chapter.

These last two groups correspond with the first group of three—Abel, Enoch and Noah, both being occupied with reference to God. A glance at the structure will be sufficient to show this.

We are now in a position to attend to the rendering we have given above of the remainder of the 35th verse, which, in our last chapter, we saw was wrongly divided so as not to sufficiently and properly distinguish the two groups.

We must therefore break up the verse, and commence this last group with the words

"But others "

It is not merely "and others." A great demarcation is made, by the word "but," between the conquering and the suffering group ; between those who overcame through faith in God's power to strengthen, and these "others" who were overcome and remained faithful in spite of all, through their faith in God's power to sustain.

This brings us to the heart of our subject, and shows us the nature of the faith in question.

It is remarkable that no mention is made of the "faith" of those in this last group. There is in the former group ; " Who, through faith, subdued kingdoms, &c."

Here, it is simply, "But others were tortured," &c., with no reference to their faith ! At the end of all it is added in words, which include them with the whole of the "great cloud of witnesses" from Abel onward, "and these all, having obtained a good report through faith."

How can we account for this seeming omission in connection with those who suffered the loss of all things ? What does the omission say to us ?

Is it not to tell us this, and thus to emphasize the necessary difference between this last group and all the others who are mentioned in this chapter ?

It was not "through faith" that these suffered, in the same sense that those overcame and wrought wondrous works by their faith which was given to them as the gift of God.

In this last case they suffered *on account of their faith.* The former overcame through believing what they had *heard* from God, these latter *were overcome* on account of their own faithfulness to God. Of course, they were able to endure only through God's sustaining grace. But the fact thus emphasized points us to the one feature which covers the case of this whole group.

Thousands of people have suffered in similar ways

because of their sins and wickedness as men among men. Those who were not worthy of the world have been tortured, have had mockings and scourgings, bonds and imprisonments. They have been slain in war and executed by the sword for offences against the state and against their fellows. But these, "others" who are referred to here, are in a different class altogether; for, of these "the world was not worthy" (*v.* 38). While some suffered for their faithlessness to their fellow-men, these suffered for their faithfulness to God.

We are to distinguish this fact. It affects all that we have to say. It bids us look for the true reason, and for the practical lesson for our own selves. We bring God in, and all is clear. It was steadfastness in their belief of what they heard from God which brought all their sufferings from man.

Men had no other quarrel with them. Men had not been injured by them. The tortures and sufferings which they endured were all and wholly on account of man's rooted enmity against God and His Word. This it is which enables us to understand the words used.

Let us look at them:

"But others were Tortured"

The word "tortured" means beaten or cudgelled to death. The Greek word is *tympanizō* which means *to beat on a tympanum* or drum. This was an instrument of torture, being a wooden frame resembling a drum on which criminals were stretched to be beaten to death.* See 2 Macc. vi. 19, 28, 30; vii. 9 (which we shall have to refer to later).

Not accepting the [proffered] liberation; *i.e.,* on the

---

* Probably, the beating of drums was conjoined with this, in order to drown the cries of the sufferer.

condition of apostatizing in order that they might attain (or obtain) a resurrection, better and far preferable to a release from torture procured by a denial of their faith.

The word " better " must be taken as referring either to the restoration to life mentioned in the earlier part of the verse (see 1 Kings xvii. and 2 Kings iv.) ; or, " better " than the redeeming of it for a while, from temporal death, on the conditions prescribed.

The Greek reads " not accepting THE redemption,* *i.e.*, the deliverance, procured on account of satisfaction given, which, in this case was recantation and apostasy.

Far " better " than ransom at this price was death itself in view of resurrection of which they had heard from God, and believed.

Certain as were their present sufferings, God's Word was no less certain, and their faith enabled them to prefer the certain future and glorious resurrection to a continued life on earth, especially in the times in which they were then living.

It was " better " than a resuscitation or regaining of their present life, to be again subject to death, and perhaps to torture.

They had *resurrection* as their hope, as all godly Jews had. Paul himself says before his judges : " I . . . have hope toward God *which they themselves also allow* that there shall be a resurrection of the dead both of the just and unjust." (Acts xxiv. 15). That " hope " was based on their " faith " (Heb. xi. 1), and their faith was based on the Word which they had " heard " from God.

---

* The word is *apolutrōsis*, which occurs 19 times in the N.T., and is rendered " redemption " 9 times (Lu. xxi. 28. Rom. iii. 24 ; viii. 23. 1 Cor. i.30. Eph. i. 7, 14 ; iv. 30. Col. i. 14. Heb. ix. 15), and " deliverance " once, in this passage.

Josephus tells us how " every good man . . . believes that God hath made this grant to those that observe these laws, even though they be obliged readily to die for them, that they shall come into being again, and, at a certain revolution of things, receive a better life than they enjoyed before " (Josephus *Against Apion* ii. 31. Whiston).

It is of course possible that the word " better " may refer to the resurrection " of the just," and " of life," as being better than that " of the unjust " or, "of condemnation." But the word may be " better," used of two good things, one of which is better than the other ; rather than of one good—and the other evil.

This is why we have sought out a reference for the word, more in harmony with the context.

There can be little doubt that the Apostle referred to the case of " Eleazar one of the principal scribes " (in the days of Antiochus Epiphanes). " A man already stricken in years, and of a noble countenance, was compelled to open his mouth to eat swine's flesh which had been offered to a false god. But he, welcoming death with renown rather than life with pollution, advanced of his own accord to the instrument of torture [the *tympanum*] but first spat forth the flesh. When his friends had besought him to spare his life, he steadfastly refused and went straightway to the instrument of torture." (Read 2 Macc. vi. 19-31).

That *resurrection* was the hope that sustained those who thus suffered is shown by the account of the mother and her seven sons, as recorded in 2 Macc. vii. who were scourged * (*v.* 36) as well as tortured.

---

*Not the same word as in *v.* 35, but the ordinary word for scourging (*mastix*), so rendered only in Acts xxii. 24. Elsewhere rendered " plague " (Mark iii, *v.* 10, 29, 34. Luke vii. 21).

The second son in the midst of his tortures exclaimed to Antiochus "Thou, miscreant, dost release us out of this present life, but the King of the world shall *raise up* us, who have died for His laws unto an eternal renewal of life" (2 Macc. vii. 9).

"Likewise, the third son, who when he put forth his tongue to have it wrenched out as his brother's had been," stretched forth his hands courageously, and nobly said "From heaven I possess these ; and for His laws' sake I contemn these ; and from Him *I hope to receive* these back again" (*v.* 11).

The fourth son, in like manner, "being come near to death he said thus : ' It is good to die at the hands of men and look for the hopes which are given by God, that *we shall be* raised *up again by Him* ; for, as for thee, thou shalt have no resurrection unto life'" (*v.* 14).

If these were the hopes of godly Jews who had returned from the home of Babylonian traditions which would do away with resurrection as a hope, we may be sure that those who suffered under Jeroboam, Ahab, Jezebel and Manasseh had the same blessed hope, and looked on resurrection as better than release from torture at the price of apostasy.

"And Others"

b. "Had Trial of Cruel Mockings and Scourgings"

" And others received trial of [cruel] mockings and scourgings,
as well as of bonds and imprisonment " (v. 36)

THE word rendered "others," here, is not the same
as in verse 35. There, it means "others" of the *same*
kind as those mentioned and referred to throughout the former part of the chapter; having the same
precious faith, believing the same words of the same
living God.

Here, it refers to *different* classes of sufferers among
those same believers.

They had the same faith and the same faithfulness,
but they suffered in different manners from those
referred to in the immediately preceding clause.

The former suffered tortures with a view to apostasy.

The latter experienced trials in consequence of their
faithfulness.

The words of the A.V. "had trial" are very expres-
sive, and beautifully idiomatic for reading in a Version.
But this is not sufficient for those who desire to get
beneath the surface.

We have given the more literal rendering "received
trial," which may otherwise be expressed by "were put
to the test," or "experienced." And, what this test
was, or these trials were, is described in the long list
which follows.

The trials and mockings referred to here were not on
account of anything in the private life or in the public
conduct of these sufferers.

Many who are " of the world " have been mocked, in our modern sense of the word, by those who are " of the world." Every day, in the spheres of the world's amusements and politics, such trials and mockings are stock in trade of a very large class of people. But, these sufferers endured scoffings and scornings on account of their believing what God had said and caused to be written in His Word. This was a very different thing. The former may be well deserved ; and those who experience them may find many to sympathize with and encourage them.

But these scoffings were endured alone, and only through faith—"as seeing Him Who is invisible."

Nothing short of a living faith in the living God can enable any to endure the experience of such trials.

They had to be endured, often, in loneliness and isolation, and in the solitary prison, as is intimated in the words which follow ; with no surrounding friends to support, encourage, and cheer the sufferers with their words and prayers.

If we look for examples, we note one as early as Judges xvi. 25, in the person of Samson ; and, though his trials were not of the same exalted character, being brought on by his own sin and folly, yet, in their source, they were the same, for they came from his having heard what God had spoken concerning him, and believing what he had heard. His prayer in the prison showed that he knew the true relation in which he stood to Israel's covenant God.

But it is in those that were more or less types of Him Who is " the Faithful Witness " that we see the true examples, specially referred to in these words of Heb. xi. 36.

In 2 Sam. xvi. we see David, the type of David's Son, and David's Lord—David's root and David's off-spring, rejected by his own household—experiencing " the cruel mockings " spoken of him.

His faith enabled him to endure. His submission in receiving it " from the Lord " is wonderful.

When suffering under the cursings of Shimei, and urged by Abishai to execute summary vengeance, David replied " Let him alone   .   .   .   the Lord hath bidden him " (v. 11). We see the echo of these words in Psalm cix., where we have this scene referred to, and made prophetic of the then yet future mockings of Messiah. In vv. 20 and 27, it was received as from the Lord ; and faith in Jehovah's word enabled David to say " Thou Lord hast done it." " This is Thy hand."

In other Psalms also these mockings are prophetically referred to. We must never forget that David was a prophet and, therefore, spake beforehand of the suffer-ings, death, and resurrection of Messiah. This is dis-tinctly declared by the Holy Spirit through Peter in Acts ii. 30-33. Forgetting this, many modern critics, when they meet with references to the restoration of Zion, or return from the captivity, &c., immediately assume that such passages in the Psalms are by a much " later hand " ; but, on such matters, as well as on others, modern critics are " willingly ignorant," and would not willingly part with any so-called " discrep-ancy," or what may appear a " difficulty " to them, lest they should lose an argument against the inspiration of God's Word.

The " mockings " endured by David were typical of those of Messiah ; and there are evidences that, in many instances Jeremiah's sufferings are also to be regarded as types. In chap. xx. 7 he says "I am in derision daily, every one mocketh me," * for since I spake, I cried out . . . because the word of the LORD was made a reproach unto me and a derision daily."

In Lam. iii. 14 he adds : "I was a derision to all my people, and their song (or mocking song) all the day."

These words agree with similar passages in the Psalms which refer to Messiah.

Indeed, if we carefully compare many passages of Jeremiah with those in the Gospels, we shall see this point very clearly.

All who believed God, and were faithful witnesses for Him, were typical in measure of Him Who alone could be called " THE faithful witness " (Rev. i. 5).

Micaiah (1 Kings xxii. 24) was hated and suffered, in consequence of his faithfulness to what he had heard and believed and uttered from God.

Nehemiah suffered in the same way from the scoffings of Sanballat and Tobiah (Neh. iv. 1-4).

In fact Jehovah sums up the sad history of Israel in 2 Chron. xxxvi. 16, where it is written : "they mocked the messengers of God, and despised His words, and misused (or scorned) His prophets," &c.

It all came to a head when "the Faithful Witness" appeared, and spoke the words He had received from the Father. The Parable of "the Vineyard let out to husbandmen" reveals the sad condition of the nation : beating, stoning, killing the messengers who had been sent to them, and, above all, slaying the beloved Son Himself (Matt. xxi. 33, &c. Mark xii. 1, &c. Luke xx. 9)

---

* The former part of this verse can be understood only by noticing the force of the Hebrew idiom, by which one is said to do what he permits to be done.

In the lament of the Saviour over Jerusalem (Matt. xxiii. 34-37), He foretold that it would be as it had ever been : "behold, I send unto you prophets, and wise men, and scribes ; and some of them ye shall kill and crucify; and some of them shall ye scourge in your synagogues and persecute them from city to city," &c.

What thoughts must have filled the Apostle himself as he penned the inspired words fulfilling this prophecy : —" and others were put to the test of scoffings and scourgings; as well as of bonds and imprisonment—" when he remembered how he himself had helped to fulfil them when he " made havoc of (or, ravaged) the assembly, entering into every house (or house by house), and dragging men and women, delivered them up to prison " (Acts viii. 3) ; and, " breathing out threatening and slaughter " (Acts ix. 1), " destroyed them that called on this name in Jerusalem " (v. 21) ; and persecuted this way unto the death, binding and delivering into prisons both men and women" (Acts xxii. 4). " I punished them (he says) in every synagogue and compelled them to blaspheme " (Acts xxvi. 10, 11).

With what feelings (we repeat) must he have penned these words as they were given to him by the Holy Spirit.

How well we can understand his feelings, when he says he "used to wish himself anathema [cut off] from Christ " (Rom. ix. 3), so great was his hatred of that name.

But, we have to remember, that in all this he was most religious (Phil. iii. 5, 6. 1 Tim. i. 13), for it has been religion—false religion—which has ever sought to destroy those who believe God.

"And Others"

c. "Bonds and Imprisonments"

THESE are the concluding words of verse 36 which was the subject of our last paper.

" BONDS AND IMPRISONMENT "

awaited those who were faithful to the God Whom these sufferers believed.

We have already referred to Micaiah (1 Kings xxii. 26), and we might mention Hannani the seer, who was put in prison by Asa, in his rage (2 Chron. xvi. 10); and Jeremiah (Jer. xxxii. 2 ; xxxvi. 5) who, when put into the pit of the dungeon, sank into the mire (xxxviii. 6).

All this suffering was brought on in consequence of faithfulness ; and this faithfulness was the fruit of their faith : for it is, and ever has been, that the absence of faith in God leads to unfaithfulness to God.

And, if we ask why all this cruelty was so conspicuous in Israel, and is still, in Romanism, the answer is that, in both cases, the religious power was one with the civil power. Hence its bitterness, and its unrelenting character. In Romanism we see the true successor of Israel's persecuting spirit. Both are visible to this day.

For centuries Rome wielded the civil power; and even to-day wherever this is combined with religious power as it is still in some countries, alas ! we see the same results.

The "Christian religion," as such, is no different in spirit and character from " the Jews' religion." All the persecutions of Rome have been inflicted in the name of " the Christian religion," and it would be much the same in our own day if it were not for the protection which the civil power affords us.

Paul himself had to appeal to the civil power of Pagan Rome for a justice which he could not procure from his religious brethren according to the flesh.

Religion condemns from its *feelings;* not from the principles of law or equity. When it *desired to have judgment* against Paul, Festus answered " It is not the manner of the Romans to deliver any man to die, before that *he which is accused have the accusers face to face, and have licence to answer for himself concerning the crime laid against him.*" (Acts xxv. 15, 16).

Many of our readers have reason to wish that their own Brethren knew something of the justice of Pagan Law. How many are daily condemned without any such " licence." In the " whisperings and backbitings," which abound throughout the sects, characters are blasted, and reputations ruined without any such opportunity of answering for one's self.

Hence we need to-day as much as ever—(for religion will be the same to the end)—the same living faith in the living God.

Nothing else will stand us in any stead.

" *Semper eadem* " (always the same) is the motto of religion, and the Apostle experienced it. It was this that caused him to say " all . . . are turned away from me" (2 Tim. i. 15). He refers to those among whom he laboured most effectually and for a longer period than any others (Acts xix. 10). And at the end of his life and ministry he had to say " No man stood with me ; all men forsook me " (2 Tim. iv. 16).

He suffered in a more refined way than those whom

he dragged from their homes and delivered to prison. And it was probably more acute. For, in prison, the iron may enter into the flesh; but, in thus being forsaken, it enters into the spirit. But it hurts just the same!

Oh! to have a living faith in the living God. "He abideth faithful."

Hence, the Apostle could immediately add to his sad confession: "Notwithstanding, the Lord stood with me and strengthened me."

The Word of the Lord was not bound. That is why he could add "that by me the preaching might be fully known, and that all the Gentiles might hear. And *I was delivered* out of the paw of the lion. And the Lord *shall deliver* me from every evil work, and will preserve me unto His heavenly kingdom to Whom be glory ever and ever. Amen" (2 Tim. iv. 17, 18).

The struggles of opposing worships were always of the fiercest. Nothing in the world has ever been so cruel as *religion!* More blood has been shed and more lives sacrificed in the name of religion than in any other cause. It is the same in modern times as in ancient; the same in the days of Antiochus as in the reign of Manasseh; the same under Diocletian and others as under Antiochus; the same under Ferdinand in Spain and under Mary in England, as under Diocletian.

The same is seen to-day, without shedding of blood, or breaking of bones, but not without breaking of hearts, among those who inherit the same religious nature and instincts.

Only among those who are endeavouring to "*keep* the unity of the Spirit;" do we discern "the bond of peace." It is among those who are seeking to *make* their own bodies that we see strifes, envies and divisions, and excommunications.

This spirit is seen in all systems of religions, in all ages.

The Apostle, of course, is referring to the establishment of false religion in the kingdoms of Israel and Judah which we may be quite sure was not accomplished without persecution.

We know that, under Jezebel's religious tyranny in Israel, the outward worship of Jehovah was, for a time at least, extinct.

We know from 2 Chron. that Jeroboam, who first introduced another religion into Israel, robbed the Levites of their possessions and property, and prohibited them from carrying out their duties in the worship of Jehovah.

They emigrated in a body to Judah; "and, after them, out of all the tribes of Israel, such as set their hearts to seek the Lord God of Israel, came to Jerusalem, to sacrifice unto the Lord God of their fathers" (2 Chron. xi. 14-16).

Another and a greater exodus is mentioned as coming "out of Ephraim, and Manasseh, and of Simeon," in the reign of Asa, king of Judah (2 Chron. xv. 9).

In the reign of Hezekiah also "divers of Asher and Manasseh, and of Zebulun humbled themselves and came to Jerusalem" (2 Chron. xxx. 10).

These events show how severe was the pressure of the persecutions carried on by the idolatrous kings of Israel, Ahab and Jezebel, Ahaz and Manasseh as well as under Jehoiakim and Zedekiah.

So that it was not merely under Antiochus Epiphanes

that religious persecution was so severely felt. It is only that we have further details given of them in Jewish secular history in the books of the Maccabees and by Josephus.

Josephus tells how, when " Antiochus had built an idol-altar upon God's altar, he slew swine upon it, and so offered a sacrifice neither according to the law nor the Jewish religious worship in that country. He also compelled them to forsake the worship that they paid to their own God, and to adore those whom he took to be gods, and made them build temples and raise idol-altars in every city and village, and offer swine upon them every day . . . He also appointed overseers, who should compel them to do what he had commanded. And, indeed, many Jews there were who complied with the king's commands, either voluntarily or out of fear of the penalty that was denounced; but the best men, and those of the noblest souls, did not regard him, but did pay a greater respect to the customs of their country than concern as to the punishment which he threatened to the disobedient ; on which account they every day underwent great miseries and bitter torments, for they were whipped with rods, and their bodies were torn to pieces, and were crucified while they were still alive and breathed . . . and if there were any sacred book of the law found, it was destroyed, and, those with whom they were found, miserably perished also (Josephus *Antiquities* xii. 5, 4).

It has been the same sad story through all the ages : not merely in Israel and Palestine, but in Rome, and wherever Romanism has had power, in every part of the world. Rome brought religious tortures to perfection and made persecution a fine art.

How many tens of thousands perished for their faith in God and His Word has been computed, but will never be known till "that day" of recompense shall come, and "the day of vengeance of our God."

Blood has been shed in wars of conquest, but the conquered had at least the opportunity of self-defence, as well as of overcoming. But it is religion that has never given any quarter, and has exhibited all the hatred and enmity of Satan himself against the people of God and the Word of God.

Jews suffered as well as, or even more than Protestants, throughout the persecutions of Rome in Europe.

The Armada that sailed from Spain was not for political conquest, but for religious supremacy. Thumb-screws, and similar instruments of torture found in the vessels sailing under the orders of Rome,* were not weapons for honourable warfare, but for *the subjugation of the conscience,* and *the extinction of liberty.*

These are, and ever have been, the two aims and objects of religious persecution.

The spirit of them is seen in the religious intolerance of modern Christian and so-called Protestant sects, who suffer not their members to worship outside their own bodies, without making them feel certain pains and penalties, often resulting in excommunication, and extending as far as surveillance of the private life and associations which bring "a visit" from those who assume and usurp an authority in defiance of the simplest laws of Christian liberty. Even those outside, like ourselves, are made to feel the secret power of religious boycotting which is as rife and rampant in some "Christian" sects as in the political sphere.

---

*Still preserved, and to be seen in the Tower of London.

Let a member of such sects dare to learn and discover some new truth from the Word of God, which happens to be different from what has been determined on by the sects themselves, and at once he is made to experience the worst features of "religion," and to realize, even in his private life, the power of a secret inquisition, which is as real as that of Rome, and whose tortures, though not physical or in the body, are as acutely felt, and may have after-effects on bodily health and mental powers.

In our own day, though "the powers that be" are able still to protect us from the grosser outrages and physical tortures of former days, they are yet unable to reach those which are animated by the self-same spirit, and are more refined in their character, being calculated to produce their own peculiar mental and spiritual effects.

The same "like precious faith" is required in us, as much as it ever was by the saints of old, if we dare to believe God in what He has revealed in His Word.

The irreligious world has formulated its Eleventh Commandment. A breach may be made and tolerated in any or all of the other ten; but "Thou shalt not be found out," is more important than all, in the eyes of the world and is certain to bring down the world's condemnation.

It is the same in the religious world. It has its Eleventh Commandment: "thou shalt not differ in opinion." All else will be tolerated; but once this command is broken, the unpardonable sin has been committed.

We repeat therefore, once again, that nothing but a living faith in the living God "will stand us in any stead when we thus have to face religious intolerance."

Oh! to believe God; and "cease from man."

Let us remember these "others." They have no name; let us be content to have none.

Those who through God-given faith have been enabled to do great wonders may be known and named, and endured, and even praised by the world. But, there are "others" who must be content to walk with God— unknown by the world, and suffering for what they have learned from the Word of God, and for daring to believe Him instead of the traditions of men.

"And Others"

d. "They Were Stoned" (vs. 37)

THIS is a fourth class of those "others" who exhibited faith's power in enabling them to suffer FOR God.

They were stoned, not as criminals who had sinned against man, but as sufferers who had resisted man in their faithfulness towards God.

Stoning was one of the prescribed methods of inflicting punishment, and there are nine cases of death from stoning recorded in scripture, and nine is the number connected with judgment.

1. The blasphemer (Lev. xxiv. 14).
2. The sabbath-breaker (Num. xv. 36).
3. Achan (Josh. vii. 25).
4. Abimelech (Judges ix. 53).
5. Adoram (1 Kings xii. 18).
6. Naboth (1 Kings xxi. 13).
7. Zechariah, the priest (2 Chron. xxiv. 20-22).
8. Stephen (**Acts** vii. 58).
9. Paul (Acts **xiv.** 19, 20. 2 Cor. xi. 25).

Of these, only Naboth and Zechariah come under the heading in our verse 37 of Heb. xi. ; and both are important.

It is the more needful for us to consider well the case of

NABOTH THE JEZREELITE,

inasmuch as it has been the aim of modern criticism to make out that Naboth suffered merely from personal considerations and selfish motives.

Surely, the Holy Spirit, in giving these words to Paul, must have intended our thoughts to go back to

415

such an example as that furnished by such a notable case as that of Naboth. This may be the reason why the enemy has sought to be-little and explain away the whole subject.

It has been urged* that "when Ahab requested Naboth to exchange his vineyard for another which the king would give him, Naboth, in the independent spirit of a Jewish landholder, refused. Perhaps the turn of his expression implies that his objection was mingled with a religious scruple at forwarding the acquisitions of a half-heathen king. Jehovah forbid it me that I should give the inheritance of my fathers unto thee," as though the emphasis were placed on "thee."

But, this is not the case, so far as the Hebrew is concerned, nor was it the case so far as Naboth was concerned. This is the view taking by a modern critic who cannot see beyond the "letter," and fails altogether to reach the "spirit."

The history shows that the emphasis is to be placed on quite a different matter, namely, the faithfulness to Jehovah's law, which is by this very incident shown to be known and in full operation at that time ; while the modern critics are endeavouring to make us believe that the Pentateuch was written five centuries later.

The event, therefore, at once rises before our eyes, in all its significance and importance.

The structure of Ahab's reign, if we may refer to that given in *The Companion Bible* sets this out, and shows very clearly that the incident connected with Naboth's vineyard is the second example of Ahab's "Personal Evil."

---

* Smith's *Dictionary of the Bible*, article "Naboth," by the late Dean Stanley.

AHÂB'S REIGN (1 Kings xvi. 29—xxii. 40)

Q | R | xvi. 29-. Introduction.
   | S | T | xvi. -29-33. Personal evil.   Idolatry.
   | | U | xvi. 34—xx. 43. Public events. War with Syria.
   | S | T | xxi. 1-29. Personal evil.   Naboth.
   | | U | xxii. 1-38.   Public events.   War with Syria.
   | R | xxii. 39, 40.   Conclusion.

Then it is shown that the portion marked *T* is thus divided by the Holy Spirit.

PERSONAL EVIL (1 Kings xxi. 1-29)

T | Q¹ | 1—16.   The evil committed.
    | Q² | 17—29.   The evil to be judged.

We need not show the further expansions of these two members.   It is sufficient for us to be thus informed that the primary fact shows that this scripture is not written to eulogize Naboth's faith, but to exhibit a second example of Ahab's personal evil.

Naboth's faith is there all the same, and it is not until we reach Heb. xi. 37 that we are directed to it, as an example of faith's power in enabling Naboth to suffer FOR God.

Yes it was for God.   The opening words of 1 Kings xxi. give us the key and the clue to the whole matter. There the revelation of Ahab's personal evil begins with the mention of Naboth.

"Naboth the Jezreelite had a vineyard."   The verb rendered "had" means to "become," and compels the rendering "a vineyard came to be Naboth's [by inheritance]."   This at once tells us that this vineyard was not Naboth's by *purchase*, but by *inheritance*, and the law of God left him in no doubt as to his duty toward it. That law told him that he held it under trust; and, that he could deal with it, only according to requirements of Jehovah's law, which was clearly laid down for his instruction.

The law is given in Lev. xxv. 23, 24. "The land shall not be sold in perpetuity (*i.e.*, absolutely, or beyond recovery); for the land is Mine; for YE are strangers and sojourners with Me. And in all the land of your possession ye shall grant a redemption (*i.e.*, a repurchase) for the land."

This was why Naboth declined King Ahab's demand. The words show us the lofty nature of the stand he took; "Jehovah forbid it me, that I should give *the inheritance of my fathers* unto thee."

It is clear from the context that Ahab required a total alienation of the inheritance, for he offered to give Naboth "a better vineyard than it," or the "worth of it in money."

But why do the modern critics wish to get rid of Naboth's obedience to Jehovah's law, by introducing the personal element, and making his refusal turn on the feelings of "a Jewish landholder"?

Why? Because it is held that the law was not given till some centuries later, and this incident, rightly understood, shows unmistakably that this law was in such full force that Ahab did not dare to take the vineyard without showing good cause, and a semblance at least of right.

This was the point of Jezebel's plot. She pretended to obey another law, the law of blasphemy, by which not only might Naboth be got rid of, but his property would revert automatically to the king. That this was the law is clear from the case of Mephibosheth, on account of the treason of Ishbosheth his father. David voluntarily restored the forfeited property to Ishbosheth's son (2 Sam. ix. 7). Not only was the property forfeited, but Mephibosheth's life also was forfeited. Hence he was in hiding at Lo-debar (2 Sam. ix).

In Naboth's case, not only was his life unjustly taken on account of the false witness on which he was condemned, but it is clear, from 2 Kings ix. 26, that his sons' lives were also taken. This was on the precedent of Josh. vii. 25.

The law of Moses had to be adhered to in all points, for the king had no power to inflict the punishment of stoning.

The law was moreover observed in proclaiming a fast ; for the Mishna and Gemara explain that criminals were usually executed on days of solemnity "that all the people might hear and fear" (Deut. xvii. 13).

In any case, we lift the case of the stoning of Naboth out of the mere hypothesis of not wanting to sell an ordinary piece of land to a "half-heathen king," on to the very highest level of obedience to the law of Jehovah ; and at the same time, furnish the evidence that that law was well known, and acknowledged as being, in that day, part of the social system in Israel.

This is a conclusion worthy of the scripture record. Naboth "believed God" as his forefather Abraham had done ; and he submitted to be stoned to death rather than disobey Jehovah's law. This was faith indeed. We do not read that he made any defence or offered any violent opposition. He heard the two witnesses (for the law of Deut. xvii. 6, etc., was again strictly carried out); he knew their witness was false ;

yet, he suffered in silence, and is here, in Heb. xi. 37, referred to and placed among those "others" whose belief of what they had "heard" from God enabled them to suffer for His sake.

Among these "others" stands out the case of "Zechariah the son of Jehoiada the priest" who was stoned for his faithful witness on behalf of Jehovah's written law (2 Chron. xxiv. 20-22). Jehoiada his father had rendered signal service to Joash the king. Indeed, Joash owed his life to Jehoiada; for, it was he whose wife Jehosheba rescued Joash as a babe "from among the king's sons that were slain" by Athaliah, and put him and his nurse in one of the chambers of the house of God and hid them for six years.

Zechariah had his father's faith, for Jehoiada, during those six years, witnessed to the truth of Jehovah's word that "the king's son shall reign as THE LORD HATH SAID of the sons of David" (2 Chron. xxiii. 3).

Zechariah his son exhibited a like precious faith when he appealed to the king and the people saying: "Why transgress ye the commandments of the LORD?" It was still faith in what "the LORD hath said."

This was the true witnessing which makes him worthy to find his place here, in the great cloud of witnesses who suffered death rather than fail to witness for God.

It is this Zechariah whom Jehovah specially raised up and sent to bring His people again unto Himself from their idolatrous ways; and of whom it was written "they testified against them."

We have before called attention to the rendering of these words in the Latin Vulgate, authorized by the Council of Trent: "*quos protestantes*," *i.e.*, who were witnesses against them. Rome is thus compelled to be the first to use the word "protestant;" while, ignorant of her own Bible, she declares that the name was invented at the Reformation (at the diet of Spiers)

May the Lord make us faithful " witnesses for " those truths which we have "heard" from Him; and ready to suffer, if need be, even with our lives, as true " protestants " have ever been.

There is another Zacharias, the "son of Barachias," whose death we read of in Matt. xxiii. 35, and Luke xi. 51, but he was not stoned. He was a prophet, while the one of whom we have been speaking was a priest. Doubtless it was for his faith.

The stoning of Stephen must surely have been present to Paul's mind, while he was being inspired to pen these words. He could but remember how he had "consented unto his death," and "held the clothes of those who stoned him" (Acts vii. 58; viii. 1). What his thoughts and feelings must have been, we can scarcely imagine.

He must indeed have needed precious faith in those other words which formed a special part of his gospel "having forgiven you all trespasses" (Col. ii. 13), and have rested on Him, "in Whom we have redemption through his blood even the forgiveness of sins"(Col.i. 14).

And, when he was himself stoned (Acts xiv. 19), he knew what it was to suffer for Christ's sake; and needed all the faith of which he afterwards wrote to those same " Hebrews " (Acts xiv. 19 ; 2 Cor. xi. 22, 25), in this chapter which we are considering.

Many of our readers, we are sure, are among these "others," but they have "like precious faith" to sustain them. If it was sufficient for those who " were stoned," it will surely be sufficient for any suffering which we may be called to endure through our faith in and faithfulness to God's Word, which through grace we have heard.

"And Others"

e. "Were Sawn Asunder"

As we approach the close of the great "cloud of witnesses," it seems as though the examples of those in the second of these last two groups who *suffered for God* were so many more than those who *conquered through God* (in the former group), that no names are given. The apostle was evidently "moved by the Holy Ghost" to hasten on to the conclusion of his theme.

Those in this last group are so numerous, and the manner of their suffering so various that one kind after another is mentioned—as though it were impossible to include them all. The description "and others" is pathetic in its brevity, and full of significance. We can scarcely find any record of many of them in the Old Testament.

Tradition tells us that Isaiah was "sawn asunder"—but nothing is said about it, or any other so suffering in the Bible. Its origin is in the Jerusalem *Gemara*.* There we read, how, in the days of King Manasseh, Isaiah fled and took refuge in a cedar tree, whereupon the cedar swallowed him up. The fringes of his garment were seen and they betrayed him. When Manasseh was told of it he commanded the cedar tree to be sawn asunder. When the king's orders were obeyed the prophet's blood gushed forth, etc.

It is added, that this is what is referred to (in 2 Kings xxiv. 4), as that "which the LORD would not pardon."

---

* *Sanhedrin.* The *Gemara* is the commentary of the *Talmud*, while the *Mishnah* denotes the text.

There is no record of any individual cases of those who suffered in the ways here stated, in the historical books of Scripture. Hence, some modern critics desire to bring the references down to the time of Antiochus Epiphanes.

But there is no need to do this. Quite enough is said in 2 Kings xxiv. alone to account for all the horrors recounted in these verses. We read there, how Jehovah removed Judah out of His sight " for the sins of Manasseh, according to all that he did ; and also for the innocent blood that he shed : for he filled Jerusalem with blood ; which Jehovah would not pardon " (vv. 3, 4).

It is sufficient for us that, whether Isaiah thus suffered or not, there were others that did ; and if he did not suffer thus in his own person, his prophecy has suffered in this manner ; for modern critics do not hesitate to cut his book asunder and say there were two Isaiahs— one of whom wrote from i. 1—xxxix. 8, and the other from xl. 1, to the end. This is a crime as great as Manasseh's for Isaiah was only " a man of God," but his book is part of " the Word of God."

The Lord Jesus referred to *both* parts of his book and makes no such distinction between them.*

This is nothing in the eyes of modern critics who dare to commit a sin similar to that of Jehoiakim (in whose days was executed the judgment pronounced on Manasseh's sin). Jehoiakim cut up the word of God with his penknife ; these men cut it up with their pens. That is the only difference. The result is the same.

* Of the 60 quotations from Isaiah in the New Testament, 24 are from the first part (chs. i.-xxxix.), and 36 from the latter part (chs xl.-lxvi.). Of these 60 quotations, several are quoted more than once, so that there are 45 separate passages ; of these, 16 are from the former part and 29 are from the latter part.

They call themselves "critics," which means *able to judge ;* but they judge without evidence. They do not understand the laws of evidence, so that the only and sufficient answer to their blasphemies is—"they say so."

Whoever they were that were "sawn asunder," the fact that remains for us is that they were able to endure even this manner of death "through faith." They "believed God" instead of man, like their father Abraham, and men resented it by thus putting them to death.

f. "Were Tempted"

There are many suggestions as to the "reading," and the rendering of this word.

This furnishes us with a good example of the principles which govern the doings of modern critics. Their human reason cannot understand why a so apparently mild expression should follow such "torments, and ways of dreadful death." Through not understanding what is meant by the Greek word here used, they are "surprised" at finding it here ; and they say : "This surprise having been all but universally felt, various have been the *conjectures* resorted to." (1) "Some are for leaving out the word altogether, its very form was suspicious" *epeirasthēsan* coming so soon after *epristhēsan* (=were sawn asunder), "might have been a mistake for it." This is said because the critics fail to see the beautiful Figure *Paronomasia* (two words having a similar sound with different meanings, to call our attention to the emphasis intended). "It might have been a marginal gloss of some dull student." (Of course the modern critics are never "dull.") With them it is always the book that is wrong. It never dawns on them that what is wrong is with them.

It has seemed to many critics that some mention of *fire* might well be expected here, so that they have conjectured *eprēsthēsan, epurasthēsan, eparthēsan, eprathēsan, epēreasthēsan, espeirasthēsan, esphairisthēsan, epreasthēsan, etaricheuthēsan, epurōthēsan, epuristhēsan, eneprēsthēsan, enepuristhēsan."* Our readers will see that the critics are prodigal with their conjectures.

Others have *thought* that *mutilation* was more probably intended, and have conjectured *epērōthesan* Many other *conjectures* may be seen in authors whose names are given. Luther read *eparthēsan* (= were thrust through).

After citing these Alford says on his own account " *If any conjecture is to be made* (and he puts this sentence in italics) I would say that either the omission, or *eprēsthēsan* would appear to me the most probable."

And all these *conjectures* are indulged in because (he says) " As it stands, I do not see how any appropriate meaning can be given to the mere enduring of temptation, placed as it is between being sawn asunder and dying by the sword."

Those words, " I do not see," are the key to the whole matter. Thus is the Word of God, quite apart from Textual Authorities, brought down to the bar of human reasoning.

From what we have to say as to the real meaning of the word in question our readers will see that there is no reason to doubt the correctness of the A.V. rendering, " were tempted."

And we have to keep in mind that this temptation or trial was in connection with their " faith," not with their " works." They were tempted not to commit crimes or immoralities, but to abandon their faith in what God had said, by listening to promises of deliverance, or heeding threats of diabolical tortures.

Like the temptation of our first parents, it was the Word of God that was in question. " Hath God said " was the only " trial " in their case ; and it has been the same trial of faith through all the ages. Promises were made to them that they should not die, and that they should be as God. They believed Satan's lies, and they fell. Their fall consisted in *unbelief*.

These " were tempted " as they were. Tempted, so that they should not believe God's promises ; tempted to doubt His goodness ; to disbelieve His Word. They were tempted, as our first parents were, by false promises ; promises of liberty, of honour, and of promotion ; and these were tried (as our first parents were not), by threats of tortures and violent deaths ; but " through faith " they were more than conquerors.

It was religion by which these " others " were tempted and tried. Religion tempted them to believe its dogmas instead of God's words. Religion tempted them to forsake God.

It was not the irreligious world, with its vanities or politics, that thus tempted these " others."

The world goes to war, and throws down an honourable and an open challenge to a trial of strength. It does not use secret arts or instruments of torture in a trial of faith. That is reserved for the sphere of religion. It has ever been so. Life and wealth and honour were frequently offered in the midst of unimaginable tortures to induce believers to forsake the God Whom they believed.

Micaiah knew what it was to be thus "tempted" when Zedekiah, the son of Chenaanah, smote Micaiah upon the cheek . . . and said . . . put this fellow in prison, &c. (2 Chron. xviii. 23, 26).

Jeremiah knew what it was to be thus tried, when "Pashur, the governor of the house of the LORD, smote him and put him in the stocks." How he was tried with mental tortures is recorded in the rest of the chapter (*vv.* 12-18). At any moment he might have secured immunity from his trials by holding his peace.

In chapter xxxviii. 6, we read how (because of the word of the LORD which he spake), they "took Jeremiah and cast him into the dungeon . . . that was in the court of the prison: and they let down Jeremiah with cords. And in the dungeon there was no water, but mire. So Jeremiah sunk in the mire."

We may be sure that these instances were by no means solitary or exceptional cases of trial and suffering and temptation to escape all by turning away from God and His Word.

Paul himself knew what this meant when he said before Festus how he "shut up many of the saints in prison and . . . compelled them to blaspheme" (Acts xxvi. 10, 11). He does not say that he succeeded. He uses the imperfect tense, which may have a tentative (as well as a frequentative sense *used to compel*). Hence it may mean that he *attempted* and *wished* to compel them to apostatize. Like all unbelieving Jews of his time, that was his object. He was a zealot in "the Jew's religion," which, like all other religions, filled him with hatred and madness against all who differed.

This was and is the spirit of the religion of Rome,

and it is worthy of note that the phrase "to put the question" gave the name to the Inquisition, for that is the very meaning of the word. To "put the question" meant to examine by torture, with the view of forcing their victims to change their faith.

The very word *peirazō* is the root of the word here, "were tempted," *i.e.*, tried by questioning.

The word would be well understood by the Hebrews to whom the Apostle was writing. It must have had a sinister significance in their ears and their memories.

From the first Epistle of Peter we know that these "temptations" were still being endured by believing Hebrews. . . He speaks of "the trial of your faith being much more precious than of gold that perisheth, though it be tried with fire, might be found unto praise and honour and glory at the appearing of Jesus Christ" (1 Pet. i. 7).

This word, "tried," has been taken heretofore as a verbal form; but, the use of this very expression is found in the Papyri used as an Adjective in the sense of *genuine.**

Hence, the expression (*to dokimion*), means *your tried faith; i.e.*, your faith which has been *tried*, and *found genuine*.

In that day, the temptation was to abandon Christ as their Messiah and Saviour. In older days it was to abandon the worship of Jehovah for the idolatry of the heathen. What temptations were endured at the hands of Jezebel, Athaliah, Ahaz and Manasseh, no tongue can tell.

---

* Is is found on pawn-tickets and marriage contracts written about the same period of these Epistles. See Deismann's *Bible Studies* (T. & T. Clark, Edinburgh, p. 259, &c.).

Elijah's words give us a faint idea of them, in his reply to the word of Jehovah which came to him in Horeb, the mount of God (1 Kings xix.) And we know the details of the temptation presented to Hananiah, Mishael and Azariah, in Dan. iii. Theirs was a typical example of our subject, " were tempted." With the burning fiery furnace before them, we know they stood steadfast in their faith, and went into that furnace not knowing they would be delivered.

True, they were delivered, but it was not their *faith* which delivered them. Their faith made them without care as to the result.

This was the manifestation of their faith, and it was this that proved it to be *genuine.* The point of our subject is not faith's power to overcome through God, but faith power to suffer for God.

We are not all Daniels, nor are we all tried with his trials. God had His own purpose to serve, and His own ends to accomplish in the deliverance of Daniel and his companions in captivity.

He may have no public end to serve in our case. It may be our lot to be among these "others ;" but the same precious faith will enable us to endure.

He may not "send His angel" to deliver us from trial here and now, but He is going to "send Jesus Christ," and therefore we rejoice with joy unspeakable and full of glory, receiving the end of our tried faith, which is more precious than of tried and genuine gold which perisheth.

"And Others"

g. "Were Slain With the Sword"

IN verse 34 we read of those who "*escaped* the edge of the sword."

But there were others who "were *slain* by the sword."

It was the same sword, and the same "precious faith," in each case; but how vast the difference.

In the first of these last two groups it was faith overcoming *through* God. Here it is faith suffering for God.

In the former case, faith overcame through believing what God had promised.

In the latter case, faith suffered in consequence of believing what God had said.

But it was the same precious faith; it "came by hearing"; and the hearing came by the word of the same God.

The Greek of Hebrew xi. 37 is literally, "by the slaughter of the sword they died." It might even be rendered "they were butchered by the sword."

This was specially the death which kings had power to inflict. They could not punish by stoning (as we have seen in the case of Naboth. The laws of God given to Moses were carried out by the properly constituted tribunals for such cases).

Execution by the sword was the only form of death which the king could constitutionally inflict.*

Jezebel could get rid of the prophets in this way; but she could not get rid of Naboth without a formal

---

*Maimonides. *Hilc. Sanhedrin* Ch. xiv.

430

tribunal, and a legal sentence of death, albeit it was procured by false witnesses.

She could "cut off the prophets of Jehovah' (1 Kings xviii. 4) ; and what this means we learn from Elijah's lips in xix. 10, 14. "They have slain thy prophets with the sword."

It is astonishing how alert the modern critics are to discover, if possible, by any ingenuity, some fault with the Word of God.

One asserts that "one prophet only perished (he means, only one prophet perished, and not more; he does not mean that he "only perished" and nothing else happened to him) by the sword in the kingdom of Judah, viz., Urijah (Jer. xxvi. 23)."

This is one of numerous examples which show that the statements of modern critics must always be verified. We cannot trust them to the smallest extent, not even in giving a reference. We must verify even this. "The wish is father to the thought," and their "wish" is so strong that they put their "thoughts" for serious facts!

Our Lord said "O! Jerusalem, Jerusalem, thou that killest the prophets . . . which are sent unto thee" (Matt. xxiii. 37). So another critic at once questions the statement, and asks for evidence that the "true prophets had been put to death in the holy city."

We can at once satisfy his thirst for knowledge by referring him to Jer. ii. 30, where Jehovah charges Jeremiah to "Go and cry in the ears of Jerusalem . . saying: 'your own sword hath devoured your prophets like a destroying lion.'"

Those who have this "wish" to discredit the statements of God's Word readily gulp down the thoughts of man, and treat them as facts and truths; but our readers will believe nothing that they say; and will examine every assertion, and verify every reference. The one resultant fact will be—"they say so."

On the other hand, the more we search, the more we learn; and the more we are able to learn, and lean hard on the smallest details of the Word of God; and very often the efforts of modern critics result in our discovering things that we should not perhaps have otherwise noticed.

We have an example in the present case.

On looking further at the words used, we find that in 1 Sam. xxii., 18, where it says that Doeg, the Edomite, "slew" 85 priests; the word *mūth* means *to put to death*. But in *v.* 21 we learn the manner of their death, when Abiathar told David "that Saul had slain the LORD's priests:" the word "slay" being *hārag, to slay with the sword*.

This fact led to a further discovery, viz.: that the Jerusalem *Gemara* (the Jewish Commentary on the Talmud) explains that this word (*hārag*) was understood as the equivalent for beheading: "The prescription respecting those slain with the sword: they cut off his head with a sword, according to the manner of the kingdom (*i.e.*, by the execution of the king's orders). It goes on to explain that the head was sometimes "struck off with an axe." It was so, either with the sword or axe, in the case of John the Baptist by Herod Antipas (Matt. xiv. 10, Mark vi. 16, 27, 28, Luke ix. 9), and James the brother of John by Herod Agrippa (Acts xii. 2). It was this death that Peter, at that time, escaped.

Our verse (Heb. xi. 37) gives the equivalent for this technical term (*hārag*).

We are thus led to some light that is thrown on Rev. xx. 4 "the souls of them that were beheaded," which explains the expression in Rev. vi., 9, "the souls of them that were slain."

Of course, the word "souls" is used here tor "persons," and the Genitive is that of Apposition—the expression meaning, "I saw the slain ones," and in Rev. xx. 4 "And I saw thrones, and those beheaded; and they [*i.e.* the beheaded ones] sat upon them [*i.e.* the thrones] : on account of the testimony of Jesus and on account of the Word of God, and those who had not done homage to the beast, nor to his image, and did not receive its mark upon their forehead, and upon their hand; and they lived [in resurrection] and reigned with Christ a thousand years."

This verse is the fulfilment of Chapter vi. 9 where John says "I saw underneath the altar the souls of those who were slain for the word of God and on account of the testimony which they held."

Here the words have the same meaning: "souls" are put for "persons"; and, the Genitive is the Genitive of Apposition, *viz.*, "Souls, *i.e.*, those who had been beheaded for the word of God," etc.

The use of the word "souls" here is the same as in a vast number of passages of which Gen. xlvi. 27, furnishes an example: "All the souls of the house of Jacob which came into Egypt were three-score and ten."

Indeed, it has exactly the same meaning as in some thirteen other passages where the Hebrew for "soul" (*nephesh*, Greek *pseuchē*), is translated, "the dead." (Lev. xix. 28; xxi. 1; xxii. 4. Num. v. 2; vi. 11); "body" (Lev. xxi. 11; Num. vi. 6; xix. 11, 13;

Hag. ii. 13); "dead body" (Num. ix. 6, 7, 10). Why did not the translators render it "dead body" in Rev. vi. 9; and xx. 4? Why this inconsistency? Why render it "dead body" in Num. ix. 6, 7, 10, and "soul" in Rev. vi. 9, and xx. 4?

In the latter passage it was the dead bodies of those who had been beheaded for their faith, who lived again in resurrection, and reigned with Christ a thousand years.

We are aware that there is a Various Reading with regard to the statement in the next verse about "the rest of the dead," about which there are some who labour under a great mistake. We often hear it said that the words "lived not again until" form no part of the true text, and ought not to be there at all. But this is not the case. It is not a question whether the words should be there or not, but whether we should read *anezēsan heōs* ("lived not again until") or *ezēsan achri* ("lived not till").

Practically, all the textual critics prefer the latter reading; but this does not make any difference to the sense; for *ezēsan* means the same thing. The verb *zaō* frequently means *to live* in resurrection life; and that necessarily means *to live again*, whichever form of the verb we take. Our readers have only to refer to the following passages to see this for themselves.

In Matt. ix. 18, "My daughter is even now dead: but come and lay Thy hand upon her, and she shall live," *i.e.*, *live again*, as she had lived before.

In Mark xvi. 11, "They heard that He [Christ] was alive," *i.e.*, *alive again* in resurrection.

In Luke xxiv. 5, "Why seek ye the living (*i.e.*, Him That *liveth again*) among the dead?" And verse 23 "saying that they had seen a vision of angels which said that He (Christ) was alive," *i.e., alive again.*

So we may compare Acts i. 3; ix. 41; xxv. 19; Rom. vi. 10; xiv. 9; 2 Cor. xiii. 4; Rev. i. 4, 18; ii. 8; xvii. 14. The only question about Rev. xx. 5 is, not whether "lived again" should *be in the text* or not, but whether it is the same word as in verse 4, where we read "they lived and reigned with Christ a thousand years." If it is, then it means "they lived (again in resurrection life), and reigned," &c. So that it comes to the same thing, and the supposed Various Reading is not worth talking about.

In Rev. vi. 9, John saw (in a vision, be it remembered), those who had been slain; and, likewise in vision, he heard what they are represented as saying.

In Rev. xx. 4, he sees (again in vision, for the " until " has not come to pass even yet, nor has the promise made to them in vi. 9, been yet fulfilled), these same dead persons alive again, sitting on thrones and reigning with Christ.

And we learn the additional fact as to the manner in which they had been slain; they were "slain with the sword," in other words, they had been " beheaded."

How could "souls," apart from the body, "sit" or "reign"? How could they "live" except by being raised from the dead, and living again in resurrection life?

It is strange how traditionists, and rut-ualists, will cling to the most absurd and inconsistent interpretations to suit something they have learned from someone else; and yet will not allow others the same liberty of believing what they have heard from God. They insist on taking " souls" in Rev. vi. 9 and xx. 4 *literally*. But they will not allow Romanists to take " this is my body " literally, nor will they allow Ritualists to take " we have an altar " literally. In these cases they are quite correct, for these *are* both Figures of Speech. Their inconsistency lies in taking " souls " in Rev. vi. 9 literally, when it is just as much a Figure of Speech, and is used of *the whole person.*

When they speak of an employer of labour employing a certain number of " hands," they understand and use the word " hands " in its figurative sense ; " hands," *a part* of the person, being put for *the whole* person.

When they read in Rev. xviii. 13, how Great Babylon is to be punished because (among other things) she traded in the bodies and souls of men," they understand this of the slave trade, and indeed agree to the accurate rendering of the word " bodies," as meaning slaves, referring to Ezek. xxvii. 13, where it is written, " they traded in the persons of men." In Ezekiel, the word rendered " persons " is the Hebrew *nephesh* (souls), which is again put as a part of the person, for the whole person, as in Rev. vi. 9.

Even so should they understand the word " souls " as being put by the same figure (*Synecdochē*) as *a part* of the person for *the whole* person.

The great fact about these " persons " here, however, is the manner of their death. They had been " beheaded," in other words, they had been " slain with the sword."

Thus our understanding of this expression in Heb. xi. 37, throws light upon Rev. vi. 9 and xx. 4.

In the passages in Revelation they are not the same persons, of course, as in Heb. xi. 37, for these have not yet been " slain with the sword."

Heb. xi. 37 refers to the Old Testament history to which reference is made throughout the chapter, while Rev. vi. 9 and xx. 4 refer to events which have not yet taken place; for the beast who thus beheads them has not yet arisen; the time for his revelation has not yet arrived; the apostasy has not yet come to a head.

It is on its way. Many are the "signs of the times" which furnish evidence of this.

We are exhorted thus with regard to it: "Let no man deceive you by any means FOR [that day (*i.e.* the Day of the Lord) shall not come] except the apostasy shall have come first, and the lawless one, the son of perdition, shall have been revealed," &c. (2 Thess. ii. 3).

So that the beheaded ones have not yet been beheaded; and, what John saw in Rev. vi. 9, was not merely in a vision, but in a *prophetic* vision—a vision of what has not even yet taken place, so that he could not have actually seen the beheaded ones themselves.

They will suffer for their faith, as those referred to in Heb. xi. 37; and their faith will enable them to suffer for God, as did these "others" in Old Testament times.

It is all a question of believing God. He has spoken: and, such is the natural man's enmity to God, that all who believe God rather than man have suffered, and must expect to suffer, and will yet suffer, at man's hand.

This is the secret cause of all the suffering of these "others." The form of suffering has varied with the times.

In the Old Testament the only form of death exercised by the king was beheading; and, as at the French Revolution, so hereafter, in the persecution which the Beast will carry out, this form of death will be its great characteristic.

Nothing but a living faith in the living God will carry the faithful through it. All else will be useless. Church membership and church ordinances will alike be of no avail; all earthly props will fail, and He Who hath spoken will alone be the support of those who believe what He hath said.

"And Others"

h. They Wandered About in Sheepskins and Goatskins

GREAT pains are taken by some to show that these words refer to the garments worn by the prophets. We read of such garments as worn by Elijah in (2 Kings i. 8), and John the Baptist (Matt. iii. 4; Mark i. 6); and of false prophets being similarly clad in order to deceive (Zech. xiii. 4). But the context, in Heb. xi. 37, forbids such a reference as this.

The times referred to are evidently times of trouble, in which, to escape from the hands of men, such wanderers, driven out by dire necessity, were compelled to use the skins of animals instead of ordinary clothing. Such clothing is mentioned here to show us to what distresses those who believed God were reduced.

The point for us to bear in mind is not the mere necessity, as such. Many have thus gone about and been reduced to wear whatever they could obtain, and this, because of their own poverty produced by misfortunes, or sins; or, on account of crimes against society, or offences against the state.

But, not for any of these things were these wanderers thus clothed. Man, in his natural enmity to God, would not tolerate the society or even the existence of "others" who believed God, and hence regarded them as being "contrary to all men."

This is the reason why they were thus clothed. They could not approach men, in order to procure any other kind of clothing which men prepared and wore.

They were driven out to share the lot of wild animals, and were reduced to wear their skins instead of clothes woven by men.

This form of suffering is mentioned here to show, on the one hand, the cruelty of religious persecutions; and, on the other hand, the mighty sustaining power of faith.

What power indeed was this! It was not merely the compulsion such as that which enforced the wanderings of society's outlaws. It was the result of deliberate choice, like that of Moses (vv. 24-26). Any day, any one of these wanderers could have rejoined his fellow men, enjoyed their society, and shared their comforts; but, they preferred this lot to apostasy. They, like Moses, "chose rather" to suffer these afflictions, than to give up their belief of what they had heard from God.

This is the whole case before us. It was proof of the mighty compelling power of faith in God, that placed them in this position, and gave them strength not merely to endure it, but to prefer it to that which they had given up for it.

This is further enhanced by the words

i. "Being Destitute, Afflicted, Tormented"

or, being destitute, being cruelly harassed, being evil-intreated."

These were additional sources of suffering, aggravating the circumstances which necessitated their being thus clothed.

David and Elijah both knew, in their day, what it was to be thus destitute; and to wander about, and to be afflicted, and evil-intreated.

David only had to throw in his lot with Saul. Any day he could have gone back and become a courtier in the royal palace of Saul. But, he had "heard" the words spoken by God, through Samuel His prophet. Samuel, in obedience to God, had anointed David to be King, after He had "rejected" Saul (*cp.* 1 Sam. xvi. 13 with *v.* 1 and 12) "The Spirit of Jehovah came upon David from that day forward."

David therefore preferred to wander, conscious of Jehovah's presence with him.

He would rather be destitute of the greatest glories and the greatest honours that Saul could confer, than be destitute of the tokens of Jehovah's presence in his trials and afflictions. The Psalms abound with testimonies to the depth of his suffering and the height of his joy in God.

It was not all suffering; for, there was the compensating and sustaining power which enabled him to "count it all joy."

We are not called thus to wander and suffer, but we have similar tests of our loyalty to God. David's followers had not "heard" God speaking to them; they had only "heard" what God had spoken to David, and of David; but they believed God, and were content to suffer with David.

They had gone to him—"everyone that was distressed, and every one that had his creditor, and every one that was bitter in soul, and David became a captain over them" (1 Sam. xxii. 1, 2).

We, who were once distressed, on account of our sin; we, who had a creditor whose claims we could not meet; we, who suffered from bitterness of soul which no earthly anodyne could allay; we have gone forth "without the camp" to Him. He has become our Saviour and our Lord. He is the "captain over" us.

Now, we suffer with Him, and our wanderings are under His eye. We believe what we have "heard" from the true David about his anointing, and his future reign.

We have no part or lot with Saul's party. All our loyalty goes forth to the true David—"David's Son and David's Lord," and we believe—as we hear—that "if we suffer with Him, we shall reign also with Him" (2 Tim. ii. 12).

Believing what He has thus promised, we are prepared to endure anything here in view of the glory which is soon to be revealed.

We must note the parenthetical remark thrown in just here :

j. "Of Whom the World Wasn't Worthy" (vs. 38)

The world thought that these wanderers were not worthy of a part in their world, but the real fact was just the opposite. The world in which these wanderers lived was not worthy of them.

How full of meaning are many of these parentheses of scripture. Some of them contain a mine of truth and teaching.

This one has become a proverb among ourselves. Whether it was already a proverb then we cannot say. But here it is a statement of scripture truth. The world was, indeed, not worthy of them. Men of the world could not understand them, then, or now.

Men of the world could go over from one party to another, and even become mercenaries of either side;

they could have changed their religion if it paid them
to do so. But, here were men who could go through
any suffering and endure any hardship and privation
rather than give up what they had "heard" from
their God.

Truly the world in which they lived was "not worthy
of them." Nor is the world worthy of such to-day.

After this parenthesis, the subject is again taken up
for the conclusion of the list of these "others."

k. "They Wandered in Deserts, and in Mountains and in Dens, Caves of the Earth" (vs. 38)

It is not the same word for "wandered" as in verse
37. There it is *to wander about (periēlthon)*, here it is
to wander up and down (planōmenoi).

The reference is to those who hid in mountains, and
dens, and caves (holes) and cavernous retreats, such as
those hundred prophets whom Obadiah hid by fifty
in a cave, and fed them with bread and water
(1 Kings xviii. 4).

The reference may take in a later fact in Israel's
history recorded in 2 Maccabees x. 6, where we read
"they kept the feast eight days with gladness, like
the feast of the tabernacles, remembering that not long
afore they had held the feast of the tabernacles, when
as they wandered in the mountains and dens like
beasts."

Josephus also gives a terrible account (*Antiq.* xii. 6, 2)
of how nearly a thousand men, with their wives and
children, were smothered by fire, in the caves whither
they betook themselves, rather than fight on the
sabbath day.

Those referred to in Heb. xi. 38 are not the only ones who have experienced the particular forms of suffering here described.

The Waldensian Valleys could tell how, in later days, that " great cloud of witnesses " was added to by those who believed God rather than man.

It was the same faith that enabled them to endure and suffer for God. The times were different, and the persons were different, but, the same faith had heard the same solemn truths from the same Word of God, and the faith that came by that " hearing " produced its own precious fruit in the lives and in the deaths of those who believed what they had heard.

General Reflections

Verses 39, 40

" *And these all, having obtained a good report through faith, received not the* [fulfilment of the] *promise ; God having provided* [marg. foreseen] *some better thing for us, that they without us should not be made perfect* " (Heb. ii. 39, 40).

THESE verses must be among those to which Peter referred when he said, speaking of Paul's Epistles, there " are some things hard to be understood." For they confessedly present no small difficulty.

Moreover, we feel sure that they are also one of those passages of which he goes on to say, " they that are unlearned and unstable (*i.e.*, uninstructed, and not established) wrest (*i.e.*, twist) unto their own destruction " (or loss).

Now, our own earnest desire is not to suffer loss. Therefore, we feel the need of a full share of " instruction " ourselves.

Those who " oppose " have the same great need of " instruction " (2 Tim. ii. 25) ; and, from verse 15, we are plainly told, that this instruction can be obtained only from a rightly divided Word. Only thus can we learn " the truth."

So we will now learn together.

We must first rightly divide this whole Scripture (Heb. xi.) according to its structure, for the structure of a passage is ever its best and surest commentary. Only from *its whole scope* can we get at the meaning of the *words* which go to make it up.

445

As a whole, the chapter is obviously composed of *four* large members (or groups of verses) arranged in alternation :—

  | 1-12. Particular examples of faith.
   | 13-16. General reflections.
  | 17-38. Particular examples of faith.
   | 39, 40. General reflections.

If we desire to learn more, and apply the microscope (as it were) to these larger members, then we shall see their perfection and beauty more clearly, in *Alternation* and *Introversion.*

A | C | E | 1-7. GROUP (Witnesses FOR God)
       | F | 8-12. Abraham and Sarah.
          D | 13-16. GENERAL   REFLEC-TIONS.

          B | G | 20, 21. Isaac and Jacob.
             H | 22. Joseph.
           G | 23-28. Moses & his Parents.

A | C | F | 29-31. Israe. and Rahab.
    | E | 32-38. GROUPS(Witnesses THROUGH God)
        D | 39, 40. GENERAL   REFLEC-TIONS.

An examination of this structure will show how exquisitely each member corresponds with its fellow ; and how the " General Reflections " stand out, as though inviting us to compare them, and to see how the former, and longer reflections (*vv.* 13-16, marked D) will help us to understand the shorter and latter reflections (*vv.* 39, 40, marked *D*).

We notice, at once, that they have the same " catch words ": "these all . . . received not the promise." This is the great fact, which is thus emphasised.

Each member must be closely compared with its fellow ; and the one must be used to interpret the other so that we may supplement each and get the whole teaching of both.

The great outstanding fact is thus pressed upon us, so as to show us the special blessing and characteristic of " faith " (*i.e.*, believing what we have heard) is that it carries us beyond the grave.

It shows us how *faith* is thus the very *opposite* of *sight*, and gives us the meaning of the words " we walk by faith, and not by sight." This statement in 2 Cor. v. 7, illustrates precisely what is recorded in these " General Reflections " in Heb. xi., *viz.*, that all these were examples of faith, in that they did not walk by what they saw with their eyes, but by what they heard from God ; and thus saw by faith what was invisible.

Noah was " warned by God of things not seen as yet." But he did live to see them.

Other patriarchs died in full faith that they should yet receive what God had promised them, having "seen (the promises) afar off."

Moses was strong and stedfast, not fearing the wrath of Egypt's king, because by faith he could " see Him Who is invisible."

Even so, we, now, believing what God has promised us, that we who now live in our bodies made of earth (2 Cor., v. 1) shall one day have heavenly and spiritual bodies, not made " of the will of man " or " of the will of the flesh " (John i. 13), that is to say " not made with hands," and, therefore, not temporal, but eternal. This is why we, while in these bodies, groan, "not having received the promises," but we earnestly desire their fulfilment, and to be "clothed upon" with those heavenly bodies. We do not desire to die so that mortality may be swallowed up *of death*, but we desire our resurrection bodies, "that mortality may be swallowed up *of life*."

We know that, while we are at home, here, in these mortal bodies, we are absent from the Lord: for how can we enter into His glorious presence in our bodies of humiliation?

"There is a natural body, and there is a spiritual body" (1 Cor. xv. 44), the one is to be buried, "sown in corruption," but it is to be "raised in incorruption." "It is sown in dishonour; it is raised in glory. It is sown a natural body, it is raised a spiritual body."

While, therefore, we are in this natural body, we are necessarily "absent from the Lord," for, "flesh and blood cannot inherit the kingdom of God; neither doth corruption inherit incorruption" (*v.* 50).

When, then, shall we be "present with the Lord?" The answer is given. We are not left helpless in the darkness and the ignorance of heathenism, or tradition. It is "WHEN this corruptible [body] shall have put on incorruption, and this mortal [body] shall have put on immortality, THEN shall be brought to pass the saying that is written 'Death is swallowed up in victory'" (*v.* 54).

This agrees with 2 Cor. v. 4, where we learn that it is in Resurrection, we shall be "clothed upon with our house (or spiritual body) which is from heaven" (*v.* 2)

"that mortality might be swallowed up IN LIFE."
THEN shall we be "present with the Lord."

Till then, mortality will continue to be *swallowed up in death.*

Thus, we are assured that, walking by faith in the Word of our God, we shall be "clothed upon" by Translation, or, live again in Resurrection, when we shall be "present with the Lord." Therefore, this faith makes us "confident," yea, it makes us well pleased,* and the very thought fills us with great pleasure, that we shall one day be absent from these bodies of humiliation and, in a glorious Translation or Resurrection, be "present," yea, "for ever with the Lord."

This is the obvious "instruction" we receive from 2 Cor. v. 5-8, as to the "promise" we have received from God. We are well aware that there are those who "twist" it to their own great loss. But those who thus "oppose themselves" *need* this "instruction," and we give it "with meekness," mindful of our charge in 2 Tim. ii. 25.

To interpret this Scripture otherwise is to rob the blessed promise of Resurrection of all its power. Indeed, it is, in effect, to err like those "who concerning the truth have erred, saying that the Resurrection is past already." In Paul's day, those who thus spoke "overthrew the faith of some." But in our day these, like Hymenœus and Philetus, "overthrow the faith" of *many.*

---

* Greek *eudokeō* = well-pleased or delighted with, as in Matt. iii. 17; xii. 18; xvii. 5; Mark i. 11; Luke iii. 22; 2 Peter i. 17; 2 Cor. xii. 10; Eph. i. 5, 9; Phil. ii. 13; 2 Thess. i. 11; ii. 1 and 2; (not Titus ii. 9). With a negative, Heb. x. 6, 8, 38.

For, to substitute *another* hope, instead of Resurrection is to overthrow faith in that blessed truth. To say, " Lord, Thou needest not to come for me, and receive me to Thyself; I am coming to Thee." What is this but to overthrow faith in the Lord's gracious promise, "I will come again and receive you unto Myself" (John xiv. 3). When the uninstructed believe and teach the tradition of men instead of the truth of God, and say, we shall " ever be with the Lord" when we die, and therefore without any Translation or Resurrection, What is this but to overthrow the faith of those who would believe that " the dead in Christ," who shall rise shall be " caught up TOGETHER WITH " those who shall be alive and remain, and " SO,"* and only " SO," shall we " ever be with the Lord ?"

This " promise " is so simple, so categorical, so clear and unquestioned, that it should make us all more than willing to reconsider one or two other passages which those who are somewhat instructed consider to be open to emendation.

In any case we so believe it and understand it; and, if any, thus receiving it as the inspired Word of God, are required to believe another interpretation of it as a condition of fellowship, then we know of only two such " systems " which thus act. One is the Roman Catholic Church which arrogates to itself authority over the consciences of others, and imposes its own interpretation of Scripture as a condition of membership; and the other is that which acts on precisely

---

* The Greek *houto* means *thus, in this manner*, Matt. v. 12, 16, 19, &c., and in 1 and 2 Thess. in all the occurrences. 1 Thess. ii. 8; v. 2; 2 Thess. iii. 17.

the same "system," and yet considers itself to be different from all "systems."

It is a strange situation; and it ought to give rise to serious thought. But we need not dwell further on it. Rather, let us see how far the "General Reflections" in Heb. xi. agree with this. For, seeing the scope, we are now in a position to understand the words used in verses 13-16, and 39, 40. "These all died in faith not having received the promises, but, beholding and embracing them from afar, confessed that they were strangers and pilgrims† on the earth. For they that say such things declare plainly that they seek a country," *i.e.*, a homeland. Thus they declare themselves to be aliens, and as foreigners in this present world, while absent from that heavenly land, and from the One with Whom they desire to be.

The word rendered "country" is peculiar. It is not a country in the usual sense of the term, but, such a country as one's father dwells in, and whither we desire to journey. It is *patris*, a fatherland, or paternal home. It occurs only *six* times:—Here, and in Matt. xiii. 54, 57; Mark vi. 1, 4; Luke iv. 21, in all of which five places it is rendered *his own country*, referring to the earthly parental home of Mary and Joseph.

Here we are distinctly told that it was not the home of their earthly fathers, from whence they had come out, which they sought out and searched for (Gr. *epizēteō*). Had it been so, Abraham could easily have returned to Chaldea, and Isaac and Jacob to Mesopotamia. But no, it was a heavenly home. "For, not

---

† Note the order of these words in Gen. xxiii. 4; I Chron. xxix. 15; Ps. xxxix. 12; I Pet. ii. 11. We cannot be "pilgrims" journeying heavenward, until we know what it is to have become "strangers," (*i.e.*, aliens) as regards the world.

ashamed of them is God—God called upon (or invoked) as theirs; for He hath prepared for them a city " (*v.* 16).

When we read the word "them," we remember that this "promise" was made to each of the three patriarchs severally as well as jointly.

To ABRAHAM God said "To thee," Gen. xiii. 15; xv. 13.

To ISAAC God said " unto thee," Gen. xxvi. 3, 4.

To JACOB God said "to thee," Gen. xxviii. 4, 13; xxxv. 12; xlviii. 1-4 (in this latter verse Jehovah said, " The land whereon thou liest, *to thee* will I give it and to thy seed "), xxxv. 12; xlviii 1-4.

These passages are most conclusive, for in the Hebrew these pronouns are emphatic. Moreover, the pronouns are further emphasised by being distinguished from and contrasted with (and made additional) " to thy seed."

Therefore, the conclusion is inevitable that for them to realise this promise they must needs be raised from the dead; for " *they died, not having received the promise.*" They did enjoy the promise during their pilgrimage, and the more they enjoyed and desired it, the more they realised that they were " foreigners," while sojourning in that very land which God had spoken of.

This tells us that God must have *said* much more to them than is recorded in Genesis, because they could never have believed it unless they had "heard" about it from God. If they had not heard of it directly from God Himself, it would have been the pure imagination of their own brains, or only some tradition which they had heard from man.

We know that it could have been neither, for it distinctly says it was " by faith."

They must also have heard from God about that wonderful "city" for which they looked, that city whose Architect and Creator is God. *We*, also, have heard about it; and in Rev. xxi. 9-27, we are told about its name, its glory, and its "foundations," wall and gates.

If we believe what we have heard, then we, too, shall long for the time when it shall be seen "descending out of heaven from God" (*v*. 10).

Abraham, Isaac and Jacob, and all these who "died in faith not having received the promises, but saw them afar off," all these shall enter into it.

The city itself is yet future, for John saw it centuries later, in a vision of things which are yet to come, which will receive its fulfilment only after resurrection.

This brings us back to the great theme which is the subject of the "General Reflections" of Heb. xi.

"Abraham is dead," (John viii. 52, 53), and therefore Abraham with Isaac and Jacob, *must be raised from the dead* in order to enjoy the fulfilment of God's promise which was given for their faith, and on which He had caused them to hope.

In Matt. xxii. 31, 32 ; Mark xii. 26, 27, and Luke xx. 37, 38, the Lord silenced the Sadducees, who did not believe in resurrection, by quoting Exodus iii. 6, where God called Himself "the God of Abraham and the God of Isaac, and the God of Jacob," and this when Abraham had been dead 335 years, Isaac had been dead 186 years, and Jacob had been dead 137 years.

The only question was "touching the resurrection of the dead"; and, concerning this the Holy Spirit teaches by Paul that "If there be no resurrection of the dead then is not Christ risen. . . For if the dead rise not then is not Christ raised; and if Christ be not raised . . . then they also which are fallen asleep in Christ are perished " (1 Cor. xv. 13-18).

But the conclusive argument of Christ was that when God spoke to Moses He called Himself "the God of Abraham." This simple fact our Lord takes as an all-sufficient proof that Abraham shall be raised from the dead. God sees the end from the beginning, and " He calleth those things which be not as though they were" (Rom iv. 17) when He has determined that they shall be.

He, therefore, calls Himself Abraham's God, simply because He had purposed that Abraham should rise again from the dead.

He does not say that " all live " though they are dead : but, "all live UNTO GOD" whom He has determined to raise from the dead.

When God said to Abraham " A father of many nations *have I made* thee" (Gen. xvii. 5), it means that He had determined so to make him : not that He had then already made him so to be.

And when He said " Unto thy seed *have I given* this land," it means that He had given it *in purpose*, not that He had actually given it in fact, for Abraham at the time of Gen. xv., 18, had no seed.

Even so, Jehovah said to Moses at the bush, " I am the God of Abraham " because He had purposed to raise Abraham, Isaac and Jacob, with "all those who died in faith," from the dead, and make them live again.

We may, therefore, thus render Luke xx. 37. " But that the dead are to rise," even Moses disclosed at the bush when he called the LORD the God of Abraham, and God of Isaac, and God of Jacob.

" Now God is not [the God] of dead [people], but of living [people], for all, to Him, [are] to live."

The statement that " God is not the God of dead people " was sufficient to convince the Sadducean enemies of the Lord, of the fact of resurrection, and surely it ought to be sufficient to convince all those who believe Him and love Him. If the dead were already, and at that very time, living in some other state or sphere, the argument of our Lord would have been no proof of resurrection.

That Abraham himself believed the dead would rise and live again is shown also from verse 17, where he was willing to offer up Isaac, and is reckoned as having done so (Gen. xxi. 12, Rom. ix. 7). He did it " accounting that God was able to raise him even from the dead," and thus, simply because God had said " in Isaac shall thy seed be called."

Therefore, interpreting verses 39, 40 by verses 13-16, we are able to understand exactly who are meant by " them " and " us." The former were those who had " died in faith," the " us " were those then living, to whom the Apostle was writing. The " them " were those who had " fallen " asleep, and the " us " were those who might be " alive and remain."

The same statement is made concerning the very same two parties in 1 Thess. iv. There we are assured that the " us," *i.e.*, those who should be alive should not precede those who had " fallen asleep " but, that, though their resurrection would first take place, yet " we " (the living) should be caught up " together with them " to meet the Lord in the air, so to be ever with the Lord.

Here (Heb. xi. 40) the same truth is put the other

way. God had foreseen some "better thing" for the "us" who should be alive and remain : and that was, that they should be caught up without dying ; so that those who had died would not be made perfect [in resurrection] before the Lord should "descend from heaven."

That this is the meaning of "made perfect" is clear from Luke xiii. 32. Where the Lord, referring to the His Resurrection, says "the third day I shall be perfected."

There is no perfection in death, or in the grave. The body returns to dust, as it was, and the spirit returns to God Who gave it. Both are imperfect until they are re-united in Resurrection. Therefore, the dead in Christ will be imperfect, *i.e.*, unraised, until the Lord shall descend from heaven. Thus, "they" (*i.e.*, "those who died in faith), without us," shall not be made perfect (in Resurrection). And "us" (*i.e.*, "those who are alive and remain") have "the better thing" which God has foreseen and provided for them.

"Not without us" in Heb. xi. 40 is synonymous with and equivalent to "together with them" in 1 Thess. iv. 16.

The Apostle in Heb. x. 37 had assured them that "yet a little while, He that shall come, will come and will not tarry. Here then was to them at once the good thing and the better thing.

There is, therefore, no need to introduce the "Mystery" into an Epistle where it is not once mentioned. All is perfectly clear upon the surface of the Word, without it, and is suited alike to the time when, and the persons to whom this Epistle was written.

Each of the Elders in Heb. xi. believed what they heard from God; and there was more to be heard as God continued to speak, by His prophets; and still more when He spoke by His Son (Heb. i. 1, 2).

It was the same faith, though the hearing (or, what was heard) was different.

And now, in the day in which our lot is cast, God has spoken again by Paul (2 Tim. i. 8), "the prisoner of Jesus Christ," for us Gentiles, and shown us the things which could not be spoken by Christ: and, it is our duty to believe what we have heard, and to look foward to the "things to come" which have been thus written for our learning.

Conclusion

AT the outset of these papers we stated that the particular examples of faith might be likened to a series of family portraits in which each had one feature perfect: one being remarkable for the eyes, others for the forehead, the nose, the mouth, etc., while, at the end, there was One with every feature perfect, and Who combined in Himself, the perfections of the whole.

These elders, who "obtained a good report through faith," are now (in ch. xii.) spoken of as a great "cloud of witnesses."

The words "report" and "witnesses" are cognate, and refer (in the Greek) to witness borne, and given with the mouth, or by the laying down of the life. They have nothing whatever to do with the eyes.

These elders bore testimony through their faith; and the whole of chapter xi. is given in order to encourage those to whom it was written to endure the great combat of sufferings. And the argument is that others had endured and been engaged in the same combat in former days.

The examples chosen are those which exhibit this endurance, which only a living faith in the living God could produce.

Moses and the others all "endured as seeing Him, Who is invisible." And now (in ch. xii.) we have the greatest example of all, and are exhorted to run our course *with endurance*, looking away from all others who thus endured, to Him Who for the joy set before Him *endured* the cross, despising [the] shame, and on the right hand of the throne of God hath taken His seat.

"For consider Him Who hath *endured* such contradiction by sinners against Himself . . . If ye *endure* chastening, God dealeth with you as sons."

This is the scope of these chapters—the power of faith to endure suffering ; and, to wait God's time.

This is why the greatest example of all is left to the last, because He is perfect in this as in all beside.

He is called "the author and finisher of our faith," but this rendering does not give us the full force of the Greek. He is called faith's *archēgos* and *teleiōtēs*. The former word means *princely-leader*. It occurs four times and is rendered "*prince*" in Acts iii. 15; v. 31; "*captain*" in Heb. ii. 10, and "*author*" in Heb. xii. 2. The latter word occurs nowhere else, but it means Him Who brings us through to the end, and Who is thus the Leader and the Victor, the beginning and the ending, the First and the Last—completing and perfecting all.

Moreover the word "our" is not in the Greek, and we may just as well supply "their," or leave it out altogether.

"These all died"; but He "remaineth," "the same yesterday, and to-day, and for ever."

These exhibited only one feature of faith, but He exhibits the whole in fullest perfection.

He offered unto God "a more excellent sacrifice than ABEL" (xi. 4), and His blood "speaketh better things than that of Abel" (xii. 24). He "obtained witness that He was righteous," and God testified His gift, by accepting His life in substitution for that of His people.

He "walked with God," as ENOCH never walked.

"He pleased God" as Enoch never did (xi. 5, 6) ; for He could say "I do always those things that please* Him" (John viii. 29).

He has "prepared an Ark (even Himself) for the saving of His house" as NOAH never did, by which all His household will be carried safely through the waters of judgment.

He was a stranger and a sojourner upon earth, as ABRAHAM never was. He walked with the Father as before men. He "went out" to do the Father's will, well-knowing whither He went, and the end and purpose and object of that will. While with the Father He could say "I go to do Thy will" † (Ps. xl. 7), but in Heb. x. 7, after He had come, and done the Father's will, the Holy Spirit uses a remarkable word (*hēchō*) which means emphatically "I have come," thus quoting His own scripture, and adapting it to the different time and circumstance. ‡

From Him "sprang there, even from one"—tne One Who died for them "so many as the stars of the sky in multitude, and as the sand which is by the sea shore innumerable" (xi. 12).

He, the only-begotten Son of the Father, acquiesced in the Father's will. "They went both of them together" (Gen. xxii. 6, 8), as Abraham and Isaac never went. He accounted that the Father was able to raise Him up, even from the dead ; and, at the very opening of His ministry, He announced the fact (John ii. 19-22).

---

* The same word as in Heb. xi. 6.

† In Ps. xl. 7, the verb means either "come" or "go."

‡ There is no mis-quotation by the Apostle, but the perfect liberty of the Divine author : a liberty claimed and used by human authors in quoting their own previous writings.

He announced "things to come" as ISAAC and JACOB never did (Matt. xxiv.); and before His death He told His Apostles how those things should be shown and made known in due time (John 16. 12-15).

He waited God's time as JOSEPH never waited; and made mention of the blessed truth which has ever since been the hope of His people.

He has given a commandment which Joseph could not give. Joseph could give commandment concerning his own bones, but not the bones of other people. But our Joseph knew the Father's will, "that of all which He had given Him He should lose nothing, but should raise it up again at the last day" (John vi. 39).

He *refused* all honour from men, and the glories of the world; and "*chose rather* to suffer affliction with the people of God"; and to "*esteem*" reproach; and to "*endure*," as MOSES never did or could. (Heb. xi. 27; xii. 2, 3).

He will subdue all the kingdoms of this world so that they shall one day become His. (Rev. xi. 15).

He "wrought righteousness"; yea, a perfect righteousness—a Divine righteousness, for all His people (Phil. iii. 9).

He "obtained promises," yea, "exceeding great and precious promises" (2 Peter i. 4), as none other ever obtained.

He has wrought deliverances for His people, and has accomplished a work which ensures final victory over all enemies.

He has delivered, and doth deliver, and will yet deliver us from all our enemies. (xi. 33, 34. Compare 2 Cor. i. 10. 2. Tim. iii. 11, 12).

He will raise us to life again (xi. 35. 1 Cor. xv.).

But, on the other hand, He "had trial of cruel mockings and scourgings, yea, moreover, of bonds and imprisonments" (xi. 36).

("Of Whom the world was not worthy")

Thus are we invited to look away from all others unto Him; to "consider Him," that we may behold the perfections of our Princely-leader, and contemplate Him Who is the beginning and the end of all faith; its Author and Giver, its object and its subject.

Blessed and wonderful as are the particular examples of the various features of faith in ch. xi, yet here, in ch. xii., we have the one perfect example excelling and embodying them all, and manifesting His glory to our wondering eyes.

May we exhibit, each in our own humble sphere, "like precious faith," that we may be enabled to endure, and wait for the day when we shall inherit, in glory, all the promises which grace has given to us.

OTHER BOOKS BY E. W. BULLINGER

THE BOOK OF JOB

An exposition of the earliest written book of the Bible. This work contains a new translation by Bullinger, as well as practical insights into how we can enjoy peace with God both now and in eternity.

ISBN 0-8254-2291-4	200 pp.	paper
ISBN 0-8254-2292-2	200 pp.	deluxe hardcover

COMMENTARY ON REVELATION

The pastor, teacher, and serious Bible student will find this book both practical and profound in its literal acceptance of God's Word. This is not a collection of other men's views "warmed over." You will find other commentator's views not merely parroted, but challenged. You will be challenged in every chapter to either confirm your views of interpretation or to accept Bullinger's creative and masterful insights.

ISBN 0-8254-2289-2	738 pp.	paper
ISBN 0-8254-2290-6	738 pp.	deluxe hardcover

THE COMPANION BIBLE

The most complete one-volume Study Bible available in the King James Version. Notes within the text give valuable insight into the original Greek and Hebrew languages. Alternate translations, explanations of figures of speech, cross-references and an introductory detailed outline of each book and chapter are among the many features which pastors, preachers, seminarians and Bible students will find helpful.

ISBN 0-8254-2203-5	2,160 pp.	hardcover
ISBN 0-8254-2288-4	2,160 pp.	bonded leather

HOW TO ENJOY THE BIBLE

A basic introduction to the study of the Bible. Bullinger brings to the reader insights on the Bible and its background. Chapter subjects include: the object and subject of the Word of God, rightly dividing the Word of God, first occurances of select words in the Scriptures, figures of speech in the Bible, and interpretation and application. *How to Enjoy the Bible* will shed light on the Bible and its content for the serious student of the Scriptures.

ISBN 0-8254-2213-2	466 pp.	paper
ISBN 0-8254-2287-6	466 pp.	deluxe hardcover

NUMBER IN SCRIPTURE

An invaluable guide to the study of Biblical Numerology, or Numerics. The first section reveals the amazing designs involved in the numbers and numerical features of the Word of God which give evidence to their Designer. The second part covers the spiritual significance and symbolic connotations of those numbers which repeatedly appear in the same or similar contexts throughout the Bible.

This thrilling and provocative study will provide a storehouse of knowledge and ideas for ministers, teachers and Bible students.
ISBN 0-8254-2238-8   312pp.   paper

THE WITNESS OF THE STARS
Building on ancient astronomical sources and current scientific data, the author displays how the constellations witness to the accuracy of biblical prophetic truth. Numerous celestial charts and diagrams are provided to lend vivid support to his conclusions. With the Psalmist one discovers, "the heavens declare the glory of God and the firmament showeth His handiwork," encouraging Bible students to look upward for the coming of Christ.
ISBN 0-8254-2245-0   212 pp.   paper

WORD STUDIES ON THE HOLY SPIRIT
An in-depth study of the Holy Spirit and His work by one of the greatest Greek and Hebrew scholars of past days. Includes a complete list and exposition of 385 occurrences of *pneuma* as found in the New Testament
ISBN 0-8254-2246-9   224 pp.   paper

Available from your Christian Bookstore, or:

kregel
PUBLICATIONS

P.O. Box 2607 • Grand Rapids, MI 49501-2607